Crash to Paywall

Crash to Paywall

Canadian Newspapers
and the Great Disruption

BRIAN GORMAN

McGill-Queen's University Press

Montreal & Kingston • London • Chicago

© McGill-Queen's University Press 2015

ISBN 978-0-7735-4591-5 (cloth)
ISBN 978-0-7735-4592-2 (paper)
ISBN 978-0-7735-9760-0 (ePDF)
ISBN 978-0-7735-9761-7 (ePUB)

Legal deposit third quarter 2015
Bibliothèque nationale du Québec

Printed in Canada on acid-free paper that is 100% ancient forest free (100% post-consumer recycled), processed chlorine free

This book has been published with the help of a grant from the Canadian Federation for the Humanities and Social Sciences, through the Awards to Scholarly Publications Program, using funds provided by the Social Sciences and Humanities Research Council of Canada.

McGill-Queen's University Press acknowledges the support of the Canada Council for the Arts for our publishing program. We also acknowledge the financial support of the Government of Canada through the Canada Book Fund for our publishing activities.

Library and Archives Canada Cataloguing in Publication

Gorman, Brian, 1950–, author
    Crash to paywall : Canadian newspapers and the great disruption / Brian Gorman.

Includes bibliographical references and index.
Issued in print and electronic formats.
ISBN 978-0-7735-4591-5 (bound).–ISBN 978-0-7735-4592-2 (paperback).–
ISBN 978-0-7735-9760-0 (ePDF).–ISBN 978-0-7735-9761-7 (ePUB)

    1. Newspaper publishing – Economic aspects – Canada. 2. Journalism – Economic aspects – Canada. 3. Newspaper publishing – Canada. 4. Electronic newspapers – Canada. 5. Canadian newspapers. I. Title.

PN4914.F5G67 2015   071'.1   C2015-903772-7
                                                              C2015-903773-5

Set in Sabon 10.5/13 and Avenir.
Interior book design and typesetting by James Leahy.

For Diane, Patrick, Connor, Sean, and Katie

Contents

Acknowledgments ix
Preface xi

1 Introduction: Postmodern Times 3
2 History: Hot Lead and Cold Cash 22
3 Critics: A History of Truculence 59
4 Business, Part One: The Daily Abyss 95
5 Business, Part Two: Grim Harvesters 118
6 Technology: Sacred Tablets 148
7 Craft: A View from the Shop 193
8 Conclusions: Neo-postmodern Times 235

References 265
Index 291

Acknowledgments

First, I would like to thank my editor, Mark Abley, for doing such a magnificent job of mentoring, editing, and advising. For all of that, and for his bottomless patience, I am eternally grateful. I have met many editors in my time and he is as good as they get. I would also like to thank copy editor James Leahy for his help in fine-tuning the manuscript, and for his patience with my occasionally prickly attitude. The book is much better for his input.

Next, I want to thank my doctoral adviser, Dr Christopher Dornan of Carleton University, whose advice, insight, and constructive criticism went a long way toward making this project possible, as well as Drs Michael Dorland and André Turcotte, also of Carleton, who provided invaluable encouragement and advice. Thanks, as well, to Concordia University Distinguished Professor Emeritus Dr Enn Raudsepp for throwing his support behind this project.

Also, though it almost seems redundant considering how remorselessly I have rummaged through their work, I need to say thank you to the giants upon whose shoulders I have tried to stand, the dedicated reporters and industry observers who worked so hard every day to put the unfolding craziness into perspective and context – and often did so under financial fire. Their first draft of history was, as journalism is at its best, chaotic, contradictory, frustrating, confusing, brilliant, and riveting.

And then there are the three dozen or so journalists, news industry executives, and scholars who agreed to be interviewed for this book. Their extraordinary generosity in sharing their time and ideas is greatly appreciated.

I also would like to thank the people at McGill-Queen's University Press: executive director Phili[p] Huijstee, graphic designer Da[vis] and the MQUP marketing t[...] board. Writing may be a lonel[y] effort.

Thanks also to my colleague[s] Studies at MacEwan Universit[y] for their feedback, input, chall[...]

Finally, a big thank-you to t[...] my manuscript (in one case tw[...] tive criticism.

Preface

The starting point for this project was an off-hand comment by the publisher of the *Ottawa Sun* in the mid-1990s. The price of newsprint had shot up, and he was speculating on how nice it might be to run a radio or TV station, where expenses consist of an office, a broadcast tower and a handful of employees. Looking back, I think that sentiment probably was widespread among publishers, and their desire to transform the business into another type of broadcasting industry may have helped take newspapers to where they are today.

The publisher was John Paton – now CEO of the US news organization Digital First Media, formerly the Journal Register Co. In 2009, he was responsible for the Ben Franklin Project, in which the newspapers in the Journal Register chain were put out for one day using freeware, shareware, crowd-sourcing, and citizen journalism. That year, Paton was named publisher of the year by *Editor and Publisher* magazine. In the fall of 2012, his company went into Chapter 11 bankruptcy protection for the second time. It has since, through merger, been reborn as a publisher of 800 digital and print products.

I also remember Sun Media tech guru Wayne Parrish – now a senior executive at Postmedia Network Inc., Canada's largest newspaper chain by circulation – doing a show-and-tell at the *Sun* in the mid-1990s to brief newsroom managers about the company's new Internet site, Canadian Online Explorer, or CANOE. Mostly, I remember him talking about giving away newspaper content to draw readers into "virtual shopping centres." Several years later, Parrish told me: "The essence of the Internet was that they could do all of that themselves … To be a middle-man in that world, where you didn't sell anything, where you only facilitated sales, and yet you had no particular competitive advantage to doing that … It never quite made sense."

It seems to me that those two moments were eerie glimpses of key milestones on the road to today, like disturbing, ghostly shadows caught in the corner of the eye – or gut feelings ignored in the heat of the moment and regretted in the clear light of morning.

The "death-of-news" panic that began in 2008 has resulted in the popular portrayal of a business instantly rendered obsolete by digital technology, and being forced into extinction by a "broken business model." However, a closer look at the press coverage reveals more complex circumstances, which beg to be placed into the context of fifty years of media theory and criticism. As several observers have noted, the discourse has been dominated by a point of view that is business-focused, Western-centric, and cyber-utopian, and that suffers from a severe case of historical amnesia. As a result, much of the public conversation has excluded such constituencies as small dailies, the ethnic press, community newspapers, alternative publications, online news organizations, the emerging online world newspaper, and the business in such nations as India, China, Argentina, Brazil, and sub-Saharan Africa, where daily journalism has been surviving, and in some cases thriving. It also has largely avoided addressing the possibility that many news organizations were, at least in part, suffering the consequences of years of arrogance, in terms of undervaluing their product, taking their advertisers for granted, underestimating the intelligence of their readers, and abdicating their social responsibilities.

A striking characteristic of the conversation is that it has largely ignored many years of criticism, as if there were an unspoken agreement that the circumstances that precipitated this crisis blew away years of shortcomings, such as: a tendency to practise "safe" journalism that appeals to the affluent and provides a pleasant climate for advertising; a preoccupation with the rich and the powerful; a widespread abandonment of investigative reporting. At the same time, the economic situation has, as *Daily Beast* founding editor Tina Brown put it, provided timely "air cover" for corporations that have financed acquisitions with debt, while tying themselves to shareholder expectations of unrealistic profits – to the point that many profitable newspapers were forced by heavily mortgaged parent companies into rounds of layoffs that undermined the brands that were supposed to carry them into the digital age.

There is no question that new technology has presented large challenges for mainstream news businesses – not the least of which is the way the Internet has undermined traditional forms of advertising. Yet, the newspaper industry has largely been the author of much, if not most, of its misfortune. As Mount Royal University communications professor David Taras told me, "This wasn't murder; it was suicide."

Because of the focus on industrial imperatives, the conversation about the great promise of the new technology, in terms of the practice and craft of journalism, has been reduced almost to a sideshow, when it could be argued that it should be at the centre of the discourse. Rather, the loudest part of the discussion of technology has involved ways to monetize Twitter, drive circulation and page visits with Facebook, cut costs by deploying unpaid bloggers and citizen journalists, and invent new forms of advertising that will bring back retail and corporate advertisers. Yet, often in unlikely corners of the Internet, pioneers are experimenting with new ways to tell stories with video-game technology, multimedia, and interactive graphics. A new breed of data journalist has discovered that free online information can be mined for new stories and new perspectives on old ones. And – perhaps the most radical concept of all – there are journalists who are discovering that bloggers and citizen journalists comprise a resource that, as *Guardian* editor Alan Rusbridger put it, is "not about replacing the skills and knowledge of journalists with ... user generated content. It is about experimenting with the balance of what we know, what we can do with what they know, what they can do" (2010). Finally, some publishers are waking up to the fact that there will be no new advertising bonanza, and they should have been selling what they were giving away. They had been slicing away the bones, muscle, and brains of their business, not the fat.

To a certain extent, this book is an extension of the questions and misgivings newsroom workers were having in the 1980s and '90s about the way their craft and livelihoods were being managed. When that so-called "perfect storm" (which may be the most overworked catchphrase of the past fifteen years) broke in 2008, and the focus shifted to the "broken business model" (which may be the runner-up), I began to wonder what had happened to all the previous concern and criticism about the way chains and their managers were running newspapers. It seemed to me that the situation was neither perfect nor a storm, in the sense of being an unavoidable or unexpected act of God. And the people who broke the business model seemed to be using the situation to obscure two decades of bad decisions, to put even more money into their already bulging pockets and, in the worst cases, to strip the carcasses they made. The hope that chains might finally break apart under financial pressure was dashed as heavily indebted media companies managed to remain intact, continuing to siphon money away from journalism. My employer at the time, the Tribune Company, entered Chapter 11 bankruptcy protection in December 2008. Yet my pay cheques continued until I ended my association with the company in July 2012 – some six months before Tribune emerged from bankruptcy protection. Although I was grateful, I have to admit the situation puzzled me, especially in 2010, when the *New York Times* ran a lengthy feature that portrayed Tribune management as living like depraved feudal lords, looting the company and vandalizing the news (Carr 2010).

Often, the survival of chain management appeared to be a threat to the existence and evolution of the news business, as executives claimed massive bonuses, newsrooms were slashed, and properties were closed or changed hands. Yet even the news organizations that were embracing the new technology and making dazzling contributions to the art and science of online journalism were suffering, while they searched for ways to make money from an audience conditioned to expect free information. There was, and is, nothing definitive to which we can point as a solution to the strange paradox of dwindling paid circulation and exploding unpaid readership. There is no perfect example of intelligent management, fine journalism, and tested business strategy. Everything is transitory; something that appears to be working in this quarter is reported as a failure in the next, only to bounce back in the third. Even the measure that appears most obvious, the paywall, is rendered murky and uncertain by the complexities of Web flow and traffic, and by the ugly, unavoidable logic that years of cutbacks by desperate or greedy managers have left many news organizations with very little to sell that a reader might consider worth buying.

What the developments of the past few years mean for the future is anyone's guess. And those who predict with great confidence a world in which the Internet has transformed the public conversation into something wonderfully or horribly strange are similar in one sense. They usually tend to ignore the one perfect lesson about the future that we have learned from the past: just about every prediction will be wrong. As the saying goes, The future ain't what it used to be.

Crash to Paywall

1

Introduction: Postmodern Times

One of the more dramatic by-products of the recent economic crisis was what amounted to a prolonged and very noisy nervous breakdown on the part of the so-called mainstream media. It started in 2008, and quieted down considerably after 2013, though the mantras of "broken business model" and "perfect storm" persist, as in, "A perfect storm of economic catastrophe and technological innovation has destroyed our business model."

In this narrative, readers and viewers were abandoning newspapers and television – or, at least, young desirable ones were – so advertisers were turning away from these "dying" media. However, largely because of the abundance of time and space online, Internet advertising revenues weren't coming close to living up to the promise of the dot-com bubble of 1997–2000. In a strange contradiction, readers had migrated to the Web, creating audiences of a size that news companies had never imagined possible, yet advertisers were turning away. Or, to be more precise, classifieds had been reinvented and retailers were recreating their ways of doing business – and traditional advertising was no longer a major part of the plan. As many publishers have pointed out, moving advertising online amounted to trading dollars for nickels ... or pennies.

Much of the reporting and analysis of the situation drifted toward two poles: democracy would lose its centre and society would tear itself into unconnected pieces; the old "gatekeeper" culture of the mainstream media would be swept aside by a new, free, "citizen" journalism and the old, unresponsive, corrupt electoral politics replaced by an ongoing political conversation of the culture. At one extreme, observers were conjuring up visions of a democracy seized by a sudden inability to speak clearly to itself, a civil society transformed into a marketing culture, and a politics of polarization, atomization, commodification, and alienation. At the other, cyber-utopians were predicting a wired citizenry rising up and replacing the old media with a new, conversational, fully engaged wiki-journalism in which everyone could be reporter, editor, and publisher, and information would be collected and shaped by the people who consume it. The people would seize the machinery of communication, and electoral politics would be replaced by an ongoing participatory democracy.

As several observers have pointed out, there is an uncompromising, evangelical tone to much of this conversation. Yet even a casual examination of the discourse reveals a maze of contradictions, generalizations, omissions, and highly suspect conclusions. Left out was a discussion about what had been wrong with journalism – and what had been alienating readers and advertisers – at least since the 1970s and about concerns with the nature of commercial journalism that date back to the days of the penny press.

Many of the stories told during this period simply outline the financial struggles of several large media companies, and a lot of the analysis applies that information to the newspaper industry at large – ignoring data in other stories that showed smaller newspapers and individual holdings of large media companies turning a profit and foreign newspaper industries thriving. In some cases, stories contradicted their own headlines. For example, one headline described a generation that was uninterested in the news, and had abandoned print and turned to the Internet. Yet the story contained figures that indicated more young people than before were reading newspapers, yet not as many as were getting news online, and most were getting news online from newspaper websites or from newspapers through aggregators (Kawamoto 2009).

One striking aspect of the story has been Big Media's unwillingness to consider that much of the damage may have been self-inflicted. Many metro dailies had long lived in a monopolistic fool's paradise: advertisers and readers had nowhere else to go, so the money just rolled in. At the same time, business had taken precedence over journalism for so long that many metro dailies had stumbled into irrelevance long before the Internet came along to kick away their legs. Yet, for the most part, the industry continued to blame reader and viewer boredom on online competition, the frivolous interests of young audiences, Google-bred attention deficit – anything but dull content. As *Globe and Mail* media reporter Steve Ladurantaye told me, "There are some really shitty newspapers that are being used as examples of the problems with the print industry, which makes no sense ... That's not talked about enough: that these papers have cut so deep that they're just not making something that somebody wants to read."

As Robert McChesney and John Nichols have pointed out, the debate over the future of the news business "has, for the most part, been presented as a matter of mechanics and ledgers rather than one of turmoil of journalists and danger for democracy" (2010, 19). The commentary and reportage over the past six years have provided considerable support for that view and have revealed a strange and often solipsistic historical amnesia. The crises of the recession are rarely taken as part of a long-standing set of financial problems involving overextended parent companies, runaway debt, shareholder expectations, cost cutting, and a consequent erosion of quality. Yet, it would seem logical that these factors should be part of any conversation about the state of the industry.

By harking back to a long tradition of media criticism and analyzing a mass of the news and commentary about the industry published over the six-plus years from late 2008 to early 2015, we can see that most of the challenges facing journalism predate the Internet by at least a decade, and many by a century or more. The current fixation on "mechanics and ledgers" obscures a long-standing and ongoing set of issues, and the story is much more complex, more nuanced – and more hopeful and pessimistic at the same time – than much of the commentary might imply. Although the Internet has proved to be a powerfully disruptive force to the old, institutional models of journalism, it has invigorated and extended the reach of the best of the old brands, and enabled new forms of journalism and storytelling. The Internet may have put the tools of communication into the hands of the many, but it has also given control of the message to the few, and made possible government and corporate surveillance beyond the darkest fears of the most dystopian among us. At the same time, it has seen the emergence of a new Big Media, controlling search engines, social networks, and online sales that were unimagined as little as a decade ago. Many of these new media mammoths are moving into traditional newsgathering.

Big-city dailies have been punished most by technological disruption, and the small dailies and community papers have fared well in weathering the storm. However, the best of the brands – such as the *New York Times, Financial Times, Wall Street Journal,* and *Guardian* – are evolving into massive international news organizations, and many of the others are in the process of rediscovering the value of local news. Yet it seems unlikely that the small dailies and community newspapers will continue to escape online competition; the potential of digital media is just too powerful to remain unexploited at that level – especially as more journalists find themselves thrown out of secure employment and into a saturated job market.

As many cyber-utopians argue, the Internet may yet fulfill philosopher-educator John Dewey's vision of an involved public and a Great Community rising from the Great Society. However, it is at least as likely to produce a larger and noisier version of journalist-essayist Walter Lippmann's "bewildered herd" of uninvolved citizens, who are barely competent to elect governments to rule them. As we have seen with recent disclosures about the US National Security Agency and the government-corporate assault on WikiLeaks, the Web has the capacity to make government surveillance and censorship more extensive and intrusive. At the same time, the online world can be a playground for special-interest groups that wish to manipulate the public discourse.

"There's a lot of utopianism in the defenders of the Internet," Carleton University professor emeritus Stuart Adam says. "That there is a chance to explode out of this phenomenon new levels of democratic participation and richer conversation, and so on. The problem ... is, not withstanding their optimism – the idealization of democratic procedures and so on – they still have to face the reality that these are also systems of power and control."

To a certain extent, this book is an extension of a central discourse about the public and the news media, and their relationship in a functioning democracy that has crystallized around some of Lippmann's and Dewey's writings: the questions of how involved in the democratic project we can expect the citizenry to be, and to what extent and in what ways the news media can be expected to advance this cause. This involves a set of questions that have dominated the discussion of the news business since the invention of mass media in the nineteenth century:

- To what extent is a media company a private enterprise, and to what extent is it a public trust?
- Is journalism an art, a business, a public service, or all three?
- Is it realistic to expect the news media to act as an agent for the democratic project?
- Should journalists, as individual craftspeople, be deployed as agents for *any* political, cultural, or financial project?
- Is journalism primarily a cultural activity?
- Can the business, artistic, and political aspects of journalism be reconciled?

To this, we could add a question that has become a recurring refrain in the age of online discourse: Are the traditional news media still a necessary component of the public sphere?

The concepts of communication as an instrument of public policy, public opinion, and public sphere have evolved over the centuries, but we are no closer to unravelling their contradictions and conflicts than were Plato and Aristotle. In fact, with a collapsing print media and a cacophonous digital one, we may be further than ever from reconciling power and the public good.

There is much to suggest that the news business suffers rather than benefits from what sociologist Michael Schudson has called "a creeping desire to define journalism normatively, as a field with a mission" (2003, 14). One of the most powerful expressions of that creeping desire was *Four Theories of the Press* (1963), a surprisingly influential work that has taken a central place in much postwar thinking about the role of the news media in a modern society. Its most influential section, "The Social Responsibility Theory," was a direct offshoot of the Hutchins Commission report, a late-1940s, US industry-sponsored exploration of ways in which commercial media could be made accountable to the public good. Scholars such as John C. Nerone (1995) have pointed out that the *Four Theories* wasn't so much a set of theories as four expressions of one world view: Western liberal thought. John C. Merrill (2002) has argued that the Social Responsibility Theory can as often be used to justify the suppression of free speech as the promotion of it – something that has begun to play out in government attempts not just to control but to harness the Internet.

For example, Yochai Benkler identified the attacks on WikiLeaks by US government and corporate agencies as a manifestation of "those systems of control that developed in the second half of the twentieth century – to make the press not only 'free,' but also 'responsible'" (2011). And British Prime Minister David Cameron's response to the Edward Snowden NSA leaks was to warn the *Guardian* newspaper that unless it were to "demonstrate some social responsibility [by withholding information Parliament wished withheld], it will be very difficult for government to stand back and not to act" (Osborn 2013).

At the same time, over the postwar period, balance, often taken to obsessive, or even ridiculous, extremes, came to be mistaken for objectivity, and an ongoing explosion of punditry led to the talking-head TV journalism that, along with a preoccupation with soft news, characterizes much of the output of the all-news networks and most of the blogosphere. The period is also characterized by the rise of ownership by chains and public companies, and a corporatization of newsroom management – documented by many critics writing in the 1990s and 2000s. All of this has eroded confidence in the news media, as we see with survey after survey placing the profession at the lower levels of public esteem.

One thing made clear by the current discourse and the interviews I conducted for this book is that, despite the crisis, things have not changed enough to break many large companies out of patterns that impair their ability to evolve and meet new challenges. Commentators from across the political spectrum have argued that the press has alienated much of its audience with its limited notions of what is political, what is necessary for a democracy to function, and who owns the concept of free speech. Many critics go so far as to say that much of the mainstream press has evolved into a de facto publicity machine for state and corporate interests, and that it frames the public conversation according to the desires of those special interests and contrary to those of the public. This is a point of view found in the earliest writings of Lippmann and echoed by modern critics such as Noam Chomsky, Edward S. Herman, and Robert McChesney, as well as myriad online voices – particularly in criticism of the North American press response to the Iraq War, the sub-prime mortgage crisis and, in Canada, the erosion of democratic principles at the federal level.

Against the backdrop of the discourse about the dying old media and rising new media are some taken-for-granteds that beg to be challenged. Among them are: the widespread and self-fulfilling belief that print is a dead or dying medium; the idea that amateur "citizen" journalists can replace the dwindling corps of professionals; the notion that the newspaper – and magazines, film, and television – will all be replaced by new media; the drive to constrain journalism by a narrow definition of "professionalism," which would preclude participation by gifted amateurs, natural talents, and autodidacts; the cyber-utopian assumption that online media are the exclusive domain of the pure at heart, and despots and opportunists are inherently technologically incompetent.

This book is by no means a Luddite attack on the satanic mills of the digital age. Rather, the aim is to sift through the rough draft of history, to incorporate a range of oral commentary, and to fashion a narrative from a Canadian point of view, which places the current discourse into a long-term context. Also, by uncoupling the financial narrative from those of craft and technology, we can differentiate between economic failure and journalistic success – which often inhabit the same space at the same time.

In January 2010, Tina Brown encapsulated much of the recent criticism of the press when she wrote on her Internet news aggregator the *Daily Beast* that the claim that digital devices are killing newspapers and ending investigative journalism is "a load of Spam." US dailies are dying, she wrote, because "they were so dull for so long a whole generation gave up on them" (2010). Brown's comments fit into a history of discontent with what has lately come to be derisively called the "mainstream media," and it extends back roughly a century. So, an exploration of the current "crisis" in journalism must be framed by a tradition of criticism that reaches back almost a century: from Lippmann's landmark essay, *Liberty and the News*, to the *Daily Beast*.

As Robert McChesney and John Nichols (2010) point out, much of our current discourse on the state of newspapers is rooted in the belief that corporate ownership of the media has always been the dominant business model, and that its decline must also signal a decline in journalism. Similarly, much of our thinking about the press is fixed to the doctrine of objectivity, "an ideology of distrust in the self" (Schudson 1978, 71) that has only come into vogue in the news business over the past half-century or so and was clouded by the mistaken belief that objectivity meant neutrality, and that every story had to be balanced by giving equal weight to opposing points of view. This confusion of mindless balance with objective inquiry is also largely responsible for the separation of fact and analysis, which, as Eric Alterman (1982) and Schudson (1978) have pointed out, gave birth to the punditocracy that rules so much of the news media.

If we are to contemplate a future for journalism, we must understand its past, particularly its recent past, through the postwar era of objectivity, balance and social responsibility, through chain ownership, public companies and convergence, and the notion of news, information, or "content" as a financial resource. And we need to establish that there is a history before that recent past. In acknowledging that journalism has evolved from coffee-house news sheets to partisan, state-supported press, to populist yellow journalism, to balanced, stenographic medium of record, to an amalgam of amateur and professional enterprises, we give ourselves licence to imagine a future that likely will involve similar evolution.

As several commentators have pointed out, one thing that is striking about the current climate of gloom is how the lines have been blurred between business and craft, economics and aesthetics. As contradictory as this may sound, the recent financial crisis was much more a problem of the chains and conglomerates than of their individual holdings. Many chain-owned newspapers might have been much better fit to deal with the economic crisis if they hadn't had to service their parent companies' debts and satisfy the expectations of shareholders. Individual news organizations might have been saved the waves of newsroom layoffs that devalued the product that they recently put behind paywalls. "No doubt papers need to charge for what they have online," *Columbia Journalism Review* deputy editor Ryan Chittum says. "But have they gutted themselves to the point that they don't have anything worth paying for?" Yet the inference taken from the economic meltdown was that what is bad for owners is bad for newspapers, and what is bad for newspapers is bad for journalism and journalists. The other side of the argument is that bad decisions by industrial-scale media owners created a deadly environment for journalism and a lot of opportunities for the imaginative, the agile, and the dedicated.

As *Journalism Studies* editor Bob Franklin has written, there is an "evident Manichaeism" in the prognoses being presented for newspapers (2008, 631). On one hand there are those who profess to have determined with scientific precision the date newspapers will cease to exist – as one did with the prediction that the last daily would roll off the presses in 2022 (Australian 2010). Meanwhile, in 2008–9, after US dailies lost 10.6 per cent of their circulation, others pointed out that reducing circulation by 10 per cent could actually be a good thing, if you were to raise your cover price by 11 per cent, because you cut production costs while maintaining your income (Gross 2009). And the 2009 year-end figures for the *New York Times* seemed to bear that out: daily circulation down 7.3 per cent; Sunday circulation down 2.7 per cent; revenues up 6.7 per cent. So, depending on whom you read in the catastrophic years of 2008 and 2009, you could have drawn the conclusion that the end was nigh, or that dailies experienced a small decrease in profitability in the face of the worst economic downturn since the Great Depression – and one for which executives at General Motors or Chrysler would have been happy to trade their children. Sales and profit figures have since indicated that this downturn was no mere dip in the income charts for the newspapers, but a fundamental change in the economics of publishing and advertising. However, we'll never know how much of the downturn was the result of newspaper owners advancing their unprofitable digital products at the expense of their profitable print ones – and deploying the full promotional power of their organizations to convince readers and advertisers that ink on paper was a dead medium.

Alterman (2008a) has argued that the stresses between the network society and the mainstream media are an extension of the so-called Lippmann-Dewey debate: the mainstream media are the Lippmannian gatekeeper or watchdog, speaking down to the great unwashed; the wilder, less organized, and reader-driven Internet fulfills in the virtual world the concept of the conversational society expressed by Dewey and more recently by James Carey and the proponents of public journalism. That comparison is interesting in that it also reflects the Manichaean outlook Franklin identified: it implies that one must side with Lippmann or Dewey, because the former is an anti-democratic Platonist bent on removing the public from the public sphere, as Carey (1997a) put it, and the latter is an idealistic dreamer seeking a great community in the Aristotelian ideals of a great common sense, while forgetting that Aristotle warned that democracy could only exist within the reach of the human voice, and that society at large needed the firm hand of a sovereign on the levers of power. Also, it involves two basic assumptions: print is a dead medium or at least in the final stages of terminal illness; news on the Internet is inherently more democratic and less institutional than news in print, and is destined to remain thus.

This sort of high-concept rhetoric commands us to choose sides and become technological stereotypes. We can embrace the Web and give ourselves over to social media, exposing all our warts, blemishes, crevices, and mounds on Facebook, tweeting out every banality that comes into our heads and developing the attention spans of Labrador retrievers. Or we can be grumpy old hoarders: sitting surrounded by piles of newspapers in smelly apartments, muttering to ourselves, staring at the television, and waiting to die and be eaten by our twelve cats. Yet, going by how old media have always adapted to competition from new media, there is considerable probability that words – on paper and on screens – will likely remain the preferred method of delivery for certain types of information or narrative. Certainly digital multimedia is here to stay and will continue to transform the ways we tell stories and transmit information.

There has always been an enormous middle ground between these contrasting points of view, as British culture critic Raymond Williams (1983) demonstrated in his dismissal of "old democrats" such as Dewey and "new skeptics" like Lippmann. This is especially pertinent at a time when utopian communitarians in Dewey's mould perceive the Internet as a political and social panacea. The gap between cynicism about a rational public and wide-eyed belief in collective wisdom, Williams argued, is an avenue for special interests to exploit communication for their own ends. We're all susceptible to manipulation by people shrewder and less scrupulous than we, he warned, and we'd be best not to forget it, or imagine that we can build machinery that will protect us from it. "Williams believes that both these attitudes ... communitarians and realists ... leave the door open for con artists and hucksters," communication scholar John Durham Peters writes. "Williams warns us against the dangers of both realism (cynicism) and blind faith (folly) in democratic attitudes. The standoff between innocence and experience only leaves the door open for exploitation by hard-headed opportunists" (2003, 224–5).

Similarly, Schudson (2008) points out that there is more evident Manichaeism in the way Lippmann is exploited as the embodiment of the elitist gatekeeper and Dewey as the prophet of the conversational society. It was never so cut and dried, and it is as possible to use Dewey and Lippmann to argue one point of view as it is to set them in opposition. It may be more important that they agreed that if, as Dewey wrote, "a public exists, it is surely as uncertain about its own whereabouts as philosophers since Hume have been about the residence and make-up of the self" (1954, 116–17). Where they differed was in the solution to public malaise. The way Lippmann's biographer Ronald Steel put it was that Lippmann saw the public as "a Great Beast to be tamed," and Dewey, as a "force that could be educated" (1980, 218).

The tension between those points of view lives on in the division between cyber-utopians and skeptics. The first group argues that the huge surplus of information we have at our disposal empowers citizens to come together in their free time to govern themselves. The second warns that democracy may be poorly served by an atomized online society that has all but abolished the physical public sphere and has replaced civil discourse with partisan ranting and facile pronouncements about truth being relative and opinion as valid a form of information as fact. (The first group appears to forget that the digital age has almost abolished free time for all but the richest and the poorest of us – and that the latter are more concerned with feeding themselves than with self-government.)

"Societies – especially democratic societies – are one great, roiling, ongoing, fractious, cacophonous conversation," says Carleton University journalism professor Chris Dornan, a long-time analyst of the Canadian media business. "The conversation is not simply fractious, but it is now fractured as well, because when the [Ottawa] *Citizen* was the only game in town, if your interest was the affairs of the city in which you lived, you basically had to read the damned thing. So everyone had a common touchstone. They may have disagreed with it. They may have detested it. But everyone was exposed to this daily compendium of information. That is no longer true."

Meanwhile, many recent commentators have questioned whether we should be analyzing the press, rather than blaming the audience, to find the reasons for falling reader interest. Dornan puts it this way: "The newspaper increasingly resembles the local cable company, which is just another infuriating monopoly – and a bland one. There may have been a time when people loved their newspapers. A newspaper would be a genuine daily jolt of interest and excitement. But those days are long gone."

To put it another way, as Raymond Williams argued, we should never assume that the mass is not a public simply because it fails to share the interests of those who govern it, or of those in the media who choose to champion the interests of the powers that be. People are highly political when their interests are involved, and their "inertia and apathy" are the only weapons they have to use against those who refuse to address those interests (1983, 316).

Though the recent recession started toward the end of 2007, the panic in the press didn't begin in earnest until mid-2008. At that time I began collecting daily news reports, magazine articles, and commentary on the subject of the "death" of newspapers and journalism. I followed the narrative as it unfolded through the economic collapse and bounce-back, hoping, at some point, to draw a reasonable conclusion on at least the immediate future of the craft and the business. As of mid-2015, the so-called crisis has subsided somewhat, the flood of predictions, prescriptions, and eulogies has slowed to a trickle, and the chains have returned to business as usual – or at least to their focus on leveraged acquisitions, bottom lines, cost cutting, broken business models, and saviour technologies. With one exception. In 2012, news organizations such as the *New York Times* and, in Canada, the *Globe and Mail* admitted that they could never do business the way television networks do, and set up metered paywalls, charging regular readers a monthly or annual subscription fee for access to the content on their sites. They were soon followed by such companies as Torstar, Postmedia, Quebecor, and Gannett. This change of strategy presents obvious difficulties for companies that followed the ideology of cost cutting through the recession. They have found themselves with severely limited value to place behind their new paywalls. Notable among the holdouts was the *Guardian*, a limited-profit company owned by the Scott Trust, which has used high-quality free content to transform itself from a British national daily newspaper into a world information source.

Some of that flood of commentary over the past six years contained the same criticisms and complaints highlighted by Tina Brown and – at least in terms of the concern about readers turning away – echo works such as John Miller's *Yesterday's News* (1998), Doug Underwood's *When MBAs Rule the Newsroom* (1995) and Ben Bagdikian's *The Media Monopoly* (1992). Yet the relevance of that criticism was obscured by a fog of facts and figures that treated the downturn in the fortunes of the business as being mostly, if not solely, the result of sudden technological and economic upheaval. This wave of gloom has been treated as something entirely separate from the previous thirty years of media history, in which criticism focused on other factors that were perceived to be affecting circulation and alienating readers: blandness created by chain ownership; timid management; unimaginative editorial leadership; too much focus on political gamesmanship over issues; trivia and pseudo-events presented as news; drab, awkward writing; interests too closely aligned with the rich and powerful. Some of those factors have figured prominently in several recent audience surveys conducted in Canada and the United States (*State of the News* annual reports; Canadian Media Research Consortium 2004 and 2008), as well as in the current criticism that has taken notice of historical precedents. Also, a perceived ongoing crisis of management long ago became something of an obsession among working journalists, such as this senior reporter, who requested anonymity for fear of management reprisal, who told me:

> Local papers have deteriorated primarily not because of the structure but because of decision making by senior management. To connect the dots more clearly, it's really quite simple thinking: You load up your balance sheet with debt. You've got to service your debt. So how do you do that? You plunder the cash flow of the newspapers within your chain, thus denying them the financial resources to reinvest in their product, to improve their product, improve their coverage. That's effectively what we've seen [at Postmedia] from Day 1 under the Aspers [of Canwest] to the present day, under the current ownership.

As for online commentary among journalists, a particularly good example is this one, from a Quebecor employee calling her or himself RMP, posted on the *Toronto Sun Family* website:

> I have sat in board meetings where senior executives have been more interested in the quality of the food that was served than in the business being discussed. I have seen exceptional employees

tucked into quiet corners and incompetent ass-kissers promoted. I have seen the exodus of talent and witnessed quality newspapers turned into glorified flyer carriers ... I am not sure how much longer I can remain in an industry that is being systematically cannibalized by delusional management. I can only hope that an industry "leader" finally comes along that is willing to listen to the voices crying out in the wilderness. (2010)

Eric Alterman has written off most US news executives as "completely off their respective rockers" (2008b), and Underwood's *When MBAs Rule the Newsroom* (1995) is an entire book about management practices that undermine quality journalism. In fact, a steady stream of similar criticism has been flowing through the pages of trade journals and various books on the industry, such as Ben Bagdikian's *The New Media Monopoly* (2004) and John Miller's *Yesterday's News* (1998). Today, Miller says that the long-term practices of news executives have led to the "logical outcome" of dwindling circulation. "You're cutting reporters. You're cutting back coverage. You're trivializing the news. It goes on and on. Newspaper readers are pretty smart. They know when they're getting superficial news." As we will see from the debt figures, circulation statistics, and layoff numbers in chapters 4 and 5, these criticisms are not the generalized ravings of the disgruntled.

Most of the end-time predictions for the industry fail to take into consideration that virtually all of the injuries to the newspaper business model – or, perhaps more accurately, "revenue model" (Picard 2010, 18) – have been self-inflicted. Newsroom budgets were long ago hobbled by the accumulation of debt resulting from the wave of acquisitions by large media companies over the past two decades and by shareholder demand for return on investment. Compounding the problem were the decisions to give away the daily paper online and not to move classifieds online before competitors, such as Craigslist and Kijiji, could take over the field. Huge debts (for example, Tribune's $13 million leviathan, which dragged a mostly profitable collection of daily newspapers and TV stations into bankruptcy protection) have starved many media companies, creating a short-sighted, bottom-line-focused management that has consistently sacrificed technological innovation and quality of content for cost of production. In some cases, proprietors and managers fail to see their news-media holdings as anything other than commodities to be traded, sold, or harvested in a game of profit maximization that has no point other than short-term gain.

Yet newspaper readership has been growing in such countries as China, India, Brazil, and Argentina. News companies – particularly ones that resisted the temptation to slash editorial staff – are building gigantic online audiences. For example, in March 2014, the *Guardian* website topped 100 million unique monthly visitors (as recognized by an IP address and at least one other means of identification, such as a cookie or sign-in) – which included 24.1 million from the United States (theguardian.com 2014). That year, the company's Web enterprises turned their first profit, of US$36.6 million (Chambers 2013), without charging readers for access to any content. "The *Guardian*'s approach to digital advertising goes against the grain and it is paying off," advertising researcher Daniel Knapp told bloomberg.com in July 2013. "The *Guardian* is positioning itself as a global media brand." At the same time, community newspapers and small dailies across North America survived the recession quite nicely by sticking to a print product filled with local news.

Digital applications for smart phones and tablets – some of which bear a strong resemblance to the printed page – are drawing people away from the Web and to proprietary content. Metered paywalls have put circulation revenue back on the balance sheet. Internet technology has demolished the financial barriers to publishing startups; nowadays, owning a press and a building are liabilities that make a company more vulnerable to the competitor with a laptop and a WordPress page. Technology has opened up new ways to tell stories and has made it possible for even the smallest communities to enjoy graphic, audio, and video content that used to be available only to city audiences.

This book looks at the state of the craft, business, and technology of journalism over the transitional period from 2008 to 2015, from the crash that led to the collision of systemic and cyclical crises in the industry to the raising of paywalls to monetize growing readership, to the development of native advertising (sponsored content, or what were once called advertorials) as an antidote to shrinking display advertising and vanished classifieds. Partly, it's a sorting and ordering of the flood of commentary – mostly in the popular and industry press – over those years. I have tried to sift out the obvious hyperbole, self-interest, and repetition of much of the commentary, highlighting the apparent contradictions and reconciling them where possible. The book also incorporates interviews with forty people in the news business, as well as industry observers, mostly from Canada, but including several from the United States. Thirty-five of these conversations took place during the summer of 2013. Four were conducted at earlier dates and for other projects but contain nuggets I thought were interesting or dramatic or that helped illustrate certain points. One consisted of an email exchange with a former colleague in March 2015. Most of the interviews followed the same rough line of inquiry: What went wrong? Why? Who, if anyone, got it right? What makes you hopeful? What is your prognosis? These conversations were acts of journalism, rather than works of social science. Therefore, they were open-ended and answer driven, and tended to go wherever the participants wanted to take them. The result is a blend of official story and insider observation.

In some cases, the interviewees have retired or moved on to new ventures; two have died. To avoid confusion, I mostly refer to them by the position they held when I spoke to them. Their new situations are listed parenthetically in the "Interviews" section of the references.

Roughly 88 per cent of the interviewees were white males, and there were no people of colour. If this reveals a prejudice, it's a subconscious one, and one shared by Nieman Journalism Lab's recent project, *Riptide*, an online oral history of technology and the media which, at the time of writing, involved interviews with sixty-one people in and around the US news business, 90 per cent male, only two of whom were men of colour. As one of the project's authors told the *Washington Post*'s Andrea Peterson, the industry leaders were "regrettably overwhelmingly white men" (2013). In Canada, the dominance of the industry by white men is as regrettable, and may be even more overwhelming. Ryerson University professor emeritus John Miller, who is also a former *Toronto Star* deputy editor, spent much of his academic career studying diversity, or the lack of it, in Canadian newsrooms. "When I left [the *Star*] in 1986 to go to Ryerson, all of a sudden I was out in the city," he says. "And the first thing I noticed was that the city had changed. You could see it. And one of the first bits of research I did was to ask, Why don't I see the city in the pages of the newspaper?"

My list of interviewees reflects a perhaps single-minded pursuit of another form of diversity. I went fishing for opinions and insights from a range of people who reflected a cross-section of the industry and of scholarly research. The subjects came from Alberta, British Columbia, Ontario, Quebec, Washington State, New York, and Washington, DC. I spoke to top executives and editors at both of the major Canadian national newspaper chains, as well as the *Toronto Star* and *Globe and Mail*, founders of such Canadian online enterprises as *The Tyee* and *OpenFile*, and the chairman of one of the largest chains of community newspapers in the country, which also owns papers in the Pacific Northwest and Hawaii. The scholars with whom I spoke are involved in the political economy of the news media, and they come from Calgary, Montreal, New York, Ottawa, and Toronto. I also talked to media reporters in Canada and the United States, and several newsroom workers. Though the women to whom I spoke all had interesting things to say about women in the media, that was not the main focus of their interests, and they were chosen for their expertise in the subject matter and not because of their gender. They were: Lucinda Chodan, vice-president, editorial, for Postmedia Network Inc. and editor-in-chief of the Montreal *Gazette*; Stephanie Coombs, the managing editor of the *Edmonton Journal*, at the time, the only major paper in the country whose top executive consists almost entirely of women; Catherine McKercher, a former Washington correspondent for Canadian Press, a full professor of journalism at Carleton University, and probably Canada's most distinguished researcher in the area of newsroom labour; Kathy Muldoon, director of print journalism at Sheridan College; Karen Unland, head of the *Edmonton Journal*'s Capital Ideas project. Only one person insisted on anonymity, a senior reporter with decades of experience who feared that his/her experience, seniority, and salary had made him/her an expensive luxury in the eyes of management.

As for the absence of voices from French Canada, that is the result of my focus, which is on the newspaper industry in English Canada and the English-speaking world. In some instances, the problems faced by the news organizations in Quebec reflect those in the industry at large. In others, they are the result of the grotesquely dominant position of one company – Quebecor – on the landscape of a media that is unique on the continent in terms of its insularity. As Mount Royal University communication professor David Taras says,

"I cannot think, with the exception of Italy, of another democratic society that has that kind of concentration: the biggest TV network; the biggest book publishers; the biggest magazine publishers; the biggest event promoters; the biggest cable operators; the biggest Internet service operator. It's incredible."

The press is useful as a running, day-to-day commentary on the world, but its main weaknesses are that it usually fails to provide context and rarely revisits stories to update them. As Lippmann wrote: "The press is like the beam of a searchlight that moves restlessly about, bringing one episode and then another out of darkness and into vision" (1993, 229). So, what emerges is a patchwork of random pieces of information that need to be compared, contrasted, reconciled to one another, and stitched together into a whole story.

In patching together these fragments, I don't propose to deliver a prescription for the revitalization of the daily newspaper, or for its perpetuation on the Internet, and none of the people with whom I spoke pretended to have all the answers. To my mind, the argument unfolds in favour of both new *and* old media. A pre-Internet world would be a drab and frustrating place for anyone who has come to enjoy the pleasures of instant access to masses of information and entertainment at the touch of a fingertip, and for anyone who relishes a future in which the audience is allowed to contribute to the conversation. The masses of data, the global reach, the rush of imagination, debate, and opinion are things that have made the Internet as essential to our way of life as electricity or running water.

At the same time, there are aesthetic and functional pleasures of print that other media cannot deliver. Daily papers, magazines, and books will likely survive simply because some forms of graphic, photographic, and literary presentation are more pleasing – or more fun – in print than on a computer or tablet, because people read differently in hand than they do online, and because no medium can satisfy every informational need or deliver every kind of reading pleasure. For comparisons, one need look no further than video games, film, and television. Anyone who ever predicted video games would replace film or TV forgot about the pleasure of a story told well, of giving oneself up to the experience, of climbing aboard and enjoying the ride. Anyone who says television is dead hasn't been paying attention to the flood of important drama turned out by the US cable networks. The audience may be fragmented and the technology in flux, but TV is more vital than at any other moment in its history. People continue to read novels, though film is more than a century old. Radio and movies continued to flourish, albeit in altered form, after the advent of TV. Further proof of a continuum may be taken from the facts that, in 2010, *Atlantic Monthly* posted the most profitable month in its 153-year history (Kinsman 2010), and, despite the recent collapse of *Newsweek*, ad spending actually rose in the US print magazine industry in 2012 and was projected to dip only slightly in 2013–16 (Chittum, 2012c). The success of long-form journalism at such sites as the *New York Times*, the *Washington Post*, the *Guardian*, *Salon*, and *Slate* also shows that at least some people go looking for quality over quantity when they go online.

Yet, the core criticisms of the news industry remain, and they remain important.

2

History:
Hot Lead and Cold Cash

Most press critics and journalists are familiar with Thomas Jefferson's statement that he would prefer "newspapers without government" to "government without newspapers" and would legislate that "every man receive those papers and be capable of reading them." Less often repeated is what Jefferson had to say about the Fourth Estate after he had spent some time as its target: "The man who reads nothing at all is better educated than the man who reads nothing but newspapers." Jefferson's comments can be taken as a model of our mixed feelings about a free press: necessary to maintaining the free flow of information in a democratic society, yet often irresponsible, aloof, and insensitive.

Also, it is important to remember that Jefferson was not talking about the press as we know it, but about something that was more like talk radio, all-news networks, or blogs. What we consider news has evolved over the past two centuries, along with the business and technology that make it. Most newspapers of the eighteenth and early nineteenth centuries were partisan journals of ideas and argument, produced for the social and political elite. Michael Schudson describes them as "histrionic, cheerleading, one-sided, rationalizing, ridiculing and disparaging" (2008, 1037). So, Jefferson was praising, and condemning, "the newspapers' capacity as a forum for debate (and sometimes slander), not exposé" (Shafer 2009d). He was talking about the conflict of opinions and the marketplace of ideas, not raw information.

This chapter is by no means a comprehensive examination of the history of journalism. Rather, it points to specific milestones to provide a brief compilation of precedents for what is going on in the news business today. By exploring the evolution of the Canadian, US, and British press, we can establish that journalism has evolved over time through many business models and aesthetic and literary styles, driven by public demand, technology, social conditions, and business opportunities. Also, much of the current upheaval comes into perspective when you place the technological and commercial development into some kind of historical perspective, and look at how technology has repeatedly helped transform business and craft.

The story is by necessity rambling, because the parallel technological, financial, literary, and aesthetic developments intertwine, and the threads don't always unravel chronologically. Still, throughout the history of the news media, evolution in one area has consistently sparked response in another. For example, the spread of literacy in the United States created an audience for a mass medium that was made possible by the development of the steam press and financed by advertising – and this gave birth to literary and investigative traditions of modern journalism, which, in turn, helped manufacture the mass audience and helped create popular culture.

Though journalism is a bit more than four centuries old, the news business as we know it is less than half that age. It has been only in the past 200 years or so that gathering facts and writing about them have come together to form a type of employment. Until the mid-nineteenth century, newspapers in the United States, Britain, and Canada were dependent on political patronage and closely associated with specific parties – and often filled with essays that might have looked more at home in a journal of ideas than a modern newspaper. In the latter part of the nineteenth century, spurred by the rise in literacy among the general populace, the press evolved into a commercial enterprise built on a unique two-tier manufacturing process: news is moulded into content that is sold to readers, who are collected into an audience, which, in turn, is sold to advertisers.

As several commentators have pointed out (Kesterton 1984, Schudson 1978, Starr 2004, Teel 2006, McChesney and Nichols 2010), the fortunes of North American journalism over the years have been largely dependent on technology and government support. New technologies and cost-saving developments have repeatedly created favourable circumstances for the growth and evolution not just of the business, but of the craft of journalism as well: from the flatbed press to postal systems, to rotary presses, to steam presses, to the telegraph, to stereotyping, to radio, newsreel, and television, to cold type, photo engraving, and offset printing, to computer editing and pagination, to online publishing and mobile apps. As well, government support – advertising, postal subsidies, tax breaks, and legislative protection – has long helped ensure the financial health of the news media.

As historian Elizabeth Eisenstein points out, before the sixteenth century news delivery was a function of the Church: "As communion with the Sunday paper has replaced church-going, there is a tendency to forget that sermons had at one time been coupled with news about local and foreign affairs, real estate transactions, and other mundane matters." Eventually, however, lay printers took over the dissemination of secular news, first with news sheets distributed in the coffee houses of seventeenth century London, and later as one-man newsrooms for whom "the dictum 'nothing sacred' came to characterize the journalist's career" (1979, 131). Thus, the news severed itself from the Church and aligned itself with politics and business, in tandem with what was occurring across Western society at the time. What we see as the birth of the mass media was at the time regarded as a divisive force – much as the Internet is viewed in some quarters today. Early critics argued that the evolution of print media would cause a shift in the way people participated in public life, from personal connection as part of a community to detached involvement as a sovereign citizen. "By its very nature, a reading public was not only more dispersed, it was also more atomistic and individualistic than a hearing one" (132).

Over the course of the eighteenth century, monthly journals gave birth to weeklies, which in turn gave birth to dailies, and it was with the introduction of reliable mail service in Europe and the United States that the earliest forms of journalism emerged. Advances in printing, religious conflict, and the rise of the nation-state and the expansion of commerce had created a sufficiently turbulent environment for "more autonomous forms of communication even before free expression received legal protection" (Starr 2004, 23). The conversation of the culture was well under way before printing technology was adapted to provide a medium for it, and before governments were pushed to create mechanisms to protect it, such as the Canadian Charter of Rights and Freedoms or the First Amendment to the US Constitution.

In the United States, publishers benefited from a federal government mandate established in 1792, which required the postal service to carry all newspapers that wished to use the system and to offer them special low rates. This, combined with the absence of a stamp tax on ink and paper, created favourable economic conditions for the rise of newspapers in the late eighteenth and early nineteenth centuries. Paul Starr notes that between 1790 and 1835, the number of American newspapers grew from 106 to 1,258 (2004, 86). At the same time, the new US government had established an extensive postal system – 443 post offices in Massachusetts alone. By 1830, the USPS was delivering roughly a quarter of all newspapers consumed in the United States, and roughly 2 million more newspapers a year than letters; two years later, 95 per cent of the weight of all mail consisted of newspapers yet accounted for only 15 per cent of revenue (89–90).

The earliest newspapers in Canada came from the US northeast (Kesterton 1984, 1). The first was the *Halifax Gazette*, founded by Bostonian Bartholomew Green in 1752. Similarly, in Quebec, the first English paper was the *Quebec Gazette*, founded by a pair of Philadelphia printers in 1764, a year after the Treaty of Versailles ceded Quebec to Great Britain (2). By the time of the Revolutionary War, a decade later, newspapers were being published in all of what would become the six eastern provinces.

However, the Canadian industry developed much more slowly than its US parent, partly owing to a rudimentary postal system that offered no subsidies for newspapers. As of the 1830s, between the Ottawa Valley and the Atlantic coast, "there were more than 100,000 people, but only seven post offices ... rates were high, and the volume of postal communication was low" (Starr 2004, 89). With small populations and low levels of literacy in the Canadian colonies, circulation was tiny and advertising spare and primitive. So, early Canadian newspapers were highly dependent on government patronage – in the form of contracts to print various forms, edicts, announcements, pronouncements, and proclamations. W.H. Kesterton describes the "pioneer papers" as "innocuous" in character, "unremarkable" in appearance, and, since they were published in colonies under authoritarian rule, more or less subservient to the wishes of the sovereign (1984, 7–9). Still, the Canadian newspaper business grew, though not as robustly as its American counterpart. In 1813, 20 news sheets were published in what were to become Central, Eastern, and Atlantic Canada; by 1857, there were 291 (11).

This pattern of development would persist through the nineteenth and twentieth centuries, with Canada lagging behind and, more or less, echoing developments in the United States. However, there was one key difference, the constant chafing against a larger, dominant culture: Britain, and then the United States. At first, this took the form of a press polarized by foreign rule, and later by a growing demand for protectionist policies to keep Canadian media companies from being absorbed or drowned out by their larger, stronger, and wealthier neighbours to the south.

The North American press of the eighteenth and early nineteenth centuries is routinely described as having been made up solely of partisan, party-controlled newspapers competing for readers' hearts and minds. The reality was more complex. In the United States, "[s]ome editors still adhered to the old ideal of a neutral, open press, and many others were partisan only in the sense of identifying with a party's viewpoint" (Starr 2004, 84). In Canada, this was tinged with a growing loathing among many of the colonials – particularly the francophones of Lower Canada – for governors sent from England. As it had earlier in the United States, a growing movement for responsible government was finding voice in the newspapers of the day, countered by another for the status quo of colonial rule. As a result, by mid-century, Canadian newspapers were identified by their position on responsible government. "As views became increasingly doctrinaire, most of the important journals became known either as Reform or anti-Reform" (Kesterton 1984, 14).

The few commentators on the history of Canadian newspapers have pointed out that it was this political polarization that gave birth to the chain ownership that has marked the Canadian industry throughout its history. The creation of every anti-Reform publication in an important centre created a need for a Reform journal to counter it. "Early newspapers were powerful weapons in a perpetual battle but they were not necessarily implements of public opinion as later ones were, for they most often preached to the converted" (Fetherling 1990, 78). Political rivalries made for commercial warfare, and the "stronger newspapers gobbled up the weak ones, to the point that only a handful remained to fight for control of the expanding and immensely wealthy markets" (97).

In the United States, the 1830s was a period of revolution in journalism that "led to the triumph of 'news' over editorial, and 'facts' over opinion, a change which was shaped by the expansion of democracy and the market, and which would lead, in time, to the journalist's uneasy alliance with objectivity" (Schudson 1978, 14). Though by this time the majority of newspapers in the United States were weeklies, the daily newspaper had begun its rise. In 1830, the United States had 650 weeklies and 65 daily newspapers; ten years later, there were 1,141 weeklies and 138 dailies (13). But it wasn't simple growth that changed the face of the newspaper business. Rather, it was a development born out of technology and demographics: the penny press.

In Canada, the papers were still engaged in debate over responsible government, with the major innovations being that they had begun to report on Parliament and to devote space to local news. However, when it came to publishers aiming their product at newly educated masses, Canada was slow to adapt. Perhaps this was because the country, like Europe, trailed the United States in education and had yet to experience the working-class immigration that was flooding the US Eastern Seaboard.

By the 1850s, the illiteracy rate in the United States was 10.7 per cent among white Americans and 22.6 per cent in the general population. In comparison, approximately 60 per cent of the European adult population could neither read nor write (Starr 2004, 105). In English Canada, though literacy was rising sharply, the rate was still lower than in the United States. In Quebec, illiteracy stood at an appalling 73 per cent (106). Newspaper publishing remained a business for gentlemen aimed at influencing other gentlemen, and the Canadian newspaper publisher remained grounded in "political passion, rather than commercial desire to attract the eye of potential readers" (Kesterton 1984, 18).

South of the border, a massive change was sweeping the business. In the 1820s and '30s, most states had moved to extend the vote to all adult white males. Thus there was a large new class of citizen, with "new reasons to pay attention to the news, and political parties had new reason to pay attention to them" (Starr 2004, 130). This meant a new clientele for the press, which moved quickly to address this audience. The first of the new breed of daily was the *New York Sun*, founded in 1833. It was followed in the next two years by the creation of competing journals in New York, and similar ones in Boston, Philadelphia, and Baltimore. These were the "penny papers," so called because they sold for one cent a copy, rather than the usual six cents. Their focus was on local news. They aimed to entertain and agitate as much as to inform and influence, and their target audience was drawn from the newly educated middle and lower classes that were swelling the cities of the East. The penny press helped usher in an age of public opinion, something the British statesman Richard Cobden called the "distinguishing feature of modern civilization" (quoted in Briggs and Burke 2005, 157).

The objective of the penny papers was profit. Unlike the traditional papers, their success depended more on newsstand sales than on subscriptions, and since they were priced for shallow pockets, their success depended on their ability to build large circulation. As a result, the penny press was responsible for several innovations that led directly to the modern omnibus daily newspaper – not the least of which was the front page as we know it. From a dull collection of announcements, ads, and letters, the front page became, as one Canadian Prairie publisher put it, the "display window of [the] store of news ... filled with good samples" (Sotiron 1997, 19). So, ads, editorials, and notices vanished from the new front page, to be replaced with pictures, stories, and headlines designed to grab and hold a reader's interest. Newspaper editors became more than fixers and pundits; they were also advertising copywriters, graphic artists, and ghostwriters, dressing up and marketing their wares to the masses.

Another thing this new mass audience created in the press was the concept of economies of scale, and this "opened up opportunities for a journalism of a different kind" – one that was highly competitive and technologically advanced (Starr 2004, 131). "The penny papers aggressively sought out local news, assigning reporters to cover the courts and even 'society.' They also actively solicited advertising and engaged in vigorous competition to print the very latest news." As is the case throughout newspaper history, business drove the adaptation of technology. In 1835 the *New York Sun* became the first US newspaper to use a steam-driven press. The *Baltimore Sun* was one of the first papers to use the telegraph to get the news quickly (Schudson 2003, 76–7). When the *Sun* was founded in 1833, there were eleven newspapers in New York, with a total circulation of 26,500. Two years after adopting the steam press, the *Sun* was printing and selling almost that many copies alone (Starr 2004, 130).

Just as a "democratic market society" (the "replacement of gentry rule by mass democracy") gave birth to the penny press (Schudson 1978,

57), it was the penny press that gave birth to modern journalism. Before the penny papers, the average newspaper was a small business run by a publisher-editor with a few, usually unpaid, correspondents contributing essays or letters. This gave way to large, hierarchical organizations in which reporters, for the first time, were employed to gather and write about news. "As news was more or less 'invented' in the 1830s, the reporter was a social invention of the 1880s and 1890s" (65). The interview – the central activity of modern journalism – wasn't introduced into American journalism until 1859, when Horace Greeley talked to Mormon leader Brigham Young for the *Salt Lake Tribune*. At first, the process was regarded as manufactured and untrustworthy, and as an invasion of privacy. In 1869, the magazine *The Nation* grumbled that the interview was "the joint product of some humbug of a hack politician and another humbug of a reporter" (Boorstin 1982, 15). However, by the time of the First World War, "it was the mainstay of American journalism, although it was still rare in Europe … It fit effortlessly into a journalism already fact-centered and news-centered, rather than devoted to political commentary or preoccupied with literary aspirations. Interviewing was one of the growing number of practices that identified journalism as a distinct occupation with its own patterns of behavior … By the 1920s, this pattern produced a self-conscious professionalism and ethic of objectivity" (Schudson 2003, 81–2).

Another creation of the penny press was the inverted pyramid: a storytelling process in which the facts are presented in declining order of importance, and the narrative moves from generalities to specifics, like telling the punch line first in a joke. It also involves flashier, more direct writing: shorter sentences, active voice, transitive verbs, and sparing but sensational use of adjectives and adverbs. As one *New York Times* news executive said, journalism was coming around to the belief that "stark fact, simply told was more powerful than any purple writing" (Teel 2006, 45). The causes most commonly cited for this development are: readers' interest fades as an article goes on, and with this style of writing they could read only partway through and still be reasonably well informed; it made stories easier to trim to remove overset or accommodate late ads. However, from a cultural perspective, the inverted pyramid also fit well with "a world of increasingly independent and cocky journalists who were prepared to name on their own authority what aspect of the news could be judged most important" (185).

Investigative or accountability reporting also came into style at the turn of the twentieth century. This muckraking was the work of zealous and aggressive journalists supported by a new media capitalism run by "wealthy upstarts at odds with respectable society" (Starr 2004, 258). US President Theodore Roosevelt coined the term "muckraking" in a speech comparing journalists to the man with the muck rake in John Bunyan's *Pilgrim's Progress*. This was a man "who could look no way but downward, with the muck rake in his hand ... who in this life consistently refuses to see aught that is lofty, and fixes his eyes with solemn intentness only on that which is vile and debasing" (1906). As a Progressive, Roosevelt had been at first sympathetic to the work of muckraking reporters – but, like Jefferson, his point of view darkened when they turned on him.

The Progressives called upon government to wipe out the corrupt political bosses, rein in the trusts and tax the robber barons; the muckraking journalists were "the watchdogs" of that movement (Steel 1980, 36). They also were the main weapon of "a new level – or at least a new form – of power available through the medium of journalism" (Starr 2004, 258). Muckraking reached the peak of its power in the early twentieth century at magazines like *Everybody's* and *McClure's*, where such writers as Ida Tarbell, Upton Sinclair, and Lincoln Steffens became stars with ambitious investigations of social issues, corporate influence, and political corruption.

Though the intensive research that gave it power came with the magazine writers, in spirit, muckraking was born in the pages of such Pulitzer and Hearst papers as the *New York World* and the *New York Journal-American*. For obvious reasons, this style of reporting had great resonance with the middle and working classes, the main clientele of the penny press. "Exposing the corruption of political machines, detailing the stranglehold of the giant corporations, crying shame on the cities where immigrants and blacks were exploited, these journalists roused the middle-class conscience and made reform a mass movement" (Steel 1981, 36). Reuters media columnist Jack Shafer (when he was writing for *Slate*) once called for a renaissance of this yellow journalism (so named for a popular comic strip of the era, *The Yellow Kid*). "The yellow newspapers were looking out for immigrants; they were looking out for the powerless," he told me. "They didn't do it perfectly. Mr Pulitzer was probably more conscientious than Mr Hearst. And there was real engagement. Even [*Times* owner]

Adolph Ochs, by 1905–6, is saying complimentary things about the ability of the yellow newspaper to engage readers in stories about power and policy that a *New York Times* really couldn't."

In Britain and Canada, the development of a popular press lagged by roughly half a century. By 1872, the largest newspaper in Canada was the *Toronto Globe*, with a circulation of around 20,000 (Sotiron 1997, 5). Owned, published, and edited by Reformer and "polemicist" George Brown, the *Globe* was "required reading among the educated and business elites" (Hayes 1992, 46–7), and was not intended for a mass audience. However, "the idea of the American popular press worked powerfully in the imaginations of Canadian editors and readers alike," and in Toronto, news vendors had grown prosperous selling imported US penny papers, particularly the fat, entertaining Sunday editions (Gabriele and Moore 2009, 339). Yet, it wasn't until the beginning of the twentieth century that Canadian newspapers began to reach a public, as opposed to the kind of select constituency to which the *Globe* spoke.

Perhaps not coincidentally, by 1891, the literacy rate in English Canada had reached 85 per cent (Sotiron 1997, 39) and the popular press had begun to emerge. Canada's first penny papers – in the country's largest cities and the main gateways for immigration – were the *Montreal Star* and *La Presse*, and Toronto's *Telegram* and *Daily World*. Weekend papers in Toronto were the *Saturday Globe* and the *Sunday World*, founded in 1889 and 1891 as a response to the popularity in the Toronto market of the Sunday papers from nearby Buffalo, NY. Due to strict Lord's Day laws across the country, the Saturday papers became the common weekend editions in Canada, as opposed to the Sunday papers of the United States and Britain. "The Lord's Day Alliance in particular was largely successful in keeping the Sabbath a day of rest in Canada, especially in Ontario. Though they and other groups lost the battle against streetcars running in Toronto and other cities ... they did manage to reaffirm prohibitions against almost all Sunday labour and trade, including newspaper publishing, in federal legislation passed in 1906" (Gabriele and Moore 2009, 341).

At the turn of the twentieth century, the *Montreal Star* was the largest paper in the country, with a circulation of 52,600. Yet most Canadian newspapers remained journals of discourse and debate. "With the exception of these dailies in Toronto and Montreal, newspaper content was dominated by political news, verbatim reports of parliamentary debates, dry commercial information and accounts of events in foreign places" (Sotiron 1997, 5). Some sixty years after the birth of the penny press in the United States, most Canadian papers were still organized the way they had been since the late eighteenth century.

> Until the 1890s newspaper operations were usually modest even in the largest cities, and this was reflected in news coverage and in the number of people they employed. A commentator on the two Vancouver newspapers of the 1890s noted that "there was a lack of balance about them, a lack of variety and a lack of the features that are considered necessary to-day to attract and maintain reader interest. There was little world news in either of them, and the local news ran quite largely to politics with appallingly long reports of political meetings and sessions of the legislature and quite often of court proceedings, and City Council sessions." In 1884, one account noted, most newspapers only needed "an editor and two or three other men." (17)

By the 1910s, though, the situation had changed drastically. Canada had begun to industrialize, and newspapers began to operate as businesses. The Canadian flag-bearer for the aggressive, sensationalistic style of the penny press wasn't even founded until 1892. That was the *Toronto Daily Star*. What was to become Canada's largest-circulation and arguably most powerful daily started life as a strike paper founded by printers who had walked out of the *Toronto News*, which had billed itself as a "paper for the people" (Harkness 1963, 28). The *Star* floundered for the first two decades of its existence, going through four owners and barely amassing a circulation of 7,000 by 1899 (24). "[U]nrespected, uninfluential, and almost unread" (20), it was Toronto's "smallest, poorest, and most discredited newspaper" (24). That changed rapidly after 1899, when the paper was bought by a consortium acting on behalf of Prime Minister Wilfrid Laurier, who wanted a Liberal evening newspaper in Toronto (19). The *Star* was placed in the editorial hands of Joseph E. Atkinson, who agreed to accept the position on condition that the paper be "conducted solely in its own interest as a newspaper enterprise ... hampered by no other considerations" (21).

On the one hundredth anniversary of this refounding of the paper, *Star* publisher Beland Honderich wrote an essay crediting Atkinson with inventing the Canadian mass-circulation newspaper. When Atkinson took over the *Star*, Honderich wrote, Canadian newspapers tended to be serious or popular. But Atkinson believed "it would be possible to develop a newspaper that would be soundly popular in its appeal and at the same time find ample room for the presentation of the serious interests of human life" (1999). In the 1930s and '40s, under the guidance of Atkinson, who had risen to the post of publisher, and his editor-in-chief Harry Hindmarsh, the *Star* became the largest newspaper in Canada, and "the last home of razzle-dazzle journalism ... A penchant for cheesecake, huge headlines, full-page pictures, charitable activities such as the Fresh Air Fund and the Santa Claus Fund, startling newspaper stunts, and off-trail and frequently left-wing causes gave the paper a liveliness and variety that readers could not ignore" (Kesterton 1984, 86).

The *Star*'s blend of serious political commitment, muckraking, and sensationalism was adapted from Joseph Pulitzer's *New York World*, which through the 1920s matched human interest, crime, social crusading, and city news with one of the most respected editorial pages in the United States – edited by Walter Lippmann, writing "in shades of grey for an audience that wanted black and white" (Steel 1980, 218). The Pulitzer and Hearst papers in the United States had long since discovered that there were extraordinary profits to be made in promoting the social causes of the common person, and in exposing and exploiting the indiscretions of the rich and famous. In the same way, the *Star* served the needs and interests of Toronto's swelling immigrant population. If the *Globe* was the paper of the Protestant ruling elite, the *Star* spoke to the predominantly Jewish and Catholic working class, which was growing rapidly. Although the *New York World* folded in 1929, the *Star* flourished into the twenty-first century as "a truly populist paper ... a potent mix of commercialism and piety" (Hayes 1992, 59).

In such swelling cities as Baltimore, Boston, Montreal, New York, Philadelphia, and Toronto, it was not an act of social conscience to embrace the working class. It was good business. So, because the penny papers in these places sought a working-class clientele, they "endorsed policies and political causes that working people believed in. Whether their sympathy for the masses was sincere or not, sponsoring the causes of the relatively powerless served their interests" (Schudson 1995, 5). Pulitzer put it this way: "An able, disinterested, public-spirited press, with trained intelligence to know the right and courage to do it, can preserve public virtue without which government is a sham and a mockery" (cited in Teel 2006, 1).

As in Canada, the British popular press was slower to evolve than it had been in the United States. Asa Briggs and Peter Burke credit its rise to the Education Act of 1870, which set up schools that brought literacy to "hundreds of thousands of boys and girls," creating "a buoyant demand for reading matter very different from that on offer to an educated public" (2005, 159). And this created what the literary critic Matthew Arnold described as a "feather-brained" style of journalism aimed at attracting members of a newly enfranchised populace who were more interested in crime, entertainment, and scandal than the issues of the day (160). Although the penny papers in North America represented the democratizing of information, in Britain, they created a press for the educated elite and another for the lower classes, a schism that persists today between the quality papers and the sensationalistic tabloids.

The spread of literacy fuelled the growth of an industry that was to help define the urban life of the late nineteenth and early twentieth centuries. Industrial journalism mapped and reflected societies, propelled change, and amplified the conversation of the culture. It even helped reshape city cores, as the newspaper building took its place alongside the concert hall, library, city hall, and railroad station as a hallmark of the twentieth-century urban landscape. And here again we can see the influence of technology. As the emergence of a reading public is the cause most commonly given for the rise of the penny press, Schudson raises the intriguing possibility that it was technology that made literacy necessary, indirectly creating a mass audience. People need to be able to read advertising signage, leaflets, and publications to navigate the complex great society. So they "learn to read when reading becomes important" (1978, 36).

The spread of literacy across class lines might have been expected to democratize the press. However, there is another interpretation: that literacy gave rise to a media that herded people into a consumer corral, as "the ideal of an informed public [gave] way to the realities of the market" (Briggs and Burke 2005, 159). The German philosopher Jürgen Habermas (1991) has argued that, through the commercialization of communication in the nineteenth and twentieth centuries, capitalism, which had demolished feudalism, began to "refeudalize" the public sphere by reversing the process of public opinion from one that is formed by private citizens acting as a community to one formed when private enterprise frames the discourse to suit its needs (195). Then – through public relations, advertising, and a co-operative news media – capitalism impresses that discourse onto the crowd. This, Habermas argues, has led the press from being a manifestation of culture, a means of education, and a transmitter of the public opinion to a seller of entertainment and a manufacturer of a debased consumer culture. This plays into the various theories of hegemony, which define modern society as a "marketing culture" in which the aim of all communication is the sale of a product, an idea, or a belief, creating what critics on the left have called a state of false consciousness, or "mind colonization" (Nader 1997, 720).

At the same time, Habermas argues, the newsroom was undergoing a refeudalizing process of its own, in which the roles of editor and publisher changed from one of equals to "one of employer and employee" (1991, 183), placing commerce in the ascendant position, with communication subordinate. "The separation of public and private spheres implied that the competition between private interests was in principle left to the market as a regulating force and was kept outside the conflict of opinions. However, in the measure that the public sphere became a field for business advertising, private people as owners of private property had a direct effect on private people as the public. In this process, to be sure, the transformation of the public sphere into a medium of advertising was met halfway by the commercialization of the press" (189).

Schudson argues that there is a flaw in Habermas's thinking: he fails to take into account the fact that the commercialization of the press is only half the story. "Journalism as an occupational field became professionalized at the same time that it became commercialized as a business enterprise" (2003, 69). This professionalism armed journalists with stronger convictions, greater interest in the running of their publications and newscasts, and a more powerful ethical foundation for their demand to have a say in the forming of editorial policy. And this, he writes, acted as a counterbalance to commercialization.

On the other hand, it also has been argued that the news workforce never was entirely defeudalized. As we have seen, the newsroom evolved from "a single entrepreneur, usually flanked by a small coterie of foremen and managers who exercised power personally" to a complex hierarchical organization. The one thing the two organizations have in common is that they are designed to exploit journalists' feelings that their work is a "sacred calling" by claiming "a public service mandate that allowed publishers to submerge their profit motive within an appeal to their newsworkers' sense of duty" (Solomon 1995, 119). Although unionization and a heightened sense of professionalism in the business combined to improve conditions for newsworkers through the twentieth century, the pressure on profits created by the Internet has filtered down to a shrinking and beleaguered workforce. "New technologies and media mergers improve newspaper corporations' leverage over newsroom workers" to the extent that their situation is reverting back to that of the nineteenth century, when newsworkers were poorly paid – often less than so-called crafts workers – and badly treated, and enjoyed no job security:

> In the late 19th century, U.S. capitalism's transition to a corporate phase drove the commercial press's development, enlarging newsroom staffs and fuelling an increased division of labour. At the same time, the rising costs of owning a newspaper were moving ownership of the means of production beyond the financial reach of most newsworkers. Underlying these changes in political economy was a long-standing ideological component, one that infused newswork with a thoroughly individualistic, middle-class ethos. Caught between their public service ethic and their self-image on the one hand and their employers' capital accumulation strategies on the other, newsroom workers suffered. Today, as corporate capitalism becomes increasingly global, newsroom workers again face worsening work conditions. So, like their counterparts of more than a century ago, today's newsroom workers increasingly are coming to view their work as combining a sacred trust with a temporary job. The consequences for the public sphere – in a country that identifies itself as having a well informed citizenry that is becoming even more so, by moving onto an information superhighway – are unpleasant, at best. (131)

As the term "information superhighway" indicates, that was written in the mid-1990s, long before the technological disruption plunged the industry into its current state of despair. As we shall see, the consequences of technology on the newsroom workforce have been anything but positive in terms of quality and quantity of employment. However, what Solomon failed to foresee was that the new technology would also provide power tools for gathering information and communicating it, and would reduce the cost of publishing to the point that, once again, anyone can found a publication. In the corporate setting, though, Solomon was tremendously prescient: if anything, technology has made the conflict between sacred trust and income more pronounced. As Carleton University journalism professor Catherine McKercher says: "We have to keep in mind that journalists have been under this pressure for pretty well as long as there have been journalists ... For some reason, we're more likely to work for free than to really admit that we work for the money."

If the nineteenth century was characterized by commercialism, professionalism, and technology, the twentieth was marked by consolidation of ownership, a fixation on balance and professionalism, and continuing technological innovation – alongside a fear that technology had begun to turn against the print media. In terms of circulation, the latter half of the twentieth century was a period of long decline, even though it was also a period of constant revenue growth.

In Canada and the United States, "the 20th century newspaper story ... is a story of consolidation and centralization. Its inevitable result is the replacement of the multi-newspaper city by the single-newspaper city" (Kesterton 1984, 97). In 1900, there were seventeen two-newspaper towns in Canada. By 1966, the number had shrunk to nine, and there were seventy-five cities with only one daily. By 1913, the Canadian newspaper industry had reached its peak in terms of the number of dailies, with 138 (78), and the move toward concentration of ownership was well under way, as publishers began to expand their holdings. "Until World War I the drive toward monopoly at first concentrated on price cutting and combinations to restrain competition. During the war, the purchase and amalgamation of competitors became the preferred strategy" (Sotiron 1997, 6). By 1980, 74 per cent of English-Canadian newspapers, and 90 per cent of newspapers in Quebec, were in the hands of the chains (Kent 1981, 2–3).

At the same time, the audience for newspapers was shrinking, under attack by new competing media, an ongoing condition in the twentieth and twenty-first centuries that began in the 1930s with radio news. Even in the face of the Great Depression, radio exploded across Canada and the United States, creating the second North American continental medium, after consumer magazines. For example, in the United States by 1935, there were 30 million radio sets in homes, and more than 600 stations broadcasting (Kesterton 1984, 171).

In Canada, there was a growing worry that the national conversation was being dominated by foreign voices carried across the border on radio signals. This led to the Broadcasting Act of 1932, which brought about the creation of the Canadian Broadcasting Corporation/Radio-Canada in 1936. Though many Canadian newspapers owned and operated private radio stations – such as CJGC, by the *London Free Press*, and the *Toronto Daily Star*'s CFCA – many "newspaper proprietors grew almost irrational in their fear of radio," a dread that was transferred to television in the 1950s (Fetherling 1990, 110). As well, radio presented the first opportunity for politicians to appeal directly to a mass audience without having to subject themselves to mediation. The most famous example of this was US President Franklin D. Roosevelt's famous Fireside Chats of the 1930s. As politicians today use YouTube, Facebook and Twitter, Roosevelt turned to radio to bypass what he saw as a right-wing bias in the print media, and to "restore direct contact between the masses and their chosen leaders" (cited in Teel 2006, 167).

However, there was evidence that broadcast news actually helped newspaper circulation – if the newspapers delivered the right content. One of the first big TV news events in the United States was Gen. Douglas MacArthur's return from Korea in 1951, after his firing by President Harry S Truman. TV cameras followed MacArthur from the moment he arrived home to when he gave his "Old soldiers never die" speech to Congress. However, one survey showed that, rather than undermining circulation, the coverage drove Americans to their daily papers. "Televised news events seemed to increase readers' curiosity about these events, pushing them to buy the newspaper to read about what they had just seen" (Davies 2006, 52). This implied that people wanted more than the unvarnished facts. Television was whetting the public appetite for nuance, detail, and interpretation. The "increasing 'threat' of broadcast news, coupled with inescapable societal conflict, helped propel newspapers into new ways of reporting and presenting news – and prompted what might have been the best and most varied journalism in American history" (McPherson 2006, 1).

Still, circulation began to slide with the introduction of TV, and continued to do so through the century and into the next. For example, in the mid-1950s, Canadian newspaper companies were selling one copy for every household; by the late 1990s, the figure had dropped to just over 50 per cent. In a late-1990s poll, 34 per cent of respondents said newspapers were very important to them, down from 45 per cent ten years earlier (Miller 1998, 11).

Nineteen forty-five was the high-water mark for daily newspapers in the United States, with 1,749 dailies selling 48.4 million copies a day and $216 billion in ad space over the year (Davies 2006, 3–4). That year was also the point at which people began to turn away. Through the late twentieth century, television was drawing readers away by quickly and painlessly delivering the headlines that were all many people read anyway. At the same time, as *Newsweek* magazine put it, radio "stalked the nation like a zombie, long dead but somehow still alive" (112). Forced out of the network entertainment game by television, radio had remade itself as a portable medium for teenagers who wanted to take their music to the beach, and for adults who wanted news and music on the move, in the car, workshop, or kitchen. Also, with the contraction of the US national commercial radio networks, the medium concentrated more on local news and discussion, further fragmenting the newspapers' target audience. In Canada, the situation was somewhat the same in private radio, though the survival of CBC Radio as primarily a news and public affairs network further complicated things for the newspapers – something the CBC continues to do with its free website, which offers powerful competition for the newspapers' pay sites.

Superficially, things still looked good. The number of US papers remained relatively stable, and circulation continued to climb, reaching its all-time high of 58.9 million in 1960, a healthy increase of some 21 per cent from 1945. However, the population had grown from 139.9 million in 1945 to 180.7 million in 1960, an increase of 29 per cent (US Census Bureau 1999, 868). So, over those years, readership had actually shrunk by 8 per cent relative to population. At the same time, newspapers in Canada and the United States were growing in physical size – driven by increasing demand for advertising. In 1945, a typical mid-size US daily averaged a twenty-two-page edition on weekdays. By 1962, this had grown to fifty pages, and, though most of that growth was given over to advertising content, the editorial news hole had increased from 12.3 to 19.7 pages (Davies 2006, 112). Advertising growth was driving profits and fuelling an increase in news coverage; however, as we shall see, a good part of that increased news hole went to create advertiser-friendly sections filled with fluff.

It wasn't until the late 1970s that newspaper owners and publishers began to respond to the fact that circulation was static or shrinking. In Canada and the United States, circulation continued to decline in relation to the growth of population. In 1970, 63 million American households bought 62 million newspapers daily; in 2002, 56 million papers were purchased by 106 million households (Teel 2006, 115–16). There had been several closures of prominent, mostly afternoon, dailies, such as the *Montreal Star* (1979), and the *Ottawa Journal* and *Winnipeg Tribune* (1980) in Canada, and the *Philadelphia Bulletin* and *Washington Star* (1981) in the United States. Yet, in the 1980s, newspapers in both countries posted record profits; the survivors in one-newspaper towns were enjoying a bumper harvest of advertising. This apparent paradox is easily explained, Ben Bagdikian writes: "Disappearance of competitive newspapers always causes losses of sales. When dailies merge, the surviving paper never keeps all the readers from both papers; some readers are interested only in the paper that has disappeared and other readers who used to buy two or more papers a day when they were available can buy only one when there is a monopoly" (1990, 196).

In Canada, this weeding out was also accelerating a process that would lead in the 1990s to extraordinary concentration of ownership. Two main factors contributed to this development: geography and law. The main population centres of the country are spread across some 6,500 kilometres along the US frontier. So, in most parts of the country, it is uneconomical to cluster newspapers into regional chains, as many are in the United States. Similarly, because of the distances involved, national newspapers, such as the London dailies that had come to dominate the market in the United Kingdom, were impossible to distribute in North America until the early 1980s, when satellite technology allowed such papers as the *Globe and Mail*, the *New*

York Times, and the *Wall Street Journal* to create national editions, and for the Gannett Co. to launch USA *Today*. The second factor is a 1965 amendment to the Income Tax Act that was designed to keep US border stations from siphoning off advertising from Canadian television broadcasters. It also effectively bars non-Canadians from owning Canadian newspapers. Any company that advertises in a medium held by a private company that is more than 49 per cent foreign owned, or a public one more than 25 per cent foreign owned, is not permitted to claim advertising expenses as a tax deduction. This means a foreign-owned newspaper would operate with a debilitating handicap in selling advertising in the Canadian marketplace, and it is unlikely any large media company would be attracted to invest in an enterprise it could not control.

In the United States and Canada, the trend toward concentration of ownership began in the first decade of the twentieth century. One model of chain ownership was established by Edward Willis Scripps, whose business strategy was to establish "cheap new dailies for underserved audiences, especially urban workingmen" (Teel 2006, 5). The other, more enduring, style of expansion was established by Frank Munsey, the "gravedigger," who made a fortune of $40 million by purchasing newspapers and finding ways to squeeze greater profits from them, and then using those profits to finance further expansion (29). Chains that followed Munsey's style of acquisition and management include the Hearst, Copley, and Gannett companies in the United States, and, in Canada, Thomson, Southam, FP, and Hollinger – and Quebecor in its later years under Pierre Karl Péladeau. In Canada, only the Sun chain and Quebecor under founder Pierre Péladeau (who died in 1997) followed the Scripps formula, founding new dailies in Toronto, Edmonton, Calgary, Ottawa, Montreal, and Quebec City (and, briefly, Philadelphia).

As the first chains started to gobble up independents, media critics began to sound alarms. As early as 1928, the editor of the *Nation* wrote that chain ownership was causing a decline in the quality and originality of US newspapers. The symptoms of chain dominance were: "a lack of individuality; growing conformism dictated by media magnates; increasing preoccupation with entertainment, comics, and feature stories; and growing influence of advertising departments over editorial and news decisions" (111). Defenders of the industry responded with the argument that the commodification of news and the economies of scale made consolidation of ownership inevitable. As we will see in the next chapter, this chorus and counter-chorus remained a salient feature of the discourse about journalism through the twentieth century and into the twenty-first.

In the United States, between 1945 and 1965, the number of daily papers owned by chains almost doubled, from 365 to 750 (Davies 2006, 118). As in Canada, one of the main forces driving consolidation was tax law. On one hand, publishers could avoid paying tax on earnings that were reinvested, and buying other newspapers was a way to increase earnings and reduce tax at the same time. On the other hand, taxes on inheritance and income encouraged heirs to sell family-owned papers (119). In *The New Media Monopoly*, Ben Bagdikian points out that in the early 1980s, fifty large US media companies "dominated American audiences," and twenty dominant newspaper chains. "By 2003, five men controlled all these media once run by the fifty corporations of twenty years earlier" (2004, 27).

Critics of chain ownership continued to complain that this was fostering blandness and monotony, a sense that every paper in every city was being stamped out on the same assembly line. "A single owner concentrates energies, skills and managerial and journalistic resources on one newspaper and has the power (and often the economic motivation) to reinvest surplus profits in the long-term strength of that paper and its relationship to that one community. A chain owner does the opposite" (Bagdikian 1990, 226).

In Canada, by the early 1980s, increasing concentration of ownership had caused enough concern that the federal government created a Royal Commission on Newspapers, chaired by Tom Kent, to investigate it. The Kent Commission inquiry was the result of a massive shudder in the business that had been decades coming. In the 1960s and '70s, the largest newspaper company in Canada, in terms of circulation, was FP Publications, which owned such major dailies as the *Victoria Times* and the *Colonist*, the *Vancouver Sun*, the *Albertan* in Calgary, the *Winnipeg Free Press*, Toronto's *Globe and Mail*, the *Ottawa Journal*, and the *Montreal Star*. In second place was the Southam chain, with such holdings as the *Province* in Vancouver, the

Edmonton Journal, the *Calgary Herald*, the *Winnipeg Tribune*, the *Windsor Star*, the *Hamilton Spectator*, the *Ottawa Citizen*, and the *Gazette* in Montreal. In terms of number of dailies owned, the largest chain was Thomson, which began the 1970s with forty-one daily newspapers and ended the decade with thirty-eight (Hallman, Oliphant, and White 1981, 43). Thomson's holdings were exclusively small-circulation dailies and community newspapers, but they were very profitable.

In 1980, FP foundered after expensive strikes in Vancouver, Victoria, and Montreal. In September 1979, roughly seven months after resuming publication after an eight-month labour dispute, the afternoon *Montreal Star* closed, a victim of changes that were sweeping the industry. Afternoon papers had been struggling through the decade and, by the early 1980s, were on the verge of extinction across the continent – victims of an audience move to the suburbs, competition from television, and late-afternoon traffic congestion that delayed delivery and forced earlier and earlier deadlines. Victims of technological disruption, evening newspapers could not compete with the evening television news, which had created a new news-consuming habit in the population.

In February 1980, FP was bought by Thomson, which almost immediately launched the national edition of the *Globe and Mail*, and sold the *Albertan* to the Sun chain, which converted it to the *Calgary Sun*. Then, on one day in August of that year, Thomson closed its newly acquired FP paper, the *Ottawa Journal*, and Southam closed its *Winnipeg Tribune*. This left Thomson with a monopoly in Winnipeg and Southam with one in Ottawa. At the same time, Thomson sold its share of the *Gazette* and Pacific Press, which ran the *Vancouver Sun* and the *Province*, to Southam, giving that chain two additional monopolies. Finally, Thomson merged its Victoria dailies into a single paper, the *Times Colonist*. "This meant that Thomson and Southam controlled more than three-quarters of the total Canadian circulation," David Hayes writes in his history of the *Globe and Mail*. "And head-to-head competition between dailies had disappeared from every city except Toronto and St. John's, Newfoundland. It amounted to a wholesale restructuring of the $2.5 billion Canadian newspaper industry" (1992, 163).

Foreshadowing a future in which audience targeting would play an increasingly greater role in media-company strategy, tabloid newspapers were founded in Montreal, Quebec City, Toronto, Edmonton, Calgary, Winnipeg, Ottawa, and Halifax throughout the 1960s, '70s, and '80s – practising what the Kent Commission called "extreme product differentiation."

> Whereas in the past the general approach to competition had been to aim a newspaper at a broad middle-ground of readers, the new approach is to segment potential readership with certain characteristics, certain interests and certain needs capable of being served by a new paper, and at the same time of specific interest to advertisers. The word most commonly used in this new phase of newspaper competition is "demographics" ... there are more markets in the larger cities than had been thought. Find one, reach and reflect it, sell it and you can build a successful newspaper in the teeth of intense competition. The new approach is about 10 years old in Toronto and older in Montreal. (Hallman, Oliphant, and White 1981, 11)

That wasn't *quite* true. In Montreal in the 1970s, there may have been more head-to-head competition on all levels than anywhere else in the country. As well as the English mainstream *Star* and *Gazette*, the tabloids *Le Journal de Montréal* and *Montréal Matin* had been fighting for readers. And, from 1974 to 1976, *La Presse* was competing with the Parti Québécois daily *Le Jour*. It was only in 1979, with the closing of the *Star* and *Montréal-Matin*, that English and French Montreal became monopoly cities. The dominant dailies were the *Gazette* and *La Presse*, with the blue-collar *Le Journal de Montréal* and the elitist *Le Devoir* occupying specialty niches.

When Hayes writes that only two cities in Canada had competing dailies, he overlooks Vancouver, where the *Sun* and *Province*, though owned by the same company, competed as broadsheets until 1983, when the *Province* was converted to a tabloid. It also could be argued that, by going national, the *Globe and Mail* established the kind of product differentiation that allowed it to coexist rather than compete with the *Toronto Star* – though the *Globe* maintained a Toronto edition. Direct, head-to-head competition exists today in Canada only with the two national papers. In the United States, it lingers in a few places, such as New York (with the *Post*, *Daily News*, and *Long Island Newsday*), Detroit (the *News* and *Free Press*, under a joint operating agreement), and Chicago (where the *Sun-Times*, though a tabloid, competes directly with the broadsheet *Tribune*).

Thomson and Southam remained the dominant chains in Canada until the mid-1990s, when the former began to reorganize itself and discard newspapers and Conrad Black's Hollinger Group acquired the latter. At the time, Black said he foresaw "one more mighty cycle of newspaper profits left, at least" (Miller 1998, 90). In 1995, his main newspaper holdings were the *Chicago Sun-Times*, the *Jerusalem Post*, and the *Telegraph* in England. In Canada, he was proprietor of Sterling Newspapers, which ran tiny dailies, mostly in British Columbia, and UniMedia, owner of Quebec City's journal of record, *Le Soleil* and the tabloid *Le Droit* in Ottawa. Within eighteen months, Black acquired forty papers by swallowing up Southam, most of Thomson's Canadian holdings and the Armadale group in Saskatchewan, owners of the *Regina Leader-Post* and *Saskatoon StarPhoenix*. He also founded the *National Post* to compete with the Canada-wide *Globe and Mail*. No one else in Canada was interested in buying daily newspapers, or had the resources to acquire them, and the Income Tax Act kept the big US companies from moving north. So, the number of players had been fixed by circumstance.

The 1990s closed with an attempted hostile takeover of the Sun chain by the *Toronto Star*'s parent company, Torstar, which failed when Quebecor, at the time one of the world's largest printing companies and owner of *Le Journal de Montréal, Le Journal de Québec,* and the *Winnipeg Sun,* stepped in with a higher per-share bid. Quebecor's competing bid was partly engineered by Sun management and was welcomed by employees as salvation. It turned out to be anything but. *Toronto Sun* founding publisher Doug Creighton told me in 2002, two years before his death and long after the dust had settled, that he had never regarded the takeover as a case of Quebecor riding to the rescue of Sun Media. "I knew the old man fairly well," he said of Quebecor founder Pierre Péladeau. "Péladeau's sons, I suspect, have never been called white knights before – and don't think for one minute they'll ever get called that in the future."

That completed a total realignment of the newspaper business. Two predatory chains – Hollinger Inc. and Quebecor – controlled 66.1 per cent of Canada's newspaper circulation, and two more – Torstar and

Thomson – held another 21.3 per cent. The total owned by the four companies: 87.4 per cent (Wilson-Smith 1998).

Then, in 2000–1, the Canadian media industry reorganized itself yet again. This time, the name of the game was convergence, the belief that marrying content providers to delivery systems would lead to the birth of big profits. Canwest took over most of Hollinger's Canadian holdings – including thirteen major Canadian dailies and the *National Post* – merging them with its Global Television Network as content providers for print, TV, and the Canada.com website. In 2002, the company sold off many of the smaller properties, such as the *St Catharines Standard* and the *Kingston Whig-Standard*, to the newly formed Osprey Media.

Meanwhile, BCE Corp. – which already controlled Bell Telephone, the Sympatico-Lycos Web portal, and the satellite TV company Bell ExpressVu – took control of the CTV network and its group of broadcast and cable channels, and formed an alliance with Thomson to jointly operate the *Globe and Mail*, giving it television and print content providers for the Internet, as well as the means with which to bring the content into homes.

Finally, Quebecor won a bidding war with Rogers Cable for control of the Quebec cable provider Groupe Vidéotron – which included the TVA television network. And that, aside from some minor manoeuvrings, was how things stood until the recession of 2008, which destroyed Canwest, realigned the Canadian television landscape, and saw Quebecor acquire Osprey.

A long, deep recession in the early 1990s sent an industry that had grown accustomed to record profits into shock. In Canada and the United States, the newspaper business was increasingly dominated by publicly owned companies whose shareholders had grown accustomed to return on investment of 20 to 40 per cent of revenue (Fink 1996, 17). In the United States, the gold standard was Gannett, which at least until the mid-1990s, demanded 30 to 50 per cent profit margin from its publishers (Underwood 1995, 98) and went eighteen years (1967–85) in which each quarterly profit was greater than the one before it (Bagdikian 2004, 184). Another major acquirer of media properties was the Chicago Tribune Co., which, over the course of the decade, bought up a host of TV stations and newspapers – including the *Los Angeles Times*. By 2008, the company had run up a debt of $13 billion, which was to make it the most spectacular media casualty of the most recent recession.

On an international level, the great acquisitive force was Rupert Murdoch, an Australian-American who, over three decades, acquired and discarded major papers in the United States and Britain, ranging from the *News of the World*, the *Sun*, and the *Times* in the UK to the *Chicago Sun-Times* and the *New York Post*, and founded TV networks on both sides of the Atlantic, most notably Fox and Fox News in the United States.

Amid all this acquisition activity – propelled by ever-increasing corporate debt – display advertising had been dropping off. A 1994 survey done for Canadian publishers by consultant Len Kubas revealed that of the six factors that determine newspaper success, four were in decline: circulation, readership, advertising lineage, and public image (Miller 1998, 11). Between 1990 and 1995, Canadian industry advertising revenues dropped 27 per cent, from $2.2 billion to $1.6 billion, and then plunged another 5 per cent in 1996 (13). This was partly fuelled by a floundering retail industry, partly by advertisers focusing on demographic data to target preferred customers, and partly by the combination of high newspaper ad rates and dwindling audience share.

Yet, even with the recession of the early 1990s, newspaper profits remained high compared to other industries, 12 to 15 per cent for many, and still in the 25–30 per cent range for some – compared to General Motors' 4.3 to 4.4 per cent and Exxon's 5.8 to 9.4 per cent (Fink 1996, 17). By the late 1990s, advertising lineage and revenue had rebounded, but Canadian dailies were earning only slightly more from ad sales than they had been before the recession. "Some of the new business comes from advertising inserts, a credit not to any renewed faith in newspapers but rather to a vigorous lobbying campaign by the newspaper industry that persuaded the federal government to get Canada Post out of the lucrative door-to-door delivery of flyers. A list of advertisers who by and large ignore newspapers today includes such household names as Procter and Gamble, McDonald's, Seagram's, Ford Motor Company, Coca-Cola, Nissan, Kodak and Campbell's Soup. They are saying something scary to publishers: 'You're not worth our money'" (Miller 1998, 11).

The situation was more or less the same in the United States. Carl Sessions Stepp, senior editor of *American Journalism Review*, summed it up this way:

> Today's editors live ... in an oddly paradoxical age. Newspaper profits are rocketing, but circulation – and confidence – continue to slip. In the most pessimistic circles, something approaching a deathwatch is on, and even the optimists can be caught looking over their shoulders, or, worse, gazing at the backsides of competitors that already seem to have surged past them. In a sober-up-or-else comment at this year's American Society of Newspaper Editors convention, Intel Chairman Andrew Grove warned that newspapers could be three years away from meltdown. "Nothing sharpens the awareness of a situation like the sight of the gallows." (1999)

A year earlier, in Canada, *Globe and Mail* publisher Phillip Crawley had pointed out that although newspaper readership was growing in the developing world, circulation was "down in the U.S. by five per cent, the European Union by four per cent and in Canada by 10 per cent ... The newspaper business in the developed world is a mature business – one with lots of new competition such as the Internet, 24-hour TV news, and all-news radio ... once popular afternoon dailies, traditionally read by blue-collar workers, continue to close as the proportion of white-collar workers rises. Since the recession of the early 1990s, many papers have reduced some forms of circulation not required by advertisers" (1998).

As this postwar decline was taking place on the business side, important changes were happening in the newsroom. In tandem with the rise of the commercial newspaper industry, especially in the 1950s and '60s, objectivity had been emerging as the core belief of modern journalism. As well, as Schudson (1978) points out, there was a major change in journalists' attitudes toward their work. They stopped seeing themselves as craftspeople and became professionals.

When journalism became modern, professional, and respectable, the newspaper industry turned its back on the literary and muckraking traditions of the penny press, and adopted a quasi-scientific approach to newsgathering that was designed to bolster its new view of itself. Beginning in the mid-nineteenth century, reporters "began to see themselves, in part, as scientists uncovering the economic and political facts of industrial life more boldly, more clearly, and more 'realistically' than anyone had done before" (71). This was an attitude born of a time of great faith in science to tame nature and impose logic upon the world. Two of the most important words in the Victorian vocabulary were "authority" and "progress" (Briggs and Burke 2005 96), and all fields were finding it necessary to establish, or certify, their credentials and exclusivity. In the 1870s and 1880s, at least 200 "learned societies" were founded in the United States, ranging from the American Chemical Society to the Geological Society of America, to the National Statistical Association (Bledstein 1976, 86). "In the mind of mid-Victorians, professionalism ... embodied a more radical idea of democracy than even Jackson had dared to dream ... a liberated person seeking to free the power of nature within every worldly sphere, a self-governing individual exercising his trained judgment in an open society" (87).

In the case of journalism, this professionalism manifested itself in the doctrine of objectivity. Ideally, Neal Gabler writes, this means that the journalist enters into research with an open mind, explores all the facts, considers all the angles, and then presents conclusions supported by those facts. "The roots for this go back more than a century, when the journalistic extremists of the yellow press era, William Randolph Hearst and Joseph Pulitzer, controlled American newspapers. Progressives decided to fight back against these press lords' sensationalistic, propagandistic papers that traded in scandal and used their pages to promote pet causes – most famously, Hearst's desire to provoke a Spanish-American war. The Progressives called for a new, professionalized journalism, in which reporters wouldn't be advocates who took sides so much as observers who collected facts" (2013).

Unfortunately, he adds, "it was a very short distance from so-called objectivity, in which one might be forced to take sides by the facts, to balance, in which one avoided taking sides by presenting the arguments for each." Thus, balance usurped the role of objectivity simply because balance requires no defence: it is neutral, bland, and safe. It also is often misleading and can easily play into the hands of the hucksters and opportunists that Raymond Williams warned against.

Before the penny press, there had been no division between fact and opinion: the newspaper owner-editor-publisher was a pamphleteer, journalist, and pundit, and occasionally a politician as well. With the invention of the penny press and of the reporter, news and opinion had been segregated, as had business and editorial. If there was an opening shot fired in the battle against the subjective narrative, it came in 1851, with Henry J. Raymond's front-page launch message for the first edition of the *New York Times*. "We do not mean to write as if we were in a passion unless that should really be the case; and we shall make a point to get into a passion as rarely as possible" (Alterman 1982, 26). Raymond was reacting to the excesses of his former employer, Horace Greeley's *New York Tribune*, which had invented the editorial page but had not purged its news pages of opinion (25). Compare Raymond's remarks to the inspirational mission statement laid down in 1835 by James Gordon Bennett for his *New York Herald*, and you get a glimpse of the recurring struggle in journalism between the cold, scientific detachment favoured by Walter Lippmann and the passionate involvement advocated by John Dewey and, much later, the public journalism movement: "My ambition is to make the newspaper press the great organ and pivot of government, society, commerce, finance, religion, and all human civilization." Bennett also believed that a newspaper could "send more souls to heaven and save more from hell than all the clubs and chapels in New York" (Briggs and Burke 2005, 155).

It was the *New York Times* that set the standard for the modern newspaper – and by extension the all-news TV network – in that it was not so much dedicated to objectivity as to the appearance of objectivity (Alterman 1982, 27). That appearance of objectivity, as many observers have noted, became "the emblem of American journalism ... an improvement over a past of 'sensationalism' and a contrast to party papers of Europe" (Schudson 1978, 9).

Unfortunately, however, many newspapers' idea of objectivity was a timid one, in which cranks, lobbyists, and special-interest operatives were given equal time with scientists, politicians, NGOs, and genuine experts. The most commonly cited indictment of balance is the case of Senator Joseph McCarthy and his campaign against the communists who were supposedly infesting all levels of US government and culture in the 1950s. Every time McCarthy spouted the numbers of communists in the State Department or other federal agency, a stenographic press obediently quoted him uncritically. In the same way, the tobacco industry was able to use questionable "experts" to deliver quotes to the media. This created just enough uncertainty to keep cigarettes on sale and the companies profitable for years after medical science had conclusively proved that smoking caused heart and lung disease. That approach later became the model for climate-change denial – and goes a long way toward explaining how Donald Trump has become a Fox News visiting expert on political science, economics, and climatology. Balance was mistaken for objectivity and, because balance is so easy to pervert, objectivity was discredited in the minds of many journalists and observers of the industry.

It was also in the mid-twentieth century that journalists began to aspire to the sort of refinement Walter Lippmann had brought to the craft. Lippmann got his feet wet in journalism as an apprentice to Lincoln Steffens at *McClure's* but quickly broke with the muckrakers, arguing in his 1914 book of political analysis, *Drift and Mastery*, that the job of engineering society should be left to technicians and statesmen who work dispassionately and without appealing to the baser instincts of the public. He was a political theorist, essayist, and adviser to the powerful. One of his biographers wrote, "The first American president to praise Lippmann and then break with him was Theodore Roosevelt; the last was Lyndon Johnson" (Adams 1977, 9). With Herbert Croly, Lippmann founded the *New Republic*. He also wrote a pair of books, *Public Opinion* and *The Phantom Public*, expressing, among other things, a dismal view of the people's capacity to engage intelligently in public life and of the press's ability to inform them. He is often presented as the opposite of John Dewey, who believed in the power of communication to transform society into community and forge crowds into publics. Through his work as editorial page editor at the *New York World*, and later as a highly influential syndicated columnist, Lippmann cast the mould for the modern opinion-page columnist and TV pundit.

"Pre-Lippmann ... reporting was seen as a job for winos, perverts, and those without sufficient imagination to become successful gangsters" (Alterman 1982, 22). But, thanks to journalism schools in universities and a growing corps of highly educated reporters and pundits/public intellectuals like Lippmann, the second half of the twentieth century saw journalism become a profession for serious-minded university graduates (Schudson 2003). In 1957, *Time* magazine more or less summed up the evolution of the press with this description of the sudden transformation of the *Toronto Daily Star*: "The *Toronto Star* turned grey one day last week. Banished overnight were the sensation and sudden death once trumpeted in blazing, two-inch headlines. Staffers were forbidden to mention the nude bodies and sanguinary scenes that once covered Page One; crime reporters could no longer identify criminal suspects until they had been formally charged ... young [publisher] Joe [Atkinson] ordered drastic cutbacks, told editors to drop far-flung junkets" (Harkness 1963, 383). In 1961, new *Star* publisher Beland Honderich put a fine point on it when he told a group of editors, "The basic function of a newspaper is to inform, to tell the public what is happening in the community, in the nation and in the world. You will notice I did not use the word 'entertain'" (Gerard 2005).

As a *Houston Post* executive put it in 1950, North American journalism was shifting its emphasis "from scoop to scope" (Davies 2006, 29). After the Second World War, the North American popular newspaper found that its readers were demanding information and analysis that could help them make sense out of international tensions, galloping scientific innovations, and a booming economy. So the "old tried-and-true formulas for news" – crime, sex, money, and politics – were being "crowded by labor, industrial, and science news" (16).

As the creed of objectivity pushed opinion and interpretation from news writing, the op-ed pages grew fatter and more powerful. "Absent a professionally sacred faith in objective news gathering, there would be no call for political pundits to comment on it" (Alterman 1982, 28). To put it another way and one more directly relating to the dogma of balance, "Objectivity is an ideology of distrust in the self" (Schudson 1978, 71). In this atmosphere, journalism abandoned the interpretation and nuance of literary journalism and the passionate moral imperative of muckraking and replaced them with stenography and analysis. Objectivity provided a new model of journalism for the era of the man in the grey flannel suit. "The rakish self-image of the urban journalist gave way to a buttoned-down image of the White House correspondent, one who might even give occasional political counsel to an aspiring senator or presidential candidate" (Schudson 2003, 86–7).

Lippmann was a classic example of this kind of insider/observer, and he believed journalism should aim to be a collaboration of sober fact-gatherers and thunderbolt-hurling pundits – like Walter

Lippmann. Alterman argues that Lippmann was the prototype for every newspaper opinion-page pundit who came after him. Tom Wolfe, who worked in Lippmann's home newsroom, the *New York Herald-Tribune*, called him "the archetypal newspaper columnist ... For 35 years, Lippmann seemed to do nothing more than ingest the *Times* every morning, turn it over in his ponderous cud for a few days, and then methodically egest it in the form of a drop of mush on the foreheads of several hundred thousand readers of other newspapers in the days thereafter" (1973, 12).

While Lippmann and his progeny were ruling the op-ed pages, Wolfe writes, reporters who saw themselves as storytellers were chafing against the tyranny of the "pallid little troll of understatement" (17). And reporters weren't the only ones who had a problem with that beast. For example, in a speech at Carleton University in 1989, *Toronto Star* publisher Beland Honderich stirred up controversy by coming right out and admitting that he thought balance was not a desirable characteristic of a newspaper: "No self-respecting newspaper deliberately distorts or slants the news to make it conform to its own point of view. But you cannot publish a newspaper without making value judgments on what news you select to publish and how you present it in the paper. And these value judgments reflect a view of society – a point of view if you will – that carries as much weight, if not more, than what is said on the editorial page" (Gerard 2005).

This brings us to Dewey and his descendants, and their exhortations that communication is culture and that journalists should behave as if they were citizens and artists. Dewey writes that journalism as a "responsive art of communication must take possession of the physical machinery and circulation and breathe life into it" (1954, 183). The art is in the accurate and insightful rendering of reality, and the ability to fashion the profound out of found objects. This involves "the imposition of the narrative line upon disparate images, by the 'idea' with which we have learned to freeze the shifting phantasmagoria which is our actual experience," Joan Didion writes. "We look for the sermon in the suicide, for the social or moral lesson in the murder of five" (2006b, 185).

Yet often, social scientists, journalism educators, and some journalists impose a bland, bureaucratized professionalism on journalism and refuse to see it as an art form or even as popular culture. In his influential essay "Notes towards a Definition of Journalism," G. Stuart Adam complains that the field is often studied as if it were a "found thing," something to be described and defined uncritically, like a product of nature, when it must be approached as a "made thing" in which we ask such questions as, Is it any Good? or, Does it fulfill its mission?

> Professional practitioners are inclined to define journalism in terms of limited newsroom conceptions and thus jettison any consideration of journalism's poetics or its ambitious forms; sociologists, communicologists, and political scientists are inclined to read journalism functionally rather than intrinsically and thus contribute to the leveling impulse that originates with the practitioners. Neither the practitioners nor the social scientists are sufficiently inclined to lift journalism out of the bureaucratic settings in which journalists are likely to operate and imagine journalism as the best journalists do as they make news judgments, engage in reporting, and compose accounts of the world. (2006, 345)

The concept of news as popular culture may deflate some pompous views of the news media – journalists as guardians of democracy or educators – but, again as communication theorists Elihu Katz and David Foulkes point out, communication scholars of the radio age saw newspapers as providing "ritualistic activity, orientation to everyday living (and dying), conversation starters and the like" (1962, 378). Thus, news "becomes the central storehouse for the various national conversations" of the culture (Schudson 1995, 179).

There was a short-lived movement in the United States that tried to take possession of the machinery of journalism and retool it to manufacture popular art. In the 1960s and '70s, a generation of reporters began to question the creed of balance and the trustworthiness of power. Schudson argues that this grew out of what literary critic Lionel Trilling called the "adversary culture" of modern writing, in which the hero stands at a remove from society, offering a vantage point from which to critique and revise it. Many young journalists, like young people in the society at large, were better educated and more inclined to set themselves up in an adversarial position to a society they had come to distrust. Having grown up on often iconoclastic post–Second World War cinema and literature, written largely from the outsider's perspective and concerned with social justice, and having witnessed the empowerment of the working classes in North America and England, these journalists were often contemptuous of "straight" society and rebellious toward a newsroom culture they saw as grey and unquestioning of authority (1978, 176–7).

Some of the most important venues of this New Journalism were mainstream magazines such as *Esquire*, the *Saturday Evening Post*, and the *Herald-Tribune*'s Sunday magazine, *New York*. The last was spun off as a glossy weekly in 1968, a year after the *Herald-Tribune* folded and, under star editor Clay Felker, remained an important forum for New Journalism through the 1970s. However, the natural environment for this new style of journalism was the underground press – such periodicals as the *Village Voice*, Boston's *Phoenix* and *Real Paper*, the *Los Angeles Free Press*, *Rolling Stone*, *Ramparts*, and *New Times*.

Similar to the way the Internet is putting the levers of publishing power into the hands of the peasantry today, technological innovation had made it possible for a new generation to create publications that focused on cultural and political subjects that the mainstream press refused to take seriously. Offset printing, photo engraving, and cold type made publishing, easy, fast, and cheap. No longer did a publisher need presses, engravers, and hot-lead typesetting equipment on premises. Words, pictures, and layouts could be delivered to one end of a printing house and a pile of newspapers picked up at the other. The result was a rash of feisty, stylish, and often aggressively strange prose, typography, and layout, and a sense of literary and graphic experimentation that influenced a generation of writers, photographers, designers, and editors. The *Seattle Post-Intelligencer* described the field as ranging "all the way from little sheets explaining how to make a Molotov cocktail to large publications that are so serious they are Dullsville" (McPherson 2006, 25). This description of New York's *East Village Other* could be applied to the entire underground press of the 1960s and early '70s: "The *Other* doesn't separate fact from opinion. Its journalism is unabashedly, militantly, interpretive: pro pot, peace, sex, psychedelics and subversion; anti most of what remains in switched-off American society" (25). Although the one thing these journalists had in common was contempt for the mainstream media, their call for a more investigative and interpretive style of journalism resonated with many older colleagues, who saw change as a way to deal with the competition of TV news, the "unblinking eye" that was cornering the market on apparent objectivity (Schudson 1978, 181).

Wolfe describes how in the mid-'60s journalism experienced an awakening of the "lower class" of letters: the "day laborers who dug up slags of raw information for writers of higher 'sensibility' to make better use of." The revolution came from the lowest social order, the freelancers who wrote for Sunday supplements, slick magazines, and the alternative press. "[A] bunch of these lumpenproles ... with no literary credentials whatsoever in most cases ... they're using all the techniques of the novelist ... and on top of that, they're helping themselves to the insights of the men of letters while they're at it ... and at the same time, they're doing their low-life legwork, their 'digging,' their hustling, their damnable Locker Room Genre reporting" (1973, 25).

Meanwhile, two events in the 1970s placed journalism at odds with a power establishment with which it had formerly identified: the publication by the *New York Times* and *Washington Post* of the "Pentagon Papers" in 1971, which brought into question the US involvement in Vietnam; the *Post*'s investigation of the Watergate break-in by the Committee to Re-elect the President and the subsequent cover-up by the Nixon administration in 1972–73. This changed journalism, in that news organizations "that had once cooperated routinely with government began to see 'national security' as a euphemism for 'stay out of my business because I could be embarrassed by publicity'" (Schudson 2003, 88). As the Internet often does today, the alternative press was, to a certain extent, setting the agenda for the mainstream media – in some cases leading the way with investigative work that forced the mainstream dailies to respond by being more aggressive. However, investigative journalism gave the newspapers an alternative to the New Journalism: "a format more palatable to mainstream journalists concerned with objectivity" (McPherson 2006, 50).

New Journalism lived on, mainly in books and at some magazines and sporadically in the better dailies. Investigative or accountability reporting – always risky in terms of potential legal costs – became rare, as newsrooms shrank, reporters became more pressed for time, and bottom line–minded publishers pushed their workforce to manufacture more news in less time with fewer staff. At the same time, the underground newspaper gave way to the alternative weekly, a self-consciously hip, inner-city giveaway that was often little more than a delivery vehicle for display advertising, event listings, and racy classifieds. Similarly, "adversary journalism passed out of favor almost as soon as editors began to worry about giving readers what they want, and they surely didn't want more bad news" (Miller 1998, 231). For the mainstream press, the result was a return to balance.

To be fair, owners, publishers, and editors had compelling reasons to back away from the concept of journalism as art. There's no question that artists are harder to find and require a great deal more policing and grooming than fact-gatherers. And the last thing anyone wanted was a newspaper filled with the pretentious ravings of semi-talented hacks who fancy themselves grand stylists. At least a plain, facts-only approach could be counted upon to be coherent after editing, and a few good editors can turn even the most turgid prose into something readable. In an article revisiting Tom Wolfe's New Journalism classic *The Electric Kool-Aid Acid Test*, Jack Shafer praises writers such as Wolfe, Didion, Norman Mailer, George Plimpton, Terry Southern, and Gay Talese for "restoring strong narrative, detailed reporting, and point of view to American feature journalism." He also laments the fact that so much attention was paid to style and technique that many writers forgot that the foundation of all New Journalism narrative was extraordinarily detailed reporting. One unfortunate by-product of the movement was "two generations of boneheads who thought the lesson of the New Journalism was to pound on the exclamation key while writing yourself into the story" (2006). Even Hunter Thompson – whose gonzo journalism may have been responsible for encouraging more of those boneheads than any other form of the genre – had this to say about Wolfe: "The only thing new and unusual about Wolfe's journalism is that he's an abnormally good reporter; he has a fine sense of echo and at least a peripheral understanding of what John Keats was talking about when he said that thing about Truth & Beauty" (Weingarten 2005, 124).

Extensively researched and elegantly wrought journalism still exists in the pages of such high-end general-interest magazines as *Atlantic*, *Harper's*, the *New Yorker*, and, in Canada, *Maisonneuve* and *The Walrus*, and online at such sites as *Slate* and Vancouver's *The Tyee*. An example is the three-part series "American Ground," which William Langewiesche wrote in 2002 for *Atlantic* about the terrorist attacks of 11 September 2001. Fanatically well researched and vividly written, the series succeeded where all the punditry and sober reporting, and even all the pictures and films had failed. Langewiesche *shows* readers what it was like: to be inside the buildings when the planes struck; to be on the stairs when the buildings collapsed and hear floors crashing down on one another in rhythmic succession overhead; to be a firefighter rushing against the tide into the doomed towers; to pass through the subterranean mass of concrete, metal, and dust, to the flooded PATH train tracks. Langewiesche proves Shafer's argument that "narrative is the finest container ever devised to transport ideas, especially transporting ideas over time" (2006), not to mention Thompson's observation that the main thing that distinguishes excellence from mediocrity in journalistic writing is "abnormally good" reporting.

This brings us back to the ideal of objectivity, as opposed to the illusion of balance. As Tom Wolfe wrote, objectivity is not only desirable but, in the hands of experts, it is inevitable. The conceit that one is an artist – as opposed to a stenographer or educator – can't help but produce objectivity the way Gabler describes it: "[T]he proof of one's technical mastery as a writer becomes paramount and the demonstration of moral points becomes secondary. This passion for technical brilliance has lent [feature writers] a strange sort of objectivity, an egotistical objectivity but an objectivity of sorts in any case" (Wolfe, 1973, 50).

3

Critics:
A History of Truculence

As we saw in chapter 2, the period from 1945 to the recession of 2008 was one of contradictions for newspapers: declining circulation and growing profit; rising professionalism and falling morale; technical advances and technological threats. Those years were also marked by growing concern about the uses and misuses of mass media in a modern society, from the US Commission on Freedom of the Press (the Hutchins Commission) and its direct descendant, *Four Theories of the Press*, to a series of government inquiries in Canada, to the works of a horde of pessimistic critics in the 1990s and 2000s – many of whom were echoing concerns expressed by the likes of Walter Lippmann and John Dewey in the 1910s and '20s. Most of the concern and criticism had to do with the role of a free press in a democratic society, and how to balance the public service aspect of the news business against the drive for profit.

Harvard political scientist Pippa Norris once wrote that political communication comes in three forms: civic engagement, agenda setting, and persuasion (1999, 11–19). Each presents problems for journalism. Civic engagement involves explaining to the public the issues and the parties' positions, and mobilizing citizens to vote. This implies a bland, pure-service role that the public may no longer need, or wish, the press to play – or which needs to be reinterpreted and expanded upon. The Internet, political parties, interest groups, citizens' movements – as well as various forms of traditional and alternative media – have proved quite capable of getting unadorned information about platforms and policies to the people, stimulating discussion, and promoting voter involvement. From a business perspective, this places the mainstream news media in the financially suicidal position of selling something everyone else appears to be giving away. From a service perspective, civic engagement sets up the press to play the role of "gatekeeper" or educator, and to be seen by the public not as uncovering, illuminating, and delivering information, but as controlling and interpreting it for what the members of the press – or the people who own one – perceive to be the common good. Perhaps the most deadly effect has been that, from a professional or craft point of view, it tends to impose a humourless, pedantic, almost anti-narrative tone on storytelling, which readers and viewers often find patronizing, off-putting, or soporific. As *Wall Street Journal* feature writer William E. Blundell put it in the newspaper's handbook:

> Too many reporters do not see themselves as storytellers but as something else. Some are lawyers, in effect. They believe their job is to convince people of the rightness or the wrongness of things as they have determined it, so their copy has a didactic or shrill tone. Fixated on ideas, they lack humility in their work. They may talk down to the reader or talk at him, but they seldom talk *with* him as the storyteller does. (quoted in Starkman 2014, 91; italics in original)

Agenda setting is even more problematic, because it moves journalists uncomfortably close to the machinery of power, which they are supposed to be watching. This involves a fundamental concern about the media and democracy: that, as Lippmann wrote in *Public Opinion*, the press can't tell people how to think, but it can tell us what to think about (1997, 206–7).

The third type of political communication, persuasion, implies that the press can be used to educate and enlighten, or to mobilize and proselytize. In its positive imaginings, this outlook has its foundations in Dewey's vision of journalists, social scientists, and politicians coming together to take on the role of artist-educators and mobilizing the public into a continuous public debate, what James Carey called the conversation of the culture. In the late 1990s, that ideal found expression in the public journalism movement, which has declined in influence since its heyday, perhaps because it never proved to be a cure for waning circulation, turned out to be fairly expensive to implement, and has been enthusiastically – perhaps too enthusiastically – adopted by online citizen journalists. It also was never quite clear how a watchdog press could remain on guard while helping out with the project.

One thing the three forms of communication have in common is that they begin with the belief that there is a state of political grace to which we all should, or could, aspire. The debate is over whether it is the press's duty to lead us into that state of grace or to keep democracy safe for us while we're at the movies or driving the kids to soccer practice. Much of the discourse about the news business – dating back to Lippmann's *Public Opinion* and *The Phantom Public*, and to Dewey's *The Public and Its Problems* – has been grounded in those two viewpoints of the news media's role in democracy. At the same time, the fortunes of the press, and the concern about it, have run parallel to a similar concern about the health of democracy and the state of the public sphere. Do citizens have the potential to form an engaged public? Or are we, as Lippmann put it, just "a bewildered herd" (1993, 145) that can be manipulated into voting for tyranny or chaos, an uninformed majority with the power "to deprive tomorrow's majority of its rights" (1963, 56)?

As several observers have pointed out, forces within the craft and outside it – particularly the social sciences – have attempted to impose a formal mission on journalism, to put it to work as a persuasive force for agenda setting, or as a means to rally civic engagement. The most influential case is probably *Four Theories of the Press*, a guide to the press and "the social systems in which the press functions" (Siebert, Peterson, and Schramm 1963, 2) written in 1956 by University of Illinois communication scholars Fred S. Siebert, Theodore Peterson, and Wilbur Schramm. It is a slim book that presents the idea that the news must always take on the character of the political system in which it lives – thus eliminating from the discussion alternative, underground, or dissident press. It maps out the three types of journalism that existed at the time, according to a political history of the postwar period, and sets down a blueprint for a fourth system, designed to harness a free-enterprise news business and make it work for the common good.

In 1995, another group of University of Illinois communication scholars, led by John C. Nerone, gathered to reassess the *Four Theories* and pose the question of "whether the whole enterprise needs to be rethought" (30). Nerone argues that the theories are, for the most part, not theories at all, but rather "one theory with four examples ... Its theory, to paraphrase, is that, in its structure, policy, and behavior, the communications system reflects the society in which it operates and that society can be categorically defined by a coherent philosophy. That is the basic postulate of the book" (18). That overriding theory is grounded in liberal tradition and a neo-liberal world view, growing out of a postwar concern about the rise of totalitarian states in the twentieth century.

Three of the *Four Theories* consist of: an Authoritarian concept of the press, growing from "centuries of authoritarian political thought from Plato to Machiavelli" (6); a Soviet Communist Theory for the Marxist countries; a Libertarian Theory for Western Europe and North America. Merrill and Nerone (2002) argue that these examples have the virtue of offering a quick, simple survey of twentieth-century political systems (for, as the *Four Theories* itself points out, the Authoritarian Theory can be applied to fascism). As such, the book has survived as a mainstay of journalism programs across North America because it presents "a wonderful gift for students struggling to understand how a complicated world is *supposed* to operate." But it does so by invoking an "outdated canon of political philosophy" that flattens out differences among liberal thinkers and demonizes or discredits all non-liberal thinkers (135; italics in original). For example, the book neglects to define Marxism, communism, or the difference between the two, and never considers that "Marxist country #1 was different from Marxist country #2" (133).

The central premise of the fourth model, the Social Responsibility Theory, is: "Freedom carries concomitant obligations; and the press, which enjoys a privileged position under our government, is obliged to be responsible to society for carrying out certain essential functions of mass communication in contemporary society" (74). That it is poorly defined and full of contradictions and troubling consequences is reflected in the fact that it remains highly contentious a half-century after it was written. It also is distinctly jingoistic in tone, in that it claims that "the U.S. was at least developing [from Libertarian] to Social Responsibility and [implies] that other systems were irresponsible" (133). There is also the possibility that it can be used to justify the repression of free speech, or to co-opt the press to serve a special interest:

Look at the public journalists in the U.S. and the growing criticism of an "irresponsible press." Look at the meritocratic and paternalistic governments of Southeast Asia, especially Singapore. Look at the socialist states of Vietnam, China and Cuba. Look at theocratic states such as Iran and to a lesser extent Egypt. Look at the paternalistic Arab kingdoms such as Saudi Arabia. Look at the unstable states in most of Africa. Their strict, often draconian press control is always justified by dragging out the concept of "social responsibility." (134)

In the age of the Internet, we can add to those examples the aggressive attacks by government and online private enterprise on WikiLeaks after the Bradley (now Chelsea) Manning leaks, and the response to Edward Snowden's release of National Security Agency (NSA) files. Yochai Benkler describes the official and "vigilante" response to WikiLeaks as an enforcement of the systems of control that ensure a free press remains "socially responsible" (2011, 46). Meanwhile, reacting to the Snowden leaks, British Prime Minister David Cameron called on the British press "to show 'social responsibility' in the reporting of the leaked NSA files to avoid high court injunctions or the use of D notices [official demands not to publish] to prevent the publication of information that could damage national security" (Watt 2013). Developments like these, Benkler writes, represent a "fraying of the relatively loyal and safe relationship between ... government and its watchdog" (2011, 46).

Theodore Peterson, who wrote the Social Responsibility Theory as well as the one on the Libertarian press, prescribes six duties for the press: "(1) Servicing the political system by providing information, discussion, and debate on public affairs; (2) enlightening the public so as to make it capable of self-government; (3) safeguarding the rights of the individual by serving as a watchdog against government; (4) servicing the economic system, primarily by bringing together the buyers and sellers of goods and services through the medium of advertising; (5) providing entertainment; (6) maintaining its own financial self-sufficiency so as to be free from the pressures of special interests" (Siebert, Peterson, and Schramm 1963, 74).

So, the *Four Theories of the Press* comprise a useful teaching tool and rallying point for idealists, but they represent just one world view: free-market liberalism. And, rather than being a product of impartial scholarship, they embody the values of that liberal world view, essentially the story of Western civilization as told though its "great books and great thinkers" (Nerone et al. 1995, 17). Yet, as Nerone argues, the theories are oversimplified and fail to allow for, or explain, areas of overlap – such as Thomas Hobbes, whose masterwork, *Leviathan*, proves that it is possible to "share all the fundamental postulates of 'Libertarian Theory' as presented by Peterson and still call for authoritarian policies" (20). Lippmann also could be taken as a case of overlap. His writings wander from Authoritarian to Libertarian, to Social Responsibility and on to a revival of Natural Law. Dewey lurches from Libertarian in his spirit to Social Responsibility in his objectives. And how does Italian Marxist Antonio Gramsci fall in with the Soviet Communist Theory, when he denounces a state-influenced news media as a de facto press office for the ruling elite?

The Social Responsibility Theory is the direct descendant of *A Free and Responsible Press*, the 1947 US report on freedom of the press prepared by the Hutchins Commission, a panel convened at the request of Time-Life publisher Henry Luce and chaired by University of Chicago president Robert Hutchins. This, in turn, was the culmination of two decades of attempts by the US news business and its critics among a growing journalism academia to codify a set of standards for the conduct of journalists and their employers. For example, in 1923, the American Society of Newspaper Editors (ASNE) adopted a code of ethics, the *Canon of Journalism*. Unfortunately, ASNE represented only newspaper editors in cities with populations of more than 50,000, and the *Canon* didn't provide for any means of enforcement. During the same period across the United States, journalist groups were organizing to set ethical and professional standards. The result, H.L. Mencken wrote, was that "the journalist was beginning to think of himself as a professional man" (Teel 2006, 117). Unlike the other professions, however, he was not bound by any recognized, widespread set of professional standards. There were no licensing commissions, bar exams, or Hippocratic oaths for reporters and editors.

The Hutchins Commission was, in part, a reaction to some severe criticism that had begun to appear in postwar US academia, such as *Your Newspaper: Blueprint for a Better Press*, published by the 1945–46 class of Harvard's Nieman Foundation for Journalism, which accused daily newspapers of serving only "the class interests of their owners." Another, harsher critic was Ralph J. Cosman, director of the journalism program at the University of Colorado, who issued a "10-count indictment" of the press, which foreshadowed the work of Hutchins a year later (Davies 2006, 27).

Similar to the Motion Picture Production Code, the Comics Code, or the US TV networks' departments of standards and practices, the aim of the Hutchins Commission was to head off government regulation by articulating an industry response to the growing criticism. Large media companies had been growing in size and power since the First World War. There was a fear that the press barons running those companies presented, at least in potential, a dangerous alternative to democratically elected power, and that sensationalism and trivialization of the news posed a serious threat to democracy. The libertarian approach to the media, the criticism went, had led to "tendencies toward monopolization in the media ... and that commercialization produces a debased culture and a dangerously selfish politics" (Nerone et al. 1995, 77).

Over four years, the commission interviewed 275 journalists and observers, and in the end made a number of recommendations for the government, press, and public, which it boiled down to five "ideal demands of society for the communication of news and ideas." They read like a blueprint for the Social Responsibility Theory of the press, dictating that the media should: deliver a truthful, comprehensive, and intelligent account of the day's events in a context that gives them meaning; serve as a forum for the exchange of comment and criticism; project a representative picture of the constituent groups in the society; present and clarify the goals and values of the society; provide full access to the day's intelligence (Hutchins et al. 1966, 31). Unlike the Social Responsibility Theory, Hutchins did not mandate a role for the media in facilitating and preserving capitalism, and it did take social diversity into account.

Given that those statements more or less comprise an outline of best practices, one might have expected the US industry to collectively grunt approval and carry on. However, even though the report was the work of an industry-created committee, the response was not favourable. Publishers and editorialists denounced it as the beginnings of state control. Journalists accused the commission of being elitist – it consisted of twelve intellectuals and no journalists – and of "inviting government regulation, of unfairly lumping in radio and movies with the press, and of failing to conduct elaborate research" (Davies 2006, 23).

However, the US press, having an interest in enhancing its professional image, ended up adopting most of the commission's recommendations, "in practice (if not in theory)" (Nerone et al. 1995, 78). "Vestiges of social responsibility can be found all along the way, long before the Hutchins Commission. But who is to say this was social responsibility rather than just good business?" (83). Long before *The Four Theories of the Press*, such publishers as Pulitzer and Hearst, and the *Toronto Daily Star*'s Hindmarsh and Atkinson families, had grown very rich and powerful addressing issues of social conscience.

Yet, for all their adoption of the principles of social responsibility, the growth in power and reach of the big media companies has repeatedly tripped alarms for academic theorists, industry critics, and government. Acting on similar concerns to those that brought about Hutchins, Canada has assembled three government inquiries into the control and operation of the press by big business. In the UK, there has been long-standing concern about the conduct of the tabloid press, which culminated in the recent phone-hacking scandal and subsequent government hearings and court proceedings.

In Britain, the press tends to take itself less seriously as an agent of democracy and perhaps a little more seriously as a form of popular culture. At its lower levels, it enthusiastically embraces the idea of news as excitement, titillation, and entertainment. As a result, there has been strong criticism of a press that, at those lower levels, can be rabid and irresponsible by North American standards, and not only degrades the conversation of the culture but does so with undisguised merriment. Curran and Seaton (1997) note that the postwar press in Britain was faced with two options, neither of which it chose to pursue: follow the American example of social responsibility and journalistic professionalism, or adopt the European model and encourage competition through subsidies, grants, and tax concessions to help sustain media outlets and stimulate competition. There are two problems with the first option, the authors argue. The way in which it "seeks to compensate for monopoly and chain ownership is in practice a way of legitimating the market system," and the "evils" of chain ownership are much less apparent in Britain, which still has a healthy range of political points of view, at least among its four main national dailies. That option also "has radical implications in that it celebrates objective journalism and professional autonomy and runs counter to the hierarchical, partisan tradition of the British national press." The latter option, they continue, is difficult to implement because it also clashes with the British tradition of having no press policy (294).

As if to prove the condition is chronic, the following quotation from Raymond Williams, two decades earlier, could serve as a eulogy for all doomed attempts to tame Big Media:

> There is now no difficulty in agreeing that there is a crisis in the British press ... When it comes to remedies, of course, this unity does not last, and we have a familiar situation of British society over the last twenty years, in which there seems to be an almost functional relation between general recognition of the need for change and a persistent inability to make any real changes. Thus our years are punctuated with deep crises, decisive turning points, in-depth enquiries, radical reorganisations and bold new starts which, as they settle, and as the general problems persist, fade into the angry banalities of cynicism and frustration. This mood, which is now so prevalent, does not exclude, however, the further opportunism of yet newer starts, yet broader turning points, yet in-deeper enquiries. The crisis, at most levels, comes to feed on itself. (1978, 15)

In Canada, the hand wringing over concentration of ownership has lasted almost a half-century. The striking of official inquiries has become a periodic make-work project for politicians and bureaucrats, and the accomplishments of those inquires could be recorded on a Post-it note. To the media organizations and their apologists, the criticism of chain ownership represents the alarmism of old-fashioned thinkers mired in the quaint notion of the locally owned newspaper, which has become an anachronism in a global world. Yet, the feeling persists among many critics that a "market-driven media system is unlikely to overcome its own biases in favour of affluent consumers, consumerist lifestyles, and seemingly apolitical but sometimes socially corrosive entertainment" (Hackett and Zhao 1998, 158).

Three major news-media inquiries have been conducted in Canada: a Special Committee, chaired by Senator Keith Davey in 1970; a Royal Commission on Newspapers, chaired by Tom Kent, in 1982; a Report on the News Media, by the Standing Senate Committee on Transport and Communications, chaired by Senator Lise Bacon, in 2006. They all investigated the concentration of ownership in the newspaper business and its implications for commerce and democracy, and delivered a number of recommendations, which have been ignored. The notable exception is the system of provincial press councils that grew out of the Davey Committee and to which members of the public can appeal when they believe themselves victims of media injustice.

Onetime *Toronto Star* ombudsman Borden Spears, who sat on the Kent Commission, might have been writing a conclusion for all the reports with this comment on the effects of chain ownership on the craft of journalism: "The process of corporate growth, by concentration into larger groups within the industry, has been accompanied by a reduction in the diversity of news and comment that is the vital element of a free society. The quality of what remains has not improved, and in some respects has declined ... Innovation, creativity, even a desirable degree of eccentricity give way to the pressures of uniformity" (1984, 4).

Compare that to this quote from the report of the Davey Committee, fourteen years earlier: "The most insidious effect of journalistic monopolies, however, is the atmosphere they breed. Every reporter soon learns that there are only a few newspapers where excellence is encouraged. If they are lucky or clever, or restless, they will gravitate to those newspapers. If not, they will stay where they are, growing cynical about their work, learning to live with a kind of sour professional despair. Often, you can see it in their faces. Most Canadian city rooms are boneyards of broken dreams" (1970, 65–6).

And, finally, to the Bacon report, twenty-two years after Kent: "While the committee recognizes the importance of sustainable news media organizations, it does not agree that the unfettered free market is as optimal or benign as its proponents sometimes argue ... The Committee has seen evidence that there are news media organizations with excessively dominant positions within individual Canadian markets. Such concentration of ownership could have negative consequences for the public interest. The lack of appropriate regulation has led to the present situation" (Bacon 2006, 7).

The most famous of the inquiries, the Kent Commission, came into being to deal with accusations that, by closing the *Ottawa Journal* and the *Winnipeg Tribune*, the Thomson and Southam newspaper companies had colluded to eliminate competition. With 77 per cent of Canada's dailies in the hands of chains, the commission recommended that proprietors be limited to no more than five newspapers, the circulation of newspapers owned not exceed 5 per cent of the circulation of all dailies in Canada, and the point of publication of any acquired newspaper not exceed 500 kilometres from any other paper under the same ownership (Kent 1981, 239). York University professor emeritus of communication Fred Fletcher, who authored a research report for the Kent Commission, told me: "What we wanted to do was get the nation to consider journalistic competition to be as important as economic competition. There was pressure to do it. The competition legislation referred only to advertising and advertising rates, and competition for business."

The Kent Commission recommendations resulted in the proposed Canada Newspaper Act of 1983. It was scuttled in part by newspapers' lobbying in the name of free speech and editorializing about the spectre of government control of the press. In his commission's report, Kent wrote: "In a country that has allowed so many newspapers to be owned by a few conglomerates, freedom of the press means, in itself, only that enormous influence without responsibility is conferred on a handful of people. For the heads of such organizations to justify their positions by appealing to the principle of freedom of the press is offensive to intellectual honesty" (Kent 1981, 217).

Looking back on the commission some fifteen years later, Kent admitted that the recommendations had come "to nothing except the production of useful material for journalism students." Still, he argued, the moment had been ripe for change, but the federal government of the time displayed a failure of political will: "Powerful vested interests can be overcome, when the public interest is asserted against them, because there are moments when circumstances temporarily weaken them. That was true of the newspaper industry during the transactions of 1980" (1996, 22).

The striking of the commission, Fletcher says, was a necessary response to something that would soon become a clear and present danger. "What we worried about was that Southam was a publicly traded company that had a 14 per cent return on investment, and the industry average was about 21 per cent ... We thought that what was going to happen to Southam was that Thomson – or somebody we hadn't imagined, like Conrad Black – would buy it. And that's what happened. But one of the purposes of the commission was to create legislation to prevent that from happening."

As several commentators have observed, media concentration tends to ebb and flow, and specialty television and the Internet have certainly provided far more diversity than any of the inquiries anticipated. Unfortunately, there has been little discussion of the quality of this diversity, or if there is true diversity of content among the variety of formats. For example, the increasing concentration of ownership of television networks and specialty stations – to the point that virtually all Canadian private English-language television is controlled by three corporations – has provided a wonderful opportunity for parent companies to extract more profit from content by reusing programs across platforms. In the Bell Media world, a nature show that airs on Discovery Canada can be rerun on Discovery Science, Discovery World, Animal Planet, and CTV. A drama that airs on Global can be repurposed for Showcase, Slice, and even History (if there is the slightest historical content). Yet observers who simply count channels constantly come to the conclusion that there is more variety than ever on the TV dial, even when the standardization of programming may, in fact, be producing less. In the same way, newspaper chains that centralize functions such as federal and provincial political reporting, foreign affairs, editorial writing, analysis, major league sports coverage, and TV and film criticism produce the illusion of plenty while delivering less – as do the aggregation sites, which simply rerun news gathered by newspapers, TV networks, and wire services.

Many commentators, especially on the left (Gramsci, Williams, Noam Chomsky, Edward S. Herman, Robert McChesney, Ben Bagdikian), have concluded that news corporations "influence their audiences' perception of public life, including perceptions of politics and politicians as they appear – or do not appear – in the media" (Bagdikian 1990, 5–6).

This is not a novel concept. In 1920, in the *New Republic*, Walter Lippmann and Charles Merz published "A Test of the News," a content analysis of the *New York Times*'s coverage of the Russian

Revolution from 1917 to 1919. The authors analyzed more than one thousand editions of the *Times* over a period of thirty-six months (2007, 154) and discovered that the paper had been handed most of its information by the US State Department and anti-Bolshevik Russian agencies. The authors accused the paper of filtering that information through the ideology of the paper's owners and managers to present an unfavourable view of the Bolsheviks. "The chief censor, the chief propagandist," they wrote, "were hope and fear in the minds of reporters and editors" (158). Warning that "the reliability of the news is the premise upon which democracy proceeds" (159), they argued that a journalist who readily accepts facts handed down from official sources is about as useful to the public as "an astrologer or an alchemist" (172).

Roughly seventy years later, Herman and Chomsky used content analysis to paint a picture of a North American press that designates whether a subject is "worthy" or "unworthy" according to the ruling ideology. For example, in comparing the *New York Times*'s coverage of the Khmer Rouge in Cambodia (a murderous regime that was Maoist, and therefore hostile to the United States, and tended to receive unfavourable coverage) and Indonesia (a US ally, whose brutal treatment of East Timor was almost ignored), they concluded that the close relationship between the people who own the media and those who "fund them as advertisers" plays "a key role in fixing basic principles and dominant ideologies" (1988, xi).

This observation tends to be reinforced by the way mainstream journalism reflects and enforces reigning societal values. Daniel Hallin describes the world of journalism as being "divided into three regions, each governed by different journalistic standards." He calls these the spheres of "consensus, legitimate controversy, and deviance." The first is "the region of motherhood and apple pie," and, inside it, journalists feel free to act as partisan commentators, upholding the values of their society and acting "as advocate or celebrant of consensus values." In the second, "balance and objectivity reign as the supreme journalistic values." This is where journalists feel compelled to present the various sides of an issue as being of equal weight and importance. Finally, on the outer fringes, lies the sphere of deviance, a "realm of those political actors and views which journalists and the political mainstream of the society reject as unworthy of being heard" (1989, 116–17).

Many worthwhile topics of discussion have lived at least for a while in the last zone. Topics in the sphere of deviance, Schudson (1995) points out, are accepted as being so far outside mainstream thought that they can be freely dismissed or ridiculed in print or on the air. The example he uses is the women's movement of the 1960s and early '70s – when newspaper columnists referred to feminists as "women's libbers" or "bra burners," and wrote "witty" opinion pieces about their place being in the kitchen. A more recent example might be the near-hysterical response to Barack Obama's suggestion during the 2008 presidential campaign that Americans "share the wealth." This triggered a discussion in the US media about whether Obama's comments were socialist, and never about what socialism is or how it works, an understanding of which seems rather important to the discussion as it was being framed. An example of a story that moved from the sphere of deviance into the sphere of legitimate controversy with uncommon speed might be the Occupy Wall Street movement of 2011, which was treated at first as the exhibitionism of kooks and political extremists. Then, online news sources such as *Truthdig* picked up the story and it became the aggrieved 99 per cent rising up and demanding accountability from the privileged and irresponsible 1 per cent. A cynic might be inclined to conclude that the mainstream press quickly came to realize that the latter narrative was expressing the feelings and opinions of its readers and viewers.

Central to Hallin's analysis is that this sort of structure tends to trivialize or isolate eccentric, novel, or contrarian positions, limiting or slowing their entry into the public discourse, or keeping them out entirely. Schudson explains it this way: "The chain owners are not so much politically conservative as risk averse, which generally comes down to the same thing" (1995, 175). Bagdikian and Chomsky have both described the process that produces ideology in a media organization as one of indoctrination into that sphere of shared values. This is Chomsky's: "those who occupy managerial positions in the media, or gain status within them as commentators, belong to the same privileged elites, and might be expected to share the perceptions, aspirations, and attitudes of their associates, reflecting their own class interests as well" (1989, 8).

Logically, one might expect owners and publishers to hire news executives who share their values and who, in turn, hire reporters and editors who share theirs. The average media baron, the argument goes, has no time to dictate the editorial policy of each newspaper under his command – much less vet each story that appears in each paper. This argument implies a benign neglect on the part of the top management of newspaper chains: as long as the papers turn a profit, they are free to pursue any editorial policy and practise any management philosophy they choose. However, as David Taras points out in his book *Power and Betrayal in the Canadian Media*, it is not necessary for an owner to have his hand in the daily running of newspapers, because owners hire managers in their "own image." He quotes David Radler, then president of Conrad Black's Hollinger Inc., which controlled dozens of Canadian newspapers in the 1990s – including most English-language big-city dailies outside Toronto: "If editors disagree with us, they should disagree elsewhere" (1999, 213). Any organization that wants to enforce a set of standards and practices throughout its operations need only select a handful of "right-thinking" individuals and place them in key positions.

In 1999, Taras pointed to three developments that he argued had transformed much of Canadian journalism into a collection of mouthpieces for the new right: the rise of neo-conservative pundits such as Diane Francis, William Watson, Peter Worthington, Barbara Amiel, and David Frum; the expanding power of Conrad Black and Paul Godfrey, then head of the Sun Media newspaper chain; the emergence of right-wing think tanks such as the Fraser Institute. In fact, Taras was breaking one development down into its components: the control of most of the nation's print media by companies that choose to pursue a neo-conservative agenda. He went so far as to write that most of the print-media political discourse in Canada was being narrowed to reflect the viewpoints of Godfrey and Black, whom he defined as right-wing corporate ideologues. Thus, Taras argued, "a right-wing agenda dominates public debate" (22).

The game is not much changed today, though some of the players are retired or have been traded. Godfrey is chief executive officer of Postmedia Network, the remnant of the Southam/Hollinger/Canwest chain – and is in the process of taking over Sun Media, which would give it a kind of dominance over the industry that has not been seen since the Hollinger days. Sun Media is a division of Quebecor, majority-owned by the very right-wing Pierre Karl Péladeau, who in 2011 launched the Sun News Network, a Fox News–type forum for neo-conservative ideology – which died of audience neglect in early 2015.

Black is out of the media business – except as a writer of exquisitely florid opinion pieces and co-host of a low-budget talk show on Vision Television.

Except for Black, the players' power has grown. Péladeau was named chairman of the board of Hydro-Québec in April 2013 and remained vice-chairman of the massive Quebecor media conglomerate, which, as Taras pointed out in chapter 1, controls the largest commercial TV network, the largest cable provider, the largest Internet provider and the largest publishing company in Quebec. During his tenure at Hydro Québec, the *Globe and Mail* reported, Péladeau was "the only chairman of the board of a government agency" who sat on select cabinet committees with Quebec Premier Pauline Marois and Parti Québécois cabinet members (Robillard, 2013). He resigned that position to run as a PQ candidate in the 2014 provincial election and was elected MNA for Saint-Jérôme. Upon going into politics, Péladeau placed his business holdings in a blind trust – undoubtedly run by like-minded individuals. At the time of writing, he was running for leadership of the PQ, which would make him opposition leader in Quebec's Assemblée nationale.

Postmedia, meanwhile, now controls some 200 media properties across the country: large and small dailies, community papers, specialty publications, and websites. These include both dailies in Vancouver, Edmonton, Calgary, and Ottawa, two more dailies in Toronto, both large dailies in Saskatchewan, and the only English-language daily in Montreal. Yet, Godfrey has described the potential to merge Sun Media's *Canoe* website with Postmedia's *Canada.com* as "the jewel of the deal," creating a Canadian Internet player that can compete with the new global corporate behemoths that have emerged online (Flavelle 2014). "In some ways, everything is the same, and in some ways everything is different," Taras says. "One of the things that has happened is that the Internet is a winner-take-all environment. We have a few monsters that basically dominate the horizon and tens of millions of small players ... So, you have huge players like Amazon, eBay, Facebook, and so on, and then millions and millions of minnows who don't have much of an audience at all."

Political analyst Lawrence Martin has repeatedly pursued the argument that the ideological bent of the Canadian media is out of step with the prevailing views of Canadians. Writing in 2003, after Conrad Black had divested himself of his major newspaper holdings, Martin echoed what Taras had written in 1999: that almost all of Canada's press – specifically, Canwest, the *National Post*, the *Globe and Mail*, and the Sun chain and Quebecor in general – were right-leaning and pro-American. And most of the major commentators and pundits "slant right." Yet, "Canadians, as opinion samplings suggest, haven't migrated rightward in big numbers. It is a question of balance, and the balance – does the NDP have a chance in this media environment? – is gone. The impact on traditional Canadian values can only be corrosive" (2003).

Yet the major news chains have displayed a perplexing stubbornness to consider broadening the discourse to appeal to a wider audience. For example, when I asked Godfrey how he planned to revitalize the Postmedia newspapers, he replied: "The only way you can get to that is by making sure that you get the best journalists. We've tried to get back into the swing of things by getting Christie Blatchford to write for us, getting Andrew Coyne to write for us. In the last couple of years, we've been able to make sure that we retain people like Terry Corcoran and Peter Foster, and Conrad Black in our chain." Blatchford is a right-wing court reporter and law-and-order enthusiast; Corcoran is an extreme-right-wing business writer and climate-change denier; Foster is a twenty-five-year veteran of the *Financial Post*; former media baron Black is old, pedantic, and frequently very angry; Coyne is a widely respected but solidly establishment voice. This is not a roster of youthful, independent, freewheeling progressives whose writings are filled with surprises. In contrast to the economically fuelled social conscience of the penny press and muckraking magazines, it's as if Canada's new media barons were paralyzed by their ideology.

In the United States, the Fox News Channel has made gold out of an ideology that is almost comically intense. The network's slogan, "Fair and Balanced," is a response to a perception among US conservatives that most of their country's media businesses have a liberal bias. By favouring the far-right agenda, the network argues, it balances the debate and creates fairness for what it contends is an under-represented point of view. However, one would be hard-pressed to find anything in the North American media that is as far to the left as Fox and the now-defunct Sun News Network are to the right. It's a considerable stretch to argue that poorly financed fringe publications like *Mother Jones*, *The Tyee*, or *Truthdig*, or moderate-centrist broadcasters such as CBC, NPR, or MSNBC present an alternative.

The current situation harks back to the 1920s, when Lippmann, in *Public Opinion,* foreshadowed Chomsky by noting that newspaper publishers are businessmen who tend to sympathize with the advertiser and mistrust the loyalty of the reader, and "honestly see the world through the lenses of their associates and friends" (1997, 206). Lippmann's misgivings about the press date back to one of his earliest works and extend through most of his life. In fact, he produced a defining statement of media criticism in *Liberty and the News*, his earliest book on the subject: "So long as there is interposed between the ordinary citizen and the facts a news organization determining by entirely private and unexamined standards, no matter how lofty, what he shall know, and hence what he shall believe, no one will be able to say that the substance of democratic government is secure" (2008, 7).

It's a shame Lippmann didn't live to meet A. Roy Megarry, publisher of the *Globe and Mail* in the late 1980s. He once urged publishers to "stop kidding themselves that they are in the newspaper business and admit that they are primarily in the business of carrying advertising messages" (Miller 1998, 30). Megarry's comments describe how owners and publishers of the 1980s and '90s were fine-tuning the two-tier newspaper manufacturing process, to place the emphasis on the advertiser rather than the reader. In this world, editorial material is no longer there to sell newspapers by providing a service to the reader but exists as bait, to deliver consumers to commerce. Thus, sections that could provide useful information, criticism, discussion, and analysis – such as travel, fashion, food, real estate, automotive, entertainment, and business – are turned into congenial environments for advertisers. "The fashion section ... is an annual flood of gushy promotion of exotic garments, all in a 'news' section ... The same is true of travel and usually food sections ... The growing trend among newspapers to turn over sections of the 'news' to the advertising department usually produces copy that is not marked 'advertising' but is full of promotional material under the guise of news" (Bagdikian 1990, 165–6). It is easy to understand how this focus on the ratio of "eyeballs" to advertising has led to accounting formulas that focus on minimizing the cost of content as a way to raise the bottom line – and to see what a short step it is from creating environments for advertising to using editorial staff to create advertorial, or native, content.

The tensions in the news business of the 1980s and '90s weren't solely between business and editorial. There was serious strain among the various players in the newsroom itself. Balance, again misidentified as objectivity, had re-emerged as a convenient tool for a new breed of editors who wished to tighten their control of the lumpenproles under their command. Many were dedicated, as Spears (1984) noted, to stamping out "innovation, creativity, even a desirable degree of eccentricity" and replacing it with uniformity. Philip McLeod, then editor of the *London* (ON) *Free Press*, might have been writing an epitaph for the New Journalism when he said: "Sometime in the early 1970s, newspaper reporters started thinking of themselves as writers. But their job is to dig out information that somebody has asked for. We're in the reporting business. If you want to write, go work for [*sic*] a book" (Underwood 1995, 173).

McLeod's attitude towards his staff wasn't unusual or notably unenlightened by 1980s or '90s standards. Resentment was so widespread that a 1991 US national survey found that "inept managers" were the leading cause journalists gave for leaving the business (McPherson 2006, 111). Newsrooms that had been accustomed to editor-managers were finding themselves being run by manager-editors. Some were career newsroom managers who had spent little or no time in the field as reporters; some were journalists who had been co-opted into a management style with an emphasis on budget, graphic design, promotion, and management by objective. The last involved yearly contracts in which editors would establish for their publishers annual goals – usually involving things like budget control, circulation growth, personnel deployment – everything but editorial excellence. The result was a widespread decline in the quality of journalism. As Underwood wrote in *When MBAs Rule the Newsroom*:

> Many journalists are finding it tougher to question authority out in the world when they are being pressured to become loyal corporate soldiers inside their organizations. To fit into the newspaper's design and packaging needs, preplanning is essential and reporters are expected to fulfill their role within the system dutifully

and without complaint. Editors, who need to allot space in the news pages well in advance, prefer stories that are predictable, come in with plenty of lead time, and fit the preconceptions that have already been discussed in editorial meetings ... No matter how fervent their protests, the lives of newsworkers have become increasingly circumscribed by performance standards and management systems designed to insure greater productivity, by bosses trained in the new techniques of scientific management, by readership surveys, and by editors who have joined the marketing team. (1995, 63)

By the mid-1990s, newspapers were turning to the "total newspaper approach" to lure back readers. In this strategy, the news and business departments of dailies coordinate their activities to market their product. This is "a boon to business-side people, whose influence within the news organization has expanded greatly" (16). One manifestation of this approach was the significant role focus groups, surveys, and polling came to play in editorial leadership. Critics complained that newspaper managers sometimes seemed to expend more energy asking readers what they wanted to read than delivering it. Alison Carper defines this as a particularly self-serving form of false empiricism: It's quite a simple – albeit expensive – matter to hire consultants to carry out content analyses, set up focus groups, design surveys, or create study groups, or to redesign the product to make it "more accessible" or "youth friendly." The problem with much – if not most – of this sort of research is that it is not objective. It's client-directed. So, the aim is to satisfy editors' and publishers' hunches and prejudices, and not to uncover any objective proof of anything. As a result, the researchers' "pretenses to scientific rigor are undermined by their own subsequent pronouncements" (1997, 61–2).

Even when it is objective, market research can get in the way of solid newsroom management by shifting the focus to what readers liked yesterday, rather than what they will like tomorrow. The result is boredom: you give readers what they already have, and never surprise them with something new. As former *Philadelphia Inquirer* editor Charles Layton wrote: "Over the past 20 years, at their annual conventions, and in their trade magazines and in-house publications, news executives have spoken more and more of the need for journalists to think like marketers. As if it were easy, or possible, to know in advance what people want to read. As if the average citizen, in a brief telephone survey conducted by a part-time, poorly paid, not-very-well trained surveyor, could articulate that. And as if compelling content somehow originated with readers and not in the individual mind of a journalist with interesting things to say" (1999).

Not surprisingly, many editorial workers who formerly had been untouched by corporate planning would have preferred it remain that way – as is illustrated by these quotes, about a decade apart, from articles in two trade magazines:

The first is from Bill Gloade's "Stress Has Significant Presence in Newsrooms," *Editor and Publisher*, 12 November 1983: "Fifteen years ago, editors were editors. Today, they are editor-managers. They direct the editing of the newspaper with one hand and, with the other, they are deeply involved in business management. This editor is expected to carry on in the best traditions of journalistic excellence, but also is expected to share the responsibility for the newspaper as a 'profit center.' Many editors discovered that this dual obligation created unfamiliar stresses" (quoted in Underwood 1995, 29).

The second is from John McMillan and Jonathan Kwitny's "The High Cost of High Profits," *Washington Journalism Review* (June 1990): "We too often have corrupted the city desk with those 'endless imbecilities of high command.' Instead of talking to a reporter, the city editor audits time cards. Instead of editing copy, the city editor writes a memo about expense accounts. Instead of reading the competition, the city editor goes to a management meeting ... I submit that we run the risk of alienating our basic resource – reporters" (31).

The feeling among many observers of the 1990s was that economics was fuelling a poisonous brew of caution and desperation, a constant search for a no-risk editorial panacea and an obsession with managing expenses. In most newsrooms, though profits were high, there was a growing sense of concern about sliding circulation. Meanwhile, newspaper chains were creating large debts through acquisition and leveraging profits with public stock offerings. The main effect was to place more pressure on companies and individual media holdings to service debt and perform up to the "rising tide of shareholder expectation – a demand for ever-improved return on investment that's relentless whether a newspaper is publicly owned or privately held ...

However a family that owns a privately held newspaper often has lived for generations in its town and feels a responsibility to ensure the newspaper serves its town well. Shareholders of publicly owned companies usually have no more commitment to newspapers than to any other investment, and often they live far from towns where their companies' newspapers are published" (Fink 1996, 19).

In 1986, merger banker Christopher Shaw said the profit margin of a daily monopoly newspaper could be raised from 15 per cent to 40 per cent in two years through cutting costs and raising advertising rates and subscription prices. As Bagdikian wrote: "No one will buy a 15 percent margin paper without a plan to create a 25 to 40 percent margin. If long-term profits and stability come from local news and larger portions of detailed and analytical news, why have newspaper publishers gone in the opposite direction? The reason is not irrational if short-term profits are the goal ... Unfortunately, short-term profits are now imperative in the major media almost without regard for the future of the media institutions. Newspapers no longer depend solely on their readers. They must satisfy advertisers, Wall Street investors and parent corporations" (1990, 200).

To a certain extent, publishers were reacting to a long line of prescriptions for the ailing industry. One of the most notorious was the 1980 US Newspaper Research Project, *Changing Needs of Changing Readers*, a $4 million undertaking made up of some seventy research projects conducted over three years. In it, researcher Ruth Clark urged editors to revamp newspapers to help readers cope with their lives – to produce, in the vernacular of the period, "news you can use." She said readers: craved good news; were busy and wanted news in easy-to-digest nuggets; liked newspapers that were well organized, well designed, and easy to navigate; wanted predictability, with anchored features and standard placement of articles (Underwood 1995, 7).

The belief that Clark had found the antidote to TV-bred short attention spans led to a series of trends that gained momentum when the Gannett newspaper group deployed virtually all of Clark's recommendations in its founding of USA *Today* in 1982. With its bite-size stories, soft-feature content, chatty reader friendliness, obsession with weather, and flashy layout, America's first mass-market national newspaper was "the quintessential product of modern corporate media engineering."

Critics of USA Today complain that the only vision at the heart of the newspaper is a marketer's vision. They condemn the newspaper for its overemphasis on packaging, graphics, brief text, factoids, flashy color, and news summaries in lieu of in-depth reporting. But editors *en masse* have followed the newspaper's lead in appealing to busy Americans who (their research tells them) aren't taking the time to read. In a report for APME [the US industry society, the Associated Press Media Editors] in 1983, more than 100 newspapers reported a variety of changes in news editing, reporting and production as a result of competition from USA Today. (96)

As the *New York Times* put it, USA Today was "loudly mocked and quietly mimicked" (McPherson 2006, 31), leading to a continent-wide epidemic of fact boxes, splashy colours, and chatty stories.

Then, in 1984, at a convention of the American Society of Newspaper Editors, Clark fired off another shot and sent the herd stampeding in a different direction. This report was quickly nicknamed *Ruth Clark II*, and in it she revealed that readers no longer wanted news they could use, but craved material that would help them understand a complex world: hard news, health, and science and technology (Underwood 1995, 11). At around the same time, Leo Bogart, retired executive vice-president of the US Newspaper Advertising Bureau, released the results of a 1983 survey of 1,310 US newspapers. He found that, since 1979, two out of three had made substantial changes to editorial content and design, and 71 per cent to graphics and layout. One-third had altered significantly the ratio of hard news to features – opting two to one in favour of more "reader-driven" features, as well as more sectionalizing, regional zoning, and marketing to upscale readers (10). None of the tinkering had turned the tide of declining circulation. By the mid-1980s, Bogart, like Clark, was reporting that readers craved more substance in their daily newspapers, and less how-to and self-improvement material. The real pressing issues facing newspaper publishers, he said, were pricing, delivery, service, and conditions over which newspaper executives had no control, such as the price of newsprint. Bogart argued that newspapers had the best chances for renewal if they concentrated on performing their traditional functions well and forgot about the graphic and marketing gimmicks. He wrote, "It's fantasy to believe that a newspaper can be packaged like a bar of soap or a can of dog food, or even like a television news program. Its symbolic texture is too complex for that; its elements are too rich" (11).

Yet, as Carleton University's Chris Dornan points out, the trend among chain newspapers remained towards blandness and uniformity: "You could kidnap somebody, chloroform them, drop them into a city. They wake up. You give them a local newspaper and, as long as you removed any mention of the specific place, they wouldn't be able to tell what city they were in."

In a chain, sameness is driven partly by editors who don't want to miss the big stories that run in sister papers. Partly, it is driven by the simple reality that sameness saves money – content can be recycled across several publications. And partly, the blandness lies in the nature of the one-newspaper town, where the economic pressure is towards controlling journalistic quality, not encouraging it. As Yochai Benkler writes, "Where there is one outlet, providing content that is highly mobilizing to 30% of the audience but alienates 70% is a bad strategy. You gain a strong commitment to 30%, but if you are a local monopoly, those 30% have no real options and would have bought your product anyway, while the 70% who might have bought a bland informative media product will be turned off" (2011, 374). Benkler further points out that such a strategy works in a monopoly situation, but falls apart when the mass deserts the media, and it becomes more economical to go after the highly committed 30 per cent than to try to woo the 70 per cent that has dispersed into smaller groups. Companies that have grown accustomed – if not addicted – to monopoly profit margins cut costs to maintain them, assuming readers will go on buying the depleted product and advertisers will go on buying space in them, because they are the only game in town.

"The publishers were used to these big profit margins, and that's the way we operated," says *Globe and Mail* media reporter Steve Ladurantaye. "Going back to my time at the smaller papers, we were making solid profits. But that's not the message you hear in the newsroom and it's not the message that's being put out into the community. The message is that things are tough and we need to clamp down, and give you less and charge you more. There seemed to be this idea that that could go on forever: that we could just give less and charge more, and it would just sustain itself."

Through the 1980s and '90s, a chorus of critics levelled attack after attack on the news business "for being shallow, confrontational, inaccurate or incoherent," as Canadian academic Roger Bird put it. In 1997, with an eerie foreshadowing of the sloganeering that would dominate the discourse a decade later, he delivered a fairly prophetic if premature obituary titled *The End of News*. Its thesis was that news had become "less reliable and less relevant ... destined to occupy a smaller and smaller part of our cultural map. Information is becoming more important than news to those who have money and power" (1997, 1).

Underpinning much of this conversation was a sense that some ineffable characteristic that connected a newspaper with its audience had been lost. In 1999, the US Project for Excellence in Journalism commissioned Carl Sessions Stepp to compare American newspapers from the early 1960s to those of the late '90s. Stepp found the papers of the '60s to be "homely and drab," often badly written, disorganized, "jam-packed with short items, overflowing with local names, places and activities." The average length of a story was six inches and written in the old-fashioned inverted pyramid style, with one or two longer, more reflective pieces being the norm (Stepp 1999).

Through the 1980s and '90s many, if not most, media observers and critics had argued that the modern attention span had shrivelled, and readers wanted information quickly and concisely. This appeared to be borne out by the greatest success stories in modern North American journalism – the creation of the tabloids *Le Journal de Montréal* and the *Toronto Sun* in Canada in the 1960s and '70s, respectively, and of USA *Today* in the 1980s. Yet, Stepp's research indicates that readers have long expected newspapers to be concise in most stories, and to offer in-depth analysis only for the two or three most important issues of the day.

Second, Stepp's statement that the old dailies were "overflowing with local names, places, and activities" echoes something community newspaper editors and publishers have been saying for decades: a newspaper must connect with its readers. "That's the secret of community newspapers," Black Press chairman David Black told me. "Always has been: faces and names." Stepp's research showed that the newspapers of the late '90s were more comprehensive, offered more in-depth reporting, were more conscientious in getting the story right, were better organized, and were more attractive in terms of photography and graphic design. Yet, he invokes that sense of loss that permeates so much of the discourse:

> Beyond the hard data, a close reading ... yields signs of the newsroom anxieties that have been documented elsewhere in the *State of the American Newspaper* series, and which I have seen first hand in a decade's worth of editorial consultations. These include increased mistakes in copy (tied to such factors as reduced quality control and overstretched copy desks), demoralization over rising productivity demands in an age of downsizing and cost cutting, and a clash between marketing and public-service mindsets. Forces like these have plunged the industry into a crisis of confidence at a time when many papers are, arguably, at a peak in terms of quality. Yet one wonders at heart if it isn't an intangible that should be an even greater worry: the question of personality and connection – that essential and ephemeral quality that can make the difference between readers speaking fondly of "our paper" or simply "the paper." (1999)

Stepp is invoking James Carey: "'My newspaper' of older usage became 'the newspaper'; it had severed its allegiance and contact with the public" (1997b, 249). Carey's fellow proponent of public journalism, Jay Rosen, has argued that reporters and editors had taken to sitting in the grandstands and "jeering the idiots." This approach created "a sorry spectacle, a game of 'who's up and who's down,' a public comedy played by villains and fools, scored by journalists who believe they're above it all." Rosen accused newspapers, when they are not preaching to the converted, of creating readers that "find only further estrangement in the news, which treats politics as a game to be played by insiders and pros" (1999, 224). Similarly, in Canada, John Miller complained that readers were becoming repelled by the negative tone of daily newspapers: "Traditional journalism follows a script, identifying, decrying and demanding solutions to problems encountered by covering other powerful vested interests in society. Frequently, it adds to society's confusion, hopping from one dose of bad news to another as if it were delivering bodies to what one editor calls the emergency room of the mind" (1998, 218).

As the twentieth century was coming to a close, Rosen wrote that journalists were faced with the question, "Do they want merely to entertain the public or engage it?" He invoked James Fallows, Washington editor of the *Atlantic Monthly*, from his book *Breaking the News: How the News Media Undermine American Democracy*, who predicted that chasing readers would lead to a race to the bottom. Once "people see no point in paying attention, journalism will have to transform itself into something else: entertainment. But the press cannot hope to compete with the entertainment culture, with its lurid diet of celebrity news and sensationalism. In flunking the political test before it, the press will fail commercially as well" (1999, 224).

Another criticism of the news media at the turn of the twenty-first century was that many were interested only in an affluent audience. Observers, mainly on the left, complained that this was creating an echo chamber for the rich and powerful, and disenfranchising everyone else. Robert McChesney, for one, argued that the abiding concern of the mainstream press was the perpetuation of the status quo: "The media system is linked ever more closely to the capitalist system, both through ownership and through its reliance upon advertising, a function dominated by the largest firms in the economy. Capitalism benefits from having a formally democratic system, but capitalism works best when elites make the most fundamental decisions and the bulk of the population is depoliticized" (1999, 3).

Many late-century critics described this pursuit of the affluent as a disaster for newspapers, society, and democracy, that the process of appealing only to the well off "leads to news content that is less and less relevant to blue-collar citizens who were once reliable newspaper subscribers. The newspaper, in short, in its upscale move, has significantly authored its own irrelevance" (Schudson 1995, 182).

While owners convert their papers into "primarily carriers of advertising, advertisers want affluent readers between the ages of 18 and 49" (Bagdikian 1990, 199). This means newspapers control the readership by gearing their coverage to reflect the audience in affluent neighbourhoods, where they promote their circulation. At the same time, they cut back on reporting of neighbourhoods without the desired demographics, primarily where low-income people and the elderly live. "The 'unwanted American population' that is systematically discouraged by advertising-supported media is not small ... 50 percent of all American families" (199).

This was an important concern in Canada, too, where the 1990s saw an astonishing level of concentration of ownership. One owner, Conrad Black's Hollinger Inc., controlled all the quality broadsheets outside Toronto, Winnipeg, New Brunswick, and Halifax, with only the national edition of the *Globe and Mail* to offer any competition. *Ottawa Citizen* editorial page editor Peter Calamai – who was dismissed after the Hollinger takeover in the mid-1990s – described Black as a man who "thinks what matters is speaking directly to the people who have influence, speaking directly to the people who have their hands on the levers." Black's wife, newspaper columnist Barbara Amiel, went so far as to tell a meeting of the Canadian Association of Journalists that the "newspapers that will survive and prosper are those we take up-market" and that it was "time for newspapers to turn into cultural, literary and public affairs experiences for those large numbers of sophisticated readers who want that experience" (Miller 1998, 78).

Anyone who likes newspapers would have to at least partly sympathize with Amiel's comments, especially in view of the industry's growing blandness over the years, when so much energy was expended in chasing the lowest common denominator. However, it is worth noting that the "sophisticated readers" of which Amiel spoke were almost certainly economic and power elites, as opposed to a broad spectrum of the intellectually or politically engaged.

There are signs that newspapers have simply moved their old strategies online. At Postmedia, ideas lean towards sponsorship and native advertising, and programs to build communities among the affluent, such as the *National Post*'s "Gastropost," aimed at Toronto foodies, and the *Edmonton Journal*'s "Capital Ideas" network of entrepreneurs. "Advertisers are asking for different ways of reaching buyers, and one of them is native advertising or sponsored content," says Lucinda Chodan, editor of the Montreal *Gazette* and Postmedia's eastern-region vice-president of editorial. "Newspapers have always accepted that ... I'm saying that there are ways of envisaging things that have those three elements: journalistic interest / integrity / values. Editorial values, reader interest, and potential revenue, and doing that with integrity – and labelling the stuff that is advertorial – is really crucial to our continued survival."

As for the drive to capture the well-heeled reader, *Globe and Mail* editor John Stackhouse showed that the lure of the rich is ever strong. In a letter to staff, he wrote that his paper's target audience is people with a household income of at least $120,000 a year "and retired or young people who either had, or are on their way to, a six-figure income" (Kimmett 2013). At the same time, the paper's publisher, Philip Crawley, has reaffirmed the faith in giving readers more of what they liked yesterday. As we have seen, the idea of pinpointing the reader's interests has been a long-running quest for newspaper publishers. "But in an online world ... the key is 'predictive analytics.' The *Globe* now employs data analysts who can determine what kind of content gets read and how 'engaged' readers are with that content. They can measure how many page views an article receives, how long a reader spends reading it and many other variables that were simply not possible until recently" (Basen 2013).

Although Stackhouse admitted to me that there is a danger in focusing too closely on what readers liked yesterday, he argued that "there's an equal danger of producing material that no one's interested in and pretending that someone is interested in it. This was the curse of daily newspapers: that many journalists and editors thought what they were publishing was of great interest because half a million people were buying their paper. They discovered half a million people were buying their paper for the classifieds, comics, and puzzles – that journalism was just the coating."

Many observers have also argued that late twentieth-century newspapers had no choice but to follow the affluent. There were "dramatic changes" in the structure of newspaper audiences, with cities growing out and annexing affluent populations, and with other affluent residents fleeing farther from the city cores. Conrad Fink writes that "roughly two options are open to a newspaper that is anchored downtown ... adjust to market change and follow the affluent, recapturing them in the suburbs, or ... wither and die" (1996, 37).

However, many newspapers appear to have stayed resolutely out of touch with their audiences. For an audience of minivan-driving suburbanites whose main concerns are good highways, clean streets, garbage pickup, taxes, schools, and children's sports, newspapers can be a baffling compendium of downtown insider information geared to people who eat in fad restaurants, drink interesting little wines, ride in taxis, and attend the theatre. As retired academic and former

Toronto Star deputy editor John Miller said in chapter 1, one of the problems with journalism is that journalists have far too little contact with the people they write about – or for. "I used to get in my car and drive to work and never leave the building all day, and go home. And I was one of the people directing news coverage. How stupid is that?" Similarly, a senior reporter who requested anonymity told me:

> I remember having discussions with people in the *Sun* newsroom when I lived in Vancouver and asking why we weren't going after suburban audiences. I was one of the few people who lived in the 'burbs. But people just didn't relate. People in the newsroom just didn't relate to people who lived in these outlying communities. A lot of them bought homes in Vancouver in the 1970s, got real-estate rich, and were fat and happy. But that speaks to this drifting away of the interests of your staff from the readership you should be going after. They just didn't relate to people who shopped at Costco in Langley. They were hanging out at the False Creek market and all the trendy places. They had the money to do it.

If you talk to enough journalists, you find a recurring theme of disconnection from society at large, and a fixation on the rich, the stylish, and the powerful. Many large dailies have cut large segments of the population out of the conversation and rendered their activities irrelevant to that conversation. The implications are obvious, if you consider that many social, commercial, and cultural trends in society tend to bubble up from below, and that the upper layers of society have little to gain through innovation and everything to profit by preserving the status quo. As for the newspaper business, it would seem that, by alienating vast swaths of the middle and working-class audiences, the dailies helped engineer their own decline.

It is less clear how newspaper owners and publishers could have got the Internet so wrong – especially considering that newsrooms had been receiving material electronically from the wire services since the early 1970s, and journalists had become accustomed to reading news onscreen. As we have seen, Internet-age newspaper companies have had a talent for misreading technology, from implementing the baffling audiotext systems (in which readers were invited to navigate a robot-call system to retrieve, among other things, their horoscopes), to giving away their most valuable resource online, to overlooking the value of online classified advertising. As late as the mid-2000s, the "content provider" model was more or less the only means of adaptation newspapers were considering – and, even then, often tentatively. In early 2000, newspaper consultant Christine Urban of the US company Urban & Associates warned that newspapers had been far too slow to adapt the new technology to their purposes, and their product to the new technology. She suggested daily newspapers should: develop different websites for different sections; repackage sports news in a weekly online magazine; distribute free, abridged, digest editions for commuters; accelerate their rate of innovation, bringing new projects online within six months of inception. In other words, she anticipated the highly specialized blogs of today, as well as such free commuter papers as *Metro*. "The concept of having new products designed to cannibalize some sections of newspapers is anathema," she said. "I say being cannibalized is better than being eaten by another species, and at least you still get the protein" (MacAfee 2000).

The newspapers' search for a saviour technology extends back at least to the late 1990s, when the portal was supposed to be the killer app. As Robert McChesney wrote at the time, the portal was supposed to "bring order to the Internet experience" (1999, 163). People would enter cyberspace through a portal and stay tethered to it, like an astronaut on a spacewalk, reading the news, watching video, conducting searches, retrieving email, and even buying goods. The newspaper, as proprietor of the portal, would skim profit off the top of all these activities. It could continue to sell its readers to advertisers, and deliver them to providers of Internet services, too. The fact that the notion of a portal defies the logic of the Web appears to have been lost on the media executives who embraced it. In the hopeful world of executive Webspeak, terms like "brand," "portal," "pipes," "content," and "toolbox" were thrown around like incantations, without regard for the fact that someone surfing the Web has more freedom of choice than a person browsing a magazine or newspaper, or doing laps around the TV dial. Web browsing is active, omnivorous, and omnidirectional, and the last thing the average Web surfer wants is someone to "bring order" to it. There is obvious value in mapping and helping to make sense out of the glut of information, but that's not what the portals offered to do; they were renting out space in a corral.

Reading the latest news no longer involved the linear process of receiving and digesting one news package assembled by an editorial team, or even several news packages assembled by several editorial teams, but searching and collecting fragments from a variety of sources that can span the globe and a variety of political and social viewpoints. The websites that are prospering are the ones owned by trusted brands that have created a loyal following by delivering material that enriches the lives of their readers or viewers, and helps them make some sense of all this information. And the fly-by surfers who arrive at these sites through search engines generally leave as soon as they get the information they're after.

Even at the turn of the century, many observers were less than impressed with the portal strategy. As Jordan Worth, an analyst with International Data Corp. (Canada) Ltd., pointed out, portals don't deliver anything beyond a standard newspaper-style mix of news, business, entertainment, and sports content – and editorial excellence is not very high on the list of priorities. "The kinds of things we're seeing in terms of application and content have not been terribly imaginative. That is just not where the battle is being fought" (McArthur 2000). Similarly, Wayne MacPhail, a former director of content for Bell's Sympatico-Lycos, accused Canadian websites of serving "the equivalent of airplane food – neither offensive nor exciting to anyone ... And, in some cases, the desire for blandness censors legitimate voices on the political spectrum" (2001).

Anyone looking for hard news on any of the service-provider or browser portals today will find little has changed since MacPhail wrote those words. A typical day might bring a survey of bad celebrity fashion sense, the ten scariest cars to drive, or the five foods you should never eat (portals love list stories). News you can use is alive and well on the Internet. On the other hand, newspaper websites have evolved to do pretty much what newspapers always have done: some do dazzling and surprising work; most offer only a surprising predictability and lack of imagination. As proof of their value, more people than ever are reading newspapers – and fewer than ever are paying for them. So, the circulation problem has been solved, in a way, by giving the product away online and allowing aggregators to cull the best material, sending flocks of fly-by readers to the newspaper sites. What have not been answered are the questions of how to turn a profit from the Web and how to rejuvenate the still profitable print editions. Even the paywalls are producing disappointing results in many cases. From the point of view of journalists, questions also linger about how to address that perceived slide in quality, how to return the dailies to being "my paper," and how to fund quality journalism when a large part of the audience appears to be turning away from print and proving resolutely opposed to paying for news online.

The most popular villain in most late twentieth-/early twenty-first-century news-media story is economics. Publishers, producers, news directors, and proprietors have long recognized the need to offer readers and viewers more than they can find on twenty-four-hour-news television or an aggregation site but are unwilling or unable to spend very much money on it. Pundits, wire services, and junior reporters are cheap; investigative reporters and feature writers are expensive. In a week, a columnist can crank out three to five opinion pieces, a reporter can deliver fifteen to twenty telephone-reported or press-release-based stories, and the wires will deliver hundreds of articles. Or management can assign a writer to do one or two well-researched features or investigative stories. To editors and publishers who want to deliver cheap content to a dwindling readership – and for chain owners carrying enormous debts and shareholders expecting a return on their investment – the answer is simple: keep the salaries low and the copy output high. As a result of these economic and competitive pressures, newspapers have become increasingly filled with wire stories, rewritten press releases, news stories generated by telephone reporting, and columns, fluff, and opinion pieces masquerading as news. Much of the journalism is a blend of old-fashioned essays and columns.

In the same way, all-news television and talk radio are faced with the quite frightening task of filling twenty-four hours a day, seven days a week with news content. But there often isn't enough news to fill 168 hours of television multiplied by the three main news networks in the United States and the two in Canada – a staggering 840 hours of combined airtime every week. To fill all this air, screen space and paper, there has been an explosion in panels and pundits: analysts, commentators, and experts called in to chew over every story that goes to air or print. British academic Brian McNair describes this explosion in opinion as one of the great threats to the credibility of modern journalism. "The normative functions of political news are being undermined by a proliferating commentary industry; a plethora of pundits who, drawing their cultural power from the privileged status of the journalist as licensed truth-teller, increasingly flood the public sphere with speculation and conjecture" (2000, 61).

Journalists have not been oblivious to the damage being done to their craft. Harvard researcher Pippa Norris reports that most US journalists complain that the press "pays too little attention to complex issues, blurs the distinction between reporting and commentary, is out of touch with the public and is too cynical." She quotes two senior US industry observers as saying a large majority of journalists feel the news culture has been degraded "from one that was steeped in verification and a steadfast respect for the facts, towards one that favours argument, opinion-mongering, haste and infotainment" (2000, 311).

Perhaps most famously, Joan Didion has accused journalists of alienating and boring their audience by turning politics into a game of "Insider Baseball," played at a great remove from "the actual life of the country" (2006a, 744). Journalists, she writes, focus tightly on the polls and the process of getting elected, and create a narrative "made up of ... tacit agreements, small and large, to overlook the observable in the interest of obtaining a dramatic storyline ... It is understood that this invented narrative will turn on certain familiar elements. There is the continuing storyline of the 'horse race,' the reliable daily drama of one candidate falling behind as another pulls ahead. There is the surprise of the new poll, the drama of the one-one colloquy on the midnight plane, a plot line (the nation sleeps while the candidate and his confidant hammer out its fate)" (755).

There is a fair amount of evidence that much of the audience rejects or ignores the punditry, or takes it simply as entertainment. Norris's intensive study of the 1997 British election indicates that "all the acres of newsprint which editorial writers devoted to trying to raise voters' concerns had no effect whatever" on the outcome of the election (1997, 184). Despite editorial writers' and pundits' argument that Britain's relationship with Europe was the decisive issue, the public chose to focus on domestic policies – something that implies the British news media were out of touch with their readers and viewers. In fact, Norris and her colleagues found no evidence that the press or television news were able to set the public agenda. However, their research also showed that the Conservative slide was fuelled largely by media reporting on sex scandals and incompetence, and the Liberal-Democrats' boost in support was propelled by their coherent platform and the fact that they stayed consistently on message. In other words, punditry did not influence the voters; reporting did.

Evidence also suggests that a large segment of the public is repelled by the trivialization of the news. The US Project for Excellence in Journalism has reported that "since the early 1980s, the public has come to view the news media as less professional, less accurate, less caring, less moral, and more inclined to cover up rather than correct mistakes" (2007a). Similarly, in a study of 3,012 Canadians, 80 per cent of respondents said they believed reporters' biases influence news; 54 per cent said they thought the news media tried to cover up their mistakes; one in three said they doubted the accuracy of news reports; 79 per cent said the news was often or sometimes unfair or not balanced; 92 per cent accused the news media of being at least sometimes sensational (CMRC 2004).

Following the events of 11 September 2001, many observers speculated that the news media would return to more sober, serious, issues-oriented reporting, after what many identified as a low point with the coverage of the Bill Clinton–Monica Lewinsky scandal of 1998. Yet, a year and a half after the World Trade Center attacks, Canadian Press was reporting that 62 per cent of the respondents to a Leger Marketing survey found "their media were sensationalistic and biased." In the same survey, television news was rated the most credible source of information by 40 per cent of respondents, followed by newspapers at 30 per cent (Wyatt 2002).

There were areas of concern in North American news coverage that were less readily apparent to the average reader or viewer. The US press may have grown more serious about foreign affairs, but it still, for the most part, allowed its business sections to ignore the WorldCom and Enron scandals, and completely miss the high-risk mortgage black hole that was sucking the world toward recession. "The securities fraud case of homemaking media maven Martha Stewart affected far fewer Americans than [Enron or WorldCom], yet drew more media attention, undoubtedly because of the celebrity aspects involved in her case" (McPherson 2006, 182).

Yet, significant segments of the news media believe the public wants more sensationalism and trivia, not less. Another Project for

Excellence in Journalism study showed that, between 8 February and 2 March 2007, coverage of the death of reality-TV star and nude model Anna Nicole Smith consumed 15 per cent of CNN's air time, 21 per cent of MSNBC's, and 32 per cent of Fox News's – compared with 17 per cent, 26 per cent, and 10 per cent for the Iraq War (2007b).

This is not to say that politics is all there is to hard news. The press tends to treat power politics as hard news and to trivialize most other forms of human endeavour as soft news, yet there is a world of things that people take very seriously but the press treats as lighter fare: culture (which becomes celebrity coverage); food (recipes); the multi-billion-dollar fashion industry (supermodels and runways); science and medicine (lifestyle and health); human relationships (advice and self-help); spirituality (the Sunday "church pages").

Often, the news industry has responded to shrinking readership by taking economic, technological, or cosmetic measures, or by asking audience members what they liked yesterday. There has been little emphasis on being better at telling us the stories we need to hear in order to live – perhaps because this is a slow process and almost impossible to measure in terms of progress or effect.

John Dewey argued that the public was waiting to be called into existence by "a kind of knowledge and insight which does not yet exist." If they want to create "an organized and articulate Public," he wrote, journalists need to think like artists. "Artists have always been the real purveyors of news, for it is not the outward happening in itself which is new, but the kindling by it of emotion, perception and appreciation" (1954, 166).

The job of the journalist is to make important things interesting to a broad audience, not simply to deliver the lewd, the weird, and the sensational. Yet, as *Toronto Star* business writer David Olive says, "the state of journalism is terrible, and it doesn't only have to do with technology. Did we warn our readers about the Great Recession? Did we warn our readers that Iraq was going to be a quagmire? Did we warn our readers about global warming?"

4

Business, Part One: The Daily Abyss

Between 2008 and 2013, it looked as if the newspaper industry were sinking by the bow and taking all passengers with it, and the rhetoric of the coverage reflected this. Scan the headlines for the period and you see such recurring verbs as "slash," "cut," "hit," "dive," "plunge," "tumble," "plummet," "fall," "decline," "shrink," "struggle," "slump," "die," "survive," and – a new one for this industry – "outsource." The "language of the obituary" (Project for Excellence in Journalism [PEJ] 2009) had come to dominate the tone of the conversation, and the fear had begun to feed upon itself, to the point that even positive news came shrouded in gloom. A content study by Hsiang Iris Chyi, Seth C. Lewis, and Nan Zheng for *Journalism Studies* looked at how the *Wall Street Journal*, the *New York Times*, and *USA Today* had covered the crisis. They concluded: "The coverage overwhelmingly focused on short-term changes ... rather than providing a more historical perspective ... little contextual data were featured in the coverage, particularly in relation to the state of newspapers around the world ... sourcing patterns privileged the views of newspaper management over external research or readers by a wide margin ... coverage assigned blame to advertisers, readers, the Internet but not newspaper themselves ... the overall tone of the coverage was largely negative, with more than a quarter of all stories including some 'death' imagery" (2011, 316).

The press was writing its obituary with peculiar enthusiasm. Often, newspaper owners and publishers behaved like demented impresarios, screaming "Bomb!" in front of their own box office. *Dallas Morning News* publisher James W. Moroney III put it this way in a letter to staff: "I don't know how the death of newspapers could have been any more exaggerated, especially in stories we in the newspaper business wrote about our own industry ... We gave it all we've got. And we did a great job. Everyone bought into the imminent death of newspapers. We managed to convince consumers, sell the notion to advertisers, and scare away investors" (2010).

Yet, by and large, newspapers remained profitable, even when their parent companies were on the verge of collapse. Quarter after quarter, many small newspapers reported profits, as did many newspapers that were being dragged down by the debts accrued by their parent companies. There may have been good reasons for concern, but the panic was pointless – unless self-immolation was the point. Advertising lineage was creeping downward and wasn't being replaced by online revenue. Though circulation had been exploding online and, in many cases, holding its own in print, profits were dropping off precipitously. Yet, there are more elements to the story than are embraced by the party line of a perfect storm of technology and economics roaring out of nowhere to blow away a time-tested business model.

Despite the constant cuts to staff and content, failure to engage with pre-recession criticism, and the obsessive negativity of the self-coverage, the narrative has mainly focused on the recession and technological change, and on blaming the audience for losing interest in the product (strange, considering that many newspapers were reporting a larger audience, much of which was reading for free online). *National Post* columnist, former magazine editor, and long-time observer of the news business Robert Fulford speaks for many media critics when he says, "I felt for a long while that most of our North American newspapers had become deadly in their sameness and had become less and less interesting. I remember twenty-five years ago, going through two or three American cities in a couple of weeks, and realizing I was reading the same paper, although they had different names ... There have always been a few good newspapers, but many of them have been pretty terrible for many years." Yet the all-purpose narrative is of the newspaper that serves democracy tirelessly and well savaged by predatory online competition, readers who refuse to acknowledge the value of the product, and advertisers who have lit out for the territory.

Even in its more positive manifestations, there is a tone of desperation and absolutism to the discussion. It's as if an entire industry decided that the gods had turned against it, and the only way to salvation was to have a bonfire of the vanities and walk naked, innocent, and penniless into the future. Many of the prophets of the digital age – even the ones who want to preserve journalism – seemed to be as keen on killing the print medium as they were on giving birth to a digital one.

There are those who argue that non-profit or limited-profit websites such as *ProPublica* are the answer to preserving a free press that will safeguard democracy. Some envision a world in which reporters carry cameras, microphones, and smart phones, and tweet, record, and write their stories for all media. Some publishers see a future in which the readers vote on the news, write it themselves, and buy back their own work – eliminating the need not just for ink, paper, and delivery people, but for writers, photographers, and editors, as well. And there are those who can't imagine "newspaper" without the word "daily" in front of it.

Some observers argue that newspaper companies simply became fixated on the newest, brightest, shiniest thing and, determined to have that thing, sabotaged a perfectly good product that was making a lot of money for a lot of people. "Newspaper people are not that smart," says Les Pyette, who has held editorial positions from reporter to editor-in-chief at papers ranging from the *Windsor Star* to the *Calgary Sun* and the *Toronto Sun*, and was publisher of the *London Free Press* and *National Post*. "So, if they see a wave coming, like digital: *Oh!* We've *got* to do this digital! And everybody gets caught up. It's just like when it became www.com a while back. Okay, you've got to have that, and you've got to have online advertising. Some of it – it's, Throw out the old baby that brought in $250 million. You're online for ten years and it's bringing in $30 million. Well, do the math."

In the realm of finance, the conversation mainly involves the mantra "broken business model," complaints about the whirlwind of negative conditions, and a lot of doom prophecy, anguish, and reflection on the industry's dependence on advertising to finance the practice of journalism. Much of the conversation revolves around a given: if the newspaper business dies, so goes journalism, and this would be a disaster for democracy. Much of it also centres on a management storyline that is rather self-serving: the Internet disrupted the revenue stream and is forcing owners and publishers to cut back on journalism to keep down the weight of costs so the ship can stay afloat. As we have seen in the previous chapters, there were a lot of problems with the way newspaper companies did business before the Internet, and there was never any evidence that emptying newsrooms would solve them. As the *Columbia Journalism Review*'s Ryan Chittum told me, the business strategies that had produced huge profit margins proved to be important factors in the plunge of newspaper fortunes after 2008:

> There's no doubt that the newspapers going public en masse in the 1980s was not a good thing – and the chain-ification of newspapers. Gannett is the one that everyone talks about. They were probably one of the most egregious at pumping up profit margins and putting out crappy papers. They abused this monopoly. Before everyone started going public, you still had crappy newspapers. But the rise of the chain and newspapers going public put new pressure on short-term thinking. We've seen that across the economy; it's not limited to newspapers. It's the financialization of everything, shareholder capitalism and the support of short-term stock prices at the expense of investment for the long run. Newspapers got caught up in that and it seriously hurt them. When you have these monopoly profits – What would things look like if they had invested more of that instead of kicking up dividends or buying back shares?

What colours much of the discussion is an uncompromising – and rather simple-minded – technological determinism that predicts a utopian online society peopled by pure-hearted citizen journalists, with unlimited time and funding, acting tirelessly for the good of society. The alternative vision is of big media companies colonizing and plundering the Web. Commentators such as Clay Shirky, Robert McChesney, Eric Alterman, Michael Schudson, and Jay Rosen have weighed in with everything from dire predictions to prescriptions for renewal, to Internet evangelism, as have many reporters, analysts, business writers, bloggers, media critics, and casual observers in the popular press and online. Some – notably Chittum, Steve Ladurantaye, former media reporter for the *Globe and Mail*, the late David Carr of the *New York Times*, and Reuters's Jack Shafer, formerly of *Slate* – have provided ongoing, nuanced examinations of the newspaper crisis and the evolution of online media, and the discussion thereof. Many have jumped in looking for the simplistic and the high concept and then jumped out, or have fastened onto a narrative and stayed with it. Some have had the slightly hysterical don't-say-we-didn't-warn-you tone of the vested interest. (For example, without a note of irony, a CBC *News Sunday* item in March 2009 went so far as to announce "The End of News.")

As blogger Paul Dailing writes, much of the conversation plays out like a chorus of death-of-newspaper Cassandras. "The point's not to fix anything. It's to describe the problem more dramatically than the next guy. If Steve Outing says newspapers have a 'death spiral' and Clay Shirky predicts a 'bloodbath,' the point goes to Shirky. Basically, I imagine a group of people watching a building burn down and bickering amongst themselves about whether it's a conflagration or an inferno. It's like that, but with consulting fees" (2009).

Following the discussion has often been a disorienting and bipolar experience, disheartening as much for the peculiar enthusiasm of some of the end-times prophets as for the information itself. We have heard the reflexive chanting of "information wants to be free," which neglects to reference the rest of Stewart Brand's legendary statement: "Information also wants to be expensive. Information wants to be free because it has become so cheap to distribute, copy, and recombine – too cheap to meter. It also wants to be expensive because it can be immeasurably valuable to the recipient" (quoted in Tofel 2012, 88). When Brand's words are taken out of context, they make him sound like a naive hippie ideologue inviting people to help themselves to all the music, film, and text they can load onto their hard drives. Taken as a whole, his comments are a compact assessment of the central problem of the Internet: that it is very good at taking from each according to her ability, but terrible when it comes to providing to each according to his need – with the exception of a few people at the top of a few huge online enterprises, such as Google, Twitter, Amazon, and Facebook.

At their worst, these online companies operate a virtual feudal society. For example, Facebook owns the "land" and allows a massive cyber-serfdom to live on it. We fertilize the Facebook landscape with our personal data, which is harvested and sold for profit – the way medieval serfs had to drive their cattle across landowners' fields, where the precious manure was dropped to create the most fertile farmland. And, like feudal lords, these companies' mastery of their domains is absolute.

In the end, aggregators and social media simply understood the Internet better than newspapers did. They created content-less services, which they filled with intellectual property gleaned from their users or cribbed from the media companies that paid to create it, and they made it available free online. Also, the aggregators and social media companies were adept at corralling advertisers, by mining personal data and providing targeted advertising that the old-line media companies have been unable to match. So, with no expenses incurred to create content, they were able to charge a lot less for advertising that was more effective and establish themselves as overlords of their online properties.

So newspapers have to find a way to harness the financial potential of all this expensive information, even though, as Shafer long ago pointed out, the idea that people will never pay for content has become a salient feature of "Web orthodoxy" (2009a). As Brand illustrates, it is extremely difficult to charge for intellectual property once you've started giving it away for free. One of the problems is that quality starts off being irrelevant to value, because a bad movie, game, magazine, newspaper, book or phone call costs as much as a good one – until the source develops a reputation, "because the consistency (reliability) of source makes value somewhat predictable" (quoted in Tofel 2012, 88). Brand's argument is supported by the fact that news organizations such as the *Wall Street Journal,* Thomson-Reuters, Bloomberg, and the *Financial Times* consistently turn a profit online because they have information that investors need and a reputation for reliability, and the information they provide has a tangible, financial value. Similarly, services such as *Consumer Reports,* Netflix, and iTunes have had little trouble getting people to pay for content by providing tangible value and convenience.

The three criteria for success for paid sites, Shafer wrote, are: "1) They are so amazing as to be irreplaceable. 2) They are beautifully designed and executed and extremely easy to use. 3) They are stupendously authoritative" (2009a). Yet, old media companies appear to be convinced that they can erode their product indefinitely and still provide value, or the illusion of it, to readers, and that the Web, the smart phone and the tablet are saviour technologies that will wipe away past financial and professional blunders and return everything to business as usual.

Apart from the debts accrued through decades of leveraged acquisitions and the dedication to serving shareholders over readers or advertisers, the problems faced by the news industry can be attributed to two Original Sins, to borrow a term coined by newspaper analyst Alan Mutter (2009): newspapers' decision to give away their product, their only source of value (Mutter's original Original Sin), and the failure of the industry to compete with online services that drained away classified advertising revenue, such as eBay, Craigslist, and Kijiji.

In the first case, the assumption was that the Internet would work the way television does, that a large number of viewers would translate into big advertising revenues. That didn't work out. "Lots of people came, but lots of advertising didn't," newspaper analyst John Morton wrote in 2011. "Last year, only 10 percent of newspaper advertising revenue came from online – this after a 10-year effort." Things hadn't changed very much in three years. For example, in 2013, Postmedia was earning 15–20 per cent of its revenue from electronic sources. The company is Canada's largest newspaper publisher by circulation, owning the *National Post*, the *Vancouver Sun* and the *Province*, the *Calgary Herald*, *Edmonton Journal*, *Saskatoon StarPhoenix*, *Regina Leader-Post*, *Windsor Star*, *Ottawa Citizen*, and the *Gazette* in Montreal.

Between 2008 and 2013, Canadian newspaper advertising revenue decreased by 13 per cent, yet operating expenses were down by 12.5 per cent (including a 16 per cent drop in employee salaries). So the industry showed an 11.1 per cent profit margin in 2012, compared to 12 per cent in 2008 (Ladurantaye 2013a). Ad revenue in Canada topped out at around $3 billion in 2005. It slipped to $2.5 billion by 2008, followed by a second drop in 2008–9 to a little less than $2 billion, where it levelled off, representing roughly a 33 per cent decrease in revenue since 2005 (Warnica 2013). Despite predictions that newspaper revenue would drop by 20 per cent between 2013 and 2017 (Ladurantaye 2013b), newspaper ad revenue was up by 2 per cent in 2012 (Ernst and Young 2013, 13). In comparison, the US industry lost 55 per cent of its profits in four years, sliding from $49.4 billion in 2008 to $22.3 billion in 2012 (CNS News, 2013).

"I think what's remarkable is how recent the collapse of the newspaper is," Jack Shafer says. "I mean, in 2005 they are still minting gold, still 30-per-cent-margin businesses. And, then, with the recession – which kicked their legs out from under them – what advertisers now knew was what we can do in the marketplace without advertising. And when they came back into the market I think they bought elsewhere."

Yet, rather than beefing up their product and aiming for ways to extract revenue from the masses of online readers they were attracting, most newspaper companies' best idea was to cut costs by shedding staff and impoverishing the product. The pre-recession profit margins of 20 to 30 per cent that had been spent on paying back debts or enriching shareholders could have gone a long way towards ensuring the future of newspapers – especially in Canada, where the profit margins are still equal to or better than that of most industries. "No one has ever persuaded me that you can cut your way to greatness," says John Honderich, chairman of Torstar, parent company of the *Toronto Star* and *Hamilton Spectator,* and the Metroland chain of community weeklies. "On the other hand, when you're operating revenue declines by as much as it has in our case, you've got to take steps. You've got to stay ahead of it, or else you'll end up on the wrong side."

Newspapers also failed to foresee the online competition for ad dollars, how the Internet would expand the ways in which advertisers could reach their clientele. In Canada in 2012, the Internet showed a gain of 15 per cent, for a 27.5 per cent share of the country's advertising market, and search advertising (in other words, Google) accounted for 42 per cent of that (Ernst and Young 2013, 12). On the Web, ads can be targeted through social media, user groups, or search-engine inquiries. Goods can be sold directly to consumers through sites such as Amazon or special-interest, or brand sites. Classifieds can be interactive, immediate, and free (unless one upgrades to attract more views, which is where the sites make some of their profit). Consumer information can be mined from social media, promotional pages, and their attendant content, and contests on Facebook attract "likes," which attract more views. The information that is mined through all this activity is used to stream ads directly to target users.

In this environment, newspaper ad space becomes discretionary and specialized. For example, in 2009, when Mercedes-Benz introduced a new E-class sedan, it ran big, expensive display ads on the home pages of the *New York Times, Washington Post,* and *Wall Street*

Journal. The estimated cost was $100,000 per site. However, the car company's strategy was to make a splash with the mainstream media and then immediately move to a cheaper, more focused campaign involving buying from networks: organizations that bundle ad space on websites, often selling it at a deep discount. So, rather than being the main, day-to-day buy for advertisers, newspaper websites became "the patent-leather stilettos of the online world: they get used for special occasions, but other shoes get more daily wear" (Clifford 2009).

One factor that nobody could have predicted was that the Internet would redefine the value of advertising. Advertisers had always known instinctively that their ads and commercials were reaching as many consumers they didn't want as ones they did, but there was no way to tell one group from the other. So, they continued to buy space in newspapers and magazines, and time on television, knowing that total penetration was better than none. Online, however, it became easy to monitor the reach of ads and, therefore, to target only consumers who were interested in the product. Advertisers began to see that state of affairs as normal. "User behaviour could be carefully tracked; offline it seemed suddenly much more knowable, as advertisers demanded quantification where once anecdotes had sufficed" (Tofel 2012, 44).

This was not a new concept and should not have been difficult to see coming. Newspapers were among the last media to be hit by targeted marketing. Through the 1970s and '80s, the magazine industry had seen a huge shift from general-interest to niche publications aimed at specific interests and, through the same period, specialty cable channels had wrought havoc on commercial TV networks, siphoning off specific types of programming, and the viewers that went with them.

With advertising being charged by CPM (cost per 1,000 page hits), ad sales went from a money tree to a hole in the ground. "With CPMs, what advertisers are asking for, which they never asked for before, is effectiveness," Honderich says. "Prove to us. Show us that our ad is working. Feet in the store. That kind of thing. The CPM model is there, but our line rates have been devastated. Advertisers come in and say, We'll advertise with you, but at 50 per cent of what your rate is. We have so many other options, places to go. We used to use that wonderful phrase, 'You can't buy around us,' in terms of getting to the audience. Now they can. Talk about a paradigm shift. It's huge."

As *New York Daily News* publisher Mort Zuckerman told the UK House of Lords Select Committee on Communications, the Internet may have expanded the reach of newspapers immeasurably in terms of audience, but in terms of advertising revenue it has substituted "pennies for dollars" (2008, 121). For example, in 2011 the *New York Times* had roughly 30 million online readers and a print circulation of just 900,000 on weekdays. Yet it derived 80 per cent of its profit from the print edition (Grueskin, Seave, and Graves 2011, 21). This is why newspapers across North America have moved to put their content behind paywalls, which have proved to be partial and imperfect solutions. "The problem with the paywall – for us and everyone else – is that you just can't replace the print revenue," the *Globe and Mail*'s Ladurantaye says. "It's just not going to happen. Eighty-five per cent of Postmedia's revenue comes from print advertising. You can't make up a $50,000 full-page ad for one day with a bunch of subscriptions at $10 each. The math just isn't there. Even if you strip out all the distribution costs and all the rest, the real money is in print."

In a column in the *New Yorker*, James Surowiecki observed that in the past, when companies fell into the kind of downward spiral in which newspaper companies found themselves, it was because people had stopped buying their product or service. With newspapers, thanks to the Internet, people are actually using them more: "They've just stopped paying for them, a kind of backhanded compliment to their continued relevance ... The real problem for newspapers, in other words, isn't the Internet; it's us. We want access to everything, we want it now, and we want it for free. That's a consumer's dream, but eventually it's going to collide with reality: if newspapers' profits vanish, so will their product" (2008). If newspapers hadn't committed the Original Sin, Ryan Chittum says, it would have changed the nature not only of the news business, but of the Internet as well:

> I think the original problem was credulously looking at the Internet, not understanding it, and putting all their content for free online. Had they not done that, they would have deprived what we now know as the Internet of a lot of its oxygen. It would have stunted its growth – at least delayed the reckoning day. Aggregators, blogs, you wouldn't have the sort of thing where you could get all-hour news online for free from other people, who are repurposing newspapers' and magazines' news. The Internet opened everything up

for competition, but you still have to support it with money, and ad revenue, if you don't have circulation. So, people starting up, you might have had an individual blogger here and there, a commentator, but it would have been much harder to start up something to compete with a newspaper. The *Seattle Times* has a newsroom of 400. You're going to start up and compete with that?

It is also difficult to monetize the digital news product through advertising because online audiences are wide but not deep. For example, a recent analysis of traffic to the website of a mid-size US newspaper revealed that hard-core "fans" of the site amounted to just 4.3 per cent of visitors, and "regulars" another 3.1 per cent. Yet, those two groups were responsible for 64.3 per cent of the page views. Meanwhile, fly-bys – directed to the site by a search engine or aggregator – amounted to 75.3 per cent of visitors, but only 19.7 per cent of the page views (Grueskin, Seave, and Graves 2011, 24). James Harding, editor of the *Times* of London, arguing for a paywall, allowed that charging an admission fee would drastically cut down on the 20 million visitors who were going to the *Times*'s website. However, he dismissed that loss as simply a matter of culling the "window shoppers," the fly-bys who land on a website by search engine, read a bit, and then flit off to something else (Pfanner 2010).

In other words, the online audience that publishers and advertisers care about is the same one that matters to the print edition: the readers who browse the front page, follow the headlines into the stories, and keep coming back for more. This means search-engine optimization, or SEO, is a waste of time. It also goes a long way toward bolstering the newspapers' complaint that aggregators such as the *Huffington Post*, Yahoo, Google, and the *Daily Beast* are profiting at their expense. Aggregator sites have long argued that they help the newspapers' business by promoting their work through links to the original stories that they collect from the paper's websites. However, the statistics on fans and fly-bys suggest that aggregators steal revenue from newspapers by repurposing material the dailies paid to create, posting it online and sending flocks of useless fly-bys to the original site. Meanwhile, the aggregators create the loyal audience the advertisers want, and they build it with the best material lifted from companies that pay to manufacture it.

All of this has serious implications for the method of pricing online ads by CPM rather than according to the nature and loyalty of core readership. It's as if print publications tried to include in their circulation the people who pick up the paper at the newsstand, read a headline or one story, and then put it back. Or, perhaps more pointedly, it compares directly to junk circulation derived from print copies dumped at airports and hotels. Consequently, newspaper executives have begun to talk about dedicated audience and reader engagement rather than page views. "The new jargon is audience development and audiences, and what audiences do we have and we can sell," *Edmonton Journal* managing editor Stephanie Coombs says. "When the advertising department talks about studies, they talk about ... We have to get off CPM. It's not worth it. And we have to get advertisers to understand audiences and to understand these committed local readers. That is definitely where the pendulum is shifting."

But to build that audience, you need compelling, unique content. The idea is to wean advertisers off CPMs "by focusing the advertisers' attention on the value of engagement," Postmedia chief operating officer Wayne Parrish told me. "You accomplish that by driving content so that you have a highly engaged audience, and that 14 per cent [of fans and regulars] becomes 20 per cent ... You've got to get advertisers to appreciate – which they do over time – that a single view of an ad on a Google search, the reader or audience might look at for two seconds or 2½ seconds, is ultimately less valuable than ads sitting next to something a consumer is going to consume over the course of a minute, two minutes, or four minutes. And that's the challenge."

Yet, oddly, advertisers who are concerned about wasted exposure – and complain when those dumped copies are folded into print circulation figures – are just catching up with the inefficiency of counting CPMs. As media analyst Matt Shanahan writes in his blog: "When people talk about the size of an audience, that's a sham ... The digital world has changed the revenue dynamics for publishers. In the print world, a publisher's shipment of physical media is the basis for revenue. In the digital world, consumption of media is the basis for everything ... In other words, engagement is the unit of monetization" (quoted in Grueskin, Seave, and Graves 2011, 25).

The "economics of attention" is what Richard Lanham (2006) calls it: an assessment of value measured in how much celebrity, for want of a better word, one can create. As the model for success in this new market, Lanham uses Andy Warhol, a painter, publisher, filmmaker, and marketing genius whose one theme was fame, stretched across multiple platforms. Warhol reproduced fame with his Marilyn Monroe and Campbell's soup silkscreens; he mocked it as producer and director of movies that celebrated sleaze or sneered at the audience; he wallowed in it with *Interview* magazine; he lived it, or behind a facade of it, with his life, his Factory, and his entourage. Like so much that enters the current discourse, the Warhol example serves to strengthen the argument that the salient difference between the digital age and what came before is how much easier it is to be a trader in the economics of attention, and how much more difficult it is to get anybody to pay for it. For every Kardashian family or Justin Bieber, there are thousands – perhaps millions – of aspiring celebrities whose best hope is a viral YouTube video or Vine. For the most part, fame was valuable when it was rare, and you could trade it for money. Now, anyone with an interesting, odd, or creepy persona and a Facebook page can achieve a measure of worthless fame. As someone once said, online celebrity is just like being the most popular girl or guy in high school. Usually, it is also as profitable.

When you consider that most large newspaper companies trudged into the tar pits of the recession dragging huge debts behind them, it's easy to see how financial and employment circumstances got blended into a Doomsday narrative. Just at the moment the industry needed to be innovative and daring to meet the challenges of the digital age, most companies found themselves fighting a rear-guard action against their creditors:

> The company has borrowed a lot of money to make acquisitions ... and the company's newspapers, while still profitable, throw off lower profits during a recession. This can mean that a company encounters difficulty meeting debt obligations and meeting lenders' requirements for cash flow coverage of interest payments and the like. A company can respond by renegotiating its debt ... which raises the interest rate; by eliminating or cutting its dividend payments to shareholders ... and by unloading assets ... And, most common, a company can lay off employees, eliminate special features and sections, tighten news space and cut

back circulation to reduce newsprint and distribution costs. Those actions, of course, diminish the standing of newspapers in their markets and to some extent undermine efforts to transfer strong brand names and advertising efforts to the web. The long-term impact of these actions is yet to be learned, but it is unlikely to be beneficial. (Morton 2008)

Morton has been proved right. We have begun to see the effects of those decisions, and they were not beneficial. "Thirty per cent return on investment is fine when you don't have any debt," says Raymond Brassard, the recently retired executive editor of the Montreal *Gazette*. "But when you have debt, it's nothing. It all goes to servicing the debt. So you're not really making a lot of money. And that happened across most of the newspaper companies – even the *New York Times*. They paid over a billion dollars for the *Boston Globe* and then just sold it for $70 million. It's ridiculous. But that was the way the business ran in the '80s and '90s and early 2000s ... The whole industry is a prisoner of what happened in the past thirty years on the business side."

It's not as if there were no early warnings that things were changing for newspapers' print and online operations. Right on the heels of the dot-com bust of 2000 – which coincided with what was, at that time, newspapers' most profitable year on record (Tofel 2012, 9) – there was a steady drop in newspaper advertising. Media-economics specialist Robert Picard explains that advertising revenues "typically rose higher than GDP growth in good times and fell further than GDP declines during recessions and downturns." However, "advertising did not recover after the 2001 recession, as it had in the past." When the short slump from 2001 (following the attacks on the World Trade Center) to 2003 ended, advertisers didn't follow their usual pattern of returning to their old spending habits. For example, from 1950 to 1990, newspaper-advertising growth in the United States showed a constant rise, from $2 billion to approximately $30 billion, then a short drop in 1990, followed by another constant rise, to $47.4 billion in 2000, then another drop, to approximately $40 billion. This time, however, instead of an incline, the chart shows a plateau to 2005, the year advertising revenues began a slump from which they have not recovered (Picard, 2008, 708).

Then, with the crash of 2008, an economic sinkhole opened up. Online advertising revenue stopped rising, and then began to fall, too.

The new income stream upon which newspaper publishers and owners had been banking was drying up with the old one, and economic recovery was doing little, if anything, to help. "Even though advertising has recovered in magazines, on radio, and on TV – where it had weakened during the recession – it never came back for newspapers. In fact, it keeps going down" (Mutter 2011).

Strangely, much of the reporting and commentary, especially in the popular press, reacted to these statistics as if they were the result of some sudden, unforeseen natural catastrophe. However, the business conditions that created this situation were neither unforeseen nor natural, except to newspaper companies locked into a downward spiral of cost cutting and debt management. In most cases, these were companies that flipped newspapers like condominiums and had never given much thought to the relationship between quality and profit. A few years after the takeover of Sun Media by Quebecor, I asked former *Toronto Sun* publisher and newsroom legend Hartley Steward what he thought of the way the parent companies were doing business: "Suddenly there's a lot of money distributed to a few people, and nothing really has changed. No one went out and created another paper. Nobody created an asset of value, or created any wealth ... A lot of money gets paid out and nothing is created. What's created is savings, and those are skimmed off ... You cut the shit out of the place. It's a vicious kind of a thing."

As we have seen, in the 1990s a considerable amount of advertising had begun to look for new outlets: "Procter and Gamble, McDonald's, Seagram's, Ford Motor Company, Coca-Cola, Nissan, Kodak and Campbell's Soup ... are saying ... 'You're not worth our money'" (Miller 1998, 11). With the Internet, advertisers were being offered alternatives – sometimes for the first time. For that reason, classified advertising has all but disappeared, in a little more than a decade. For example, US daily newspapers made $20 billion from classified ads in 2000. By 2011, that had dropped to $5 billion (McChesney 2013, 172). Big-city dailies that once printed entire sections of classifieds now run two or three pages of the announcements that once contributed much of their profits, and about half of those are often – prophetically, perhaps – death notices. Their online ventures are also-rans to Kijiji and Craigslist.

Leonard Downie Jr and Michael Schudson (2009) point out that, as television began to drain away display advertising from newspapers through the 1960s and '70s, newspapers became more dependent on classifieds, which the electronic medium couldn't do. However, the Internet *can* do classifieds – much better, in fact, than print. Classified ads truly are a community talking to itself and, as such, are more efficient and attractive when they are searchable, can be updated by the minute, and when the viewer can achieve instant gratification from clicking on a link or sending an email. For example, the way Craigslist and Kijiji display the time an ad was posted – a day, an hour, or a minute ago – gives the viewer a sense of being actively involved in the hunt, much the way eBay does with its bidding system. In comparison, by the time a reader gets to a newspaper classified ad, it isn't just dead; it's decomposing. And someone with something to sell can place an ad for free online, while they have to pay for newspaper space.

The newspapers never took the upstarts seriously, Postmedia CEO Paul Godfrey says. "I just think they got caught with their pants down. It was one of these rare things. Everybody slammed the door on Craigslist and Kijiji, and, before they knew it, classifieds were gone and they weren't getting them back." Godfrey's comments echo the online mythology of Craig Newmark pitching his idea for online classifieds to his hometown newspaper, the *San Francisco Chronicle*. "Only after being summarily rejected did he go on to found Craigslist and singlehandedly decimate the primary revenue source of newspapers everywhere" (Rubenstein et al. 2012). Some might say there's a poetic symmetry to the fact that, in 2009, the *Chronicle* came close to being the first big American daily in a single-paper city to fold. Its owner, the Hearst Corp., threatened to close it if it couldn't be sold, only to give the paper a reprieve and relaunch it with glossy cover pages a few months later.

So the "received wisdom is that newspapers succumbed to a stealth attack from Craigslist" (Tofel 2012, 71–2). In reality, however, newspapers across North America were experimenting with online classifieds at around the same time Newmark founded his email notice board, which evolved into what we know today. In Canada, Sun Media, the *Globe and Mail*, and the *Toronto Star* had successful automobile-sales and career sites running long before Craigslist became a household word. And in the United States, a consortium of six newspapers, including the *Chicago Tribune*, also beat Newmark to the Web, "but failed to compete effectively with a single geek working out of his apartment" (72).

The problem, Postmedia's Wayne Parrish says, is that newspapers kept making the same mistake of trying to adapt what they were already doing to the Internet, rather than inventing a new online form. They thought they could continue selling classifieds and throw in the Internet as a bonus:

> The American papers dealt with it differently and better than we did in Canada, because they recognized the power of the Craigslist kind of approach and Kijiji approach – in other words, free classifieds. And they began to invest in cars.com and classified ventures, and so on, entities that would seek their own place in the market not tethered to the newspaper franchise, and not where you sell a classified ad and then up-sell a digital ad. In Canada we took a more conservative approach ... We tended to tether our digital ads in classified to our print ads, and that turned out to be a recipe for disaster.

In Britain the situation was not much different. In 2007, before the full effects of the recession hit, executives from the *Guardian* told the House of Lords Select Committee on Communications that classifieds were slipping away at a rate of 10 per cent per year. Representatives from the *Times* of London told the committee, "the most dramatic difference for the business model over the past 10 years had been the 'decline of classified advertising'" (2008, 16). Back in the United States, in one decade starting in 1999, classifieds fell from 40 per cent to 20 per cent of all newspaper advertising (McChesney and Nichols 2010, 27), dropping 42 per cent in 2009 alone.

Traditionally, ad revenue has, on average, accounted for 80 per cent of a daily newspaper's earnings (Krashinsky 2010). However, advertising losses have been so severe that money earned through circulation – which in some newspapers is rising, partly thanks to paywalls – has passed advertising as a percentage of revenues. For example, by mid-2009, the *New York Times* reported that its advertising-to-circulation ratio of profits had gone from two-to-one to one-to-one in just three years (Chittum 2009b).

As the bad news persisted, the mood in the industry quickly went from nervous to panicky, and the panic led to an unprecedented gutting of newsrooms. Poynter's Rick Edmonds estimates that between 2007 and 2009 the US newspaper business reduced its spending on journalism by $1.6 billion annually. When it comes to replacing that investment, it "would take roughly 1,600 [non-profit news sites] MinnPosts or Voice of San Diegos to replace the spending on journalism that newspapers have cut" (2009). In 2012, the American Society of News Editors announced that the level of staffing in US newspapers was at its lowest point since the group began taking an annual census in 1978. That is, US dailies employed 40,600 editors and reporters, compared to a peak of 56,900 in 1990. That is a decline of 28.6 per cent (Mutter 2012).

In Canada over all, the income-to-debt situation (aside from Postmedia) is not as dire as it is at many of the large US chains, and, as we have seen, the drop in profits has not been as steep. However, the drop in classified advertising is comparable, as is the shrinkage in display advertising. Circulation remains problematic in most cases – although even rising circulation has done little to lure back advertisers. Between 2009 and 2012, average daily circulation at the *Globe and Mail* slipped by 4.2 per cent, from 315,272 to 302,190. Meanwhile the *Toronto Star* lost 12.6 per cent of its average weekday circulation, dropping from 409,340 in 2009 to 357,612 in 2012. Its crosstown rival, the *Toronto Sun*, dropped 10.4 per cent, from 188,863 to 169,219.

Across the country, the situation is strangely variable. The *Vancouver Sun* had a circulation of 175,572 in 2009, which dropped to 164,507 in 2012, for a loss of 6.3 per cent. Its rival, the tabloid *Province*, dropped 12.6 per cent, from 162,765 to 142,300. In Edmonton, the *Sun* lost 23 per cent of its average weekday circulation, and the *Journal* dropped 14 per cent. But papers in southern Alberta showed gains, with the *Calgary Herald* rising 2.0 per cent, from 124,607 in 2009 to 127,147 in 2012, and the *Sun* growing by 25 per cent, from 51,757 to 64,654. These numbers are mitigated by the fact that Calgary was the fastest growing city in the country, with a rate of population increase of 3.3 per cent in 2013 alone (CBC.ca 2014). So, the *Herald*'s growth lags behind that of its potential audience.

In the east, the *Ottawa Citizen* lost 11.2 per cent, from 123,856 in 2009 to 110,019 in 2012. And the Montreal *Gazette* plunged 30 per cent, from 163,501 to 113,888. Yet *Le Journal de Montréal* gained 6.8 per cent, going from 269,391 to 287,799, and *La Presse* gained 5.6 per cent, growing its circulation from 215,142 to 227,206 (all figures, Newspapers Canada 2012a). This could be at least partly explained by the fact that the French-language newspapers face softer competition – no *Guardian, New York Times, National Post,* or *Globe and Mail* to siphon off readers.

The circulation figures are reported by different audit agencies, and include paid and unpaid circulation, so it is extremely difficult to impose any strict logic on them. The reason I chose the years 2009 and 2012 is that 2012 was the most recent year for which there were records, and before 2009 only paid circulation was counted, so there's no basis for comparing, say, 2008 with 2012. It would take a major study to explain why circulation is rising in Calgary and French Montreal and plunging in Edmonton, Ottawa, and English Montreal, and why the slippage is so much less dramatic at the *Vancouver Sun* and the *Globe and Mail*. Rather, the usefulness of these statistics lies in the fact that they show there is no overall pattern to circulation growth or shrinkage, unless a page-by-page and reader-by-reader comparison could prove empirically that better papers draw a larger audience. At the same time, the statistics imply that readership is no more a factor in newspaper losses now than it was in profits before the recession.

"The disruption is also on the advertising model," Montreal *Gazette* editor-in-chief Lucinda Chodan says. "There's a lot of discussion online in publications whose business is advertising and whose audience is advertisers, and agencies and marketers. It's not just the information-delivery model that is broken. It's the advertising model that is broken, and people are talking about the death of advertising. It's a complex situation and I think it has been a very underreported part of the big disruption." Actually, it's not so much that the advertising model has broken, but that advertisers have discovered that you don't need content to sell goods, and you don't need to go through the newspaper to reach its readers. In fact, it's cheaper and more efficient if you don't. The main impact of the disruption has been on retail advertising, where you can add up the effectiveness of your campaign at the cash register. For institutional advertising, where the aim is brand awareness, the impact has been less severe. But it's mainly the big national advertisers who do institutional campaigns, and the bulk of them go to television, big national or international dailies such as the *New York Times*, and glossy, high-end magazines like *Vogue* or *Vanity Fair* – where slick advertising is an integral part of the package, and another reason readers buy them. Perhaps most important, if a video campaign is interesting enough, it goes viral on social media – which is the twenty-first-century equivalent of what used to be called a water-cooler commercial, one everyone is talking about at work the next day.

Newspapers rely on retail, and targeted advertising and online sales have made the traditional retail ad all but obsolete. There has been massive growth in search advertising, social-media promotions, and online marketing. Tied to this is a persistence of ad prices set according to the number of people who click through (CPM) and search engine optimization (SEO) driving in junk readers, who scan one story and move on. It's not so much that newspapers need to move advertisers online but that they need to realize that they're moving from an advertising medium to one where advertising and publishing have become uncoupled – probably permanently. As *Columbia Journalism Review*'s Ryan Chittum says, the changes in the environment are so great that advertising may never again play a large role in the newspaper's financial structure:

> I've been arguing for paywalls, and the argument was that most of your page views come from the core readership. And engineering all your content to go after the marginal click is insane. You want to do everything you can to keep your core readers there, and if you start dumbing your stuff down and SEO-ing it down, and going after these marginal readers, who are going to click you once and leave, it's stupid. People have talked about the tyranny of the CPM, and it's unfortunate. But I just don't know what you can do about it. The cat's out of the bag. Unless you completely close yourself off to the Internet. And the way it's gone, I don't see how you're going to say, If you want to be here, I'm going to charge this amount. I guess if you had a certain audience, advertisers really wanted to reach, maybe you could do that. But the way everything is set up now, they can go somewhere else. They have metrics on where else *New York Times* readers go on the Web. If you really need to get *New York Times* readers, you can go to NPR or whatever.

Online editions have picked up a large readership but this has failed to translate into sufficient revenue to make up for the losses in the print editions. Though online advertising revenues in Canada for 2012 were $3.1 billion (Ernst and Young 2013), only $242 million went to newspapers – less than 10 per cent of the total, and roughly 10 per cent of the newspaper-industry advertising income for the year (Newspapers Canada 2012b). In the fall of 2012, Quebecor reported that advertising revenue for the quarter had dropped by 3 per cent at urban papers and 6 per cent at community papers. As the *Edmonton Journal*'s Karen Unland says, display advertising just doesn't get through, and the advertisers know it. "All that kind of advertising is based on interruption. You came here to read this story about what's going on in the LRT yesterday that stopped everything, but instead I'm showing you a really great ad for Shaw Cable. I don't care about Shaw Cable. I care about why the LRT stopped. It shows a basic disrespect for the viewers, and people who read their news online are much less tolerant of interruption advertising. We are very good at tuning out all that stuff. So it's not effective. Display advertising is not effective any more. You need some other way to do it now."

The response to dwindling advertising revenue has been a steady stream of layoff and buyout announcements from Canadian dailies. For example, the fifteen-year history of Quebecor's Sun Media ownership was a constant trickle of layoffs and buyouts, rising to 600 job cuts in 2008. Four hundred positions were eliminated in early 2012, followed by the slashing of another 500 in November, in a reorganization that included the shutting of two Ontario production facilities and the restructuring of management so that the entire chain of hundreds of dailies and community newspapers would report to three executives. This, in turn, had followed the mass firing of senior editors and publishers across the country in October. A week after the job cuts, the paper closed two Niagara Peninsula dailies. Then, in 2013, the company closed eleven of its newspapers and eliminated 360 jobs in July and cut another 200 jobs in December. "It is very tough to announce job cuts," Sun Media CEO Julie Tremblay said in a news release in December. "But as distressing as they are for the employees involved, these restructuring initiatives are necessary to maintain our leading position and ensure the corporation's sustainability" (CBC.ca 2013a).

Sun Media also faced two drawn-out labour disputes at the company's flagship newspapers in Quebec – for fifteen months in 2007–8, at *Le Journal de Québec* and for two years in 2009–11, at *Le Journal de Montréal*. The latter resulted in a settlement of unprecedented harshness, which called for the rehiring of just 62 of the 227 workers who had been locked out by the company. For the third quarter of 2012, Quebecor had posted an $18 million profit, mostly due to its cable and cellphone businesses. That was despite a 2012 loss of $17 million on the ultra-right-wing news channel Sun News. In April 2015, Postmedia took control of all the latter's English-Canadian print media and Internet properties, all but guaranteeing another massive round of layoffs, as Postmedia seeks to boost income to help cover liabilities.

In 2011–12 alone, Postmedia, which took over the Canwest newspapers in 2010, slashed some $35 million worth of jobs, closed its national news syndicate, discontinued Sunday editions at its Ottawa, Edmonton, and Calgary papers, outsourced much of its newspaper editing and page production to a central newsroom in Hamilton, Ontario, and sold off its Toronto headquarters, which also housed the newsroom of the *National Post*. The company also announced a three-year "cost transformation plan" to "reduce legacy newspaper infrastructure costs" (Financial Post 2012). In October 2012, Postmedia announced a $28.4 million loss for its fourth quarter, partly due to restructuring costs, and announced a drop of nearly 6 per cent in revenue over the previous year. In 2013, the company eliminated the publisher's position at its ten papers, reorganizing the chain under three regional VPs, and cut a half-dozen editing positions at the *National Post*. In early 2014, the trend continued with the February closing of Postmedia's parliamentary bureau. Five journalists were laid off, and the remaining four were reassigned to the *Ottawa Citizen*'s parliamentary team. At the same time, newspapers across the chain began a new round of buyouts. Postmedia executives had announced earlier that they planned to cut $180 million from the budget that year.

In late 2009, the *Toronto Star* announced the "biggest restructuring in the newspaper's history" (Friend 2009), which ended with the elimination of seventy-eight editing jobs. However, the company backed away from a plan to outsource all its copy editing to an off-site production company. Roughly two years later, Canada's largest newspaper went through another round of staff buyouts. In the summer of 2013, the company announced it would outsource editing and advertising layout jobs to Pagemasters North America, eliminating some forty-four positions, and in the fall announced further plans to outsource advertising sales to its *Metro* newspapers division and to eliminate another seventy-five to one hundred people in editorial, and finance and administration. In mid-2014, the newspaper announced a buyout package designed to encourage older editorial staff to take early retirement, though this appeared to be an attempt to rejuvenate the newsroom rather than depopulate it. Torstar chairman John Honderich – a former reporter and editor – told me in 2013 that when he arrived at the newspaper in the early 1980s, there were 2,250 Newspaper Guild jobs; at the time he was speaking, there were 350. He also said that, over the years, 70 per cent of the cutbacks at the *Star* had been to unionized positions.

There also have been cuts at the *Globe and Mail*, a paper that might be expected to be more insulated than most by brand loyalty and the upmarket, somewhat specialized nature of its product. The paper lost sixty positions to voluntary buyout packages in 2009, as many more in the spring of 2013, and announced the elimination of another eighteen positions in January 2014.

It would take far too much space to produce a shopping list of all the layoffs at such companies as Gannett, Tribune, McClatchy, and Hearst, as well as at the smaller North American chains and collapsed community papers in the United Kingdom. However, for a time, the *Paper Cuts* blog kept a running tally of US layoffs and buyouts that revealed the magnitude of the employment catastrophe that had befallen that country's newspaper industry. The worst year was 2008, when 15,993 journalism positions were lost in the United States. The total jobs cut between January 2007 and July 2012 was 41,344.

In Canada, the Media Guild estimates 10,000 jobs lost between 2008 and 2013: 6,000 print jobs and 3,700 TV news positions (Wong 2013). Considering that the United States has roughly ten times the Canadian population, this would imply that the slashing has been more aggressive here than south of the border.

5

Business, Part Two: Grim Harvesters

If there was a sonic boom in the financial dive of the big media companies, it was the December 2008 announcement by the giant Tribune Company that it had entered Chapter 11 bankruptcy protection. Tribune was something of a textbook case of a big media company that walked into the recession of 2008 with eyes shut. An outgrowth of the *Chicago Tribune* and the product of a 2000 merger with Times Mirror, which owned, among other properties, the *Los Angeles Times*, Tribune counted among its possessions fifty websites, twenty-five TV stations, and eight major newspapers. It also owned the Chicago Cubs baseball team and had real estate holdings that included the Cubs' home stadium, Wrigley Field, and the landmark neo-Gothic Tribune Tower on Chicago's lakefront. Even though it had been slumping, this was a company accustomed to 25 per cent profit margins (O'Shea 2011, 2).

The 2008 recession hit a year after Chicago real-estate mogul Sam Zell pulled off a complicated buyout that involved employee participation and the acquisition of $8 billion in debt. This had been piled onto a large financial obligation that the already struggling Tribune Company had been carrying – for a total of roughly $13 billion. When the recession hit, the company was caught in a crossfire of plunging revenue and crippling payments – $1.4 billion by June 2008 alone (Thornton and Grover 2008).

Typically for a leveraged buyout, the Tribune acquisition was supposed to have been financed by advertising profits, inflated by cost cutting. The company eliminated 2,500 jobs in one year – 16 per cent of its workforce (Greisling 2008) – and began to sell off assets, such as *Long Island Newsday*, which went to Cablevision for $632 million.

The money went directly to servicing debt. In December 2008, after suffering a $124 million loss in the third quarter of the year, and with $1 billion in payments due, the company declared bankruptcy and sought Chapter 11 protection. At the time, Zell told the press that "factors beyond our control have created a perfect storm – a precipitous decline in revenue and a tough economy coupled with a credit crisis that makes it extremely difficult to support our debt" (Merced 2008). However, he told the *Los Angeles Times*, the company had "a positive cash flow before debt service was taken into account" (Rainey and Hiltzik 2008). For example, the *L.A. Times* had projected a $100 million profit for 2008 – down from $240 million two years previous, but still well into the black.

The shock waves rattled the industry on both sides of the Canada-US border. As Geneva Overholser, director of the school of journalism at the University of Southern California, told the *Chicago Tribune*, the collapse represented "the spectacular failure of an economic model of newspapering" (Greisling 2008). The company did not emerge from Chapter 11 until 1 January 2013. Its new CEO, Eddy Hartenstein, promised that the company would "emerge from the bankruptcy process as a multimedia company with a great mix of profitable assets, strong brands in major markets and a much-improved capital structure" (Hagey 2013). This was taken as shorthand for, We're dumping the newspapers. "We're at this point where some people are starting to think, 'It's time to cut our losses and liquidate these things,'" *Columbia Journalism Review*'s Ryan Chittum says. "You look at what Tribune's doing. They're going to spin off the papers, but they're keeping the papers' real estate and the classified. Stock. All the stuff that's worth money."

Meanwhile, in Canada, another print and television giant was running into trouble with its lenders. As we saw in chapter 3, Canwest had purchased most of Conrad Black's newspaper holdings in the early 2000s, under the standard operating plan that advertising revenue and cost cutting would produce a formula for paying off the debt acquired to finance the deal, servicing shareholders and allowing the company to grow. Much of Canwest's debt was accrued with the purchase of the newspapers for $3.5 billion, and this was exacerbated by the company's 2007 purchase for $2.7 billion of Alliance Atlantis Communications Inc. – owner of a stable of cable channels that included History Television, Showcase, and Slice. Canwest's revenues had been rising year after year, from $2.9 billion in 2007 to $3.1 billion in 2008, but its share value had dived in eight years from $20 in 2000 to 60 cents in 2008. And the company was the most advertiser-dependent media firm in Canada, with 77 per cent of its revenue coming from ads and commercials (Hood 2008). So, when advertisers cut budgets, Canwest – like Tribune but on a smaller scale – found itself with a stable of less-profitable TV stations and newspapers, and not enough cash flow to service debt. Finally, in October 2009, a little less than a year after Tribune had begun floating on its back, Canwest asked for protection under the Companies' Creditor Arrangement Act, Canada's equivalent of Chapter 11.

Unlike Tribune – a problem so large no one seemed able to fathom it – Canwest was sold off in fairly short order. In May 2010, the US investment banks JPMorgan Chase and Co. and Morgan Stanley provided $700 million in loans to back an unsecured creditors purchase of the company's newspaper holdings for $1.1 billion, placing in charge Paul Godfrey, former Sun Media CEO and current president and CEO of the *National Post*. The new company, Postmedia Network Inc., announced it would be a "digital first" publisher. As one Toronto media buyer told *Canadian Business* magazine at the time, the shortage of details gave no comfort to investors and advertisers. "It's hard to get excited about Godfrey's vague new strategy" (Watson 2010).

By the end of 2013, Postmedia's long-term debt stood at approximately $471 million. The company announced a first-quarter net loss of $11.8 million – compared to net earnings of $6.7 million a year earlier – "largely due to a $15.3 million increase in restructuring expenses, primarily associated with print production outsourcing, an increase in depreciation expense and a modest decline in operating income before depreciation, amortization and restructuring" (Postmedia 2014). That, at least, was down from the $632 million in debt with which the company had started in 2010. However, in October 2014, Postmedia agreed to pay $316 million for Quebecor's English-Canadian properties, a deal that went through in April 2015, and which was expected to drive Postmedia's debt back up to roughly $500 million and increase shareholder equity by $186 million (McNish and Nelson 2014).

One failed leveraged buyout had led to another teetering one, which in turn had led to a unprecedented concentration of ownership in the English-Canadian news media (more on this in chapter 8). In

2010, however, there had been alternatives. Several potential buyers and buyer groups had popped up across Canada – including one that wanted the *Ottawa Citizen*, the *National Post*, and the *Gazette*, another interested in Pacific Press, owner of the *Vancouver Sun* and the *Province*, and a third that was looking at the *Calgary Herald* and *Edmonton Journal*. However, Canwest refused to consider a "piecemeal" sale because the company needed to raise $935 million to cover debt and was afraid of falling short and being left with unsaleable properties (Robertson 2010). As for the company's TV holdings, Calgary-based cable company Shaw Communications picked up the Global television network and all its specialty channels, including the newly purchased Alliance Atlantis holdings.

Across the United States, many companies were in the same state. In April 2008, the *Capital Times* in Madison, Wisconsin, stopped printing and turned itself into an online publication. A year later, the Hearst Corporation's 146-year-old *Seattle Post-Intelligencer* slashed staff and became an online community paper. In 2009, the *Minneapolis Star-Tribune* declared bankruptcy and went into Chapter 11. The same year, the *Chicago Sun-Times* joined the *Tribune* in bankruptcy, and Denver's *Rocky Mountain News* folded. In 2010, Affiliated Media, owner of the *Denver Post, Salt Lake Tribune*, and *San Jose Mercury*, went into Chapter 11.

One of the most interesting stories is that of the *New Orleans Times-Picayune*. In May 2012, it printed its last daily broadsheet edition and converted itself to a combined three-day-a-week publication and online news organization. Writing in the *Columbia Journalism Review*, comedian and voice artist (*The Simpsons*) Harry Shearer, a New Orleanian "by adoption," knocked the *Times-Picayune*'s owners for ignoring the fact that "the TP enjoys the highest print penetration of all dailies in the 50 biggest metro areas" in the United States. He also put a fine point on the criticism of chain ownership, writing that "you can't care about what you don't understand."

> Here, for your reading pleasure, are two familiar clichés: 1. New Orleans is a unique city. 2. The newspaper business is changing. Several days ago, when it was announced that *The Times-Picayune* would get out of the daily print newspaper business, the second cliché kicked the first one's ass. This makes no sense to me ... New Orleans is a genuine community. Not a "community" in the sense

of like-minded gamers connected by the Internet, but in the sense of an urban space where the residents have deep connections to the place, to each other, and to the past. (Shearer 2012)

For roughly a year, New Orleans was the biggest city in North America without a daily paper; then it had two. In July 2013, the *Baton Rouge Advocate* began daily distribution in New Orleans. In September 2013, the edition became the *New Orleans Advocate*. In response to the *Advocate* invasion, the *Times-Picayune* changed course and began publishing as a broadsheet on Wednesdays, Fridays, and Sundays, and as a tabloid Mondays, Tuesdays, and Thursdays.

The return of print to New Orleans couldn't be taken as a change of heart for an industry bent on euthanizing its most profitable products, however, and as we shall see in the next chapter, Apple's 2010 unveiling of the iPad saw a return to the saviour-technology narrative. "The newspaper industry ... has rallied around a story ... that year-by year [sic] it is developing new digital products and new revenue streams to transition from dependence on print advertising" (Project for Excellence in Journalism [PEJ] 2012a). However, there didn't seem to be very much relief in sight in the short run, as online profits still failed to live up to expectations, and newspaper companies continued to slash staff and product.

Although the newspaper industry has long had difficulty improvising, innovating, and experimenting, it may finally be finding its way out of the wilderness. Certainly, the rush to establish paywalls in 2011–12 at least showed that executives had given up on the dream of an online bonanza of advertising dollars – though it remains to be seen whether they have come to grips with the fact that advertising as they knew it may be extinct. The big problem with the paywalls is that their success will surely depend on the value of what lives behind them. "You can recover from slow print advertising," *Globe and Mail* media reporter Steve Ladurantaye says. "I'm not sure you can recover from a newspaper that has no staff and no compelling content that anybody local may want to read. If you're just producing what everybody else in the world is getting, then maybe you don't need that newspaper." Or, to put it another way: "The one thing that lets them stand out from the pack is their credibility and reputation for professionalism," says Rick Gibbons, former publisher of Quebecor's *Ottawa Sun* and a victim of cutbacks. "That means invest in quality journalism or risk losing everything."

There has been so much bad news that it becomes confusing and tiresome just to keep track of it. Yet, the situation is more complex than the rush of doomsday headlines might lead us to believe. For example, the Pew Research Center's Project for Excellence in Journalism, in its *State of the News Media 2012* report, painted a picture of an industry that is still profitable – in Canada by an 11 or 12 per cent margin. Most US dailies make money, even if debt and one-time charges (such as buyouts and layoffs) have made profit "razor thin." On the negative side, many are profitable because of cost cutting, though some have chosen to take a loss rather than cut quality.

Audiences are holding up, though they're not producing enough revenue to sustain traditional newsrooms. Print circulation continues to decline, while digital audiences grow. The problem is that no one can figure out how to get those audiences to pay for the cost of the product. By the summer of 2013, Pew was reporting a number of positive signs for the business – though the authors did modify their optimism by quoting a famous blues lyric: "Been down so long it looks like up to me."

- Companies have started to experiment with new revenue streams and major organizational changes.
- Digital pay plans are being adopted at 450 US dailies and appear to be working, not just at the *New York Times* but also at small and mid-size papers, and circulation revenues are holding steady or rising. The paywall model appears to weaning the industry off "its historic over-dependence on advertising."
- Share prices of publicly traded US newspaper companies rose in 2012.
- Newspapers coming onto the market are finding buyers.
- As the US economy improves, so do newspaper profits. Auto advertising has come back, and some markets, like Miami, are beginning to see recovery in real estate and employment ads as well.

On the negative side, the authors reported:

- Print advertising fell for a sixth consecutive year in 2012 – by $1.8 billion, or 8.5 per cent.
- Growth in digital advertising – as we saw, roughly 15 per cent of newspaper ad revenue – remains slow.

- Advertising is doing no better on mobile devices than online.
- Most newspaper organizations are profitable on an operating basis, but their parent companies continue to struggle under the weight of debt and pension obligations.
- Papers are still cutting newsroom staff, with too few digital jobs being created to make up the difference. Some newspapers have ceased to be daily, and only publish three times a week. (Edmonds, Guskin, Mitchell, and Jurkowitz 2013)

Unfortunately, in Canada, we have nothing like the Project for Excellence in Journalism, so newspaper data are hard to come by here. However, a survey of the business pages reveals a similar situation, without the rash of bankruptcies and newspaper closings that the United States saw between 2008 and 2012. Without question the biggest developments took place in 2010: the breakup of Canwest, and the acquisition of CTV and its broadcast properties by BCE Inc., involving the return of control of the *Globe and Mail* to the Thomson family's Woodbridge Co. In the first instance, this meant the major daily newspapers in Vancouver, Calgary, Edmonton, Regina, Saskatoon, Windsor, Ottawa, and Montreal, and the *National Post* were into their third owner and second leveraged buyout in a little more than ten years. And this was a company trying to implement a digital-first strategy while being forced to constantly fight costs. In the case of the *Globe and Mail*, control of the newspaper was returned to the Thomsons, who had owned it from 1981, when they acquired the old FP Publications, to 2001, when BCE originally acquired control of it, along with CTV. The story of the BCE company between then and now is an extremely convoluted tale of changing strategies and the coming and going of minority investors, including Torstar and the Ontario Teachers Pension Fund. In the end, BCE returned to the vision with which it started the century – of a blended delivery and content company.

By 2013, almost all of English Canada's private television stations and networks were in the hands of three delivery companies: BCE, owners of Bell telephone, mobile, Internet, and satellite and fibre-optic TV; and the Rogers and Shaw cable companies, also major Internet, satellite, and wireless providers. In 2013, BCE expanded its holdings by buying Astral Media Inc., owners of some twenty specialty TV channels, including the Family Channel the Movie Network, and a half ownership of HBO Canada (the other half is owned by Corus Entertainment), and more than eighty radio stations. The deal had been blocked by the federal broadcast regulator, the Canadian Radio-television and Telecommunications Commission, in the fall of 2012, because it "would have created a situation where a company of BCE's size and scale would be able to exert its market power unfairly and hinder healthy competition," CRTC chairman Jean-Pierre Blais said at the time (Sturgeon 2012). That was no longer the case nine months later. "This was just outrageous to tee this up for a second time so quickly," says Carleton University communication professor, blogger and media critic Dwayne Winseck, who was one of the opponents of the deal. "They had to take a time-out, but they just ran everybody down. Nobody's got the resources to back a bid or opposition to a bid of this size in such rapid succession." Like other commentators, Winseck says he worries that, despite the troubles in the news business, consolidation of media ownership will gain momentum as it takes over the online world. "I think, they fundamentally skew the nature of our media experience. What we have is the incumbent cable and telephone companies not using their networks in a neutral and transparent way that allows people to access content wherever they like and without obstruction – a situation where networks become gateways and the incumbents use the gateways to regulate flows of content and to regulate in turn what we can and can't do with our network connections, or to put it simply, our Internet."

If you look at the products BCE and Shaw did not want to own, it implies that in-depth news is not something upon which these big media companies place much value. One by-product of BCE's growth was that the *Globe and Mail* became a single-paper entity. By divesting itself of its stake in CTV and increasing its percentage of the *Globe and Mail* to 85 per cent, the Thomson family was seen by some to be placing a powerful vote of confidence in the paper and its future. In an editorial heralding the deal, *Globe* editors quoted the company's founder, Toronto-born Roy Thomson, Lord Thomson of Fleet: "Sometimes it isn't necessary to publish a good newspaper to make money – but it is necessary to make money to publish a good newspaper." The editorial went on to say, perhaps somewhat smugly, that "economic cycles come and go. Social fads can emerge and fade. Even technological revolutions can take their toll. But strong principles, they endure" (Globe and Mail 2010).

So, even in the gloom of big-city dailies, there were scattered rays of sunlight, such as the *Globe* going into the future with owners who believe in newspapers (more on this later), and circulation rising or holding its own in the United States with the big Sunday editions, arguably the most important ones of the week in terms of the public discourse.

And it doesn't hurt to remember that, by industrial or retail standards, an 11 or 12 per cent profit margin isn't necessarily a sign of impending doom – unless you're giving it all to your creditors.

In late 2011, billionaire investor Warren Buffett sent ripples through the newspaper business by purchasing his hometown newspaper, the *Omaha World Herald*. Buffett wasn't new to the business; he had owned the *Buffalo News* since 1977 and, through his investment firm Berkshire Hathaway, held a "substantial minority interest" in the *Washington Post* and a seat on the *Post*'s board (Wemple 2012). Yet, less than two years earlier, Buffett had told the *Wall Street Journal*: "For most newspapers in the United States, we would not buy them at any price. They have the possibility of going to just unending losses" (Patterson 2009). The reason, he added, was that newspapers had ceased to be essential to readers and, therefore, to advertisers.

In some quarters, Buffett's purchase was written off as altruism, a play to keep the hometown paper alive. But then, in May 2012, Berkshire Hathaway paid $142 million to Media General to buy sixty-two small dailies in the US southeast, forming a subsidiary, BH Media Group, to run its newspaper holdings. Shortly after taking over the *World Herald*, Buffett had made it clear that he was not acting out of sentimentality. He told shareholders in Omaha that newspapers have "a decent future" if they solve at least one of the "three big problems they face": they have lost the monopoly on information that made them an essential service; they have an extremely high-cost form of manufacturing and distribution; they give away for free what they spend a fortune producing. "So far, I would say the evidence is there will be many papers who can deal with these problems … The great majority of newspapers are making money" (Bundy 2011). Specifically, Buffett was talking about small-market newspapers. "In towns and cities where there is a strong sense of community," he said, "there is no more important institution than the local paper" (Roberts 2012).

Media observer Jack Shafer took perhaps the least charitable view of Buffett's purchases, saying that it was as if "an old cow that's still a milker has been moved to a neighboring farm's pasture, where it will be squeezed until it can give no more and will then be ground into pet food." Still, he continued, the purchase of the sixty-two papers – and the titles Buffett chose to buy – was an indication of the continued value of small, local newspapers. "Aside from Richmond, Va., and Winston-Salem, N.C., most of the towns where Buffett is now the press lord are backwaters – places like Hickory, N.C., Bristol, Va., and Eufaula, Ala. These small dailies and weeklies still retain franchise status because they cover local issues nobody else does, and they make money. It's worth noting that Buffett did not purchase Media General's *Tampa Tribune*, an unprofitable paper in competition with the *Tampa Bay Times* (*née St Petersburg Times*) with no franchise value on the horizon" (2012a).

In late 2012, even though he had closed one newspaper – the *News and Messenger* (Manassas, VA) – Buffett said: "I think newspapers in print form, in most of the cities and towns where they are present, will be here in 10 and 20 years. I think newspapers do a good job of serving a community where there is a lot of community interest" (Haughney 2012). Buffett's actions highlight the fact that, while the narrative of the failing large-market North American newspaper had dominated the discourse, there were several less-told stories of areas in which the business of print was not necessarily dead.

Even among the large papers, there have been glimmers of optimism. For example, in 2009, *New York Daily News* owner Mort Zuckerman invested $200 million on new presses that would allow the paper to be printed entirely in colour. A year later, the *Globe and Mail* committed $2 billion over eighteen years to new printing presses. Though the *Globe* is a leader in Canada with online and other digital publishing, the paper's publisher announced that print "is where the future of newspapers is" (Austen 2010).

In both instances, the publishers said they were upgrading mainly to attract high-end advertisers. Interestingly, media buyer and news business analyst Ken Doctor endorsed the long-term commitment to print, which he described as "a niche for an older, moneyed demographic" (Watson 2010). Since then, the *San Francisco Chronicle*, which was one of the first papers to retrench and focus on improving its print product, has paid a small fortune to rewrite its fifteen-year contract with Canadian printing company Transcontinental, to allow it more flexibility in what and when it prints. Despite the experience of the *Times-Picayune*, newspapers have begun to rethink the concept of the daily morning newspaper, *Globe and Mail* media reporter Steve Ladurantaye says:

> Do we need the seven-day-a-week paper? That, I think is the big question. I don't think there's any doubt that most publishers are looking at reducing their publishing days over the longer term. There's still a role for print. There's still that big sit-down read. But people aren't consuming newspapers at 7 a.m. on a Wednesday morning like they used to. They're reading on their devices. They're doing other things. If you're going to put that money into print, then maybe you're probably best to invest in a well-produced, good-looking weekend paper, maybe a midweek paper. Maybe you go back to evening editions. All these things are on the table, I think. We saw the *National Post* drop their Monday edition last summer for the whole summer. [Postmedia] just dropped a ton of Sunday editions, of course ... But nothing is off the table when it comes to figuring out how to cut costs and still produce some kind of paper that you can hang your hat on and get that big print revenue.

In November 2010, *Atlantic Monthly* – which considers itself a "digital-first" company – announced the highest-earning issue in its history, and one that represented a 60 per cent jump in ad pages and a 95 per cent rise in advertising revenue, over November 2009 (Kinsman 2010). In late 2012, after the demise of *Newsweek*, Ryan Chittum trotted out figures from *eMarketer* that showed ad spending on US magazine print editions had crept up to $15.9 million from $15.5 million in 2011, that they were projected to slip only slightly, to $15.3 million in 2013, and were also expected to level off until 2016 (2012c). In other words, he wrote, *Newsweek* wasn't a harbinger; it was an outlier, the sickly runt of an otherwise healthy litter.

In August 2011, the *New York Times* repaid a $250 million loan to Mexican billionaire and minority Times Company shareholder Carlos Slim Helú three and a half years ahead of schedule (Peters 2011). The company had borrowed the money to see it through 2009.

Though it later resorted to job cuts, the *Dallas Morning News* in 2009 announced it was raising its cover price, hiring staff, and experimenting with a "premium product" approach to reduce dependency on ad revenue (Bailly 2009). The *Economist* and *Financial Times* – both British publications with a world reach – consistently reported profits through the recession by delivering high-quality, premium content, online and in print. Though it did experience layoffs, the *Winnipeg Free Press* was able to maintain positions such as movie critic, TV columnist, and Ottawa correspondent, which chains had long since centralized (Cornies 2009). Technically, the *Free Press* is part of a group (FP Publications also owns the nearby *Brandon Sun*), but that "chain" is so small that, for the sake of argument, we can consider the paper one of Canada's independent dailies. Although the *Free Press* suffered along with the rest of the industry, it still reported net earnings of $3.1 million for the first three quarters of 2012 – virtually unchanged from the same period in 2011. Digital operations for the same period, meanwhile, grew by 24.9 per cent over the same year (Free Press Newspapers 2012).

In March 2009, Seattle was a city in danger of becoming a no-newspaper town, with the *Post-Intelligencer* gone Web-only and the *Times* "holding on by our fingertips," according to the paper's publisher, Frank Blethen (Johnson 2009). By August, the *New York Times* was describing the *Seattle Times* as "resurgent as a solo act" (Pérez-Peña 2009). The *Times*, an independent owned by the Blethen family, had begun to operate in the black and its daily circulation had risen 30 per cent. In the previous year, it had cut some 165 editorial staff, and that, combined with increased revenue owing to lack of competition and being released from its Joint Operating Agreement with the *Post-Intelligencer*, had pushed it into the black. It also helped that the *Times* was an independent daily with an ownership, the Blethen family, willing to carry it through the bad times, and proud not to be a party to the "inexorable, greed-fueled feast" of the highly leveraged, publicly traded corporations (Blethen 2009).

One thing all of these corporations have in common – as Blethen so colourfully pointed out – is that they're not owned by large, heavily indebted media conglomerates, and they entered the recession in stable financial shape. By having farther to fall and being under the stewardship of owners with a strong commitment to their survival, they appear to have ridden out the slump with less difficulty than papers owned by big media companies.

However, it was in the smaller communities in the United States and Canada that newspapers were doing more than holding their own. Being the sole sources of news in their communities not only slowed their decline, but also bought more time for them to move online. Also, in many small communities, the little dailies and community weeklies remain the most important source of classified and retail advertising.

In 2009, while the newspaper business was suffering its worst year in history, advertising revenue for dailies with circulation under 100,000 fell just 3.6 per cent. As small-town Georgia newspaper editor Robert Williams Jr told Reuters: "CNN is not coming to my town to cover the news and there aren't a whole lot of bloggers here either. Community newspapers are still a great investment because we provide something you can't get anywhere else" (Ovide and Adams 2009). Another editor suggested that big papers had taken their readers for granted: "Too many newspapers have been operating in an ivory tower for too long. I answer my own phone. Some newspapers are just now trying to develop a relationship with the local communities they cover. Ours has been going on for 14 years" (Liedtke 2009b). Leonard Downie Jr and Michael Schudson sum up the situation:

> Many of those less battered by the economic downturn are situated in smaller cities and towns where there is no newspaper competition, no locally based television station and, as is the case for now in many communities, no Craigslist. Those papers' reporting staffs, which never grew very large, remain about the same size they have been for years, and they still concentrate on local news. A number of them have sought to limit the loss of paid circulation and advertising in their print papers by charging nonsubscribers for access to most of their web content. They are scattered across the country from Albuquerque, New Mexico, and Bend, Oregon, to Lawrence, Kansas, and Little Rock, Arkansas, to Schenectady, New York, and Newport, Rhode Island. Although they have not attracted many paid web-only subscribers, their publishers say they have so far protected much of their print circulation and advertising. (2009, 18)

In Canada, the situation is not much different: Torstar's Metroland chain of community papers has become the company's big money earner, and two of the country's other major community chains, Black Press and Glacier Media Group, are doing well enough that they have begun to absorb larger city dailies. In Glacier's case, the company bought the *Victoria Times-Colonist* from Postmedia in 2011. And Black, in addition to a string of small community papers in British Columbia and the Pacific Northwest, is owner of the *Honolulu Star-Advertiser*, formed when the company bought the *Advertiser* from Gannett in 2010 and merged it with its own paper, the *Honolulu Star-Bulletin*. "A lot of our papers haven't been affected at all," company chairman David Black says. "It really depends on the local economy and a number of other factors. We have a big daily over in Honolulu that is growing ... There were adjustments in the first year but now we're in our second year and it's still growing."

Even at the big-city level, when something happens that matters deeply to people, they still turn to their daily paper. For example, when the New Orleans Saints won the Super Bowl in 2010, the *Times-Picayune* sold more than 500,000 single copies – 300,000 more than its owners allowed for with its first run (Fitzgerald 2010a). A year earlier, the election of the first black US president, Barack Obama, "produced a clamor for newspapers that publishers said they had never seen." The *New York Times* printed an additional 225,000 copies of its 5 November 2008 edition, and the *Washington Post* sold 350,000 special editions, priced at $1.50 a copy (Pérez-Peña 2008).

A strong connection to the community and the production of memorabilia – something tangible that can be clipped and glued into a scrapbook – have played a large role in the success of the newspaper. As the *Edmonton Journal*'s Karen Unland says, "people like to be in the paper – and it means more for them to be in the newspaper than to be on the website ... It might not be a long-lasting phenomenon, and it might be based on the fact that your mom, aunties, and grandma *do* still the read the paper, so they make you feel special if they see you in the paper. I don't know what it is, but I know from experience that it's true." The connection between community and paper is strongest in smaller communities. The 2011 Newspaper Audience Databank (NADbank) figures showed that the communities with the highest per capita total newspaper readership were Charlottetown, PEI (metro population, 64,487), Cape Breton Island, NS (135,974), Brandon, MB

(56,219), and Peterborough, ON (173,400). Ninety-one per cent of the population in Charlottetown and Cape Breton read the print or Web edition of a newspaper on a weekly basis. For Brandon, the figure was 89 per cent, and for Peterborough, 88 per cent. By comparison, Canada's three biggest cities lagged, with 80 per cent for Vancouver, 76 per cent for Montreal, and 75 per cent for Toronto. The interesting thing about those figures is that the larger the city is, the smaller is the percentage of people reading newspapers, from tiny Charlottetown and Brandon to the largest city in the country, Toronto. This is reinforced by the fact that 90 per cent of respondents told NADBank they read their papers for local coverage. Torontonians can go to a variety of sources for news about their sports, businesses, or municipal politics. In Brandon, people have only "one source of in-depth news about the Royal Manitoba Winter Fair" (Houpt 2012b).

In contrast with the situation in North America, the British community press has collapsed, with some papers losing as much as 77 per cent of their circulation. The national dailies hold on, still selling roughly 7 million copies a day (theguardian.com 2014). Yet they are feeling the same pressures to monetize the Internet, and their conditions and solutions are complex and diverse. While the Murdoch-owned *Times* of London installed a paywall around its website in 2010, the Scott Trust–owned *Guardian* has remained a steadfast champion of free information. The paper's editor, Alan Rusbridger, has said he believes not only that free content is good business but that paywalls mean "turning away from a world of openly shared content" (Pfanner 2010).

Journalism studies editor Bob Franklin has written of "an evident Manichaeism in the different futures which unravel for newspapers," and a widespread tendency among pundits to "make unrealistic extrapolations based on declining circulations to predict, with a curiously bizarre precision, the exact date on which the last newspaper reader will vanish" (2008, 631). Francis Gurry is one such pundit. In 2011, the UN official told the Swiss newspaper *La Tribune de Genève*: "There are studies showing that [newspapers] will all disappear by 2040. In the United States it will end in 2017" (Agence France-Presse 2011). This could be taken as more hopeful than the forecast from "futurist Ross Dawson," who predicted "journalism will be increasingly crowdsourced [to] hordes of amateurs overseen by professionals" and that the newspaper would cease to exist in 2022 (Australian 2010). As Franklin puts it: "[T]he precocious pessimism and unwarranted hyperbole of those who wish to proclaim the imminent demise of the newspaper is clearly unsustainable. It articulates a curiously North American and Eurocentric view of the press which seems blinkered to the explosion of new titles and readerships in other parts of the world; the future of newspapers is more open and considerably more nuanced than some observers imagine" (2008, 631).

Likewise, Robert Picard argues that the "crisis" in journalism is particular to "some countries" of the West and that "journalism is in a growth stage" elsewhere in the world, particularly in Africa and Latin America (2010, 17). In 2008, while the bottom was dropping out of the market in North America, the *Economist* was citing figures released by the World Association of Newspapers (WAN) that showed circulation increases of 7 per cent in Argentina, 12 per cent in Brazil, 20 per cent in China, and 11 per cent in India, where there was a five-year increase of 35 per cent. And there is evidence that the growth is even greater in countries where "[g]overnments with limited resources are ill-equipped to monitor a profusion of local and regional newspapers," WAN reported. "In Mali, for example, newspapers are popping up 'like mushrooms'" (Economist 2008). Also, at a time when advertising was dropping in North America, global newspaper advertising spending was expected to increase from $125 billion in 2007 to $130 billion by 2010 (Timmons 2008).

In India, the industry is exploding, to the point where Indian companies have been stealing work from North American journalists. The *Times of India*, with a circulation of more than 4.3 million, is the largest English-speaking newspaper in the world and boasts pre-tax profits in the 25 to 30 per cent range (Auletta 2012). The Hindi newspaper *NaiDunia* went from 500,000 to 800,000 circulation in two years and projects a readership of 15 million by 2016 (Nolen 2011). *Rolling Stone*, *Vogue*, FHM, and *Maxim* have all launched Indian editions. Tina Brown and Tom Brokaw have advised aspiring North American journalists to go to India for work. And there even has been an exchange program of sorts in which Columbia University students have served apprenticeships at Indian dailies.

Perhaps most telling, Indian companies have begun to capitalize on the situation in North America, drawing work overseas by cashing in on the wealth of highly trained, English-speaking Indian journalists, who are happy to work for a fraction of what their North American colleagues earn. One example of such a company is Mind Works Global Media of New Delhi, which advertises itself on its website as "an award-winning content solutions company" that creates "real-time content across platforms for brands, institutions, and media" (mindworksglobal.com 2014). The company has provided services for a variety of North American clients, including California's *Orange County Register* and the *Miami Herald*. In the same way, the Chicago-based company Journatic farms out work to freelancers around the world, who make $10 or $12 an hour grinding out "local" stories – everything from amateur sports to garbage collection schedules. Stories from the service have appeared in such papers as the *Chicago Sun-Times*, the *San Francisco Chronicle*, and the *Houston Chronicle* (Shafer 2012b). Understandably, American journalists are concerned about being replaced by such content farms, and the development has been interpreted as one more sign that the news business sinking and dragging journalism down with it.

In Europe, where there is less reliance on advertising revenue and where circulation has been falling more slowly than in North America, there has been a range in both the levels of crisis – from non-existent to menacing – and in the measures used to deal with the situation. In 2009, while the sky was falling in North America, the sixty-two-year-old German newspaper *Bild* recorded its highest profit, and the Oslo publisher Schibstad reported that a quarter of its profits came from online activities (Pfanner 2009).

At the same time, Europeans proved to be more willing to take measures to help their newspaper industries. To try to bolster its ailing dailies, the French government unveiled a plan to provide free one-year newspaper subscriptions to eighteen- to twenty-four-year-olds. In the 2000s, the Dutch newspaper NRC *Handelsblad*, a national institution, found its circulation was dropping by 5,000 to 10,000 per year, and that young people weren't reading it. It responded in 2006 by launching a splashy digest of the paper's sexiest items, aimed at young readers. By 2008, the paper's publisher claimed its youth edition, NRC *Next*, had made a profit of $3.3 million on sales of $25 million (Levine 2009). In Belgium, a group of francophone newspapers calling themselves Copiepresse took Google to court and won a ruling that ordered the Internet company to remove their content from its aggregation site. The aim was not so much to protect or enhance profits, said the group's secretary general, but to avoid "having giants killing us" (Pfanner 2010).

Perhaps the greatest reason for optimism – at least in terms of the future of the craft of journalism – is the explosion of online readership many newspapers are enjoying, especially such emerging world dailies as the *Guardian*, the *New York Times*, and the *Daily Mail*. For January 2013, *MailOnline* reported 126.8 million unique visitors, an increase of 87 per cent over January 2012. The *Guardian* reported 77.9 million unique visitors in that month, for an annual rise of 23 per cent (Durrani 2013).

To a certain extent, the *Guardian* is the standard-bearer for one, very rare, business model: non-profit open journalism that is, as the Guardian Media Group (GMG) website puts it, "free from commercial or political interference" (2014). "Unlike *The New York Times* and *The Washington Post, The Guardian* is not ultimately part of a commercial enterprise. It doesn't need to grow financially. It just needs to not lose too much" (Starkman 2013). The Guardian Media Group, like the *Guardian* before it, is operated by the Scott Trust, which allows it to operate at a considerable loss while seeking new ways to create great journalism. While other news companies seek profits, the *Guardian* seeks sustainable losses.

Thanks to the 2014 sale of Trader Media Group for approximately $1 billion, the Scott Trust has a war chest that can sustain the Guardian Media Group until 2045, Ryan Chittum (2014a) wrote in the *Columbia Journalism Review*. That's assuming the *Guardian* continues to lose money at its 2013 rate of $51 million annually. However, as Chittum pointed out, that 2013 loss is a considerable improvement over the $73 million the organization lost the year before, and losses are continuing to drop. In fact, the Guardian Media Group is bringing in enough digital revenue to fund its newsroom of almost 700 (Chittum 2014a). As editor Dominic Ponsford of the British trade publication *Press Gazette* wrote, the long-term plan is to "protect the financial and editorial independence of the *Guardian* in *perpetuity*. I understand GMG is aiming for ongoing losses of around £20m a year. Five per cent annual return (which I am told is realistic) on £1bn would give them income of £50m a year, enough to cover the *Guardian*'s losses and keep on top of inflation. Just looking at the current

£850m could give GMG investment income of around £40m a year" (2014; italics in original). The *Guardian* is unique, but its success demonstrates that there are ways to fund great journalism, if great journalism is the goal.

Across the Atlantic, the *New York Times* not only gained ground online but defied popular wisdom by posting an 18 per cent annual gain in paid circulation to 1.87 million in 2013, passing USA *Today* to become the second-largest US newspaper after the *Wall Street Journal*. The interesting thing about these figures is that they include 667,000 online subscribers (Lee 2013). Then, in the last quarter of 2013, the *Times* picked up another 33,000 subscribers, bringing that total to 700,000. At the same time, the organization announced that it had arrested its digital-advertising decline and had slowed the drop in print advertising to 1.6 per cent (Chittum 2014b).

Meanwhile Gannett, which has been slashing and burning its way through the technological and financial disruption, had fourth-quarter results that "were basically miserable," Ryan Chittum wrote in the *Columbia Journalism Review*. Publishing revenue dropped 4.6 per cent from the same period of 2012, advertising dropped 5.9 per cent, and circulation across the chain fell by 1.6 per cent. The results reflect the fact that Gannett is a company "that has squeezed profits out of its newspapers for decades." Yet, the company is profitable – for now. "Last year, it generated 22 per cent cashflow margins, paid out $183 million in dividends, and laid off hundreds of journalists" (2014c).

The contrast between the *Times*'s performance and Gannett's is strong proof that, as John Honderich said, you can't slash your way to greatness. We can clearly attribute the *Times*'s success to the fact that it invests in quality journalism and therefore has something to sell that people consider valuable. "The *Times* still has roughly the same size newsroom as they did ten years ago," Chittum told me. "It's a different composition. They have more people doing digital-only stuff rather than print stuff – but that's what they should be doing. Their newsgathering clout is pretty much the same as it was. I think it's lower in some foreign areas, but they're still the best paper in the world. And when they charge people – when they ask for money – they've got it."

―――――――

It took a long time for the concept of Original Sin to get through to newspaper publishers, but by 2011 the lesson finally sank in. It was at that point that, "after years of talk and no action, the Canadian and U.S. industry began to embrace paywalls for digital content" and began to make the first moves towards wringing some money from aggregators (PEJ 2012a). It had become taken for granted in Web publishing that if you charged for content, readers would flee – but it was also becoming painfully clear that advertisers had already left the game and had taken most of their money with them. For example, when Wayne Parrish started pushing Postmedia's digital advisory board to consider a paywall, "he got the living daylights kicked out of him by these people, mostly in the US, who suggested it would be the downfall of the news," company chairman Paul Godfrey says.

As we have seen, in choosing to give away their content, newspapers had gambled and lost on the belief that advertising income would outweigh loss of circulation revenue. As well, by making their content free, they provided a bonanza for aggregators, such as the *Huffington Post, Daily Beast,* Yahoo, Sympatico, and Google, which could cherry-pick the best material from a variety of sources and run it, often in digest form, on their sites for free, linking to the original posts. They had minimal costs, so they could succeed with minimal advertising income. Free newspaper content also was something of a gold mine for bloggers, such as the famous Matt Drudge, who could, in effect, create op-ed pages that gathered and dissected the news produced by the papers – often while adopting an anti–mainstream media posture. In short, everyone but the dailies seemed to be profiting from newspapers' investment in news. And, according to a 2010 Pew Research Center study, 95 per cent of news stories "with fresh information came from 'old media,' and the vast majority of that from newspapers" (Fritz 2010).

By giving away their product, the newspapers had devalued it. Throughout the modern history of the publishing business, there had been a sharp divide between publications for which a consumer was willing to pay and the "advertising rags" that were given away for free. The former carried with them a stamp of quality in the sense that they had a market value, validated by their continued existence. The giveaway, on the other hand, was expected to be filled with promotional bumph designed to create a home for the ads. When the newspaper publishers decided to give away their content, it never seemed to occur to them that, in appearance at least, they might be pushing themselves into the realm of the latter. As James Harding, editor of the *Times* of London put it: "Saying our journalism is worthless and dumping it free online is not a viable economic model" (Pfanner 2010). So, an important subtext to the discourse about broken business models, debt crises, and dwindling share value was the question of who was going to fund quality journalism if the newspapers starved themselves to death with their generosity. The issue had become, as Bill Gates once put it in an open letter to software pirates, "Who can afford to do professional work for nothing?" (Isaacson 2009). So, for once, the business and editorial sides of the newspaper industry had a cause in common; where they often parted company was in the solutions they suggested.

It was in 2008 that newspapers began to talk seriously about finding a way to monetize the big audiences they were building online. However, attempts to establish subscription or pay-as-you-go systems date back to 1996, when *Slate* magazine debuted with the idea of eventually putting up a $19.95 per year paywall, which it did in 1998, only to take it down a year later. As noted earlier, the most successful paywalls have been ones created by specialty organizations, such as the *Wall Street Journal* – which erected one in 1997 – because it delivers information that has an established value to an audience with no other way to get it. When there are alternatives, it's a bit trickier. For example, in 2003, the *Los Angeles Times* put up a $4.95 paywall around its online arts and entertainment section, and took it down two years later after experiencing a 97 per cent drop in readership. Not surprisingly, there was no shortage of alternative coverage of the entertainment industry in Hollywood. In 2005, the *New York Times* put its archives and columnists behind a $50-per-year paywall, but aggregators still found a way to link and it came down two years later. In 2007, the *Financial Times* invented the metered paywall – where readers got so many stories for free every month before they had to pay. This was the model for paywalls introduced in 2011–13.

The conversation about paywalls has taken the form of an intramural argument: attracting a percentage of the audience that is willing to pay has always been what newspapers do and the only way they can remain solvent is to do it online; news has always been free, because advertising always paid for it, and asking readers to pay will just force them to go elsewhere, reduce the size of the audience – and reach of the newspaper – and make the site less attractive to advertisers. Besides, the latter argument goes, for a very small fee, aggregators will be able to take the content and make it available to everyone on the Web. It is a hard argument for anyone to win, because all the data have dual application. For example, a Harris poll conducted in 2010 showed that 77 per cent of Americans would stop reading newspapers online if they had to pay for them. At first glance, this appears to be a resounding rejection of paid content. However, as Ryan Chittum (2010a) points out, that also means that 22 per cent of Americans *are* willing to pay – compared to the 19 per cent who buy newspapers. It appears that the Internet has created a new mindset not just on the part of the audience member, who expects everything for free, but also on the part of the publisher, who expects to be able to talk to a worldwide audience of millions where, in print, a few hundred thousand would have sufficed.

In Canada, the reaction against paying for content was slightly stronger, with 81 per cent saying they definitely would not pay for content and 92 per cent saying they'd find another free site if their favourite site began charging (Canadian Media Research Consortium [CMRC] 2011b). It's not clear how to interpret those numbers – perhaps readers of Canadian newspaper websites find the information useful but not so compelling as to be worth paying for. Further, using Chittum's logic, 81 per cent who won't pay leaves a pool of 19 per cent who would. And finally, there is a hole in the research: Why did no one think to ask respondents whether they read the print version in addition to the online site, and whether they'd give up the print version for digital at the same or a lower price?

After some four years of waiting for business to return to normal, the newspaper industry finally did what radio and movies did when TV arrived in the 1950s – reinvent itself for a new reality. And, as is so often the case, no one noticed that the little guy had taken the initiative. In 2011, shortly after the *New York Times* finally rolled out its pay model, the University of Missouri School of Journalism conducted a study that found 46 per cent of US papers with a circulation of less than 25,000 were already charging for at least some online content – and only 24 per cent of larger newspapers were doing the same. Another 35 per cent of smaller papers said they had plans to start charging. "There was so much build-up to the *New York Times* pay model, and when they finally rolled it out, a lot of people were watching that. But it wasn't like the smaller newspapers were waiting for the *Times* to get its act together ... Small papers are more nimble" (Levine 2011).

As for the larger general-interest dailies, Long Island's *Newsday* was the first to erect its paywall, in October 2009. It allowed full access for subscribers to the print edition of the paper or the parent company Cablevision, or for people willing to pay $5 per week. For everyone else, all that was available were headlines and summaries of selected stories; classifieds, listings, weather reports, and obituaries remained free. By 2010, *Newsday* had reportedly signed up only thirty-five online subscribers. But more important, the publisher said, was the fact that readership in the New York area had declined by only 2 per cent, meaning that putting up a paywall had served only to drive away "the junk traffic from outside New York," about whom neither the publisher nor the advertisers cared (Chittum 2010b).

In July 2010, the *Times* and *Sunday Times* of London put a rigid, subscriber-only paywall around their website and watched circulation evaporate; only 14 per cent of Web readers were converted to subscribers (Bercovici 2010). A year later, the circulation of the *Times* print edition fell another 13.3 per cent, the largest drop of any non-tabloid British daily (Taylor 2011), and its UK Web traffic (the audience that matters to advertisers) was down 42 per cent (Chittum 2012b). The *Times* remains behind a hard paywall and has suffered for it in terms of readership. The paper reported only 1.5 million unique worldwide visitors in April 2013 (Kinstler 2013), compared to the millions reported by the *Guardian* and *MailOnline*.

In March 2011, the *New York Times* launched a metered paywall, whereby readers were allowed to read twenty stories a month for free and only be charged if they wanted to drill deeper into the site. The system also has a range of subscription rates for online, smart phones, tablets, or all-access. It is also a flexible system that allows for *Times* editors to set the meter to zero in the event of a big news story, like the World Trade Center attacks, in which the demands of public service supersede business. Essentially, the plan punishes the fans for being loyal and rewards the fly-bys for being flighty – but it works. The paper retained its trophy audience of 30 million worldwide while finding a way to get the percentage of the readers who are responsible for most of the page views to pay for their habit. "The paper has calculated, correctly, that it can keep the ad revenue while adding tens of millions of dollars from subscriptions. Traffic (unique visitors) is actually *up* 2 per cent at nytimes.com since the meter went up and it took in 6 per cent more in digital advertising in the third quarter than it did a year ago without a meter" (Chittum 2012b; italics in original). By the end of 2012, the *Times* was reporting that its subscriber base had grown by 11 per cent, to 566,000 in the third quarter – a healthy circulation by any measure. Its ad revenue had experienced an unexpected drop of 10 per cent, but the loss had been offset by subscription revenues (Ladurantaye 2012c).

Once the *Times* showed it was possible to be profitable in the digital age, the rush was on to launch paywalls. In August 2011, Media News, owner of the *Denver Post*, announced an online subscription system for two dozen of its papers in five states. In September, the *Boston Globe* (then *New York Times*–owned) put up a paywall, which allowed only subscribers to read the full contents of the paper online. In October, the *Minneapolis Star-Tribune* created a paywall, and Gannett announced plans to put paywalls around all of its eighty dailies – except USA *Today*.

In Canada, the idea swept the business. The *Globe and Mail* put up a metered paywall in October 2012, allowing free, all-platform access to print subscribers and selling *Globe Unlimited* subscriptions (for tablet, phone, and computer) for $19.99 a month. In November 2012, Postmedia, which had experimented with the strategy at selected publications, announced it would put up paywalls at its papers. By May 2013, all Postmedia dailies were behind paywalls.

In December 2012, Sun Media activated paywalls at its papers in Calgary, Edmonton, Winnipeg, Toronto, and Ottawa. The *Toronto Star* launched its paywall in August 2013, charging $9.99 for digital content. Web surfers can read as many as ten stories for free per month before the drawbridge goes up. Also in August, the *Halifax Chronicle-Herald*, Canada's largest independent newspaper, went behind a paywall.

In November 2014, the Canadian Press reported that the *Star* was reversing its ground and placing its bet on advertising. The Toronto daily announced that it would take down the wall in the fall of 2015 and at the same time launch a multi-platform product modelled on *La Presse+*, a product that "has been able to do what most Canadian media companies crave: attract a highly engaged, younger audience who use the tablet app for an average of 45 minutes a day, and up to an hour on Saturdays" (Nguyen 2014). In a memo to staff in early 2015, *Star* editor Michael Cooke announced that the paper would be hiring sixty new staff over the course of the year to produce the new tablet edition (Gillespie 2015). At the time of writing, the *Globe* had reported 100,000 subscribers, and Postmedia, 137,000 across its ten dailies. The *Toronto Star* had yet to release any online circulation figures (Baluja 2014a).

Brunswick News, controlled by the Irving family, which owns all the dailies in New Brunswick, has a universal hard paywall – though a trial subscription sells for just 99 cents for the first month. The company came under some sharp criticism from New Brunswickers for failing to lift it in June 2014, during the Justin Bourque shooting rampage in Moncton. Brunswick News ombudswoman Patricia Graham wrote a reply defending the company's decision and chastising readers for being too cheap to pay for the news: "It's encouraging to know that critics on social media were interested in viewing content from Brunswick News newsrooms. It's not so encouraging to know some people didn't want to pay even 99 cents for it. Possibly I missed it, but I didn't see anyone demanding the print edition for free. To me this underscores the major, ongoing challenge newspaper companies face with expectations around digital content" (2014).

The last daily to implement a paywall was FP Publications' *Winnipeg Free Press*, which had remained free only to Canadians until April 2015, when the paper became the first in North America to introduce a micro-payment system. FP's head of digital content, Christian Panson, told *J-Source.ca* that the company could find no precedents in the news business, so it took iTunes as its model. "We did a bunch of analyses to see what micro-payment environments look like. Apple does it with 99-cent songs, or $1.99 apps" (Braganza 2015). The *Free Press* paywall charges readers 27 cents per article.

Though the heads of all the companies have said that they finally went to the paywall reluctantly and that it was long overdue, some also made the point that it took time for the audience and the technology to catch up with the idea. "Bear in mind, around that time, a couple of other forces were starting to crystallize," says *Globe and Mail* editor-in-chief John Stackhouse. "One was the consumer willingness to pay for anything online had increased significantly because people got comfortable with it. They paid for airline tickets, booked hotels, concert tickets, and yes, music and movies. So your typical consumer – not the digital pioneer but your typical consumer – by 2010–11 was a lot more comfortable paying for something in the digital space ... Add another trend to that, which is the improvement of payment technology, which for newspapers, because of our registration system, is quite important. This is not like a one-off purchase, this is a subscription."

No one is saying the paywall is a perfect solution, but so far it appears to be the most effective way to keep journalism functioning as a business, an art, and a public service, and as a separate entity from government. Anyone with a rudimentary understanding of the Web can get around a paywall. So, the success of the structure relies heavily on the goodwill of readers who believe they're getting enough value for their money, and are willing to subsidize the source of that value. But, then, most of the new business models involve some kind of quality/loyalty relationship, whether it's the *Guardian*'s aim to mobilize hordes of news consumers under its banner, the *New York Times*'s metered paywall, or the publications that rely on friendly benefactors and a community of readers, such as Vancouver's alternative website *The Tyee*, which has thrived on a blend of audience support and sponsorship by organized labour. It has even announced a desire to create a national edition, and recently appointed an Ottawa correspondent, funded by *Tyee* readers who pledged monthly donations to pay his salary. "Those resources create a job for Jeremy Nuttall – living wages and expenses – which is a hopeful development given that the nation's largest news chain Postmedia has eliminated its parliamentary bureau, the CBC is rocked by cuts, and most other media orgs are downsizing" (Beers 2014).

In the United States, observers such as Leonard Downie Jr and Michael Schudson (2009) have suggested several alternative models: setting up partial tax-exempt status for news companies, in the form of corporations that would be able to receive tax-deductible donations and foundation grants; a push for foundations to fund journalism; university involvement in news-gathering and dissemination; government subsidies for local news. Robert McChesney and John Nichols (2010) make some of the same recommendations while advancing the concept of community ownership – like the Saskatchewan Roughriders or Green Bay Packers football teams – and the novel idea of a "Citizenship News Voucher," a $200 credit every American would get from the US federal government, which could be donated to the news outlet of one's choice. *New York Daily News* publisher Mort Zuckerman has even suggested that newspapers be allowed to subsidize themselves by offering sports betting on their sites.

Some non-profit organizations aim to provide high-quality online journalism that relies on foundation and donor funding, such as Minneapolis's *MinnPost* and the *Voice of San Diego*, and the "robust, well funded *ProPublica*," which had a budget of $9 million in 2009, just two years after its founding (Carr 2009c). Each aims to provide high-quality online journalism that relies on foundation and donor funding.

In California in 2012, under the leadership of CEO Aaron Kushner, the *Orange County Register* plunged into a series of experiments that conventional wisdom would describe as self-destructive. It repatriated pagination and editing from Mind Works in India, embarked on a hiring binge, doubling the size of the newsroom to 360, enlarged the newspaper and made it the priority product, and put the online news behind a hard paywall. The model was to charge readers $1 per day for the product on the platform of their choice (Carroll 2013). Kushner's Freedom Communications purchased the Riverside, California, *Press-Enterprise* and launched the *Long Beach Register* in August 2013. In April 2014, it founded a new daily newspaper, the *Los Angeles Register*, to compete with the *Los Angeles Times*

The year 2014 was a rough one for Freedom Communications. It closed down the *Los Angeles Register* in September and the *Long Beach Register* in December, and there were further staff reductions at the *Orange County Register* and the *Press-Enterprise* (Pfeifer and Khouri 2014). Yet, even after laying off 70 employees in Orange County and Riverside in January, the *Orange County Register* still had a staff of 370, up 10 over the summer of 2013, and almost double the 198 it had when Kushner bought the paper in 2012 (Yu 2014). There's no question that the investment shows in the product, Ryan Chittum says.

> A Monday paper is like seventy-three pages – a representative Monday paper. I think the *L.A. Times* the same day was thirty-six. They want to overwhelm you with stuff to read. Kushner's thinking is that he can charge people $30 a month and advertisers will start coming back a little bit. He doesn't think they're going to come back to where they were in 2006, but he can stop the bleeding. He's got profit margins to work with, probably 10 per cent. But he's investing scads and scads of money. I'm skeptical that it's going to work, just because he's spending so much money and you have

to think the odds are against it. It's almost like a pure experiment on whether this sort of thing can work – whether investing in the content, in the news, will actually pay off, and allow you to charge people good money for the paper.

Kushner and Warren Buffett aren't the only ones investing in newspapers. In October 2013, Boston businessman John Henry completed his $70 million purchase of the *Boston Globe* from the New York Times Co., and Amazon.com founder Jeff Bezos closed his $250 million purchase of the *Washington Post* from the Graham Family. There was momentary movement at the far-right side of the political map, too. Through the first half of 2013, rumours circulated in the business that libertarian oil tycoons David and Charles Koch were sniffing around the Tribune Company's newspaper holdings, including the *Los Angeles Times*, the *Chicago Tribune*, and H.L. Mencken's home paper, the *Baltimore Sun*. To the relief of many in the business, they lost interest and moved on to track other political quarries.

Subsequently, a new term entered the newspaper-business lexicon: the vanity owner. Now that newspaper prices are dropping, a new breed of owner is emerging – who is a lot like the old breed of penny press entrepreneur. The fear – especially in the case of highly political players like the Koch Brothers, who are known to invest heavily in ultra-right-wing causes – is that newspaper companies that are no longer viable as money-makers will become valuable as communications tools for special interests. "I think we'll see more of it," says Columbia University journalism professor Todd Gitlin. "This is the sort of thing we see a lot of in Europe. In Greece, for example, most of the press has been dominated by tycoons of various kinds. Think of [Silvio] Berlusconi as a model of the combination of political power and direct stake in economic life … I think it's definitely a possibility that the Koch Brothers and others who are more smooth and less conspicuous in their propagandistic desires will be in the business. I don't doubt it."

The crisis is far from over. Newspapers are still cutting jobs and chains are still carrying large debts – yet they continue to cling to life. Tribune is out of Chapter 11, but, at the time of writing, no one knows what will become of its newspapers. Some companies, such as Quebecor and Gannett, have spent years harvesting their print properties, to the point that they are husks of what they once were – and are unlikely to be restored to their former market positions. In the case of Quebecor, the Postmedia takeover is more likely to accelerate than reverse the gutting process. "Harvesting is the name of the game," Gitlin says. "I wish I had the confidence that something more journalistically serious would emerge, but I don't think that any extraordinary effort should be called up to keep the chains on life support. They're delivering less value all the time. The harvest strategy seems to be as far ahead as they can think."

Some newspapers, such as the *New York Times*, have seen the value in maintaining their news staff and, as a result, have something valuable that they can sell online. Others have cut so close to the bone that they may never again produce anything worth even the fees presented by a metered paywall. As Postmedia's Wayne Parrish says, "We've come back painfully to the realization over the last five years that really the content is what we do and what we create, and what we're noted for."

Finally, there is the perhaps unfair question of how great a role management has played in creating the crisis. Would Tribune have fared better without Zell? Should Gannett pay executives bonuses while it forces staff to take unpaid furloughs? *Daily Beast* founder Tina Brown has gone so far as to call the heads of media chains "feckless zombies ... who cared only about the next quarter's numbers" (2008). And Gitlin has compared relying on the "myopic, inept, greedy, unlucky, and floundering managers of the nation's newspapers to rescue journalism" to "leaving it to the investment wizards ... to create a workable and just global credit system" (2009). Eric Alterman warns that the state of the news business "is far too important to be left in the hands of a few clueless media moguls and their 'chief innovation officers.'"

> The crisis has been a long time coming. I recall sitting in Ben Bradlee's office nearly twenty years ago and listening to the legendary editor bemoan the fact that it was all but impossible to get young people to pick up a copy of the paper. And that was before we had ever heard of the Internet, much less Craigslist. Twenty years is a long time to watch your business model die. To believe in the notion that, in the midst of the cost-cutting mania that is sweeping the

business, we are likely to stumble onto a new source of profit sufficient to sustain the size of the news gathering and dissemination operations we've enjoyed in the past is akin to placing one's faith in divine intervention. (2009b)

One thing that hasn't changed, says a senior reporter who requested anonymity, is the management search for the "silver bullet" that will magically bring back advertisers, attract young readers, and return the newspaper companies to their place in the sun. "The only thing that senior management – at least in the organizations I've worked for – have refused to do is pour money back into the core product. The core product being not just simply the print newspaper, but the staff you need to deliver quality news coverage."

6

Technology: Sacred Tablets

This book could have been written without current technology, but not by me. Research has been mostly a matter of signing on, following the links and push notifications, and waiting for the stories to unfold. A few keystrokes, and up come the aggregators and blogs, government and company archives, pdfs of scholarly journals, newspaper and magazine websites, and online resources of organizations such as Newspapers Canada, the Poynter Institute, the Pew Research Centre, and Nieman Journalism Lab. With Instapaper, massive amounts of material are filed away without printing or worrying about expiring bookmarks. Of course, there are books as well – but one was available only on smart phone and a couple that I needed in a hurry were loaded onto Kobo or iPad. If anything, the challenge lay in sifting through the volume of information.

Interviews were captured as MP3s on a digital recorder, loaded onto a Macbook Pro, and run on ExpressScribe software; then, they were played, rewound, fast-forwarded, and paused with a foot pedal while being transcribed onto Word. If there were voice-transcription software that could do the job, I would cry, "Praise Jobs!" and use it, too.

Writing, editing, revising, and citing are all one fluid process thanks to Word, and the Cloud keeps everything safely backed up on a hard drive in Belgium, Switzerland, or Cupertino, California. I'm a paranoid, so another copy lives on an external hard drive on my desk and a third rides around on a memory stick in my pocket.

Spot research and verification are almost embarrassingly easy: a few keystrokes and the answer to virtually any question pops up on the screen. "What is the largest English-language newspaper in the world?" Hit "enter," and dozens of pages on the *Times of India* appear, with circulation and readership figures. One need only have the patience to read enough of the material to discern the most recent, verifiable figures.

Anyone who longs for a golden age of typewriters, carbon paper, white-out, cassette tapes, and trips to the library is demented. Yet, the trade-off is that we live with a constant nagging feeling that something *is* being lost, whether it is time to reflect, human contact, or personal security and privacy, or just that constant, gnawing worry that seems to go hand in hand with being on the receiving end of so much knowledge – that something important is getting by, buried in the mudslide of information. When I interviewed filmmaker Andy Blicq in 2011 for an article on his documentary *Crackberry'd: The Truth about Information Overload,* he told me that during the course of shooting, one thing that struck him was the sense of unease the new communication technology seemed to be creating in some users. "Some of the people we spoke to said they felt they had a lot of superficial conversations with people, but they don't have that same sense of connection. That came up a couple of times. I found it interesting to stop people in the street and have them say that they're uneasy about it. They're uneasy about how much time they spend with their technology and how that's impacting their lives. But don't you dare take it away from us."

These gadgets and applications are not complex tools. Anyone can learn to use them. For someone with the time and inclination to become adept at data reporting, the Internet has constructed the most massive library of record that has ever existed, and it grows exponentially by the day. This enables a whole new style of journalism that can turn statistics into everything from accountability research to narrative, to elaborate, interactive mapping projects, to learning games. After building his reputation by out-analyzing every pollster and pundit in America during the 2010 presidential election, Nate Silver, formerly of the *New York Times,* built a whole news service around data journalism: *FiveThirtyEight.* When he left the *Times* for ESPN, he took it with him.

However, Internet research is just the largest and most obvious benefit of technology. Computer pagination has turned every copy editor with a sense of composition and perspective into a graphic designer. New and simpler Internet applications have turned every graphic designer into a Web producer. Pocket digital cameras and Photoshop have made every reporter a reasonably competent photographer. Digital video and slide-show technology have made every photographer a writer, filmmaker, and storyteller. Smart phones have made every citizen a witness and potentially a journalist. Websites enable newspapers to be repositories of audio, video, interactive graphics, and even primitive games, and allow every television network to turn its reporting into text. The *New York Times* and the *Guardian* deliver audio and video. CBC, BBC, and National Public Radio become journals of record. Participatory technology enables journalists to turn old standbys like the person-on-the-street interview, the tip line, and the letter to the editor into new forms of communication and research: crowd-sourcing, citizen journalism, and comments fields. "We now have a platform that creates both expressive power and audience size," Clay Shirky writes. "Every new user is a potential creator and consumer, and an audience whose members can cooperate directly with one another, many to many, is a former audience" (2008, 106).

The technology can be dizzying, confusing, and sometimes terrifying, but it is never boring, and the discussion around it is rarely gloomy – although it does come with its share of moral panic, absolutism, evangelizing, nitpicking, societal concerns, and complications, and hyperbolic, repetitive, utopian magical thinking.

For the most part, technology has revolutionized and enriched the practice of journalism in ways we probably won't come to appreciate for years. The modern postal system helped create the press; electoral reform, mass literacy, the telegraph, and the steam press enabled modern mass-market journalism; the radio brought about the intimacy of the spoken newscast and the direct democracy of the Fireside Chats; television put the audience at the scene of the event. The new technology works with a speed that leaves even television and radio at the side of the road choking on dust. It allows events to be photographed, video-recorded, written, tweeted, emailed, and posted as quickly as they happen. (You will notice I left out "edited," "fact checked," and "proof-read.") And the new communication technology is so rife with opinion that it has more or less enshrined the idea that truth is relative to when it is told and by whom, and how it is interpreted. As Robert Darnton put it, "News is not what happened, but a story about what happened" (2009, 25). With its waves of images, text, and opinions, the Internet puts a very fine point on Darnton's comments. And, perhaps most important, it puts the members of Shirky's "former audience" into the conversation, and not just as sources and hecklers, but as auditors, analysts, commentators, and reporters.

Two conversations about journalism and technology have been taking place since the crash of 2008, and they are like the light and dark sides of The Force. This technology has been feared as the destroyer of Big Media, or worshipped as the machine that would save it – and is repeatedly used as "air cover," to steal a line from Tina Brown (2008), for Big Media's inability to manage a budget, plan for contingencies, and adapt to changing times. "The Internet broke our business model" has become the "dog ate my homework" of news executives everywhere.

On the other hand, unyoked from the dismal machinery of business, the talk has been about a revolution not just in the practice of journalism, but in its philosophy as well. In the shadows of the depressing discourse about debt, falling revenue, bankruptcy protection, and perfect storms, a conversation has been going on about the new technology that involves an "irreversible trend in society ... a trend about how people are expressing themselves, about how societies will choose to organize themselves, about a new democracy of ideas and information, about changing notions of authority, about releasing individual creativity and an ability to hear previously unheard voices; about respecting, including and harnessing the views of others. About resisting the people who want to close down free speech" (Rusbridger 2010).

There is also a dystopian point of view, expressed by people like Robert McChesney and Evgeny Morosov, who are becoming alarmed about the nature of discourse on the Internet. We may have achieved John Dewey's dream of a conversational culture, but it is confused, vulgar, vindictive, disorganized, discordant, and increasingly dominated by a few major players who are amassing fabulous wealth, while millions of small voices are lost in the white noise. In *Digital Disconnect*, McChesney argues that we have been blinded by the utopian fable of the World Wide Web and its new frontier of free information and unlimited discourse, and the free-market myth of "heroic upstart little-guy entrepreneurs battling in competitive free markets while the deadbeat government is on the sidelines screwing up the job-creating private sector with a lot of birdbrain liberal regulations" (2013, 97).

The struggle is over, he argues, and the Internet has been transformed into a marketing tool dominated by the likes of eBay, Apple, Google, Amazon, and Facebook. Observers such as Morozov (2011) and Yochai Benkler (2011) warn us not to underrate the ability of tyranny to evolve, and that despots, opportunists, and bureaucrats are proving as adept at manipulating conditions in the online world as they were in real space.

China has even taken to exporting its philosophy of a controlled cyberspace. In November 2014, the *Globe and Mail* reported, Great Firewall warden Lu Wei was one of the speakers at China's first-ever World Internet Conference, which featured corporate guests from around the globe. "In December, he flew to Silicon Valley and visited Mark Zuckerberg [Facebook], Tim Cook [Apple] and Jeff Bezos [Amazon and the *Washington Post*]. He appeared at a Washington Internet forum co-hosted by Microsoft and attended by senior US officials." The Internet, he said, must be "free and open, with rules to follow and always following the rule of law" (Vanderklippe 2015).

In Canada, "we've got extraordinary levels of concentration," Carleton University's Dwayne Winseck says. "We have some of the worst Internet connectivity in the world. Same with wireless: extraordinary high prices and the deployment of both of these technologies to enhance those who own the networks – the ability to control the information, to set the conditions under which we access media, to provide much of the media content themselves, to survey these networks to extraordinarily high degrees – basically gather the data to map out audiences and users, and further lock them into a kind of reified or recursive circle."

The Internet represents a continuation and amplification of the stresses and tensions over which theorists have been arguing since Dewey and Lippmann: whether we're creating a great community of universal discourse or just a larger, louder, more loutish, and even more atomized great society that, immersed in its noise and distractions, has become easy pickings for opportunists and manipulators.

While the newspaper industry has been in a state of nervous despair over finances, some remarkable technological innovations have emerged. Some – as with videotext, fax-delivery, and audiotext – will prove to be evolutionary dead ends, and others will transform the ways we use media. At the same time, there are those who believe "old technology," such as the printing press, still has a role to play.

The continuing success of the US Sunday editions and the *Metro* free commuter papers, the resurgence of the US magazine industry, and the remarkable durability of the book indicate that there may be areas where ink-on-paper is still the most desirable – and most efficient – technology.

There are obvious areas of overlap between technology and the business and craft of journalism. Hyper-local journalism, for example, is something some major dailies have put in place to try to emulate the success of community papers. Technology has enabled it by making it inexpensive, and it represents a change in how journalists aspire to do their work. The same is true of participatory and citizen journalism, and crowd-sourcing. Technology has helped these things develop as they have, but they have a powerful bearing on how journalists see their craft and how – or indeed whether – they will do their jobs in the future.

In January 2009, *New York* magazine ran an article by Emily Nussbaum, under the cheeky title "Goosing the Gray Lady." It was about "a group of developers-slash-journalists, or journalists-slash-developers" who were inventing the newsroom of the future inside the traditional workings of one of the world's most respected daily papers, the *New York Times*. The story began with a description of an online election poll, called "The Word Train." It asked readers, "What simple word would describe your current state of mind?" From a menu below the question, participants could choose from a list of adjectives and say whether they supported Barack Obama or John McCain for US president. The results ran in six rows of words, in Republican red or Democrat blue and descending sizes. "The larger the word, the more people felt that way. All day long, the answers flowed by, a river of emotion … It was a kind of poll. It was a kind of art piece. It was a kind of journalism, but what kind?" (Nussbaum 2009).

It is really not surprising that the *Times* was doing this sort of thing before most. Despite its reputation for being the "grey lady," the paper had long been one of the more interesting products in the business, in terms of creativity as well as authority. Around the time the Web was being born – and shortly after it pried itself away from the black-and-white vertical layout that gave the *Times* its reputation for clinging to tradition – the paper was using its big Sunday edition as a graphic design and storytelling laboratory. The *Huffington Post* didn't invent "mullet journalism" (business in the front, party in the back); the *Times* did. The "A" section may have been sombre and predictable, but "Arts and Leisure," "The Week in Review," "Style," and the Sunday magazine supplement were where you could find the stories that were good just for being good: a day with Jerry Seinfeld as he reinvented himself as a stand-up comic; how Steinway builds a piano; a feature on the funeral industry, with the type set in the shape of a coffin against a background of blue sky and puffy clouds; a glossy black magazine cover with the first paragraph of a story set in large white type, and the headline in small red type at dead centre of the paragraph. To anyone who was paying attention, it was clear the *Times* understood that newspapers needed to spice their public service with art, and that the job of journalism was to make important things interesting and entertaining.

Yet, what is most interesting about the story of the *Times*'s online team is that it was unfolding as the newspaper industry, and the Times company, were going through their worst financial crisis in history. Stock was plunging, advertising was dissolving, and circulation was shrinking. Even the mighty *Times* had been forced to borrow $250 million from one of its investors, Mexican billionaire Carlos Slim Helú. Things were so dire that *Atlantic Monthly* ran an article speculating that the paper might be on the verge of closing down entirely (Hirschorn 2009). Yet, while the best ideas of many other newspapers were to lay off employees and cut back on the product, the *Times* was looking for ways to expand its reach and voice. *Times* media reporter David Carr told *New York*: "This notion of 'Let's give it a whirl,' that's not how we act in our analog iteration. In our digital iteration, there's a willingness to make big bets and shoot them down if they don't work. And yet it's all very deadly serious. Other print websites can innovate because nobody's watching. Here, everybody's watching" (Nussbaum 2009).

That blend of creative freedom and management pressure appears to get results. In 2008, the *Times* Web team was producing features such as: "Casualties of War," an interactive map showing the home towns of US military killed abroad; "Lourdes of Twang," an audio-slide show that took viewers inside the Martin guitar factory; and "The Collapse Sequence," a multi-page interactive graphic reproduction of the collapse of a massive construction crane in midtown Manhattan.

Perhaps the most impressive effort in terms of pure design – and one that showcases all the strengths of the *Times*'s online team – was 2011's "The Reckoning," a beautifully designed compendium of text, audio, video, and interactive features commemorating the tenth anniversary of the World Trade Center attacks. More recently, the 2012 Pulitzer Prize–winning feature "Snow Fall: The Avalanche at Tunnel Creek" (nytimes.com 2011) blended a rather overwritten magazine feature with photo, graphic, and video sidebars to produce something more lovely than literary, but undeniably ambitious and visually stunning. It is a six-part exploration and reconstruction of what happened to a group of back-country skiers who were swept away by an avalanche in the Cascade Mountains near Seattle. It is beautifully designed and photographed, with brilliant use of video interviews, slide shows, and interactive graphics. As the Pulitzer committee wrote in the "Snow Fall" nomination announcement, "For those who had worried about the future of longer form storytelling in the digital age, the future had suddenly, spectacularly arrived" (Pulitzer.org 2013).

The *Times* may not be writing the manual on online journalism, but it consistently contributes some of the most interesting chapters – as does the *Guardian* and such online publications as *Slate* and *Salon.com*.

With "How Many People Have Been Killed by Guns since Newtown?" *Slate* redefined graphic representation as something that can shock, move, and tell a riveting story, with barely a traditional sentence. A blend of crowd-sourcing, data journalism, and interactive graphics, the installation (as good a term as any for it) consists of screen after screen of silhouettes – men, women, teens, and children – linked to a map of the United States showing concentrations of gun violence. Click on a silhouette, and you get a brief, point-form story: "August Golliday. Killed in Chicago. Shot on 12/31/13. Age 25." The only thing comparable in terms of simplicity and mute impact is the grim, black wall of the Vietnam Veteran's Memorial in Washington, DC.

The *Guardian*'s celebration of a century of commercial aviation, "In Flight," is an electronic coffee-table book that combines voice-overs, text, archival photos, and one of the most powerful Wow! effects I have experienced: a world map that shows every commercial airliner in flight over a twenty-four-hour period.

The *Guardian* is a unique publication, and it is deep into the process of another reinvention. Since 1936, owned and operated by the

Scott Trust, set up by its original owners, the *Manchester Guardian* had by the mid-twentieth century established itself as Britain's only non-London national daily. Then, in 1976, it moved south to the nation's capital and became simply the *Guardian*. With a history of outsized ambition, the paper went online in 1995. Four years later, it became the Guardian Unlimited network of websites. Today, under the banner of the Guardian News and Media Web Site Network, the *Guardian* is emerging as a powerful world journalistic force. The news organization claims to have more than 100 million unique monthly viewers (Deans 2014), roughly a third in the United States (Inpublishing 2014). The *Guardian*'s American newsroom employs some sixty journalists, and the US operation won a 2013 Pulitzer Prize for its coverage of the Edward Snowden National Security Agency leaks.

Former *Guardian* editor Alan Rusbridger described the paper's online philosophy as "of the Web, not simply on the Web … Journalists have never before been able to tell stories so effectively, bouncing off each other, linking to each other (as the most generous and openminded do), linking out, citing sources, allowing response – harnessing the best qualities of text, print, data, sound, and visual media. If ever there was a route to building audience trust and relevance, it is by embracing all the capabilities of this new world, not walling yourself away from them" (2010).

It is interesting that the best of the traditional media companies have been some of the most adventurous online. A list of Webby Award nominees and winners between 2007 and 2014 for "best news" and "best newspaper" (a category discontinued in 2010) is dominated by traditional media companies: for the three years of "best newspaper," the *Guardian* and *Times* had three nominations each, with the *Guardian* winning twice and the *Times* once. For "best news" site, the *Times* has five nominations and four wins, the BBC four nominations and two wins, National Public Radio three nominations and one win, and *Wired* two nominations and one win. Other nominees in the "news" category include the magazine *Salon.com*, the aggregators *Huffington Post* (two), *Daily Beast* (three) and *Buzzfeed*, and the news sites *Truthdig*, Reuters, CNN, CNN Money, NBC News (two), Discovery News, MSNBC, and the *Wall Street Journal* (webbyawards .com 2014). In the "news" category, aggregators and originators, and broadcasting and print, compete on the same playing field. This implies that presentation is more important than source and the Internet is not a medium; it is a space in which all media, as Rusbridger said, merge, meld, and compete for attention.

As the *Guardian*'s then managing editor Chris Elliott said in 2010, one of the most powerful forces promoting quality journalism online in Britain has been the BBC. "We have to be more aggressive and cover more things in more creative ways because we aren't just competing with other newspapers, we are competing with a BBC that is serious about journalism" (quoted in McChesney and Nichols 2010, 163). The same could be said about the CBC and Radio-Canada or NPR in the United States. The Internet has forced news organizations to compete for readers and has allowed readers to graze in an enormous field of information. "Every kind of idea gets some kind of exposure on the 'net," Robert Fulford says. "If I could just stop worrying about the money for a moment, or the employment – if I think about it just as a reader of journalism – I would say I'm much, much better off than I was twenty-five years ago. And it's because of all these changes. The *Guardian* is a good example. I choose that one because I don't like them at all. I don't like their politics. I disapprove of them. But I know they're terrific."

News companies are engaged in a wave of technological experimentation that ranges from utilizing freeware to involving readers in research and development. One of the more interesting of these was the Journal Register Company's "Ben Franklin Project." On 4 July 2010, all of the company's eighteen small-market dailies in the US east and midwest "declare[d] independence from expensive proprietary software." So, instead of using such pricey applications as Photoshop and QuarkXPress or InDesign, they put out their papers with downloadable free software such as GIMP and Scribus, as well as more familiar tools, such as YouTube, Google Docs, and CoverItLive. Journal Register CEO John Paton told the *Columbia Journalism Review* he had calculated that upgrading technology for the company would have cost $25 million. The freeware experiment helped him get that budget down to $12 million (Kirchner 2011, 45). At the same time, Paton said, the project "allowed audience members to help shape editorial story budgets through crowd sourcing" (Fitzgerald 2010b). Unfortunately, the experimentation didn't translate into profit. In September 2012, the chain's Digital First parent company went into Chapter 11 bankruptcy protection for the second time in three years after refusing to join the movement toward paid online content. In 2013, the company became Twenty-First Century Media and merged with Media News Group to form Digital First Media; Paton is the chief executive officer.

Other papers have chosen to reinvent themselves online, such as the *Christian Science Monitor*, the *Seattle Post-Intelligencer*, and Montreal's *La Presse*. In May 2014, *La Presse* announced plans to eliminate its 130-year-old print edition and become a mainly Internet-based news company. "We haven't made a decision," André Desmarais, co-CEO of the paper's parent, Power Corp., told CBC.ca. "We want the flexibility in order to do things properly. The market will determine when and if we have to completely (pull the plug on it). Maybe we could keep the Saturday and the Wednesday [editions]. I have no idea. We haven't decided yet" (2014).

The *Monitor*, a well-respected, one-hundred-year-old, limited-profit daily dedicated to quality journalism, has evolved from broadsheet and tabloid to a print and online publication. In 2009, it transformed itself from a newspaper to a brand – consisting of a constantly updating website, a daily pdf e-edition, and a weekly print edition – saving millions in production and distribution costs (Moozakis 2009). On the other hand, the *Post-Intelligencer* – 146 years old when it ceased publishing – was the loser in a long-running newspaper war, as was the *Rocky Mountain News*. Both were artifacts of the days when cities regularly had competing dailies. As *Toronto Star* business writer David Olive wrote, "The real story of the *Seattle Post-Intelligencer* and Denver's *Rocky Mountain News* is that they hung on as long as they did" (2009). However, whereas the owners of the *News* took the old route and simply shut the paper, the *P-I*'s owner, Hearst Corp., transformed that paper into something new: a news-and-opinion aggregator with "a robust community news and information website at its core" (Moozakis 2009). The site, seattlepi.com has since launched apps for smart phones and tablets.

As a quick tour of its Internet offerings reveals, seattlepi.com appears to have settled into life as a fairly typical mid-market site, with a focus on local news, sports, entertainment, and news you can use. The last time I accessed it, the focus was a picture box that could be filled with one of four main stories, depending on the thumbnail the reader clicked. The stories were "30 Classic Movie and TV Compliments," accompanied by a picture from the *Twilight* films, a nostalgia piece on old Seattle restaurants, something called "Bigfoot and Other Interview Questions," and a piece comparing the 2005 and 2013 Seahawks. Other first-screen headlines included: "Is Marijuana Legal in SeaTac Airport?" "Justin Bieber Arrested for Drag Racing, DUI," and "Anne Coulter's Pool Guy Made Her Anti-Pot." Aside from the SeaTac-pot story, the Seahawks piece, and the restaurants nostalgia article, the material could have been on the home page of any aggregator. There was no sign of anything inviting user involvement, beyond the usual comments. Anything resembling hard news was absent. In other words, the site looks like what it is: something done on a shoestring budget with a tiny staff and following all the conventions of an aggregator site geared to collecting an audience for advertisers (seattlepi.com 2014).

The same day, the website of Seattle's surviving print daily, the *Seattle Times,* ran under a traditional masthead heralding the fact that the paper was "Winner of Nine Pulitzer Prizes." It was organized like a typical newspaper Web page, with an ad for ANA airlines taking up about a third of the screen. The space that was left was devoted to: a feature on an African-American man researching the Pacific Northwest's role in the Civil War; a news story about ocean acidification; a piece about a fire in a Quebec nursing home; a weather forecast for the Super Bowl; a business item about Twitter moving to Seattle. There were three promos for Sports, Arts, and Lifestyle, and a very small "This Just In" featuring links to the Justin Bieber story, a piece on a mobster, and a story about an oil-train crash (seatletimes.com 2014). The difference between the two sites appears to be strictly a matter of resources; nothing terribly imaginative or interactive was going on at either site. The *Times*'s site reads like a fairly good, midsize city daily, and the *P-I* looks like the poor cousin that was losing the circulation war. Neither is revolutionizing online journalism.

Other initiatives range from the *New York Times*'s research-and-development group, which plays around with program and application prototypes for the paper's content (Strupp 2009) to the paper's launch of BETA620, a public beta-testing site for products dreamed up by the paper's RandD people. One of the things it offers is a browser plugin called "Test Drive" that allows *Times* readers to test out new products as they are unveiled (beta620.nytimes.com 2014).

Some newspapers, including the *Los Angeles Times,* have experimented with an application called Visual DNA, which allows a reader to create a personalized news page based on demonstrated interests, much the way Amazon compiles data on users' tastes from previous purchases, and then suggests new book, movie, and music releases (Behling 2010).

There are even experiments going on with news-producing algorithms. Prototypes have been tested with sports and finance stories. Co-developed by Northwestern University's engineering faculty and its Medill journalism school, the sports algorithm is called Statsmonkey, and it can use the running score and other statistics of, say, a football game to construct a story of the game. The copy is mechanical and predictable, but no more so than that produced by a mediocre sports writer. The aim is that 90 per cent of readers will be unaware the stories are machine-made (Bunz 2010).

Aside from BETA620 and the "Ben Franklin Project," none of the above ventures addresses what may be the most pressing issue: how to use the new technology to involve an audience that is coming to think of itself more as a public and less as a crowd. More and more members of this audience are demanding to be part of the conversation of the culture. This presents news media, particularly newspapers, with the challenge not only of reinventing the way they do business and deliver news, but of how they think about and practise their craft. The transition to participatory journalism can demand as great an effort by the performers as by the audience – if, in fact, there will be any division left between the two.

Freedom of the press, the old saying goes, belongs to those who own one. Now, thanks to the Internet, that means all of us. This has led to an explosion of blogs, alternative news sites, online magazines, citizen journalism, and sites such as YouTube that specialize almost entirely in user-generated content. From the *Drudge Report* to *Huffington Post*, to *Buzzfeed*, to *Talking Points Memo*, to *The Tyee*, and *Truthdig*, the Web is host to a growing range of alternatives to the mainstream press, the like of which has not been seen since the flowering of underground newspapers in the late 1960s. As in the '60s, some are bred of discontent with the press and its definition of Daniel Hallin's spheres of consensus, legitimate controversy, and deviance (1989). So what if the *New York Times* and the *Wall Street Journal* place the Occupy Wall Street movement in the sphere of deviance? At

Truthdig, former *Times* correspondent Chris Hedges puts it firmly in the sphere of legitimate controversy. Unlike in the 1960s, however, everyone can have a say in this conversation, even if it simply involves contributing to the comments field at the end of a news story. As a result, more newspapers are demanding that their employees pay attention to what matters to their readers. They have to; their financial lives depend on it.

OpenFile was one attempt to put readers into the reporting process. In 2010, Wilf Dinnick told the *Globe and Mail* that he was on a mission to take "the traditional model of reporting" and turn it upside down. His "ultimate journalistic wish list," he told the *Globe*, included "total transparency, a story that never dies, and crowd sourcing" (McLaren 2010). So, he founded *OpenFile*, a chain of Internet news sites that, until September 2012, served the Canadian cities of Vancouver, Calgary, Toronto, Ottawa, Montreal, and Halifax. They were, like the *Guardian*, free of charge. The first thing you saw when you opened the *OpenFile* home page was this headline: "OpenFile Is Community Powered News: You (the Readers) Tell Us What Is Important and a Professional Journalist Does The Rest."

The operating principal for OpenFile was, "What readers want is that authentic engagement with the audience," Dinnick told me a year after the site closed down. "And newspapers have never been traditionally good at that. That was the business model that *OpenFile* followed down the line. People would suggest stories. We knew what they cared about ... and people felt they were being listened to, and there would be increased engagement. And there was. On our site, the audience still beat our expectations, but what we did get was six to seven minutes per visitor on site. That's astonishing. I think the average news site gets 90 seconds."

On one day in July 2012, *OpenFile* published stories in Vancouver about an indie comic-book publisher, a competition to build public housing, and smokers violating a ban on lighting up in parks. In Calgary, there was a story about protests over the closure of an access ramp at an LRT station and a service report on saving money. In Toronto, there were two pieces about a shootout at a block party and a couple of stories about driving a cab in the city. In Ottawa, there was a poll on people's favourite outdoor space. In Montreal, the site covered a mother being deported against the wishes of her doctor. In Halifax, the lead was a sentimental piece about a historic pub being torn down to make room for a supermarket. This was not a typical chain of newspapers, with groupthink and pack journalism producing cookie-cutter reproductions with only slight variation from city to city. Each city page had its own flavour and set of priorities. And on every city page, there were two features: "Suggested Stories," in which readers got to vote for the ones they'd like to see written, and "Suggest a Story." At the average newspaper website, readers usually get involved after the fact, as critics and analysts; at *OpenFile*, they were active before the fact, as assignment editors.

As the chains receded, they became more predictable and bland, says *Toronto Star* digital editor John Ferri, who spent a year and a half at *OpenFile*. So the idea was to develop a site that could augment the mainstream media, as opposed to fielding an alternative to it. "Instead of concentrating more locally, they were losing some of that, and they were feeling more the same as you looked across the chain. And what we saw as our opportunity was that we could potentially replace entire categories of local coverage that they were slowly withdrawing from as they were cutting back their newsroom staff. Like schools, community-level stuff, really granular, local stuff. Even crime and court reporting. So the discussion was, Could we do this for them? Because they could no longer afford to do it. And our business model would be a lot cheaper."

OpenFile ran out of money in September 2012 and announced that after two and a half years online, it was suspending publication pending reorganization. Dinnick says there was supposed to be a handoff from the initial investor who bankrolled the site through its first period of growth, to a second investor, who was supposed to see it through to the next level. "He backed out. There were some staffing changes at a high level in this company, and we lost the deal. We had several problems with the way we were operating anyway. So we decided to put everything on hold. I had a whole bunch of fiduciary problems, but they were all solved. So we just put everything on pause. We're looking to come back, but not in the same way."

A similar story is that of Rachel Sterne, who founded *GroundReport* in 2005 with the idea that she could create a website that would be open-source and linked to citizen journalists around the world, and edited by experienced volunteers. In contrast to *OpenFile*, which was finding a new way to do traditional journalism, you won't find objectivity and professionalism in Sterne's operation. "Bias is what citizen journalists do well," she told the *New York Review of Ideas*. "It puts a more human face on things" (Quateman 2009). The site bills itself as "World news and opinions from the ground." Its home page advises: "You witness breaking news; publish article(s) on Ground Report; reach thousands of readers" (groundreport.com 2015). Stories are wikis, organic collections of tweets, quotes, addenda, and updates from multiple authors, and can make for compelling – if not entirely trustworthy – reading. For example, a report of an Israeli tour bus coming under attack in Bulgaria, reads, in part, as follows:

> Bulgaria: Israeli Tourist Bus Attacked
> by Global Voices July 19, 2012
> By Gilad Lotan
> At least seven people were killed in an attack against Israeli youth on a tour bus in Burgus Airport in Bulgaria.
> UPDATE: @BarakRavid:
> Bulgarian FM spoke with FM Lieberman and told him the investigation found the explosion was caused by a bomb hidden in the trunk of the bus.
> Israeli Prime Minister Bibi Netanyahu stated that "all signs point to Iran" and that Israel will respond fiercely.
> Shoshi, Israeli who witnessed the blast, said:
> "We passed immigration and got onto bus #4 outside the airport. We placed our bags, and after two minutes bus #2 went up in flames. We were evacuated into a secure room." (Lotan 2012)

The illusion is that the reader is getting news as it happens and that somehow the source is more credible because of it. Yet this Associated Press report from a day earlier has more detail, follow-up, and context, gets the spelling of "Burgas" right, and refers to the Israeli prime minister by his proper first name, rather than by his nickname.

> By ARON HELLER and VESELIN TOSHKOV
> – Jul. 18, 2012
> SOFIA, Bulgaria (AP) — Israel vowed to strike back at Iran for a brazen daylight bombing Wednesday that killed at least seven people on a bus full of Israeli tourists in Bulgaria.
> The bombing was the latest in a series of attacks attributed to Iran that have targeted Israelis and Jews overseas and threatened to

escalate a shadow war between the two arch-enemies. Iran has denied involvement in the past but did not comment on Wednesday's attack.

President Barack Obama termed it a "barbaric terrorist attack" and called Israeli Prime Minister Benjamin Netanyahu to pledge US help in finding the perpetrators.

The blast gutted the bus at the airport in the quiet Black Sea resort city of Burgas, some 400 kilometers (250 miles) east of the capital, Sofia, where the Israelis had just arrived on a charter flight from Tel Aviv carrying 154 people, including eight children.

In the first case, the audience is reading a story as it is being assembled. The copy can be rough, barely coherent, and factually dicey. But the aim is to bring readers in on the process, under the assumption that they will understand that the truth will unfold as errors are corrected and contradictions resolved. This form of storytelling is something anyone can do, thanks to an application called Storify, which allows anyone to pull together news-story excerpts, photos, tweets, even videos, and incorporate them with links into their own running commentary. However, as the AP version of the story illustrates, it hardly stands as a substitute for well-reported, well-written, and well-edited news copy.

Newspapers have always tried to feature some sort of reader involvement, at least since the eighteenth century, when British papers would run three pages of content and a blank fourth page, where a reader could write comments before folding the paper and mailing it on like a letter. Every modern newspaper has letters to the editor in its op-ed section. Many welcome contributions from readers, and have spaces set aside for personal essays, opinion pieces, and memoirs. In the 1970s, there was even a publication written by its readers: *Harper's Weekly: A Journal of Civilization*. It was an offshoot of *Harper's* magazine and took its title from a political weekly that was published from 1857 to 1916. It came out biweekly and it was not a success. In those days, a reader had to sit at a typewriter, compose a story, and put it in the mail with a cover letter. Weeks later it might appear in print. With the Internet, you bang out a few paragraphs, hit "send," and wait a few minutes or hours for it to pass the moderator, if there is one. So the challenge for newspapers today is to engage "a user who is at once switched [sic] and switched off, engaged and complacent, informed and ignorant, increasingly reliant on journalism and inclined to bypass journalism altogether. No small task indeed" (Deuze 2004, 147).

The arrival of each new communication technology seems to release hordes of evangelists and skeptics, and not a lot in between. The evangelists imagine an audience of politically aware citizens just dying to involve themselves in the public discourse, while the skeptics argue that online living has, if anything, left us even less time to be the "omnicompetent, sovereign" citizens that Lippmann debunked in *The Phantom Public* as "a false ideal" (1993, 29). More recently, sociologist Michael Schudson has taken up Lippmann's argument, pointing out that this great society in which we live is too big and too complex, and our attention spans and time too limited for any but the most dedicated citizen to be fully engaged in the democratic process. When we have free time – an increasingly rare commodity – we spend it on things that interest and amuse us. Despite decades of hand-wringing over how to engage citizens in public life, it always has been thus, and probably always will be.

One development points to the ways in which the illusion of a universally involved citizenry might open the door to the manipulator and the opportunist – and the Internet troll in all its carbuncular eruptions. Almost any story, video, or comment that goes up on the Web and is connected to user involvement is subject to remarks ranging from reasoned and well written to glib and uninformed, to stupid and juvenile, to hateful and vicious. "The protective force field of anonymity – or pseudonymity – brings out the worst in some people. They say things they would never say in the presence of flesh-and-blood human beings." Even in this case, some argue that there is value to even the basest contributions, because they show us the human subconscious "in all its snaggletoothed, pustulent glory, with a transparency that didn't exist before the Internet. And in a rather twisted way, that's a public service" (Seitz 2010). Also, as unpredictable and potentially destructive as it is, the protective shield of anonymity may be necessary because it allows people to make comments that might get them in trouble with authority. Therefore, suffering the vile, the idiotic, and the uninformed may be the price we pay for protecting the unnamed source. When you consider that some very big stories – Watergate, for example – have been pried loose with the help of unnamed sources, it is easy to understand why some journalists are unwilling to take anonymity away from their readers. Researcher Zvi Reich writes:

> The popularity of comments can highlight the characteristics of successful journalist-audience collaboration. For users, they offer the immediate satisfaction of getting published and having a part in the day's agenda, without demanding a lot of involvement or creativity to produce; users posting a comment do not even have the burden of finding their own topic. From the journalist's perspective, comments can be ego-gratifying. Unlike other user contributions, comments leave the journalist in the traditional position of the lead singer, while the audience members generally play the minor, faceless and reactive role of the chorus. (2011, 98)

There are good reasons newspapers keep, and many journalists like, online comments. As Reich points out, they do little to challenge the traditional roles of the reporter and editor, while giving the illusion of a discourse, and they occasionally provide useful leads and ideas for reporters, columnists, and editors. Comments also absorb resources, because they need to be vetted by a moderator before publication, to deal with issues of profanity, libel, slander, and malice. Other areas of contention "include their low quality, uncertain origins and frequently dubious contribution to the public discourse" (2011, 98).

There always will be journalists who regard readers as loathsome sub-creatures. However, a growing number see the audience as a resource and readers as partners. "We have ways to interact with our readers in ways that we never had before," the *Edmonton Journal*'s Stephanie Coombs says. And those ways range from "the simplest" – readers' comments – to more intricate and personal interaction through social media, she adds.

> The Facebook page: The other day, one of the [armoured car robber Travis] Baumgartner stories had over one hundred people commenting on it, which was fabulous. We had never had that before. So the reader involvement is amazing. You can put a call out in a variety of ways saying, We want your photos. And people send us photos of some event. Obviously what's good about that is that we

are talking with our readers, but also that brand loyalty. They now feel part of the process. It's not a one-way conversation any more.

As well as using moderators to vet comments, some newspapers are moving away from the totally anonymous comments section. For example, most newspaper sites require users to set up a profile and sign in before posting a comment – thus allowing the user anonymity to the public, but leaving a name and address for the moderator. In Canada, for example, the Postmedia papers, the *Globe and Mail*, and *Toronto Star* all require users to sign in before posting comments or suggestions. "If anonymity has what academics call a 'disinhibition effect,' registration goes a long way to counter it ... in essence creating what might be termed a 'reinhibition effect'" (Reich 2011, 109).

Moderation also allows newspaper sites to keep track of people who are responsible for multiple postings. One thing that was quickly discovered about Internet anonymity is how easy it can be to skew or hijack polls and conversations. It's not difficult to create the illusion of controversy or consensus online simply by stacking an online poll, debate, or comments field with the kinds of results you wish to see. There's even a word for it: "freeping." The *Ethics Scoreboard* website defines freeping as "coordinating efforts to overwhelm online polls with thousands of silly, obscene, irrelevant, or politically pointed responses. The name comes from *Free Republic*, a politically conservative activist website that has a readership especially responsive to poll sabotage requests" (ethicsscoreboard.com/list/freeping.html 2004).

CBC News Network found itself on the receiving end of a freep in 2008 when it connected itself to Facebook and the youth group Student Vote to ask the question: "What is your wish for Canada in the coming years?" The network's Paul Hambleton told a BBC seminar that it was only about a week before "two interest groups began freeping the site" one pro- and the other anti-abortion. "Our idealistic and motivated contributors lasted but a few minutes in the sea of abortion rhetoric. In the end, the top two wishes for a better Canada were a nation that supports abortion and one that opposes it. Other more genuine ideas wound up buried in the vitriol of the abortion debate. Why? Because without moderation the wisdom of the masses naturally descends to a common denominator that is determined by those with the most time on their hands. Free expression is not terribly compassionate" (2009, 36).

Free expression is also not as cheap as a lot of organizations at first thought it was. Publishers who believe "digital first" is a way to cut costs by unloading work onto the readers haven't thought things through. It takes constant attention to keep comments threads, forums, and polls from turning into mosh pits full of disgruntlement, rage, and bias. Plus, many of the more interesting possibilities of participatory journalism create work. First, it is futile and legally dangerous to allow readers' comments to go up without moderation, and a simple software filter for "objectionable" language won't do the job. Second, the more interesting participatory journalism experiments require participation on both ends. As the *Globe and Mail*'s Steve Ladurantaye says, newspapers have been treating interactivity like a mild skin condition – they're living with it, but they don't want to think about it, and they never seem to get around to doing anything about it:

> None of us actually have solid policies about how reporters should interact with readers, and it's happening all the time. Everyone is doing it on a case-by-case basis. I don't know how much you can plan for those interactions. It's 2013. Twitter [2006] is seven years old. Facebook [2004] has been around forever. We act like these things are new. But they're not. We're just cashing in now. If we're going to use them to drive traffic, we'd better figure it out quick, because mobile traffic is where it's at right now. And I think of all our traffic for our *Globe and Mail.com*, 50 per cent of it will be mobile in a couple of months from now. That's a huge, giant, big deal, because people aren't reading on their desktops any more. And, when they're not reading on their desktops, they want to interact.

There is a tendency for journalists to cling to their roles as gatekeepers. To a large extent, home-page buttons for emailing, tweeting, and liking further the illusion of participation, as do the boxes listing the most liked, commented, and tweeted stories, and the readers' comments, which are little more than glorified person-in-the-street quotes.

However, in its more serious manifestations, user participation should demand a higher level of engagement from journalists. Little professional involvement is required if readers are simply supplying cute pictures of cats or snow-laden backyard decks, or reminiscences of their tenth birthday, or if the news organizations are harvesting tweets, Instagram photos, Vines, and YouTube videos as a substitute for real reporting. At the same time, nothing is accomplished that couldn't have been done with old technology. Understandably, many journalists, having seen waves of layoffs and cutbacks, regard participatory journalism mainly as another threat to their jobs. Typical is Paul Carr's reaction to a plan by *Forbes* magazine to turn editors into "curators of talent" for reader contributions: "My conclusion was that, in the Internet world, quality, originality and exclusivity are fast becoming irrelevant. Instead, online publications increasingly treat content as low-paid, illiterate swill, commissioned by the ton to provide SEO and inventory" (2010). Done ambitiously and with an eye to enhancing the scope and reach of journalism, user participation should mean more staff, not less, and better reporting, not "illiterate swill."

As Clay Shirky puts it, "The current change, in one sentence, is this: most of the barriers to group action have collapsed, and without those barriers, we are free to explore new ways of gathering together and getting things done" (2008, 22). Thus, some newspapers are experimenting with training sessions for readers who want to get involved, to familiarize them with some of the journalistic conventions and legalities of contributing to a site (Singer 2011, 136). Others have taken to assigning community editors, coordinators, or coaches to work with readers' comments, citizen journalism, and blogs linked to their sites; in some cases, user-generated comments are contained in a subsidiary site and connected to the professional site (Paulussen 2011; Domingo 2011).

The potential for community journalism is obvious and exciting. Podcasting, multimedia, and hand-held video allow every town and village to have the kind of rich media that, until recently, have only been available in big cities. News organizations are only limited by their collective imagination and the will of their management in how well they can remake themselves as the social mirrors, town halls, and coffee houses of the twenty-first century.

For a little less than two years, the *New York Times* partnered with the City University of New York (CUNY) to create "collaborative, citizen-based, local journalism" in which two professors and ten students from CUNY set out to find a way in which Brooklyn could "report on itself" (Myers 2010). It organized a similar plan with New York University to cover the East Village of Manhattan. The *Times* discontinued the two programs in June 2012: "The sites ceased to be a priority for a news organization with no shortage of priorities, including a growing list of new Web initiatives that have been rolling out as readers continue to adapt to the paid digital model implemented by the *Times* last year" (Pompeo 2010).

At the *Guardian*, there is a "head of communities," a job that is "primarily regarded as a strategic role ... The person not only oversees a team of in-house moderators but also develops strategies for creating a 'much greater sense of communities across the site' and looks for partnerships and technological solutions to keep on top of the flood of user generated content" (Paulussen 2011, 67).

At the *National Post*, food editors have set up the *Gastropost* subsite in which readers are given "missions" to track down and photograph food. And at the *Edmonton Journal* Karen Unland runs *Capital Ideas*, in which the newspaper acts as facilitator to a city-wide network of entrepreneurs. "Constructing a community is very difficult to do well and in an authentic way," she says. "The tack that we take is that people already belong to communities, people already have interests. How can we add value to things that they do already, instead of going over the hurdle of, 'Join our conversation; send us your pictures; do your thing.' The way that *Gastropost* was able to grow to the size that it is now, they still invite people to *Gastropost*, they also go on to Instagram and find people who happen to have fulfilled their mission without knowing it."

At *OpenFile*, communities got involved in deciding what issues and events needed coverage and investigation – and trolling was not a problem, Wilf Dinnick says. "We were trying to be a service: suggest a story; peer review. Here is the story people think should be investigated or looked at. Here's what they care about. That's what we were after ... We never got fluff. The other thing to consider is what's important is the tone you set. If someone asks a question you think fits the reality of the mandate, you go with that question. We never had racism. We never had sexism. We never had anger. It was never a problem."

Similarly, David Beers, founding editor of Vancouver's *The Tyee*, says his readers have a powerful interest in important news, a good sense of what needs to be covered – and a personal relationship with the site. It may have become "the paper" everywhere else, but at *The Tyee*, readers still think of "my paper," he says. "The Internet is a collection of tribal enclaves and if you express some coherent values, you will draw people towards you. You'll draw money towards you as well."

It is clear that there is a role for readers to play in the news-gathering process, by blogging, contributing hyperlocal content, creating, and maintaining a conversation about the culture, and simply prompting journalists to ask the questions that matter to their audience. And, in a world where journalists are becoming increasingly desk-bound by the demands placed on them by reduced staffing, widening responsibilities and more emphasis on data reporting, there is obvious value to having eyes and ears on the street. This means journalists have to be open to the idea of crowd-sourcing, which uses the Internet, Twitter, and social media to expand and accelerate the reach of reporters beyond anything they could have imagined a decade ago.

In a 2011 TED talk, *Guardian* reporter Paul Lewis explained how he used Twitter to research two pieces of accountability journalism: the first dealt with allegations that news vendor Ian Tomlinson had been killed by London police in an unprovoked attack during the protests at the 2009 G-20 summit; the second involved Jimmy Mubenga, a political refugee who died while being deported from Britain to Angola. In the latter case, the official story was that Mubenga had suddenly taken ill on the flight. The truth was that three security guards had put him in a choke hold and suffocated him while trying to restrain him. In both stories, the official versions were debunked by citizens who came forward after *Guardian* journalists put out calls, via Twitter and the Internet, for witnesses. In the first case, the calls produced cellphone video that showed London police shoving Tomlinson to the ground and attacking him. In the second, the *Guardian* posted highly speculative stories designed to provoke controversy and comment, and put out a call via Twitter, which produced an American working on an Angolan oilfield, who was on the flight with Mubenga and witnessed his death. Lewis told the TED audience that this sort of story cannot be written without journalists accepting that they "can't know everything, and allowing other people through technology to be your eyes and your ears. And ... for other members of the public, it can mean not just being the passive consumers of news but also co-producing news" (2011).

User engagement is the culmination of the civic, or public, journalism movement of the 1990s and early 2000s, Mark Deuze writes. "Civic journalism as such is sometimes characterized by three steps: it reformulates the relationship between the press and the people, it emphasizes establishing connections and contacts between journalists and the communities they cover trying to address the audience as equal partners instead of 'just' consumers, and finally it emphasizes a focus on issues instead of institutions (summary from Dahlgren, 1998). Although this last item may not be typical of online journalism, the first two points could come straight out of a handbook of 'how to do online journalism'" (1999, 385–6). One of the founding fathers of the movement, New York University's Jay Rosen, says public journalism was ahead of its time, an idea in need of a technology: "Looking back from the perspective of today. I would say the civic journalism movement (1) warned that something was awry in the journalist's connection with the public, and the Internet came along and proved it, and (2) anticipated the importance of what today is called 'engagement' with a more active user."

In some cases, technology has sent us forward to the past. It was the Internet and the return to breaking news that brought reporters back to filing on tight deadlines and resurrected the inverted pyramid. Unland says that when the *Edmonton Journal* went to live online reporting in the 2000s, editors were surprised to find that reporters in their late forties and fifties adapted the most easily because they had learned their craft at a time when tight-deadline news writing was the norm across the board. Through the late 1990s and early 2000s, with the demise of the multiple-edition newspaper and the imposition of earlier press runs – often to accommodate outside printing jobs – newspapers had taken to holding over a lot of material that had traditionally been written on tight deadline, such as overnight concert and theatre reviews, and late sports stories. As a consequence, a universal ability to write fast, tight, and right had more or less skipped a generation.

SMS and Twitter have brought back the rewrite desk. For example, for the hearing of confessed armoured car robber and killer Travis Baumgartner, "we had three people in the courtroom, and two were live tweeting," *Edmonton Journal* managing editor Stephanie Coombs says. "They were sitting next to each other and coordinating their tweets. They were doing it so anyone who was on Twitter could get the news. But also, what we did was have a rewrite person in the office, an editor, take their tweets and write it into a story. That's like the old days of rewrite ... But this was so much faster."

It is a short step from civic journalism to citizen journalism, and from the press involving the user to the user involving the press. A lot of modern reporting – spot and investigative – is being done by people with no professional training, who simply feel the need to bear witness. The Arab Spring uprisings of 2011 and the ensuing civil wars in Libya and Syria were, to a large extent, reported with cellphone, Twitter, and Skype. Sometimes, citizens were taking pictures with cellphones, alongside professional photographers and videographers with expensive equipment. Sometimes, only people with cellphones were there to record a tragedy or atrocity. Occasionally, the people with the cellphones have even found themselves covering the deaths of the journalists with whom they had been working.

Like rewrite, the inverted pyramid, and reader involvement, this is not a new phenomenon. Citizens have been providing images and bearing witness for journalists as long as there have been pads, pencils, and cameras, and some iconic works of photojournalism are the work of amateurs. The famous photo of a woman grieving over the body of a dead protester at Kent State University in 1970 was shot by a photography student taking a break from his work; the horrific photos of the crash of an American Airlines DC-10 that lost an engine on takeoff in 1979 were taken by a bystander at Chicago's O'Hare Airport; the video of Rodney King being beaten by Los Angeles police in 1991 was captured by someone with a home video camera on a nearby balcony. Perhaps most famous, the iconic footage of the John F. Kennedy assassination was taken on an 8mm home movie camera by Abraham Zapruder, a Dallas garment manufacturer, who happened to be filming Kennedy's motorcade as it passed through Dealey Plaza on 22 November 1963. Thanks to technology, we are all Abraham Zapruder: the streets are filled with potential witnesses with video-equipped smart phones.

The revelation that police at the University of California at Davis pepper sprayed peaceful protesters in 2011 fits into the citizen-witness continuum. It also highlights how much easier it has become for citizens to bear witness. When campus police opened fire with their pepper-spray canisters, several onlookers captured the event with their cellphone cameras. However, rather than being sent to the media, the footage was posted on YouTube, where it contradicted the university's version of events: that unruly protesters had forced campus police to act. Then, the media picked up on it, and eventually the university president was forced to apologize. The situation highlights the fact that "police and government ... seemingly cannot get their heads around a simple enough concept that wherever one is, someone is watching and recording" (Whittaker 2011).

A near-perfect example of a combined newsgathering effort was the video footage of a gunman who shot a ceremonial guard at Ottawa's war memorial and then rampaged through Parliament in October 2014. It was captured by security cameras, a print journalist, and passersby with smart phones. Stitched together, they provided a moment-by-moment visual account of the crimes as they were being committed.

Digital technology and the Internet have enabled people to go directly to the audience without passing through the media, and to do it with a speed the news media can't always match. For example, there hasn't been a US war covered by a completely independent media since Vietnam. During the Gulf War, reporters covered combat from a distance, getting their information from daily military briefings. The situation was, more or less, the same in Afghanistan, though reporters were allowed to accompany military patrols. The 2003 invasion of Iraq started out to be perhaps the most heavily mediated and controlled armed adventure in US history, with reporters going into action "embedded" with military, who were responsible for them, and to whom they were responsible. But, once the United Sates was in control of the country, it was left to bloggers inside the military to circumvent military censorship – and they were on the Internet almost immediately. The abuses at Abu Ghraib prison were reported largely because a group of US soldiers took pictures with digital cameras and then posted them online. In the same way, a few dozen military personnel with laptops went online and created an instant Iraq War literature. *Wired* magazine described this "oddball online Greek chorus narrating the conflict in Iraq" as including "a core group of about 100 regulars and hundreds more loosely organized activists, angry contrarians, jolly testosterone fuckups, self-appointed pundits, and would-be poets who call themselves milbloggers, as in military bloggers" (Hockenberry 2005).

It was only a matter of time before an organization sprang up to facilitate this sort of reporting of information leaks. WikiLeaks, founded in 2007, was dedicated to revealing information that the powers that be would prefer left alone. And, as with traditional journalism, its access to that information was dependent on an ability to guarantee its sources' anonymity. During its most active years, WikiLeaks released data ranging from Sarah Palin's email to documents revealing the inner workings of Scientology, to protocols from Guantánamo Bay.

In 2010, WikiLeaks went high tech and high profile, when it took possession of a massive, encrypted video file, and then put out a call for a supercomputer to decrypt it. What it found under the encryption was a thirty-eight-minute video of US helicopter troops firing at civilians on the ground in Baghdad, killing twelve, including two employees of the Reuters news agency. WikiLeaks posted the entire video, as well as an edited seventeen-minute version, which was more widely seen because it was on YouTube. As for the process of decrypting the video, the organization was simply doing what the news media should have been doing, said WikiLeaks co-founder Julian Assange: "That's arguably what spy agencies do – high-tech investigative journalism. It's time the media upgraded its capabilities along those lines" (Cohen and Stelter, 2010). WikiLeaks has been criticized as often as it has been praised for its approach of not asking questions about the origins of its material before publishing it. "WikiLeaks comes up only infrequently in conversations about innovative efforts to reinvigorate journalism. Though one can make the claim that WikiLeaks' pushing of legal and ethical norms makes it marginal to such conversations, it is equally true to say that WikiLeaks is unsettling to journalists because it represents a radical shift in the way information is collected and distributed in the media landscape" (Lynch 2010, 310). That's a slight overstatement. The massive series of leaks by US Army intelligence functionary Bradley (now Chelsea) Manning sat unnoticed for months on the Internet before publications such as the *New York Times* and the *Guardian* picked up the material, edited it, and began to publish it. It was only once it was in print that it became a *cause célèbre*. "Journalism had to give the material credibility, and journalists had to do the hard work of vetting the material and analyzing it to find out what it meant. That required paid, full-time journalists with institutional support" (McChesney 2013, 195).

Also, as Yochai Benkler (2011) has demonstrated in great detail, WikiLeaks is not immune to pressure from states and markets. In fact, it has become something of an affront to the Social Responsibility Theory of the press, and governments and corporations have made occasionally strenuous attempts to force it into line. For example, the Manning leaks provoked very effective attacks by government and business that left Manning in jail, Assange seeking asylum, and WikiLeaks hobbled.

Perhaps the most vivid recent examples of how citizen journalism can fill the gaps in our knowledge has come from the civil wars in Syria and Libya. Almost daily, the Western news networks have carried images of bombing, strafing, and shelling, and of shattered buildings, broken bodies, and grieving, enraged, or victorious civilians. This sort of information flow belongs almost entirely to insurgents – since official sources have official ways of disseminating information – and is, therefore, understandably biased. In the most unsettling manifestation of direct communication, the radical Muslim group ISIS has shown remarkable proficiency in using Internet technology to manipulate the mainstream media and build a heroic mythology about itself.

Often, the setting of a story may be so dangerous or remote that the only way to get information is to pick it off the Internet, to which it has been uploaded by citizens with cellphones and cameras, who are living the story as they report it and blending citizen journalism with advocacy reporting. For example, though some professional reporters have been covering the insurrection in Syria, they have mostly been working beside citizen journalists, sometimes to tragic and surreal effect. Take the instance of US reporter Marie Colvin and French photographer Rémi Ocklik, who were killed in the Syrian government shelling of Baba Amr in February 2012. They had been working alongside Syrian Khaled Abu Salah, a spokesman for the Revolution Leadership Council of Homs. Just a few days earlier, they had reported on him. After the shelling, he was reporting their deaths, via cellphone camera: "Within an hour, his video report would be posted on YouTube, and then picked up by networks around the world. 'They were killed because of the random shelling of the Baba Amr neighborhood,' Mr. Salah said, angrily shaking the forefinger of one good hand at the camera; his other hand, wounded by shrapnel, was bandaged. 'This is a call to save the remaining residents while they are still alive'" (Nordland 2012).

Citizen journalism has proved particularly effective and valuable in times of natural disaster. When an earthquake rocked Christchurch, New Zealand, in February 2011, much of the public service communication and news reporting came via user-generated content, helping people locate loved ones, publicizing distribution points for supplies, and getting out the story of what was happening. Similarly, most of the close-up video of the catastrophic tsunami that followed the Tohoku earthquake in Japan a month later came from people on the ground, who felt compelled to record what they were trying to survive. "In a disaster UGC [user-generated content] is not here for your entertainment. It is not competing with network news for ad dollars. It does not care whether it should be pitted against professionals or win a journalism award. It is a way for people experiencing the most significant event of their lives to bear witness, to cry out their pain and their suffering and their need, to connect with people close by who are sharing their experience and to connect with people far away who, but for their voices, might mistake these events for a blockbuster movie on a soundstage" (Colbin 2011).

There are apps for that. As well as providing organizing and communication tools for civil resistance, such as the anti-globalization protests and the Arab Spring uprisings, social networks like Twitter and Facebook keep us up to date on local and world events. This kind of citizen journalism is what inspired Mark Malkoun, of Lebanon, to create an app called Completure, which bills itself as a "complete citizen and photojournalism FREE News app, from the creation of the story, to the distribution and selection." It promises to enable anyone to "create a mini-story in seconds using photos, geo-location, and a short title about real-world events" (completure.com 2014).

More recently, German Manuel Tessloff developed a smart phone app called Apparazzi that allows people to become one-person hyper-local news sources. With the app, people can cover their neighbourhood and post pictures, video, headlines, and short news items, and alert other users with push notifications. "Unlike Facebook or Twitter, where users follow people, users of Apparazzi follow places" (Deutsche Welle 2014).

There are new dangers in the amount of information being gathered, and the speed with which it becomes part of the public discourse.

For example, after the Boston Marathon bombings, a "human flesh search engine" (Sanchez 2013) fanned out across social media seeking to identify two men in a couple of grainy pictures released online. Several innocent people briefly became the world's most reviled villains, as their pictures and names appeared on blogs, newspapers, news sites, social media, and twenty-four-hour TV news.

Citizen journalism is valuable, fast, and often exciting, but to say it is a substitute for professional journalism is going a bit far, the Poynter Institute's Regina McCoombs told *Global Post*: "I don't think they answer any questions, but they raise questions and cast doubt on things people say. It's good to have them, but to say they prove or disprove anything is a stretch" (Lodish 2011).

Sometimes, doctoring the truth can seem innocent to the perpetrator, as with the case of a Syrian citizen journalist in Homs, who added smoke to a backdrop of a report to increase its dramatic effect (Flock 2012). And some citizen journalists see nothing wrong with breaking the law or practising entrapment to forward their agenda. For example, "conservative gotcha artist" James O'Keefe became famous for posing as a pimp to ensnare officials of the left-wing Association of Community Organizers for Reform Now (ACORN) by filming them advising one of his "prostitutes" to game the system. In January 2010, he was arrested for tapping the phones of Louisiana Democrat Mary Landrieu (Meek 2010).

While YouTube offers a worldwide arena for citizen journalism, it has barely begun to realize its potential. The Pew Center's Project for Excellence in Journalism took a tally of the most popular YouTube videos in 2011 and, not surprisingly, music dominated seven of the months, with Lady Gaga taking two, and the other five belonging to Drake, Katy Perry, Rock in Rio, Taylor Swift, and Amy Winehouse (the *Rehab* video spiked after her death). Three others belonged to a video game, the death of motorcycle racer Marco Simoncelli, and a homeless man with a powerful singing voice. Only two months were dominated by news: March, with the Japanese tsunami, and May, with the death of Osama bin Laden (PEJ 2012b).

The popularity of the thirty-minute video *Kony 2012*, about the Ugandan warlord Joseph Kony, indicates that there may be an appetite for current events among young people. It was viewed an average 7.6 million times a day for the first ten days after it was posted on YouTube, and 125,00 times a day over the following four months

(PEJ 2012b). Another Pew Center study showed that the Kony video revealed that younger people tend to get more news from YouTube than older people do. Those aged eighteen to twenty-nine were much more likely than older adults to have heard about Kony and his Lords Resistance Army through YouTube or social media such as Facebook and Twitter (Rainie et al. 2012). This has interesting implications for YouTube as a future news source, Amy Mitchell of Pew's Project for Excellence in Journalism told the *Globe and Mail*. "There's a new form of video journalism on this platform. It's a form in which the relationship between news organizations and citizens is more dynamic and more multiverse than we've seen in most other platforms before" (Coyle 2012).

YouTube is only the most obvious manifestation of an evolving way of collecting, processing, and disseminating journalism that involves an ever mutating and shifting network of connections and affiliations, partially dependent on media such as Twitter and Facebook to call attention to itself. That would also imply that the most important role of traditional media might be to play moderator, facilitator, truth detector, and publicist for this organic newsgathering network. One of the major duties of journalism may be to monitor the flow of information and opinion: harvesting the best of it, and trying to assure something important doesn't go unnoticed and that lies don't permeate the public record. The spread of false information on the Internet is a growing concern. Columbia University's Tow Center for Digital Journalism has released a 150-page report, *Lies, Damn Lies and Viral Content*, that explores "the onslaught of hoaxes, misinformation, and other forms of inaccurate content that flow constantly over digital platforms" (Silverman 2015, 1). The study's author, Craig Silverman, found that, driven by the needs to react instantly to breaking news and to draw eyeballs to their sites, mainstream news organizations play an important role in retransmitting misinformation online. And it is a tall order for those news organizations to set the record straight. "Fake articles are engineered to appeal to hopes, fears, wishes, and curiosity. They are not restrained by facts or reality. This gives them a leg up in creating shareable content that drives engagement" (68).

The challenge for cash-strapped news organizations is compounded by the fact that they are increasingly being forced to rely on unverified sources to keep up with their audiences' demand for a constant flow of new sensations. And there are parts of the world where important news is simply out of reach for news media whose staff have been cut to the bone. "Citizens are bearing witness themselves where it's hard for the classic Western correspondent to get to," says Edward Greenspon, *Toronto Star*'s head of new ventures. "I think that's a wonderfully good thing. It may be that we don't have political answers to it, but we're not informationally deprived, because it's a very different ecosystem. And it's a hybrid system, a much richer system where you have citizens and professional journalists both doing work, and not orchestrated to be mutually supportive, but mutually supportive nonetheless. You have some professional journalists beginning to curate that user-generated content. And that's terrific."

As the *Guardian*'s Paul Lewis told TED, this involves journalists admitting that they can't be everywhere, and allowing their sources to take on a much more active role in bearing witness to the world around them. Again, the difference lies in the timing. Traditionally, journalists came in and asked sources, "What happened?" Sources today witness something and put it out for the world to see. Then, the journalist comes by to try to verify and make sense of what happened.

By way of comparison to the old way of getting out stories that need to be told, the *New York Times* talked to Daniel Ellsberg, a RAND Corporation analyst, who in 1971 gave the *Times* the Pentagon Papers, a secret report calling into question US involvement in Vietnam. How would he handle the documents today? the *Times* asked. "I would have gotten a scanner and put them on the Internet," Ellsberg replied (Cohen 2010).

In 2009, *Forbes* magazine described the role of "social media director" as "journalism's hottest job," and talked about tweets being the "gold standard of scoops" (Smilie 2009). As the article mentioned, there's one small problem with this type of thinking: it accomplishes nothing for the news organization, beyond awarding bragging rights for being first with the least. Since then, many news organizations have come to understand that Twitter is an extremely effective tool for promotion and information gathering but, for storytelling and money-making, it leaves something to be desired. "I think it is promotion and I think it is crowd-sourcing," Torstar chairman John Honderich says. "That's basically where it goes: people getting followers and creating brands ... But again, it's an evolving technology. Are there other ways and means that will develop? I wait and see." That news organizations are increasingly demanding their reporters be active on social media also raises the question of whether the wall between news and promotion is being torn down. It could be a small step from asking reporters to promote their news organizations to requesting that they sell advertising, too.

As the *Edmonton Journal* showed with the Baumgartner hearings, Twitter can be used to relay information quickly from virtually anywhere – but then, so can email and SMS. And, as Honderich pointed out, tweets can be used as a draw to the main event, as a brand builder and a driver of traffic. However, as reading material, Twitter's banality is often numbing. Steve Ladurantaye, who now works for Twitter, was media reporter for the *Globe and Mail* when he told me this about tweets versus traditional storytelling:

> How many times do you hear people say, "I get all my news from Twitter; I don't need the media any more because of Twitter"? Obviously Twitter doesn't exist without all the back-end newspaper stuff to back it up, to click through to. But most people don't bother to click through. So the most news they're getting is about five tweets of 140 characters each. And that's the depth of their understanding of a lot of issues. I come across that a lot with my own stories. People will read my Twitter stream and think they know the story. I'll meet them somewhere and they'll start talking about my story, and it's clear they haven't read it. They just know the top of the line from five tweets sent at eight in the morning. But they think they're really, really, really, really well informed. That's a little spooky.

A 2011 HP Labs study revealed that mainstream news outlets are the main drivers of Twitter trends, which usually don't last longer than forty minutes. What keeps an issue alive is the incidence of retweets; the more substantial topics tend to generate the most conversation, and these come from the mainstream news media (Diana 2011) – which, as the Tow report showed, play an important role in the spread of misinformation, hoaxes, and other forms of truthiness, to use *The Colbert Report*'s term for high-quality fake authenticity.

As we saw with Paul Lewis's case studies, the other and probably more important use for Twitter is as a way to gather information and to tap into the public discourse. "One of the fascinating things about Twitter is the pattern of flow of information is unlike anything we've ever seen before. We don't really understand it. But once you let go of a piece of information, it travels like wind. You can't determine where it ends up but, strangely, tweets have an uncanny ability to reach their intended destination" (Lewis 2011).

That other social media monolith, Facebook, has come into focus as a powerful tool to promote journalism and build communities. A 2010 Pew Research Centre study revealed that Facebook was the second or third most important driver of traffic to news sites such as the *New York Times,* the *Washington Post,* ABC, CBS, Fox News, CNN, and the *Huffington Post* (Pew 2010). Many news organizations are finding that when Facebook drives traffic, it brings in readers who "tend to view more articles and stay around a site longer." For example, Mashable.com found that Facebook and Twitter visitors stayed 29 per cent longer and viewed 20 per cent more material than visitors arriving by search engine. "Facebook's audience is vastly larger than any single news organization" (Grueskin et al. 2011, 32).

However, there is some concern that Facebook may be setting itself up to be the world's information clearing house – or the last word in media monopoly. In March 2015, the social media network announced that it had reached deals with such publishers as the *New York Times, National Geographic,* and *Buzzfeed* to host their content. Facebook would get a cut of the advertising revenues while assuring that its users stay inside the corral when they look for news. As University of British Columbia digital media instructor Alfred Hermida told CBC, "Facebook wants to find a way to become essentially the de facto Internet for people. Facebook wants to be your world. The problem is, as a publisher, you're essentially renting out office space in their building. And then you're at the mercy of Facebook and how it organizes information on the site" (Kwong 2015).

What was once seen as an alternative solution to the problem of attracting readers, search engine optimization, or SEO, has proved to be no solution at all. Studies have shown that SEO – throwing every keyword you can think of into a headline to get it to pop up on Google – is much less useful than the kind of brand building news organizations are doing on Facebook. The *Edmonton Journal*'s Karen Unland dismisses SEO as "a Red Queen's race." "We were running in place as fast as we could and not getting anywhere. I think that page views as a metric for success is imperfect, and doesn't lead to necessarily good journalism or good business."

It is likely that the relationship between news and social media will be a long-term one. Social media are powerful tools for "bringing new readers to your journalism or, more importantly, getting your journalism to new readers," *Globe and Mail* editor-in-chief John Stackhouse told me. "It's a natural channel of communication for a lot of people ... Our Facebook community has an appetite for certain types of content, so we feed that content deliberately through Facebook."

If there is one technological bane of the newspaper – at least in the minds of those who own them – it is the aggregator. Aggregators have been called parasites, thieves, and opportunists. When feature writer Michael Wolff told Rupert Murdoch that he helped found the aggregator *Newser*, Murdoch's response was, "So you steal from me" (2009). Former *Washington Post* executive editor Leonard Downie Jr described aggregators as "parasites living off journalism produced by others" (Robinson 2010). Internet billionaire Mark Cuban told *Newsweek* that the newspapers' sites should "kill off these parasites" with code that locks them out (Lyons 2009).

To further sharpen the point that journalists really hate aggregators, the *Washington Post*'s Ian Shapiro once compared the time he put into a story – roughly two days – to the speed with which a *Gawker* writer plagiarized it. "Probably took me, you know ... a half an hour to an hour," the scalper told Shapiro (2009). Even Comedy Central's fake TV pundit Stephen Colbert got into the discussion in 2011 by striking back at the *Huffington Post* for cannibalizing his website. He did this by launching the "Colbuffington Re-Post," a reposting of *HuffPo*'s reposting of Colbert's original material. In a further dig at Arianna Huffington – who sold her site to AOL for $315 million in 2011 – Colbert immediately put his "site" up for sale for $316 million, and had Huffington onto his show to talk about it.

Huffington Post is the Genghis Khan of aggregators. Founded by Huffington, Kenneth Lerer, Andrew Breitbart, and Jonah Peretti in 2005, it came from nowhere to dominate the world of aggregation in less than five years. At the time of writing, it has at least ten international editions in five languages, and an eleventh planned for India. Huffington has been criticized for walking to success over the backs of newsgathering organizations and a pack of bloggers, who write for free. In Canada, there are two sites: one in English with separate front pages for the various regions of the country, and one in French for Quebec. The latter relies on a tiny staff, imported material from *Le Huffington Post* France, and the usual army of free bloggers. *Le Huffington Post* made news of its own when it debuted in Quebec, and several local columnists signed up to write for it, then backed out to protest the unpaid labour. Although it has achieved international status and respectability of sorts, the *Huffington Post* remains journalism done on the cheap, and still relies heavily on material scalped from other news organizations. In justification of using unpaid labour, Huffington says, "Our bloggers come and go. They write when the spirit moves them, and they do it because they want to be part of the conversation" (Dumenco 2009).

To be fair to Huffington, that's exactly the kind of reasoning media companies have always used to justify things like unpaid internships, you-be-the-reporter/editor contests, and freelance "opportunities" that pay the cost of lunch at McDonald's. These are all things major newspapers did for years, as they were pulling in 30–40 per cent profits. When it comes to the mechanics of exploiting freelancers, contractors, and students, newspapers and magazines wrote the shop manual.

The waves of loathing for the aggregators appear to have receded, partly due to the rise of paywalls, and the fact that newspapers are developing ways to block content so only subscribers can get at it. As a result, aggregators are increasingly being seen as semi-useful bottom-feeders who carry nuggets of content-bait into the general stream of conversation.

If there is one technological tool that carries most of the hopes and dreams of newspaper publishers it is the tablet – or, to be more precise, the mobile device. In a perfect world, the tablet would have been invented before the World Wide Web, and newspaper publishers would have had their dreams come true in one neat, paper-thin, plastic-aluminum-and-glass package. The allure of the tablet for newspaper publishers is obvious: it appears to offer them a way to craft their product without the cost of ink, paper, or distribution, and without giving up the proprietary information that enables them to gather customers for advertisers.

"I think it's a case of when you are a drowning man, everything looks like a lifesaver," is the way *New York Times* reporter David Carr put it when he was moderating a panel on tablets and newspapers (Jackson 2010). However, there's no denying the allure of the device, and there are those who hail it as the real saviour technology. The apps it runs (or that run it) have more in common with software or video games than with a website in that they are non-physical objects that carry the consumer appeal of physical ones. You have to load an app onto your device and, once it is there, the company that gave it to you can use it as a conduit to deliver magazines, newspapers, or books, and a variety of services. "The experience of reading a magazine – or a newspaper – on one of these mobile devices is in many ways superior to the experience of reading the printed product ... Advertisers can only exult in the visual quality of the ads, as well as the touch-through capabilities to route interested readers to more detailed information on products" (Dornan 2012, 74).

When *Newsday* introduced its iPad app in the fall of 2010, it did so with a commercial that should have been titled "News on the Fly." It showed a man having breakfast with his family and reading *Newsday* on his iPad. "The new *Newsday* app is better than paper in all kinds of ways," the announcer says, while the man looks up to glare at an annoying housefly buzzing around his head. Then – SMASH! – he bludgeons the fly with his tablet, scattering glass and bits of plastic all over the table, and scaring the bejesus out of his family. "Except for one," the announcer says, as the man picks up pieces of glass. "Get *Newsday*, in a whole new way. Every day" (YouTube 2010).

The message is clear: We can forget that confusing, disorganized Internet and throw away our newspapers, but we can still go back to the way things used to be. Even the close-ups of the iPad as the man reads it make it clear that this is an enhanced news*paper* experience. He scrolls. He turns the screen from portrait to landscape perspective. He enlarges pictures. In other words, he does exactly the kinds of things people do with newspapers. And, to hammer home the point, he gets so immersed in the experience that he tries to squash a fly with his tablet: "the same pages turning, the same staffing structures, the same reporting remit and revenue routines, but this time on a screen in your briefcase or handbag" (Preston 2011).

If you need further proof of the newspaper business's enthusiasm for the tablet, consider that even Rupert Murdoch likes it. In fact, he liked it before it existed. In May 2009, in an interview with his Fox News network, he predicted that inside two years, "you may get [the newspaper] on a panel which would be mobile, which will receive the whole newspaper over the air, be updated every hour or two. You'll be able to get the guts or the main headlines and alerts and everything on your Blackberry, on your Palm or whatever, all day long" (Agence France-Presse 2009). Roughly a year later, after Apple brought out the iPad, and Microsoft, Samsung, Sony, and RIM were scrambling to catch up, Murdoch announced plans to start a new newspaper dedicated to the device. Nothing you could swat a fly with – just plastic, glass, aluminum, and magic. Rumours were circulating about high-priced talent hired and big-name freelancers contacted. Murdoch told his news network that his "No. 1 most exciting project" was the *Daily* (Pompeo 2010). Then, when he launched the subscription-only *Daily* in February 2011, he declared that the news business had "to completely reimagine our craft" (Gustin 2011). It was unveiled at a press conference with Apple's vice-president of Internet services. Part of the announcement included a detailed description of the *Daily*'s terms of service, and the fact that it would allow one-click subscriptions and was available for either $1 a week or $40 a year.

Six months later, Apple announced the licensing of app number 500,000 – roughly fourteen months after the company had launched the iPad. At that time, only 3 per cent of the apps were news, compared to 15 per cent games, 14 per cent books, and 11 per cent general entertainment. Apparently, Lippmann's phantom public was alive and well, and haunting the digital world. One of the top US app designers complained that the mistake publishers were making was to try to replicate the newspaper experience digitally. "They have to reinvent, not redesign," he said (Preston 2011). By the summer of 2012, the *Daily* was losing $30 million per year and had reportedly been put "on watch" – that its continued existence would be re-evaluated after the US presidential election in November (Stoeffel 2012). In December, it was shut down.

As *Columbia Journalism Review*'s Dean Starkman pointed out at the time, all that the *Daily*'s death proved was that one tablet newspaper had failed to attract a loyal audience. Yet that didn't stop pundits from rushing in to perform the autopsy:

The obits were numerous indeed, and each provided smart technical reasons for the quick shuttering of Rupert Murdoch's experiment in tablet-based newspapering.

Felix Salmon says the failure proves the impossibility of tablet-native journalism and the limits generally of news applications, as opposed to more open web-based platforms.

Jack Shafer says *The Daily* didn't lose the game; it just ran out of time, as a distracted Murdoch pulled the plug on an experiment that had yet to run its course.

Slate's Will Oremus blamed the fact that it was available for most of its life only on the iPad, sharply limiting its audience.

Former staffer Trevor Butterworth blamed the paywall.

Derek Thompson of the *Atlantic* also faulted its self-contained structure, saying it doubled down on the mobile trend, but not on the sharing trend.

Alex Madrigal of the *Atlantic* offered three theses, including that it tried to control distribution and was, again, not made for sharing. (2012).

The belief that aggregators wouldn't colonize these devices was a bit naive. Organizations like *Huffington Post*, *Reddit*, and *Buzzfeed* were quick to produce their own apps. And it took a little more than four months after Apple launched the iPad for something unique to the tablet to come along. Advertised as "the world's first personalized, social magazine," *Flipboard* culls information from a variety of sources and, as PC *World* put it, combines them "into an attractive, remarkably intuitive layout that *closely duplicates the look and feel of a print publication* [my italics]." The magazine also called the app "Rupert Murdoch's nightmare" (Wilson 2010). And, then there is *Circa*, an entire app/publication built on the inverted pyramid. *Circa* stories are delivered like Pablum to a baby – one spoonful at a time. The first screen may be a headline, a picture, and a lead paragraph. Then you swipe to get another paragraph, and then another, until you lose interest and wander off looking for something else to play with. For news delivery, Postmedia's Wayne Parrish says, this is the wave of the future. "The article is no longer the base unit, or should no longer be the base unit of content. The base unit of content is a tweet or a photo, or a video, or a fax, or a quote. And it sort of builds from that base. If you think about that, if you think about the world from that perspective, then you don't focus so much on creating articles to read on a smart phone. You create nuggets or pieces of content, or pieces of information in a timely manner."

Roughly a year after the launch of the iPad, the Pew Centre's 2011 Project for Excellence in Journalism found that 27 per cent of Americans were getting their news on smart phones and tablets; traditional news companies were holding their ground and still providing most of the news being read digitally; unique visits to online news sites were continuing to grow, up 17 per cent over 2010 (Bauder 2012).

Two years after the iPad's arrival, the ten most downloaded titles for its Newsstand app were: the *New York Times*, *The Daily*, *New Yorker*, *Men's Health*, *National Geographic*, *Cosmopolitan*, *GQ*, *O The Oprah Magazine*, *Popular Science*, and *Consumer Reports*. Only two were newspapers (in fact, they're the only two in the top twenty), and one of these was losing $30 million per year. Of the rest of the top twenty, ten dealt with health, fitness, beauty, or other forms of self-help, three were general-interest magazines, two were science magazines, one was a high-tech magazine, and one was the always indispensible *Consumer Reports* (Botelho 2012).

By early 2014, the tablet had begun to make a big impact on Canadian newspaper reading habits: *La Presse* reported 400,000 downloads of its mobile app; 58 per cent of Postmedia's online traffic came through mobile apps; the *Globe and Mail* was getting 40 per cent of its readership on mobile devices (Baluja 2014a).

Meanwhile, according to Pew's 2014 *State of the News Media* report, online news agencies had started to get serious about news: 500 US digital news agencies employed some 5,000 journalists and a major growth area was foreign coverage, with *Vice Media*, *Huffington Post*, and *Buzzfeed* all having opened overseas bureaus and/or editions. The report found that "the vast majority of bodies producing original reporting still comes from the newspaper industry," but that number had shrunk by 6.4 per cent in 2012, just as online news employment was growing (Mitchell 2014). The survey also revealed that the former audience was doing its bit to help drive the agenda, with half of social media users sharing news items, and 11 per cent of all online news consumers posting content. There was no mention of whether that content was dominated by Iraq or the Kardashians.

Still, *Columbia Journalism Review*'s Ryan Chittum says, many newspapers are lagging behind in adapting to technology. "Tablets are an opportunity – and one newspapers haven't really used well yet – to turn their print subscribers into digital ones. If you can find a way that you can charge the same amount of money – just read it on their iPad or whatever ... It's digital, but it's just like a newspaper."

The emerging newspaper company strategy – at least in Canada – is a four-platform one: print, online, tablet, and smart phone. Most of the people I spoke to believe special content will be created for each, and readers' expectations will be different for each. For example, the Montreal *Gazette*'s Raymond Brassard sees mobile as "far and away the number one platform. Tablets are more leisurely, but smart phones are the workhorses of information. That's how you're going to get everything instantly. You have to be sitting down and ready to invest a little bit of time to play with a tablet."

Postmedia began to implement this four-tier strategy in May 2014, when the company rolled out a redesign of the *Ottawa Citizen* newspaper, website, and mobile apps, which make everything – print, online, or mobile – look a bit like a Windows 8 menu. While the website and phone editions remain behind metered paywalls, the tablet app is an evening paper, available by subscription or with individual editions for $1.99. It is also possible to download a digital version of the *Citizen* print product onto tablet (which seems a bit superfluous, like a Blu-Ray player that also plays VHS tapes). The major technology change is that, to read the *Citizen* on tablet, the reader downloads that edition, which is a slickly designed product that looks more like a magazine than a newspaper. It has a slide-bar navigation tool that makes it possible to thumb through the edition much the way one thumbs through a magazine. The smart phone app caters to the user who wants news at a glance, delivering the "nuggets" that Parrish talked about: short, sometimes flippant digests of news stories, as well as breaking news items updated paragraph by paragraph. Oddly, the money-making print edition is the weak link, with an icon-laden design that is almost anti-print. It also suffers from severely abbreviated entertainment, lifestyles, and business coverage, and a noticeably impoverished weekend section. Both print and tablet editions deliver sit-down reads, the latter aiming "to recapture that afternoon newspaper vibe that was mostly lost to television news some years ago," Nieman Journalism Lab director Joshua Benton told the *Globe and*

Mail (Bradshaw 2014). In October and November 2014, Postmedia launched "reimagined" versions of Montreal's *Gazette* and the *Calgary Herald*.

Meanwhile, there is a growing dissatisfaction with Apple and its Newsstand app. Though the company plays its cards close to the vest, Apple nets around 14 per cent on the average selling price of an app (Yarow and Angelova 2011). How it charges for free apps is not clear, but it is obvious that newspapers are taking a loss in giving their apps away, on the theory that free apps will drive paid circulation. The way Newsstand has been working, a publication that is sold through it forfeits the right to sell its app as a stand-alone, and many have complained that Newsstand creates a dumping ground – "the place apps go to be forgotten," as John Gruber writes (quoted in Kozlowski 2013).

If you say almost anything good about print, you're made to feel as if you're smashing looms or hollering "Get a horse" at steam buggies. As Bob Franklin (2008) argues, it is a discourse marked by dogmatism: print versus Internet. If you admit there are things about print you like, you are considered a bunion on the big toe of progress, and likely to start murdering smart phones and bludgeoning Retina displays if we don't keep an eye on you. Yet, there are all kinds of technical-minded people who actually like print. For example, Vancouver futurist and digital consultant Todd Maffin says he regularly unplugs, to clear his mind and let his ears stop ringing:

> I do it twice a year. I call it "stepping off the grid." I'll just go offline for three or four, or five days at a time. But I do find that I have to warn people that I'm about to do it. I have an email mailing list that are my closest friends. I put on my Facebook wall and send out to that email list that until such-and-such a date, I'm going to be off the grid. If you absolutely have to reach me, leave a message; I will check my voicemail once a day. And then I go for walks. I have an enormous amount of books that I want to get to. And there are afternoons where I will crawl into my pyjamas. I will get into bed. I will turn every electronic device in my home off. And I'll just read. And that keeps me going for two weeks. That gives me energy and heals the electronic world for a while. It's a

matter of finding quiet, of getting away from the dings and the dongs. Technology is very intrusive.

Bill Gates once said in a speech: "Reading off the screen is still vastly inferior to reading off of paper. Even I, who have these expensive screens and fancy myself a pioneer of the Web Lifestyle, when it comes to something over about four or five pages, I print it out and I like to carry it around with me and annotate. And it's quite a hurdle for technology to achieve to match that level of usability" (Darnton 2009, 69).

As historian Robert Darnton says, our digital fascination appears to have passed through three stages: utopian enthusiasm, in which we expect the new technology to accomplish all things; disillusionment when we find out the new technology cannot accomplish all things; pragmatism, when we accept that the new technology is still pretty good after all, even though it cannot accomplish all things (2009, 69). He further talks about past technologies that were expected to be a radical improvement over print, such as microfilm and microfiche, which degrade much more rapidly than paper and, in some cases, actually make people motion-sick when they try to read them (a library in Toronto keeps airline vomit bags near its microfilm readers). And often, when material is moved from print to microfilm, the print version is destroyed, abandoning a technology that has proved tremendously adaptable and durable for one that was a flop, and putting a great deal of information at risk of being lost forever (112–14). This raises the spectre of what an electromagnetic pulse could do to a society that keeps all its records online.

This is not to say print will always offer a superior reading experience. Though backlit screens tend to be harsh and hard on the eyes, readers such as Kobo and Kindle are remarkably similar to books and, from an aesthetic standpoint, are easily equal to a paperback. Tablet resolution is almost startling in its clarity. Smart phones are the greatest invention since the personal computer.

Still, nothing can equal the sensual beauty of a leather-and-gold bound first edition or is likely to reproduce the visual splendour of a printed coffee-table book filled with photographs and illustrations. And tablets are, at best, a second-rate way to read a graphic novel. Also, it's hard to see how a tablet can replace a thick weekend newspaper, with its pile of special sections waiting to be spread out on the living room floor and passed around from person to person. The daily *New York Times* can be reproduced on tablet or smart phone, but the *Sunday Times* cannot – and if it could, it could not be shared.

One thing we forget in our rush to digital delivery is that there are aesthetic sensibilities and conventions that make the newspaper – and magazine and book – valuable as popular culture. What makes print "such a perfect delivery vehicle for news" is its graphic design (Manjoo 2009). Print products are friendly to the eye and comfortable to hold, and combine words, pictures, and graphic design in ways that are satisfying, occasionally dazzling, and often just plain fun. And they offer escape from the "dings and dongs" of technology.

For example, in 2009, writer Dave Eggers and a "tribe of likeminded San Franciscans" created a 320-page one-shot newspaper called *Panorama*. It was printed in broadsheet format (15 by 22 inches) and had a price tag of $16 a copy. It sold out immediately, "foretelling a time when a printed newspaper will be a luxury item, a mass-niche product that many people will pay a great deal of money to get their hands on" (Carr 2009c).

Another advantage to paper is that it is harder to censor than the Internet. There's no switch you can flick to shut down all the presses in a country; yet you can do just that with websites that you want to make difficult to access, the way China does with its Great Firewall, and as Washington and its allies did with WikiLeaks. We may find that the old-fashioned *samizdat* may be the best way for dissident opinion to cut through censorship – and white noise.

7

Craft:
A View from the Shop

Financial apocalypse and technological utopianism so dominate the conversation that it often seems as if the quieter discourse about the state of the craft, which has been going on since long before there was an Internet, simply went away. Yet with the institution of paywalls comes the realization that newspapers have begun to operate in a competitive environment, in many cases for the first time in decades. As Ryan Chittum wrote, "a paywall imposes the quality imperative" (2014c). "You've got to charge people," he told me. "You've got to put out a good product; you've got to put out something that people have to read, or really want to read. You've got to charge for it, and you've got to make advertisers understand the value of it."

So, the conversation about quality *hasn't* gone away, and there are strong reasons that it should be getting more intense. The justification for complacency has evaporated, but the old complaints remain: editorial blandness and timidity; creativity squelching, penny-wise management; dollar-foolish ownership. At the beginning of the 2008 recession, Todd Gitlin argued that there were "five wolves" at the door of US journalism, not just three. Concern about falling circulation, dwindling advertising lineage, and increased competition for the public's attention had overshadowed a severe "crisis of authority" and "journalism's inability or unwillingness to penetrate the veil of obfuscation behind which power conducts its risky business" (2009).

Former *Vanity Fair* and *New Yorker* editor, and founder of the *Daily Beast,* Tina Brown put it in earthier terms. At the depths of the recession, when all the focus was on the broken business model, she wrote: "American newspapers ... needed to innovate back in the Fax Age of the 1980s but were too self-important and making too much money with their monopolies to acknowledge it ... It's one of the biggest fibs going that American newspapers are now being forced to give up their commitment to investigative reporting. Most of them gave up long ago as their greedy managements squeezed every cent out of the bottom line and turned their newsrooms into eunuchs." Brown also points out that "furrow browed" British quality dailies, such as the *Times* and the *Guardian*, long ago redesigned themselves to be more colourful and reader friendly, and that they manage to blend "'sexy' culture coverage and hip fashion stories as well as foreign reporting and brainiac columnists that make them a guilty pleasure to read" (2010).

Torontonians with long memories have some idea of what Brown is talking about. In the fall of 1998, Conrad Black founded the right-wing daily the *National Post* and gave the paper an almost unlimited budget with which to cause trouble. The editors of the new paper – many of whom had been imported from Britain, where Black owned the *Telegraph* at the time – brought with them a taste for literary journalism, a sense of irreverence, meanness, and fun, and a killer competitive instinct that, for a time, revitalized the Toronto newspaper scene.

At about the same time, the entrenched competition, the staid old *Globe and Mail*, hired a British publisher named Phillip Crawley, who in turn hired several British journalists, including editor Richard Addis, to brighten up the paper and make it more competitive with the *Post* – to fight fire with fire. The *Post* was "beautifully laid out and fun to read ... with big, striking photographs, gorgeous women and an airy, modern design ... Silly and smart-ass stories ran on the front page alongside alarmist headlines and columns that boiled the blood of left-leaning readers." The *Globe*, meanwhile, was a typical, earnest North American newspaper: an "icon of Canadian journalism ... boring and stuffy, which earned it the nickname 'the old grey *Globe*'" (Bell 2000). By most accounts, the *Globe and Mail*'s British imports antagonized almost everyone – co-workers and readers, along with the competition. But they succeeded in moving the paper slightly to the left – to offer an alternative to the *National Post*'s rabid, occasionally irrational, right-wing bias – and made the paper livelier, smarter, more interesting, more humane, and, once in a while, surprising.

With the predictable, earnest *Toronto Star*, the tabloid *Toronto Sun*, and the two British-style national papers, for a few short years – until

Canwest bought the *Post* and began slashing the budget, and the *Globe* shifted right and reverted to form – Toronto was arguably the best city for newspapers in North America. It was also one of only three or four in which dailies still had to compete for readers – and that meant they had to seek out, hire, and employ talented people. "I think the launch of the *National Post* in '98, for a brief shining period of three or four years, changed the equation, because Conrad went out and started hiring people, stealing people at significant rates," Postmedia's Wayne Parrish says. "The *Globe* got very serious about bringing in talent, and the *Star* defended its territory. And so, I think, for a period of time you had what was kind of – when I look back on it – a kind of nirvana in terms of Canadian journalism."

There's no doubt that, at that time, the *National Post* and the *Globe and Mail* were exactly the kind of compelling, thought-provoking "guilty pleasures" Brown wrote about, but it's debatable whether jazzing up the product would have made a difference to *Globe* circulation absent the competition. While Torontonians were enjoying some of the best journalism in North America, in many one-newspaper towns across Canada – including those Black had weakened to help finance and staff the *Post* – journalism was as dull, predictable, and bland as ever. "There were two schools of thought about Conrad Black," Ryerson University's John Miller says. "Yes, he had improved papers like the *Ottawa Citizen*, and he created the *National Post*, and he enhanced the salaries of the top journalists. But he was engaging in a business plan that made a lot of other newspapers suffer to pay for that." Yet, even at his worst, Black never did the kind of damage some other proprietors, such as Thomson, Canwest, Postmedia, or especially Quebecor, have done to Canadian newspapers.

As the business has been battered by bad news about circulation and advertising, newspapers have shrunk in page size and number, sections have been cut, bureaus closed, beats shut down, and journalists laid off in droves. Many newspaper publishers have remained true to form in underestimating the intelligence of their readers and have attempted to sell the cutbacks as improvements. For example, cutting the Arts section down to three pages and moving it to the back of Sports becomes, "We know you lead a busy life, so we've reorganized Arts to make it easier to find and faster to read!"

The nation's poet laureate of corporate double-speak is Quebecor, which has established a pattern of accompanying layoffs with press releases touting its greatness of vision. "That's not the type of tone you typically see when there are layoffs," the *Globe and Mail*'s Steve Ladurantaye says. "You typically see a reluctance, a remorse. You don't see that kind of brazen, bottom-line speech in that sort of thing ... 'We're blazing new trails. We're doing new things. We're doing things in a way that nobody else has. We're going to be hugely profitable. This is all for the greater good. And we're sorry that we're closing your newspaper.'"

By 2012, the cynicism had grown so thick that even Superman left the newsroom, to become mild-mannered blogger Clark Kent. Driven to despair by a management obsessed with happy news, and after more than seven decades on the staff of the *Daily Planet*, Kent finally threw in his keyboard, but not before exhaling a *cri de coeur* that plays as if it were written by an ex-newsman:

> The truth is that somewhere along the way, the business of news became the news. Growing up in Smallville, I believed that journalism was an ideal, as worthy and important as being a cop, a fireman, a teacher or a doctor. I was taught to believe you could use words to change the course of rivers – that even the darkest secrets would fall under the harsh light of the sun. But facts have been replaced by opinions. Information has been replaced by entertainment. Reporters have become stenographers. I can't be the only one who is sick at the thought of what passes for news today. I am not the only one who believes in the power of the press. The fact that we need to stand up for truth. For Justice. And yeah – I'm not ashamed to say – the American Way. (Lobdell and Rocafort 2012)

The style is ripe, and the corn grows as high as an elephant's eye, but the authors certainly haven't got their facts wrong in terms of the general feeling among the rank and file about media management. All the cutting and firing "have made a difference, eroding the quality, the essentiality, and certainly the uniqueness of what [newspapers] have to offer" (Tofel 2012, 109). At the same time, there seems to be an almost delusional belief on the part of some management that the new environment can be bent to accommodate the old ways of doing things, and bromides, resolutions, and catchphrases are supposed to somehow motivate each member of a demoralized, decimated workforce to do the work of ten. As a senior reporter who requested anonymity put it:

> Management will occasionally send these academics across the country, and they'll land in our newsroom and give a half-hour dissertation on mobile, or citizen journalism. But they often seem to be speaking from the 30,000-foot view without recognizing the limitations on our time, just from a day-to-day pragmatic perspective ... The reality of the job is that you're constantly on a treadmill. You're always two steps behind. There's always too much going on ... So, when somebody comes from head office and talks about the glories of digital media, and all these opportunities, he's talking to somebody who's way overstretched most of the time, and just trying to put out fires. So there's kind of a big disconnect.

For the brave, the independent, and the lucky, technology has opened up new frontiers of employment and agency. Anyone can launch an alternative publication, use social media and blogging to build his or her brand, and master coding that enables the creation of everything from interactive graphics to automated research tools. As Mark Deuze writes, the news workplace is offering a stable, salaried work week for fewer people, and more are finding themselves in the "portfolio workshop of the self-employed 'cultural entrepreneur'" who is "living in a state of constant change, while at the same time seemingly enjoying a sense of control over one's career" (2007, 23).

Like many digitally born utopian theories, Deuze's vision lacks nuance. He is describing an ideal state that is somewhat divorced from human reality. The fluid workforce may be a reality for some people, who move from job to job, project to project, and team to team. For many, however, change has meant unemployment, under-employment, or a scramble just to earn a subsistence living while trying to make sense of the surreal fact that senior executive compensation keeps rising while company revenues keep dropping.

It is the segment of the news business that traditionally employs the most people in the best jobs that has taken the biggest hit. North America has seen a hollowing-out of the mid-market, especially in the United States. However, in terms of national and international news coverage, that has been somewhat balanced by a rise in international dailies such as the *Guardian, Telegraph, Wall Street Journal, New York Times*, and *MailOnline*. For the most part, there has been no such substitute for the alternative weeklies across the continent – long an antidote to the mainstream journalism of those mid-market dailies. They have been hammered by the demise of classified ads. For example, Montreal was once home to four alt-weeklies in two languages. Today, there is one. The venerable Boston *Phoenix* folded in 2013; Victoria's *Monday Magazine* closed the same year. In February 2015, the Calgary alt-weekly FFWD was shuttered by its owner, Great West Newspapers. Yet, we may be seeing the beginnings of an online alternative press, in sites ranging from *Truthdig* to Vancouver's *The Tyee* and Halifax's subscription-only online news daily *allNovaScotia.com*, to *Voice of San Diego* and *MinnPost*, to *Politico* and *ProPublica*, to Glenn Greenwald's and eBay founder Pierre Omidyar's *The Intercept*.

There also is some hope to be found in the interest on the part of the big dailies in hyper-local journalism, and the resiliency of the small-market dailies and community papers. This has been less so in Ontario, where Quebecor's cutbacks gutted dozens of the small-market dailies it acquired over the years. Also on the negative side of the ledger is the strong possibility that community papers may not be doing things much better than mid-size dailies did – but the digital wave has yet to break on them. For example, when I spoke at an Alberta weekly newspaper conference in 2013, I was astonished by how little interest there was among the business-side people in new forms of journalism. They discussed such things as government advertising, better postal rates, and the cost of newsprint. But when I started to talk about using online resources to extend coverage and reach in their areas, and to bring new services to their readers, you could almost hear the eyes rolling back in their sockets. In contrast, many of the journalists seemed excited by the possibilities presented by multimedia storytelling, podcasting, and audience participation. This tension between journalism and business will be familiar to anyone who has worked in a Canadian newsroom. This is one of the few industries in which much – if not most – of management strives to *suppress* the ambition and ingenuity of its workforce.

Conrad Black is a convicted white-collar criminal, a TV personality, and a businessman who once owned a chain of newspapers that more or less dominated English Canada. So, when he is asked about the state of the news media, you might expect him to deliver the party line about the perfect storm of recession, Internet, and broken business model. But he has been brutally blunt about the state of the news business: "It's slowly collapsing under the weight of its own substandards," he told *Maclean's* magazine. As for the blame: "The buck stops with the proprietor" (Kirby 2010). Another way of putting it is the proverb, "A fish rots from the head."

As we have seen, critics of newspaper management who were harsh in the 1990s and 2000s have become brutal in recent years, with some justification. News proprietors and executives have consistently cut the quality and standards of their product, and slashed their workforces while often rewarding themselves with handsome bonuses. For example, the Gannett chain, long associated with low-cost, low-quality journalism, big profits, and shareholder satisfaction, has been identified as a premier example of "bonus excess despite miserable operations," *New York Times* media reporter David Carr writes. In 2011, a week before its flagship newspaper USA *Today* published an editorial attacking Wall Street bonuses, the company paid outgoing CEO Craig A. Dubow $37.1 million in retirement, health, and disability benefits, following $16 million in salary and bonuses over the last two years of his tenure. This is a newspaper chain that saw its stock tumble from $75 to $10 a share and its staff cut by 10,000, a company that "strip-mined its newspapers in search of earnings, leaving many communities with far less original, serious reporting" (Carr 2011b).

Another example of gross mismanagement is that of the Tribune Company under billionaire investor Sam Zell. Following the populist wisdom that the best way to deal with underperformance is to replace people who know what they're doing with people who don't, Zell drew a whole layer of top management from his radio holdings, led by former shock jock and Clear Channel executive Randy Michaels. Longtime Tribune news executive and onetime editor-in-chief of the *Los Angeles Times*, James O'Shea describes Michaels as someone who had a reputation for being a brilliant radio man, as well as a "boor" and serial sexual harasser, and whose plan for newspapers was to emulate Matt Drudge and Fox News. Michaels's plan for revitalizing Tribune included identifying "change leaders and resisters ... promot[ing] and eliminat[ing] as appropriate," and "identifying people in the company he could 'get to drink the Kool-Aid'" (2011, 289–90).

In a lengthy investigative feature for the *New York Times*, David Carr described the "sexual innuendo, poisonous workplace banter and profane invective" of the company under Michaels and his associates. "They threw out what Tribune had stood for, quality journalism and a real brand integrity, and in just a year pushed it down into mud and bankruptcy," media analyst Ken Doctor told Carr. Michaels was in charge from January 2008, a year before the company went into Chapter 11 bankruptcy protection, to October 2010. Between May 2009 and February 2010, $57.3 million in bonuses was paid to Tribune managers, "with the approval of the judge overseeing the bankruptcy" (2010).

It is difficult to reconcile a story like that with the common refrain that, if we lose these organizations, we place democracy in jeopardy. The nostalgia about newspapers' role in serving and preserving democracy is rather overstated, Jack Shafer argues, because, for management, it has always been about serving the power elite and reaping the rewards thereof. "Let's take off the rosy glasses, about the newspaper," he says. "Lots and lots of these newspapers, especially where they had a monopoly privilege, were sort of indistinguishable from the ruling elite of each of those towns. They were one of the players. Not all of them are crusading against hegemonic political order ... I'm less worried about newspapers vanishing than I am about the news."

In Canada, the situation is nowhere near as profligate, though that doesn't mean no Canadian business executives have profited from journalism's losses. At Postmedia, for example, the financial pain has yet to penetrate the executive offices. In 2013, compensation for CEO Paul Godfrey rose by 50 per cent, to $1.7 million from $1.1 million in 2012, while the chain posted a $154 million loss (Ladurantaye 2013c). Godfrey could argue that he is simply following company tradition. When Postmedia's predecessor, Canwest, filed for bankruptcy protection, bonuses of $9.8 million were approved for its executives (Gatehouse 2009).

At Quebecor, the record was one of cutbacks and consolidation, which is particularly confusing when you figure that, when it agreed to sell its English-Canadian holdings to Postmedia in 2014, the company owned 167 community papers, specialty publications, and small dailies across Canada – exactly the products that are supposedly thriving in the era of Internet competition and hyper-local news coverage. Yet, the conversational thread among employees of Quebecor's small papers at the *Toronto Sun Family* blog (torontosunfamily.blogspot.ca 2014) has been one long growl of discontent, punctuated by shrieks of fury – culminating in 2015 in a deathwatch, as employees waited for Postmedia to take over and start the next purge. The focus has been almost exclusively on layoffs, cutbacks, office closings, and centralization of editorial production and advertising sales. The impression one got reading these posts was that Quebecor had completely given up these papers' primary market advantage: their closeness to their communities. To show the viability of many of these markets, in many of the southern Ontario communities Quebecor abandoned, Torstar's Metroland chain has moved in and, in some, former Sun Media people have launched replacement publications. "[Metroland] is eating their lunch," the *Globe and Mail*'s Steve Ladurantaye says. "In Peterborough, we competed with a Metroland paper ... And we were consistently getting our asses handed to us by Metroland. And there's no reason for that to happen. It was simply a question of staffing. There's no way a daily newspaper should be the second player in a city under any circumstances. And that's what seemed to be happening with a lot of the Sun papers."

It's fairly clear that Quebecor was harvesting the operations to finance growth in other areas, and then had a going-out-of-business sale for the dead stock and fixtures. As for Postmedia, the main attractions appear to be the online properties, a few remaining physical assets, and the elimination of competition in some major centres. As former *Ottawa Sun* publisher Rick Gibbons says, Quebecor's strategy made sense from a purely business perspective. "Is Quebecor reinvesting the profits of its newspapers into growth areas, like wireless, etc.? I don't speak for the business at all, but I would suggest such a strategy would be exactly the right thing to do. Invest in growth. Quebecor has built a diverse corporation with a future much stronger and more viable in the long term than some of its competitors who are stuck knee-deep in a single media play like newspapers."

Still, harvesting is a particularly ugly strategy. Alex S. Jones writes that it is

> a business euphemism for stripping the carcass of every bit of flesh and then abandoning the pile of bones. It is a strategy designed

for businesses for which there is no prospect of salvation, and it is nasty ... For newspapers, harvesting would work this way. In the first five years, the industry-standard 20 percent profit margin might be greatly increased through cutting news staff – especially the most experienced people, who would likely be the highest paid. You would shrink the space for news, get rid of health insurance and other perks, and narrow the size to save on paper. You could save money by forbidding travel to cover news, require the remaining reporters to do multiple stories to make up for those who were laid off, cram the paper with syndicated material and wire services, avoid coverage that might anger advertisers or readers, and squeeze every dime you can out of the operating budget. The newspaper would still be produced. Its news columns would still be filled with words on paper that would look like news. But the enterprise that had been a living thing would essentially be a zombie. (2009, 162)

Jones goes on to describe a spiral in which readers and advertisers turn away but the momentum of the newspaper carries it for a few years while the company milks the final profits out of it. As Carleton University's Catherine McKercher says, "harvesting" is simply a soft euphemism for something hard and mean: "You can call it harvesting. I call it looting: When we're done, we'll just leave the carcass, and it will be somebody else's opportunity."

Often, however, even that opportunity has been polluted. Since harvesting can be a long, painful, drawn-out process, the result can be more than simply the death of a newspaper, Ryerson University's John Miller says. It can also do irreparable damage to a market. As a publication carries less and less local news, as Quebecor products did, readers lose the habit of turning to the paper to find out what is happening in their community. "They may poison the market for anybody else coming along and starting a paper. People begin to think there's nothing here. There's nothing happening. 'I don't need to stay in touch. I don't care any more. I'm too busy. I'm not even going to vote. I don't know who's running.' There's a snowball effect. It starts affecting democracy."

The financial crisis in the news business, Richard Tofel writes, is the product of an industry that was able to attract the best and brightest to the ranks of its craft, but not to the business. "The best young reporters and editors aspired to go to work at precisely the companies where the young executives with the highest potential did not" (2012, 62–3). As a result, as early as the 1970s, the craft side had begun to feel strangled by a business side that lacked vision, daring, and even "basic self-confidence, [and] tended to employ rafts of consultants, often placed minimal emphasis on innovation and frequently knew little about technologies in their embryonic stages" (65–6). For bright business-school graduates, the established, entrenched newspaper business, with its culture of risk avoidance, was not an employer of choice, as were the burgeoning high-tech industries and the instant-wealth machines of Wall Street.

If there is a measure of how far down the business has dragged the craft, it may be found in a letter former USA *Today* publisher and one-time Gannett chairman of the board Allen Neuharth sent to current USA *Today* publisher David L. Hunke in 2010. Neuharth, the architect of Gannett's method of driving up profit margins to satisfy shareholder expectations, was outraged that the paper had given over its front page to a wrap-around advertisement for Jeep. In the letter, he described it as "the low point in any decision any USA *Today* publisher has ever made." If it had happened during his tenure as publisher, Neuharth wrote, he would have led the staff in a walkout "that would leave those who apparently don't understand what a newspaper is to try to put one out without a news staff" (Peters 2010).

Out in the world, people don't often differentiate between poor news organizations and poor journalism. Journalists constantly fare poorly in public opinion surveys about the professions. To a certain extent this can be written off to kill-the-messenger syndrome: people within the craft have long taken public anger to be proof that they are doing their jobs. However, throughout the recession, public opinion of journalism has continued to slide – not a positive sign for a field trying to convince people of its value to society.

The following is by no means a complete or scientific survey of public opinion, but it does provide a series of snapshots of North Americans' feelings about their news media.

In May 2008, the Canadian Media Research Consortium released a report on Canadians' relationship with the press that updated a similar study conducted in 2003. The "two main problem areas" identified were "declining interest and increasing cynicism." A little more than half the respondents believed news organizations got their facts straight, between a quarter (aged 19–34) and a third (all ages) said news organizations were willing to admit their mistakes, and a bit more than half believed news organizations were careful to check their facts. Finally, "nearly two-thirds of Canadians said they believed the news media cover up their mistakes" (CMRC 2008). Similarly, in 2011, the periodic *Reader's Digest* poll of "The Professions We Trust Most" placed journalists near the bottom, in 30th place out of 41, just behind financial advisers, domestic cleaners, and lawyers, and just ahead of taxi drivers, mechanics, and home building contractors.

That doesn't tell us anything other than what *Digest* readers think of journalists, but, still, something odd turned up a month later in an online Angus Reid poll of 1,682 Canadian adults. The headline declared: "Even in the Digital Era, Canadians Have Confidence in Mainstream Media" (CMRC 2011b). In this poll, 90 per cent of respondents of all ages and 88 per cent aged 19–34 rated the information in newspapers as "very reliable" or "reliable." For television news, the rating was 90 per cent and 86 per cent respectively and, for online news, 89 per cent and 86 per cent. The lowest rating went to social networks and blogs, with 26 per cent and 33 per cent. Two key findings of the study were: "Professional editing inspires more confidence than 'crowd editing' on wikis and similar sites; most Canadians believe professional journalism is better at performing critical democratic functions than citizen journalism."

In the United States, public opinion of the press has mostly followed a consistent downward trajectory. In the March 2009 issue of the *New Republic*, the article "MSM, RIP" revealed that 36 per cent of Americans believed that the press "hurts democracy." Predictably the harshest critics were found at either end of the political spectrum, with left and right slamming "the same villain: the hypocritical biased elite media." Some of the criticism, the magazine reported, was creating a "poisonous atmosphere" that destroys the press's "authority in the culture." An example of typical rhetoric was this generalization from a screed by a *Huffington Post* blogger: "Beltway media really makes no effort to do anything other than parrot totally out-of-touch conventional wisdom – no matter how inane, stupid and ridiculous it is" (New Republic 2009).

The year finished on a down beat, with news from the Pew Research Center that only 43 per cent of Americans believed that losing their newspaper would hurt local civic life, and only 33 per cent said they would miss the daily paper if it were gone (Pew 2009). A year later, Gallup's annual *Confidence in Institutions* poll revealed that Americans were continuing to "express near-record-low confidence in newspapers and television news." This study claimed that "no more than 25 percent" of respondents said they had "a great deal" or "quite a lot" of confidence in print and broadcast journalism. The poll also revealed that Americans trusted newspapers about as much as they did banks, and slightly more than health management organizations and big business (Morales 2010).

In 2011, there was a slight rebound in the US press's public image, followed by more punches in the gut. In June, Gallup's Confidence in Institutions poll showed the press up slightly: 28 per cent of respondents said they had a "great deal" or "quite a lot" of confidence in newspapers, up from 25 per cent in 2010; and TV news jumped from 22 per cent to 27 per cent (Meares 2011).

Sometimes it seemed as if pollsters were working overtime to come up with novel ways for the public to express its disdain. In September 2011, Pew released a poll in which 42 per cent of the respondents described American journalism as "immoral," compared to 38 per cent who considered the business "moral." The public was evenly split – 42 per cent each – over whether the press helped or hurt democracy, and two-thirds believed news stories were often inaccurate, compared to roughly a third in 1985. Finally, only 25 per cent of respondents said they thought news media get their facts straight, and 72 per cent said journalists try to cover up their mistakes (Mak 2011).

A year later, Gallup released poll results under the headline "U.S. Distrust in Media Hits New High" and reported that 60 per cent of respondents said "they have little or no trust in the mass media to report the news fully, accurately, and fairly" (Morales 2012). The next year, Gallup's annual poll showed that only 21 per cent of Americans trusted the media, ranking the industry just ahead of politics, with only a 20 per cent trust rating – cold comfort in a year that saw Congress shut down the US government in what was commonly perceived to be a cynical power play to undermine President Barack Obama (Sebelius 2013). It is probably small consolation that yet another survey showed that Americans overwhelmingly supported the idea of a watchdog press and the practices it uses to investigate public affairs (Shahid 2011).

It appears Americans like the concept of journalism, but not the practice. Beyond that, it is pretty well anyone's guess what these statistics mean. There is probably little question that the polarized state of US politics has something to do with Americans' dim view of their news media, and, as the *New Republic* argued, it is very likely that the constant attacks on the "lamestream media" have had an effect.

As for whether trivialization of the news has lessened Americans' respect for their press, even that is doubtful. As the *Columbia Journalism Review* points out, the 2011 Gallup survey that showed confidence in the press up slightly was conducted during the full frenzy of "Weinergate" – the scandal about Rep. Anthony Weiner tweeting pictures of himself wearing only his jockey shorts. At the peak of the scandal, "when many of us had our heads buried in our hands sobbing about the state of the media, those interviewed expressed an increased level of confidence in this institution" (Meares 2011).

Finally, the 2013 report of the Pew Center's Project for Excellence in Journalism unloaded both barrels on the news business's sense of self-importance and blasted away any delusions held by publishers and owners that they could bleed their businesses back to financial health. The report found that most Americans were unaware of the financial troubles in the news business but perceived a decline in quality of their daily newspaper. "With reporting resources cut to the bone and fewer specialized beats, journalists' level of expertise in any one area and the ability to go deep into a story are compromised. Indeed, when people who had heard something about the financial struggles were asked which effect they noticed more, stories that were less complete or fewer stories over all, 48% named less complete stories while 31% mostly noticed fewer stories. Overall, awareness of the industry's financial struggles is limited. Only 39% have heard a lot or some. But those with greater awareness are also more likely to be the ones who have abandoned a news outlet" (Beaujon 2013).

If the public has a low opinion of the state of journalism, so do many journalists. In the United States, where soul-searching and breast-beating are almost basic journalism skills, the craft is constantly being deconstructed and analyzed. Even in Canada, where the culture of self-criticism is weak at the best of times, prominent journalists have begun to complain about a craft that seems to have lost its way.

A lot of the criticism has a familiar ring. Anyone labouring under the idea that political journalism had evolved since the 1990s – that the insider baseball and horse-race coverage had given way to issues-driven journalism – got a bucket of cold water in the face from Andrew Coyne in 2008. Writing for *Maclean's* magazine – and strongly echoing Joan Didion's "Insider Baseball" essay of 2001 – Coyne fired a devastating barrage of criticism at the Canadian press's federal election coverage. Members of the Canadian parliamentary press corps, he wrote, were in "mortal peril of disappearing up our own backsides." Accusing the Ottawa press corps of "hurting democracy," Coyne describes the coverage as being more of everything critics had been complaining about for years: mindless recycling of the parties' daily press briefings; chasing the polls, the "gotcha question," and "silly photo op"; the search for "defining moments" and "turning points." The question that never gets answered, he wrote, was the only one about which voters care: "Who are these people and what are they going to do to us?"

If anyone in the press was listening, it wasn't reflected in the coverage of the 2011 federal election. *Globe and Mail* columnist Lawrence Martin was as scathing as Coyne had been three years earlier. The members of the Ottawa press corps, he wrote, had become old and passive, and got "co-opted" by the establishment they were supposed to cover. "Much wonderment has been expressed recently on why stories of abuse of power don't seem to hurt Stephen Harper's government. The stories don't stick … because we in the media don't stick to them. It's episodic journalism."

In the case of Andrew Coyne's comments, those complaints go back decades: journalists, especially those who cover politics, come to identify too closely with their subjects and not enough with their readers. Many critics argue that democracy is not threatened by the demise of the newspaper, because newspapers simply haven't been doing their job very well. "It certainly is a problem if people are not getting accurate information and not getting an accurate picture of what's actually going on in the society around them," says Enn Raudsepp, Concordia University distinguished professor emeritus of journalism. "It's the old bread-and-circuses thing: If you keep people amused, they're not going to think deep and hard about the issues, and that is what the media is abetting here. They're helping amuse people rather than informing them adequately and properly."

As for Lawrence Martin's complaints, they play on more recent concerns that, by constantly pruning their newsrooms, newspapers are killing themselves. "The attention span needs to be lengthened," John Miller says. "If you really believe there's a future for local newspapers, which I do, that has to change to make them have a future. They have to lengthen their attention span on certain stories that strike a chord. But that only becomes possible when you have the resources to do it. If you're stretched so thin that everybody has to cover everything, if there are no beats and no time, if you have to feed the beast every day, you can't take a couple of days to cover a further angle of something you've already published."

In the United States, the criticism is more extensive, sometimes to the point that it is difficult to keep track of it. But the shortcomings described are mostly the familiar ones: a tendency to blow up small stories and overlook big ones; short attention span; too little focus on the readers' interests; an alliance with the rich and powerful; a fear of offending anyone.

Huffington Post blogger Tom Engelhardt points out that the problem isn't with under-reported or unreported stories – as is often charged by online press critics, who tend to assume anything they hadn't heard of is brand new to the world. Rather, he echoes Martin in arguing that the problem is the inability of a diminished press to sustain coverage of news that unfolds rather than breaks:

> Media critics often focus on the year's underreported or even "unreported" stories; and yet, enveloped in a crisis of downsizing, as ads flee newspapers and magazines, the mainstream media does still manage to report on just about everything – if, that is, you're a news jockey and willing to go looking for it. Generally, we only know about those under- or unreported stories because we've read about them somewhere in the mainstream. The real reporting crisis involves the inability of the mainstream to connect the dots, almost any dots, or display any kind of historical memory, or include in its daily reporting the sort of information that would make real sense of the "news." (2012)

As most of the discourse over the past few years focused on the "broken business model," it seemed at times as if everyone had forgotten that the journalism model had been broken at least since the

1990s, and probably since the early '80s. To a certain extent, this was owing to a widespread conviction that better journalism would never make for a return to profitability, so there was little point attempting it. There was a prevailing belief that many, if not most, proprietors and publishers "are not serious about the future of journalism; they are serious about cashing in as many chips as possible before closing time" (McChesney and Nichols 2010, 14). And the craft of journalism is unlikely to flourish in organizations that are in the process of harvesting – or looting – or believe that the future lies in a drastically reduced form of online journalism, "the creation of 'content,' meaning whatever will draw eyeballs" (Jones 2009, 171).

However, that only tells part of the story. To perhaps a greater extent, the craft of journalism has developed very bad habits – some based in business dictates and some not – that are making it difficult to adapt to the new realities. There is a fear of alienating readers, offending authority and threatening the status quo. In a monopoly newspaper town, the circumstances militate against quality. "Where there is only one outlet, providing content that is highly mobilizing to 30% of the audience but alienates 70% of the audience is a bad strategy," to repeat Yochai Benkler's analysis from chapter 3. "You gain strong commitment to 30%, but if you are a local monopoly, those 30% have no real options and would have bought your product anyway, while the 70% who might have bought a bland informative media product will be turned off by, say, a highly partisan screed. The same is not true when one is faced with a field of, for example, seven media outlets of roughly similar coverage" (2011, 374).

The result is a product determined to be as uncontroversial and inoffensive as possible – and an industry that eventually forgets how to compete. Whether a newspaper is held by a chain or by a single-paper owner, under monopoly corporate ownership, the press becomes an institution in the worst sense of the term: unassailable, unresponsive, monolithic, smug, and dedicated to its own survival.

What the reader sees is a proliferation of bland service sections designed mainly to attract advertising: gardening, travel, automotive, and homes sections. Parts of the paper that traditionally blended hard news and criticism, such as entertainment and business, become boosterish and soft. Critics charge that, even in the hard-news sections, North American media are "far too polite to be subversive," unlike their "fierce, more anarchic, less obedient" British cousins (Lewis

2007), whom former British prime minister Tony Blair once described as "feral."

In Canada, CBC correspondent Neil Macdonald told a 2005 public policy forum that Canadian journalists were "far too likely to genuflect to power" and that this had made them incapable of entertaining new ideas or concepts. "Marginal voices, or voices of those who think too far outside the conventional box, are ignored ... When it comes to challenging conventional wisdom, or, better, challenging the motives and practices of business, Canadian journalists are anemic ... They have far less in common with the poor and disadvantaged and far more in common with executives and the politically powerful" (Turner 2005). Robert McChesney and John Nichols go so far as to say that "a healthy professional journalism is incompatible with corporate culture" (2010, 44–5). As a result, North American news media have become "mindless amplifiers of government claims" (43).

When it comes to stating the case for a more feral journalism, until recently there was very little business argument to make. Newspapers that had won the circulation wars in their cities had a captive audience, and it was that audience that had value, in terms of advertising revenue. Because the reader had never been made to bear more than a token part of the cost of collecting and publishing news, the content was worthless. "Concentration wasn't the issue," York University's Fred Fletcher says. "The issue was corporate ownership. Especially when corporations had interests outside the media – being really part of the corporate elite. It didn't matter if it was one giant *Toronto Star*, or *Globe*, without another newspaper, or any other outlets, they're still parroting the same corporate line."

Now, with the stampede of competition that arrived with the Internet, newspapers have had to learn how to compete, or how to die. Unfortunately, most seem to be leaning towards the latter. For example, as we saw in chapter 3, the *Globe and Mail* appears bent on importing to the Internet the marketing focus of the 1990s: aiming to appeal only to the most affluent in society and using Internet metrics to target stories according to what people liked yesterday.

There seems to be an extreme reluctance to accept that advertising is no longer the major factor in newspapers' economic health and that reader engagement is. That would imply that a sane strategy would be to build something good that everyone wants to read – so you can sell it to a lot of people, regardless of whether they drive a BMW or ride the subway. In terms of circulation, this has worked wonderfully well for the *Guardian*. And, for the *New York Times*, reader support via the metered paywall has been the difference between declining and stable revenues. Between 2009 and 2013, the *Times* revenue held at roughly $1.5 billion per year (Chittum 2014d), which is remarkable in view of most other companies' declining incomes.

In the past, the strategy was to build and retain circulation with the advertising sections; special features such as comics pages, crossword puzzles, contests, and chess and bird-watching columns; and a type of news that could titillate without offending or challenging authority. "Stories about sex scandals and celebrities have become more legitimate, because they make commercial sense: they are inexpensive to cover, attract audiences and give the illusion of controversy without ever threatening anyone in power" (McChesney and Nichols 2010, 47).

The move by North American newspapers to identify more with power than with the powerless has led to some regrettable lapses, the largest and most disastrous of which are the US press's inability to question the invasion of Iraq, and its blindness to the sub-prime mortgage bubble. "The main reason mainstream media is under siege is because on major story after major story, they got it wrong," Jeff Cohen of Fairness and Accuracy in Reporting told the *Christian Science Monitor*. "It's because of the botched reporting in the run-up to the Iraq invasion and the totally missed financial crisis. The independent new voices have blossomed because of [the mainstream media's] content failures" (Goodale 2010). As Dean Starkman wrote in his examination of the business press's failure to anticipate the sub-prime mortgage crisis: "The Watchdog didn't bark ... How could an entire journalism subculture, understood to be sophisticated and plugged in, miss the central story occurring on its beat?" (2014, 1).

Similarly, the government of Prime Minister Stephen Harper prorogued government for three months in 2008–9 to avoid a confidence vote and the near-certainty of being toppled by an NDP–Liberal–Bloc Québécois coalition. The Canadian press did very little to challenge the Conservative Party line that a coalition was illegitimate and antidemocratic – despite a wealth of national and international precedents that proved otherwise. "When the Governor-General made her decision to sustain the Conservative government in office, she gave no explanation. Instead of demanding one, our media folded like deck chairs" (Martin 2009).

A frequently heard complaint is that North American print journalism's culture of caution and subservience, and its obsession with balance, made it ill-equipped to compete with the unpredictable, daring, and diverse Web. "Today, mainstream print and electronic media want to be neutral, presenting both or all sides as if they were refereeing a game in which only the players – the government or its opponents – can participate. They have increasingly become common carriers, transmitters of other people's ideas and thoughts, irrespective of import, relevance and at times even accuracy ... At a time when it is most needed, the media, and particularly newspapers, have lost their voice" (Pincus 2009).

When the press is perceived to have fallen down on the job, people look for alternatives – as they did in the 1960s and early '70s with the underground press and the New Journalism. The various bloggers, pundits, independent journalists, and aggregators on the Internet have provided the equivalent of a fairly powerful alternative press. Sites such as *Talking Points Memo, Truthdig, Voice of San Diego, MinnPost, Politico,* and *Global Post* in the United States have all stepped in to provide alternatives where there was perceived to be a vacuum. In Canada, the six *OpenFile* sites, the left-wing aggregator *Rabble.ca*, and a few local alternative sites, such as *Torontoist* (part of an international franchise founded by New York's *Gothamist*), *allNovaScotia.com,* and Vancouver's *The Tyee,* play, or have played, similar roles. The last may be Canada's most consistently interesting news site, a blend of original reporting, columns, and opinion that was founded by journalist David Beers as an antidote to the blandness and boosterism of Vancouver's Pacific Press monopoly owned by Postmedia.

Founded in 2003, *The Tyee* represents an alternative form of financing, in that it has what Beers calls "an angel investor" in the form of an affiliate of a West Coast labour union, whose leaders "felt like they were being shut out of the conversation." It also relies quite heavily on contributions from readers who believe they have a vested interest in keeping the site healthy. At the same time, it's something of a throwback to the old underground press and its reaction against the institutional media. Beers, who had worked at a variety of publications ranging from San Francisco Bay area alternatives to the *Vancouver Sun*, says that in Vancouver he saw a conversation that needed to be broadened. "Around 2003, when I left the *Sun*, it seemed to me that there was a media monopolistic situation in the city. Canwest owned everything. They owned all the weeklies pretty much, and they owned the *Victoria Times Colonist,* and the *Province* and the *Sun*, and the major television news station. And they owned the major Internet portal."

Beers says *The Tyee* has evolved from heckler of the establishment newspapers to "tip sheet" for the mainstream press – prodding the competition and adding depth and texture to the public discourse – to a replacement for the enfeebled old media. "We sent a reporter to Washington, who spent a week there reporting on lobbyists for the tar sands, and how they were in cahoots with the Alberta government, the Canadian government, and the oil industry. They're all working together to try to change US laws. That's a huge story. Where's the *Globe and Mail*'s bureau chief on that? There wasn't any reporting on that. So we had to send a twenty-five-year-old reporter there who did a brilliant fifteen-part series, called 'The War over the Oil Sands.' I guess what I'm saying is, I don't know if we're the tip sheet any more. We're doing the work that these guys used to do."

Beers says that when he founded *The Tyee,* he foresaw sites like it springing up across the country, but so far there have been no imitators. In October 2013, the organization announced a plan to create a national edition and asked readers to pledge a monthly contribution to help bring "The Tyee's principled journalism" to the whole country (Beers, D'Auria, Jenkins, and Smith 2013).

However, as Columbia University's Todd Gitlin says, the existence of an alternative press is no real remedy, unless there is a fully functioning mainstream media for it to influence. In the 1960s and '70s, a large, powerful institutional news media was searching for ways to counteract the erosion of its audience by television, and the underground press was an important incubator of new ideas. Today, as Beers says, the alternative may find itself having to replace rather than provoke the competition. Gitlin points out that most mainstream outlets have neither the confidence nor the resources to meet the challenge posed by the emerging competition.

The underground press was able to become a prod or a reform impulse, a reviving and re-energizing force, because the mainstream journalistic institutions were so confident in their ability to control the market. They weren't really suffering financially from the rise of the underground press. The disproportion was massive. So they had the confidence that led them to try these various measures of co-option, whether it was adding more stylish sections or hiring minorities, or talking hipper, or aiming more for the metropolitan college educated. Whatever it was, they were poised as a co-optive agency; they were primed to revisit themselves. Today, I think there's only one kind of reform that the chains, that the standard media, are interested in doing, and that is to do something briefer and skimpier with a smaller newsroom.

While we are on the subject of alternatives and replacements, it says something very bad about North American journalism that two of the most powerful and intelligent critical voices in the United States belong to comedians Jon Stewart of *The Daily Show* and John Oliver of *Last Week Tonight*. In 2009, Stewart was voted "America's most trusted newsman" in an online poll conducted by *Time* magazine, beating out ABC's Charlie Gibson, NBC's Brian Williams, and CBS's Katie Couric (Linkins 2009). Stewart and his fake-pundit/partner-in-crime Stephen Colbert had filled the vacuum created by a left that had ceded the media to neo-conservatism. Though Stewart has always been adamant that he is an entertainer and not a journalist, his power – and by extension the unexploited power of the press – is evident in the pressure he put on the US Congress to pass a bill pledging health-care funds for 9/11 first responders. In a *Daily Show* episode that featured several New York fire, police, and emergency personnel, Stewart singled out two groups for attack: the Republicans who filibustered the bill and the news media that had ignored the issue. Stewart sarcastically pointed out that the TV networks had been forced to choose between covering the Beatles' arrival on iTunes or the first responders. Shortly after the show, the bill passed. Syracuse University television professor Robert Thompson rated Stewart's performance as one of the three great moments of advocacy journalism on TV: along with Edward R. Murrow's exposure of US Senator Joseph McCarthy in the 1950s and Walter Cronkite's editorial about the Vietnam stalemate in 1968 (Carter and Stelter 2010). Similarly, Stewart may have been the first to mount an effective inquiry into the US press's failure to uncover the sub-prime mortgage crisis, with his March 2009 roasting of CNBC stock-market analyst Jim Cramer, which went viral on the Internet. He has also been relentless in his attacks on the incompetence of the US Department of Veterans Affairs. It is as if the editorial-page cartoonist had taken over editing Page 1 – and was doing a better job than the news desk.

At the same time, the mainstream media have allowed the new media, and some of their most extreme elements, to dictate the agenda. As Paul Starr (2010) has pointed out, US politicians today are facing the most partisan media since the nineteenth century. As the political culture has become more polarized, the pundit culture has become more extreme. Talk radio and news network commentators have amped up the rhetoric to levels of incivility that once would have got them banned from the airwaves. *Washington Post* columnist Howard Kurtz calls it "journalism as blood sport, performed for the masses ... The toxic atmosphere that many media outlets tolerate, and sometimes foster, is slowly poisoning the discourse" (2010a). The danger in this – when "the world of Walter Cronkite gives way to the world of Glenn Beck and Keith Olbermann" – is that society loses a vital political tool, a trusted, impartial press that is "a resource for building consensus" (Starr 2010). In Canada broadcast news has, for the most part, remained fairly impartial and responsible, although talk radio has its share of mean spirits and irresponsible blowhards. The only TV broadcaster that sought to follow the American model was the Sun News Network, which went off the air in February 2015, just shy of its fourth birthday.

Further driving the public agenda is the speed with which the news moves, combined with the fact that, as Lawrence Martin pointed out, the media have developed such a short attention span. For example, US Department of Agriculture employee Shirley Sherrod was more or less crucified in the mainstream press after neo-conservative propagandist Andrew Breitbart ran an out-of-context video online, which had been edited to present Sherrod as an anti-white racist. When the TV networks got hold of it, they ran it without investigation and Sherrod was fired. She was finally vindicated when someone bothered to look at the whole clip and realized that the so-called racist comments had been created by removing context. "The herd ... moves so quickly that snap judgments prevail and nuance gets lost" (Kurtz 2010b). It is most often, but not exclusively, arch-conservatives in the New Media that drive the agenda, operating with a game plan that dictates that anything is fair, as long as it advances the cause. We live in an age of truthiness.

For example, around the time of the invasion of Iraq, a US "presidential aide" was quoted in the *New York Times Magazine* as sneering at the "reality based community" of journalism and saying of the George W. Bush administration: "We're an empire now, and when we act, we create our own reality ... We're history's actors and you ... all of you, will be left to just study what we do" (quoted in Rich 2006, 3). The right is given even more power by the fact that, driven by their terror of perceived liberal bias, the mainstream media play into the hands of those who seek to create their own reality by manipulating the message. "In many quarters of the Old Media, there is concern about not appearing liberally biased, so stories emanating from the right are given more weight and less scrutiny. Additionally, the conservative New Media, particularly Fox News Channel and talk radio, are commercially successful, so the implicit logic followed by decision makers in the Old Media is that, if something is gaining currency in those precincts, it is a phenomenon that must be given attention. Most dangerously, conservative New Media will often produce content that is so provocative and incendiary that the Old Media finds it irresistible" (Halperin 2010).

This situation can be taken as another indictment of the cult of balance. As in the 1950s, when the US news media allowed communist witch-hunter Joseph McCarthy to run amok by blindly reporting everything he said without investigating or questioning it, today the news media allow propagandists such as Breitbart and James O'Keefe (see chapter 6), to place their agendas in front of the people unchallenged. The stupidity of balance has been repeatedly attacked as a mindless striving for a "phony objectivity in which the reporter quotes advocates of both sides of a controversy without any independent probing to discover the facts" (Jones 2009, 84). Balance can be used as an excuse for abdicating the prime responsibility of the journalist: to discern the truth. Simply parroting the controversy and leaving it for the audience to decide is an act of professional irresponsibility, and journalism, to a certain extent, has interpreted it as a virtue. As Starr says, "Democracy needs a passion and partisanship provides it. Journalism needs passion, too, though the passion should be for the truth" (2010).

Some of the more zealous advocates of public journalism and the New Media – the hard-core Deweyans – see the future as one in which the conversation of the culture has been turned from a sermon to a revival meeting, with the entire congregation on its feet: drilling down, bearing witness, photographing, tweeting, blogging, and shouting their opinions. Journalists, if they have a role, simply mediate the comments so each can be heard. Others, the descendants of Lippmann, are horrified by the idea of the swinish multitude replacing the educated few, and fearful of a future in which the facts cannot be heard above the din of rumour, speculation, bias, and emotion. If Raymond Williams were around, he might continue to warn that the two extremes create opportunities for special interests – and, if the Web's extremist bloggers, propagandists, and political and corporate shills are any indication, we should take heed. It is unlikely, and certainly undesirable, that either side will prevail entirely. However, we could, as the *Guardian*'s Alan Rusbridger argues, keep both, and produce a new kind of journalism, in which "uniquely knowledgeable and insightful" professionalism is married to the "experience, range, opinions, expertise and passions of the people who read us" (2010).

So, if the story of the business is one of crisis, and the story of technology is one of hope, the story of the craft of journalism blends the two into one of painful rebirth made necessary by business and aided by technology. As Columbia University's Todd Gitlin says, we can't let the glimmers of hope blind us to the fact that "no kind of resurrection or reclaiming of journalistic territory is going to take place painlessly or seamlessly. This is all very difficult."

Another recurring theme is that journalists need to redefine what they do so they can adapt to an audience that has lost patience with bland, balanced industrial journalism. As always, very close to the centre of the discussion is the question of objectivity, and whether it needs to be redefined or abandoned … or rediscovered.

Typically, the argument to abandon it focuses on the need to draw the audience away from the breeziness of the aggregators and the fiery, opinionated writing of the blogosphere. Often, this is interpreted as meaning journalists need to do both: be informative and breezy while liberally spicing their reporting with opinion. This is a blend Mitchell Stephens calls "wisdom reporting." With the Internet delivering more facts than we could ever use, he argues, newspapers need to offer readers a more thoughtful experience. Reporters need to do more than just gather facts; they have to analyze and interpret the news. "Outside of the small patch of the paper that has been roped off for opinion, the chances of coming upon something that might qualify as wisdom are not great. Most reporters have spent too long pursuing and writing 'just the facts' to move easily into drawing conclusions based on facts. Their editors have spent too long resisting the encroachment of anything that is not carefully sourced, that might be perceived as less than objective, to easily welcome such analyses now" (2007).

It's hard to see how that would be a formula for drawing people away from the "wisdom" that spreads like Kudzu all over the Internet. Also, the main question Stephens raises is, Why is opinion the natural antithesis of objectivity? As Neal Gabler (2013) points out, informed opinion arises from objective research: the reporter goes in open-minded, uncovers the facts, analyzes them, and comes out educated and subjective. If someone makes a comment, the writer doesn't just print it. She investigates it and, if it is false, reports that. The idea is not to express one's opinion, but to analyze the available material and do what storytellers are supposed to do: use their powers of expression and persuasion to paint a compelling and accurate picture that covers all the facets of the story. When Jack Shafer wrote in *Slate* that modern newspapers should return to the values of the penny press, he was arguing not for the excesses and sensationalism of yellow journalism, but for a return to muckraking, to objectivity with passion and fire, and a concern for the powerless and underprivileged. "I admire the adherence to the objective method that newspapers like the *New York Times* have devoted themselves to," he told me. "I say 'objective method' as opposed to 'objectivity.' I don't think that the people there are objective. But what they try to do, as a scientist would do, is to judge all the evidence and make the strongest case for what is real that they possibly can, what's humanly possible."

Shafer's call for a return to yellow journalism might also be a formula for curing the reluctance of many news organizations to challenge dogma, consensus, and received wisdom. Critics such as Ben Bagdikian (1990, 2004), James Carey (1997b), Daniel Hallin (1989), Robert McChesney (1999, 2010), John Nerone (1995), Jay Rosen (1999), and Michael Schudson (1995) have pointed out that there is a set of shared values implicit in much journalistic discourse that renders complete objectivity unlikely. "For instance, the articles that appear in mainstream newspapers are written with the undeclared assumptions that capitalism isn't inherently evil and freedom of speech is a virtue" (Jones 2009, 83). As Rosen says, part of the problem with objectivity is that journalists routinely place issues and information into Daniel Hallin's spheres of legitimate controversy, consensus, or deviance, but rarely think very much about it and almost never question the process. "*Which means they often do it badly*. Their 'sphere placement' decisions can be arbitrary, automatic, inflected with fear, or excessively narrow-minded" (Rosen 2009; italics in original).

The liberal blogger Atrios, probably giving away his age, has a term he uses for thinkers who lie in the sphere of deviance: "dirty fucking hippies" (www.eschatonblog.com). It is the way he refers to himself, and it harks back to the days when people like US President Richard Nixon and his vice-president, Spiro Agnew, could dismiss anti-war protesters as dirty, longhaired bums who needed to get a job, and then see their words in headlines around the world. The modern equivalent is "the out-of-power or online left and the way this group is marginalized by the Washington journalists." As we saw in the latter years of the Vietnam War, occasionally, "the people the press thinks of as deviant types are closer to the sphere of consensus than the journalists who are classifying those same people as 'fringe'" (Rosen 2009).

Yet, as we have seen, there was a time when newspapers found it was in their interests to align themselves with the fringe, when magnates such as Hearst, Pulitzer, and Atkinson saw profit and power in courting the immigrant and working classes. Also, in the late nineteenth and early twentieth centuries, many journalists had come from those classes and made small enough salaries that they remained there throughout their working lives. However sympathetic they may be to the problems of the average person, many of today's journalists are "upper income, living in [a] rarified world, and are becoming more removed from the problems of working-day people," CNN pundit David Gergen told the *Globe and Mail*. Gergen added that he had once urged a young woman on his staff to leave Washington and take a job on a small-town New England paper so she could "really understand what's going on, and the lives of people who are making $30,000, $40,000 a year ... And we need people who can do that" (Houpt 2012a).

But many newspapers long ago shifted their attention away from a mass audience and onto the well-heeled readers their advertisers desire. It seems hard to believe, but there was a time when most daily newspapers had labour reporters. Now, there are almost none – though the *Toronto Star* and such online publications as the *Huffington Post* and *ProPublica* are bringing them back. "Every daily newspaper in North America came to include a business section – filled with news for the investor, the manager, the executive and the employer, and flush with advertising. But not one included a labour section that addressed the employee, was attentive to working conditions, and chronicled the experience of the unemployed. There was no commercial base, no advertising constituency" (Dornan 2012, 57).

Today, with classifieds gone, and the concept of display advertising becoming a memory, many in the news media fail to see the potential of pleasing the broad mass of readers. To the press of today, "poor and working-class people are, for all intents and purposes, only newsworthy to the extent they get in the way of rich people" (McChesney and Nichols 2010, 51). As such, they are reported as criminals and victims, or the collateral damage of economic necessity. Normally, there is one day each year when the US media admit the existence of the poor, *Huffington Post* blogger Jason Linkins wrote: the day the US Census Bureau releases its annual report on poverty (2010).

The little glimmers of hope should be taken to mean only that "complete stupefaction is not upon us," Columbia University's Todd Gitlin says.

> I take the survival of the *New York Times* as a sometimes chronicler of uncomfortable news to be a hopeful sign – the very fact that it has that commitment. I just read an article in the *Times* this morning about the corruption of the garment industry safety system and the absence of it in Bangladesh, for example. For the last I-don't-know-how-many months or years, they have been on this story. It must be very expensive to do this. They have reporters on the ground. The guy who covered the factory collapse and the repression of labour, and so on does wonderful work. The fact that the descendants of a family are willing to make less money publishing the *New York Times* than they would if they published *Sex Daily* is, for me, hopeful.

Similarly, in Canada, we can take comfort from the fact that the CBC covered that story with the same tenacity and skill – following up on the fact that Loblaw's Joe Fresh clothing line was among the contractors served by a corrupt Bangladeshi manufacturer whose workforce was all but annihilated in the 2013 factory collapse. And the 2013 Michener Award nomination for the *Edmonton Journal–Calgary Herald* investigation into the foster care system in Alberta shows that even some financially hobbled news organizations still have the will to do accountability reporting.

Unfortunately, as we have seen, the *Herald* and *Journal* are owned by a very troubled chain, and the CBC is dependent upon government funding for its survival – and past Liberal and current Conservative governments alike have shown limited tolerance for anything remotely resembling criticism from the network. For example, though it was defeated, it can be taken as an open threat that there was a motion before the Conservative Party convention of 2013 calling for the "elimination of all public funding of the corporation which creates unfair competitive advantage with privately owned and operated networks and stations" (Wingrove 2013).

This atmosphere has led to a noticeable reticence when it comes to critical coverage of anything to the right of centre on the political spectrum. In fact, the response to anything that doesn't lie to the right is sometimes so reflexive that the press almost seems to surprise itself. Critics of the Occupy Wall Street coverage charged that the initial reporting and commentary were disparaging and one-sided, or too narrowly focused on who appeared to be winning or losing the public relations war. Alicia Shepard of National Public Radio complained that most of the coverage "hasn't been about the issues, it's been about who's up and who's down" (Stelter 2011). Fox News felt free to denounce the protesters as "nuts, lunatics, and fascists" and "demonic loons," while MSNBC mythologized them as "what working people are talking about." In both cases, the discourse was safer than discussing the images they were broadcasting, some of which showed people who had plunged the world economy into anarchy sipping champagne and smirking through the windows of their glass towers at those whose lives they had destroyed. Columbia Journalism School professor Dale Maharidge charges that this was just another manifestation of journalists' isolation from "real people" (Linkins 2010).

Perhaps the best argument for covering these real people – the working class and others who fall into the sphere of deviance – is that they're simply more interesting than the contented urbanites the newspapers are trying to reach with tedious stories about dream cars, quinoa recipes, and retirement investments.

North American journalists long ago came to think of themselves as part of the professional class. In the view of their British counterparts, this has made their work "self-reverential, long-winded, over-edited and stuffy … The British sometimes argue that, because American journalists have joined the establishment, they are easily duped by senior sources." British journalists cherish their status as social outsiders and "like to quote the adage of the late Nicholas Tomalin that: 'The only qualities essential for real success in journalism are rat-like cunning, a plausible manner and a little literary ability'" (Rachman 2008).

This contrast between British and American journalists has a positive and a sinister side. On the positive, most British journalists find North American pomposity insufferable or hilarious, and see North American journalists as far too cautious for the good of their craft. As Jack Shafer writes, it might be a welcome change if some of our newspapers took a cue from the British and "contained a little more blood" (2009c).

On the sinister, many British journalists – particularly the "Fleet Street reptiles" of the tabloid press – are possessed of a cynicism their North American colleagues often find unnerving. A prime example is the phone-hacking scandal that brought down News Corp.'s Sunday tabloid *News of the World* and landed its proprietor, Rupert Murdoch, in front of a public inquiry into press ethics. In 2013, eight News Corp. executives were charged with several criminal acts: conspiring to illegally intercept mobile-phone voice-mail messages; making payments to public officials in exchange for information; concealing documents, computers, and other electronic equipment from police investigators; obstructing justice. The charged included former *News of the World* editors Andrew Coulson and Rebekah Brooks, and Brooks's husband, Charles Brooks. In June 2014, Brooks and her husband were acquitted, and Coulson was convicted and given a jail sentence. There were ties between News Corp. and the

British government. Brooks was a longtime friend of Prime Minister David Cameron, and Coulson was Cameron's former press secretary – something for which the PM apologized after the sentence was reported.

The most unsavoury charge against the company was that reporters at its weekly *News of the World* had hacked into the cellphone of a murdered girl and deleted messages to make room for more. The activity on the phone gave the girl's parents false hope that she was alive. After a public outcry, in a symbolic gesture of goodwill, Murdoch shut down the *News of the World* in 2011, but replaced it with a Sunday edition of his equally excitable *Sun* tabloid.

Still, even taking the excesses into account, the British press's habit of thumbing its nose at authority can be healthy and refreshing by North American standards. As US journalist James Geary puts it, British tabloid journalism has a "certain gaudy brilliance" that harks back to the muckraking of the penny press (2006). At the same time, the quality papers – the *Times*, *Guardian*, *Independent*, and *Telegraph* – showcase some of the most literate, stylish, and intelligent writing in the field, which, as Tina Brown (2008) points out, also succeeds in being sexy, entertaining, thought-provoking, and fun. And it is difficult for anyone exposed to the bile and Pablum of much North American broadcast news not to be envious of Britons, whose main TV diet consists of the BBC. Perhaps the starkest contrast between the political and media cultures of the United States and Britain can be found in the almost fawning wartime reporting on the Bush administration and the aggressive coverage of Prime Minister Tony Blair.

> In the run-up to the Iraq war, a common criticism among British journalists was that their American counterparts tended to be far too polite and deferential to authority, to the point that many Britons considered their U.S. colleagues "incredibly soft" and "patsy-like" ... Unlike in the U.S., where journalists generally strive for at least the appearance of neutrality and balance, British papers have a long tradition of openly allying with political parties and flouting [sic] their partisan passions. Some veteran British media watchers ... say that this has a liberating effect, which, combined with the fact that Britain still has a dozen or so national dailies battling it out for readers, makes the British press (high-end papers and tabloids alike) edgier and more fun to read. (Hansen 2007)

Despite the emergence of a few world papers and alternative news sources, we are living in "a fractured, chaotic world of news, characterized by superior conversation but a decidedly diminished level of first-rate journalism" (Alterman 2008a). That raises the questions of what journalism is and who, in this world of endless conversation, can be called a journalist. Do we need, or dare, to define these concepts?

In recent years, there have been sporadic calls for the creation of some kind of professional accreditation, as with lawyers and doctors. In Quebec, for example, the Fédération professionnelle des journalistes has called for news people to be licensed (Neil 2011). The argument against this kind of accreditation is that it is exclusive and elitist, and protects lazy, insider journalism – that the "huffing and puffing about interloping amateurs all too often conceals the fact that these amateurs know as much or more about the subject as the professionals, and are not subject to being bamboozled by 'insiders' with an agenda" (Kamiya 2009).

Proponents of a stricter professionalism generally cite the propagandists who masquerade as journalists, bloggers who are unaware of, or unconcerned with, ethical and legal issues, and well-meaning citizen journalists who get themselves into trouble. Take for example these comments from Andrew Cohen, a Carleton University journalism professor and columnist for Postmedia newspapers: "Like politics and novels, [journalism] is open to anyone, which is why the unfiltered, unregulated, unedited Internet is full of trivia, scandal, prejudice and falsehood, and why a generation thinks the *Daily Show* (however clever) is the news and advertising flyers are newspapers" (2009). Cohen was decrying the coverage a rookie reporter named Amanda Lindhout received after she had spent fifteen months in captivity in Somalia, where she had gone to file freelance stories for a small Alberta daily newspaper. Representing the opposing point of view – that journalism is a field whose only standard is performance – another Postmedia columnist wrote that it was disturbing to see "one journalist attack another for excessive initiative, independence and bravado" (Selley 2009).

Meanwhile, *Daily Mail* editor Paul Dacre has touched off a debate about professionalism in Great Britain. Dacre suggests that British journalists be accredited by, and answerable to, a professional body charged with upholding press principles. Perhaps it is understandable that there would be some support for the idea of stricter controls on an industry that, in light of the *News of the World* phone-hacking scandal, appears to be evolving into a public enemy. Some media outlets have supported Dacre in principle, including the daily *Independent*, which argues that one of the functions of the regulating body "might be the issuing of a press card which could be suspended or withdrawn from individuals who gravely breach those standards" (Ball 2012). It is not surprising that the online world rose up to denounce the idea, and there were several expressions of concern that such a system would "kill off local voices holding power to account" (Geary 2012).

Cohen, Dacre, and the Quebec journalists federation are just three voices in a chorus urging some kind of professional definition of journalism. For example, there's the case of Oregon "investigative blogger" Crystal Cox, who was ordered to pay $2.5 million in damages to a Portland financial company because, in one of her blog postings, she accused one of its officers of tax fraud. The Electronic Frontier Foundation asked US District Judge Marco A. Hernandez to overturn the jury award, "as a threat to free speech, excessive [*sic*], and based on the wrong standard of defamation law" (McCann 2011). As it turns out, Cox's standards of journalism were not what you would call exacting. Her reporting was more or less a collection of unsubstantiated claims and personal attacks, giving the plaintiffs cause to sue and Hernandez reason to uphold the award. As David Carr writes, in times past she would have been someone who pestered city editors with her theories. "The Web has allowed Ms. Cox to cut out the middleman; various blogs give voice to her every theory, and search algorithms give her work prominence" (2011d).

What makes the case noteworthy is US District Judge Marco A. Hernandez's response to the issue of whether Cox, as a blogger, could expect the same legal protection as a "professional journalist" under US law. On page nine of his thirteen-page ruling, Hernandez sets out seven requirements for journalistic professionalism:

> Defendant fails to bring forth any evidence suggestive of her status as a journalist. For example, there is no evidence of (1) any education in journalism; (2) any credentials or proof of any affiliation with any recognized news entity; (3) proof of adherence to journalistic

standards such as editing, fact-checking, or disclosures of conflicts of interest; (4) keeping notes of conversations and interviews conducted; (5) mutual understanding or agreement of confidentiality between the defendant and his/her sources; (6) creation of an independent product rather than assembling writings and postings of others; or (7) contacting "the other side" to get both sides of a story. Without evidence of this nature, defendant is not "media." (2011)

Carr calls this definition "a MacGuffin," Alfred Hitchcock's name for a meaningless device that moves the plot forward in a film. That may be true as far as the specifics of Cox's case are concerned, but, in terms of setting a precedent, Hernandez's decision gives litigators a weapon they can use to discredit almost anyone who practises the craft of journalism. And one wonders why Hernandez even felt the need to write it into his opinion, since no legal shields protect journalists from the consequences of slander – as the Cox judgment shows. As *Forbes* blogger David Coursey (2012) points out, many people working in city rooms couldn't produce the credentials necessary to meet Hernandez's criteria, but they have the protection of large media organizations. The issue of "who is and who isn't a journalist may come down to just one thing: money. Who has it (typically the person who says you aren't a journalist) and who doesn't (typically the freelance journalist, even if working for a big name publication)."

Even with the support of a big news organization, accountability journalism can be a very expensive game, largely because civil law is the most powerful weapon people who are being investigated can use against those doing the investigating. As for determining someone is not a journalist because he or she doesn't work for a large news organization, as Jack Shafer said to me, "Tom Paine might not have qualified as a journalist."

There are privileges that journalists enjoy that could be a bit more problematic, such as the right to protect sources and the argument of fair comment. Clay Shirky argues that when anyone can become a journalist and journalists enjoy "certain latitude to avoid cooperating with the law ... journalistic privilege suddenly becomes a loophole too large to be borne by society." The problem lies in deciding where to limit journalistic privilege so that the law maintains its "ability to uncover and prosecute wrongdoing while allowing a safety valve for investigative reporting" (2008, 71).

So, where does society draw the line? Options such as the ones suggested by the Quebec journalists federation or by Paul Dacre could have the effect of shutting down the citizen reporters who have stepped in to fill voids left by a retreating professional journalism. For example, the collapse of the community press in Great Britain has left dozens of town councils with no reporters to watch over them. Volunteers who cover council meetings already "tell tales of obstructive council representatives and exclusion from meetings because they are not considered 'proper journalists'" (Geary 2012). The institution of some kind of press card would make it much easier for public institutions and corporations to simply ostracize people like them.

As Shirky writes, the "definition of journalism is not internally consistent but is rather tied to ownership of communications machinery" (2008, 72). When it comes to offering a definition for journalist or journalism, however, he skirts the issue with a predictably nebulous utopian forecast of a future in which everyone is a publisher.

David Coursey, writing in *Forbes*, jokingly compares journalism to pornography, invoking US Supreme Court Justice Potter Stewart's famous line: "I know it when I see it." He may have inadvertently hit the mark. It took years for courts to deal, case by case, with laws governing obscenity, profanity, and pornography. Some of the most famous, such as the serial prosecutions of comedian Lenny Bruce, the attempt to ban Allen Ginsberg's poem *Howl*, and the 1960 trial of Penguin Books for publishing *Lady Chatterley's Lover*, involved long days of expert testimony to establish the social and artistic values of the works in question. We could be in for a long series of debates like those, as we struggle to define which bloggers and citizens are journalists and deserving of protection under the law. Once again, we may be called upon to deal with questionable practices, one by one, as they come up, so we can protect the free speech that is valuable. "Defining the line between them is tricky and is best decided giving the benefit of the doubt to the journalist" (Coursey 2012).

As Shafer says, perhaps the most worrisome aspect of the idea of accrediting journalists is that we may set up a system of unwieldy rules and laws that don't work:

> I'm not wild about standardization across the whole industry when (a) you could be wrong, the standards that you pick, and you'd never know it because there would be this big bureaucratic hassle to

change your standards, and (b) you know that journalism needs to evolve and it needs competing schools of thought. The last is a sort of Orwellian worry, that if journalists agree, journalists come together to say what the standards are, that somehow somebody along the way tries to give them the force of law, which I think is always dangerous. You want to keep the government as far away from the press and allow the press to be irresponsible. Better to have an irresponsible press than a government-controlled highly ethical press.

As we have seen, the US newspaper business has lost more than 40,000 jobs since January 2007, and more than 10,000 jobs have disappeared in the Canadian news media since 2008. That has made for a lot fewer journalists and a lot more bloggers, citizen journalists, and public relations people. "The muscles of journalism are weakening and the muscles of public relations are bulking up – as if they are on steroids," *New York Times* reporter David Barstow told the *Columbia Journalism Review*. Journalists have always been outnumbered by public relations workers, but the imbalance has grown mightily. For example, in the United States in the 1980s, there were about 0.45 PR workers and 0.36 journalists for every 100,000 population; by 2008, that ratio had shifted to 0.90 PR workers and 0.25 journalists. Meanwhile, between 1997 and 2007, revenues at US public relations agencies increased from $3.5 billion to $8.7 billion – figures that take only private PR agencies into account, and not advertising agencies, corporate PR departments, or lobbyists (Sullivan 2011).

As Clay Shirky (2009) has said, the Web is breaking old things faster than new things can be built to take their place. Until those new things can be built, or the old ones adapted to the new situation, more of our public life "will occur in the shadows. We won't know what we won't know" (Tom Rosenstiel, quoted in Starr 2009). The corollary to that is that we will also be unable to avoid knowing what some people want us to know.

Paul Starr warns that we are entering a "new era of corruption" brought about by corporate and government organizations, and agencies that find themselves suddenly able to operate without supervision. He speculates that the omnibus, metropolitan daily may be a construct peculiar to a specific set of conditions and, thus, to a certain moment in history. "We may be approaching not the end of newspapers, but the end of the age of newspapers." As a central form of communication in cities around the world, newspapers gave us "a powerful means of leverage over the state, and this leverage is now at risk" (2009). The central question, from a social and political point of view, is what will replace the newspapers, if anything?

"I think, as we move along and as we move into more and more fragmented media, you're less and less likely to be confronted with different perspectives than the perspective you're seeking, which tend to be the ones that reinforce your points of view," says Christopher Waddell, director of Carleton University's School of Journalism and Communication. "The possibility of seeing something that actually forces you to think about whether your perspective on an issue is the right one or not is less likely."

The cumulative effect of the dwindling of journalistic resources, the bulking up of strategic communications, and the atomization of the audience may seem obvious cause for concern. However, as we have seen, many critics consider the point irrelevant and argue that most North American dailies long ago abdicated their watchdog role in favour of soft news, entertainment, and consumer advice. "It would be interesting to see if you could find any indices of corruption or malfeasance on the state level," Jack Shafer says, "and go back and measure the time – let's say in 1980 – when state bureaus were completely staffed compared to now, and see if there's any way to measure that the government was more ethical, more honest, more transparent than it is now. I've yet to read the compelling argument that newspapers close their bureaus and democracy goes to hell in a hand basket. It might be the case, but I just haven't seen that demonstrated."

Some new media are stepping into spaces left by the receding old media. Groups such as California Watch, the Center for Public Integrity, *Politico*, and the Pulitzer Prize–winning *ProPublica* are responsible for "an emerging ecosystem of investigative reporting" (Drew 2010). Relying on foundation funding and public donations, they publish on their own websites and offer their material, often free of charge, to newspapers and TV news organizations. Often, they do big, splashy investigations in partnership with other news outfits, as *ProPublica* did with *Law and Disorder*, an investigative series on the conduct of the New Orleans police department after Hurricane Katrina. This was done with the *New Orleans Times-Picayune* and PBS's current events series *Frontline*.

The new non-profits have to produce to survive; donors want to see results before they continue to donate. That means they need to get attention, which, in turn, means they prefer to go after sexy stories. But who covers the less entertaining but no less important stories? Carleton University's Catherine McKercher asks. "Everybody wants to cover the hurricane that blows through town. Everybody wants to cover the pop show. Everybody wants to review the movies ... But not everybody wants to go sit through a planning committee at city hall every week for fifty weeks a year ... Who's going to cover the kind of power centres in our society that don't exactly make it easy or sexy to go and cover them, and yet whose decisions have huge influence on us?"

Accompanying the decline in investigative journalism is the decreasing respect for writing as a profession – or at least a craft, McKercher says. "What I don't understand about the way people talk about journalists these days is that people in our own business, including journalists, seem to have a kind of contempt for the skill. There's a sense that anybody can do what journalists can do. It's like, 'We can get interns to do this.' Think about the best journalists you know and the depth of knowledge they have, the perspective they have, the ability they have to do an interview that actually gets new information, not just pat remarks. The ability to construct a narrative. These are, to me, pretty high-level skills."

Yet those skills continue to be devalued. As journalists have been thrown out of work, alternative means of employment have been getting more and more meagre. Magazines are paying lower rates, newspapers are using fewer stringers, and "content farms" such as Demand Media have flourished, paying writers as little as five cents a word for short pieces designed for search engine optimization, on topics such as "How to Wear a Sweater Vest" or "How to Massage a Dog that Is Emotionally Stressed" (Hiar 2010). As we saw in chapter 6, aggregators such as the *Huffington Post* are built largely on low-cost and free labour, and social networks are built for free by offering a service that collects an audience that is sold to advertisers – the same principle as the newspaper, but with the greatest expense – salaries – eliminated. As the ranks of underemployed professionals and hobbyists who will work for free swell, professional freelancers have seen their annual incomes slip by as much as 50 per cent. One California freelancer told the *Los Angeles Times* that she once earned $70,000 a year and now has to hustle to earn half that (Rainey 2010). Alan Mutter writes that he worries about "journocide," that we may lose a generation of journalists (2012).

With newspapers and TV news outlets strapped for cash, government and business have found an opening to tell their own stories, unfiltered, under the guise of real journalism. Newspapers have long known that a cheap way to fill an op-ed page was with commentary from politicians and leaders of industry – usually ghostwritten by communications staffers or contractors. Government departments also regularly provide video "news" bits promoting their activities. A lot of it is harmless promotional material – pieces on drug policy or agriculture research, for example – that, were it labelled as such, could be taken by the viewer as one facet of the story. However, as local TV news finds itself with fewer staff and often growing airtime, the pressure has increased to fill the air with something that at least looks like a local newscast. As a result, even items that come with identification are edited to "simply identify the government 'reporter' as one of their own" (Barstow and Stein 2005).

In Canada, there have been several complaints about the way the government of Prime Minister Stephen Harper has exercised control over the media by limiting access and centralizing communication in the hands of a few top-ranked ministers – especially in the community of federal government–employed scientists. When an earthquake struck western Quebec in 2010, *Ottawa Citizen* science writer Tom Spears wrote, he had to go to the US Geological Survey for comment, because "no one at Natural Resources Canada, which runs the earthquake office, was answering." Days after the fact, he filed an Access to Information request, and eventually received "a big heavy box" filled with email printouts (2010). If the Public Service of Canada is that fearful of commenting on a random act of God, we can only imagine to what else Canadians are being denied access.

The Prime Minister's Office has even taken to controlling the flow of photographs, and this has preyed upon understaffed – or in some cases unstaffed – newspaper picture desks. For example, in October 2009, a photo of Stephen Harper playing piano in rehearsal for a National Arts Centre gala was sent out, mislabelled as being from the performance that took place later in the day. It was run as such by newspapers across Canada. Earlier that year, photographers were kept at such a distance from the prime minister when he was on a tour of the Arctic that the national wire service had to rely on handout photos from the PMO to send to newspapers. News organizations have charged that "the PMO has effectively set up its own picture service" and is marketing publicity shots as news photos (Chase 2009). The situation was so tense at one point that Canadian news organizations published an open letter complaining that "transparency is replaced by slick propaganda and spin designed to manipulate public opinion" (Banerjee 2010).

More recently, TV news outlets were told they could film a Stephen Harper address to cabinet, but reporters would not be allowed in to ask questions. *Globe and Mail* columnist Elizabeth Renzetti criticized Harper for using social media to deliver a monologue while attempting to freeze out journalists who might pose unwelcome questions. "This war on information, and the reporters who are meant to convey it, is not by any means restricted to Ottawa, although our Prime Minister has a particularly strong aversion to being questioned, most recently considering a ban on a reporter who'd thrown an unscheduled question at him. The war is happening here, and in the United States and Britain, and information is not winning" (2013).

It is easy to see where we are headed if newsroom staffing continues to shrink and freelancers find themselves getting more desperate to earn a living. For one thing, "a journalist who is fearful that he can't get another job is in a weaker position to refuse to do something ethically questionable" (Jones 2009, 105). For another, it will become harder for news organizations to demand high ethical standards of writers they are refusing to pay. "Lower standards are cheaper than high standards" and if writers have to hustle for a living, "don't blame them for getting bought" (Poniewozik 2009). *Huffington Post* blogger Michelle Haimoff once put up a posting that suggested bloggers could make money by promoting the products of advertisers. Jessica Smith, who ran a consumer-advice blog called JessicaKnows.com was known for accepting favours from the people she reviewed, like the Ford Motor Company, which gave her use of a Flex after she reviewed the vehicle. "I prefer not to be critical," she told the *New York Times* (Carr 2009b).

As we have seen with James O'Keefe and ACORN, and Andrew Breitbart and Shirley Sherrod, even political activists who believe they're fighting for a good cause can be responsible for misinformation and broken lives. When news organizations are eager for cheap, easy, sensational items, the potential for mischief can be great. For example, immediately after US President Barack Obama nominated Sonia Sotomayor for the Supreme Court of the United States, identical and highly contentious (and, as it later turned out, highly edited) footage of the candidate surfaced on all the TV newscasts. The footage was not the work of newspeople, but of "political hit men," Mark Bowden writes. "With journalists being laid off in droves, savvy political operatives have stepped eagerly into the breach. What's troubling is not that TV-news producers mistake their work for journalism, which is bad enough, but that young people drawn to journalism increasingly see no distinction between disinterested reporting and hit-jobbery" (2009).

Under these circumstances, there is a distinct possibility that high-quality, impartial news may become an elite resource. In some cases, specialty publications and newsletters with a narrow focus and/or an agenda are stepping in to fill the gap in political coverage left by newspapers. As of 2009, for example, *Climate Wire* had more staffers covering Washington than Hearst newspapers (Kurtz 2009). The business press, such as the *Wall Street Journal*, Bloomberg, and Reuters, are not only healthy but "on a hiring spree." As of 2012, Bloomberg employed some 2,400 editorial staff, an increase of 300 over 2009, and Thomson-Reuters had hired 600 journalists in the previous four years (Moses 2012). As *Adweek* points out, the growth of organizations that make most of their money from subscription-only financial information raises some troubling questions. These companies do not produce "public-interest journalism" but rather news that "is geared to making, as one critic puts it, 'a handful of people even richer'" (Tobaccowala, 2010).

Always, it seems, money is cast in the role of super-hero or super-villain in the battle to save general-interest journalism. Recently, several rich men have emerged as vanity newspaper owners: John Henry at the *Boston Globe*, Aaron Kushner at the *Orange County Register*, Jeff Bezos at the *Washington Post*, eBay founder Pierre Omidyar backing Glenn Greenwald's *The Intercept*. Even journalism schools have begun to kick around the idea of acquiring newspapers they could use as "teaching hospitals" – raising the spectre of benefactors like the Koch Brothers or Donald Trump being able to influence coverage through university donations. Columbia University's Todd Gitlin says that's a risk worth taking, and probably wouldn't be much worse than the funding formula we've lived with until now. "You can't reconcile it," he says. "Universities are complicated institutions, and they're going to have Ministries of Evil as well as Ministries of Good, not to over-simplify it. There is going to be no shortage of political fights."

The non-profits face the same challenge, says *Columbia Journalism Review*'s Ryan Chittum. "I hope these non-profit news organizations can flourish. But it depends on rich people to fund them – and I just don't know how much rich people want to pay to be investigated, or to investigate their friends, and write afflict-the-comfortable stories … For the most part, billionaires tend not to be that civic spirited."

8

Conclusions: Neo-postmodern Times

If there is a moral we can take from the postwar history of the news business, it is that an organization can practise journalism in order to do business, or do business in order to practise journalism. Much of the criticism that has been levelled at the news media over the years has involved the former, a system in which the audience serves the advertiser, the advertiser serves the media company, and the media company serves the owners, executives, and shareholders. In this scheme, journalists are an expense, and social responsibility a means of preserving the status quo.

Unfortunately – or fortunately, depending on your view of industrial-scale journalism – a key element of this structure is rotting away: advertising. For decades, the backbone of newspaper revenue had been made up mainly of two types of advertising: classified and retail. Classifieds are gone. That is well documented and, for the most part, news organizations have come to accept it. Less documented and accepted is the fact that drastic changes in retailing have irrevocably altered that segment of the advertising industry as well. Retail advertising is most effective when it is focused and responds to the consumer's three basic concerns: price, availability, and convenience. Now, thanks to the Internet, shoppers can find virtually any item in minutes, pay the lowest price, and have it delivered, often in twenty-four hours. Targeted marketing, big-box stores, and Web-based sales and promotion have shattered entire retail sectors, and surviving retailers have become more careful with their money. This is understandable, when you consider that, at a 10 per cent profit margin, a retailer has to sell $5,010 worth of merchandise to make a dollar on a $500 ad.

With few exceptions, North American newspapers have long been able to neglect the fact that they are retailers themselves; now they have to relearn how to compete in a retail marketplace that is evolving rapidly in mysterious ways. No magic formula of native, or sponsored, content, billing by audience penetration, and desirable demographics is likely to bring back the easy 30 per cent profit margins. Demographics are for the most part irrelevant. Who cares how well heeled your readers are if high-end advertisers are using TV and glossy magazines for their institutional promotion and targeted advertising to move product? Unless you are the *New York Times*, the odds are that Ralph Lauren isn't going to put a multimedia display ad on your home page.

Native advertising, from a journalist's perspective, appears to be a fool's gambit of undermining a news organization's brand by using it to sell someone else's product. For example, in 2014 contract negotiations with the union representing newsroom workers, the *Globe and Mail* proposed that managers be "given the right to assign editorial employees to write and edit advertorial copy as part of their regular duties" (Baluja 2014c). Newsroom employees rejected the proposal, and *Globe* management dropped the contract provision during last-minute negotiations and averted a strike (O'Beirne 2014). In the future, one would hope management would be cognizant enough of the retail value of journalistic impartiality to avoid assigning, say, the TV critic to write a promotional feature for CTV's new season, or having a foreign correspondent produce a page on retirement communities in Ecuador. However, it is unlikely that we have heard the last of this kind of contract provision. And we should remember that there was a time when the idea of putting ads on the front page of a newspaper was beyond the pale – until revenue began to slide. Now, it is not unusual to see the real front page hidden behind a wrap-around that makes an automobile ad look like the major news of the day.

Blending editorial and advertising content is nearsighted even from a pure business perspective. Is it worth investing thousands of dollars and hundreds of employee hours in advertising content thinly disguised as news or feature material, to serve advertisers who can and will flee as soon as some other medium offers better price and penetration? On the other hand, wouldn't it be worth investing that money and those employee hours in creating content that a whole lot of people will find indispensable and convenient, and worth paying for? The drawback to the second strategy is that it is something at which you have to work very hard, constantly proving with everything you do that your product is worth the price you ask. That's the challenge retailers face every day, and newspapers haven't had to in a very long time.

Another possible scenario is that the new vanity proprietors, and the old chain ownerships, will see native content as an opportunity to promote pet causes, advance free-market ideology, and serve the interests of corporate and political friends – perpetuating the old business model. Because it is more or less the only stream of advertising revenue that offers any hope of supporting large news organizations, native content could give advertisers and special interests unprecedented leverage over the greater editorial tone of a news organization.

Advertisers have long been able to control the environment in which their messages appear. For example, airlines have long-standing arrangements with newspapers not to run their ads on a day when one of the major stories is an air crash (an entirely reasonable condition). However, real advertiser displeasure can have serious repercussions. In 1990, the independent *Kingston Whig-Standard* ran a positive review of a how-to-sell-your-own-house book – in its homes section. Real estate agents in the Kingston area were sufficiently offended by the review that they organized a boycott of the paper, which cost it an estimated $500,000 in advertising revenue. The losses, combined with competition from local weeklies, drove the *Whig* into chain ownership. The newspaper was sold to the Southam chain the same year (Yarrow 1993).

With native content, an advertiser who is making a major investment in a news organization could have the power to demand that *no* editorial material run contrary to its message, or even its politics or morality. For example, if the bulk of a news organization's income is coming from a series of advertorials on the oil sands, it is conceivable that there might be a tendency to play down or suppress stories about dirty fossil fuels, anti-pipeline protests, and global warming, and to support political parties that are in favour of cheap, dirty energy and uninterested in environmental concerns. Studies have shown that average readers often don't recognize the difference between native content and genuine editorial material, so the power of this sort of advertising may be to tilt public opinion in a direction that is not always aligned with public interest.

As for the possibility that the audience might be willing to support trustworthy, unbiased news, the argument that people won't pay for content has been demolished by the likes of iTunes and Netflix. Both services offer, for a very reasonable price, convenient, quick downloads of material that can be obtained free elsewhere, but through greater effort and with less consistent quality. You may not be able to sell albums for $20 any more, but you can sell songs for 99 cents and movies for $14.99 – and millions of them. As media observer Jack Shafer wrote, you can charge for information online if it is indispensable, authoritative, and alluring (2009a). *Consumer Reports* and various financial sites have long been able to charge for their product because many people need the information they provide; the *New York Times* has attracted some 700,000 paid subscribers for the same reasons. The *Guardian* is free, but the reason it draws 100 million visitors a month is that it is a brand people trust and a site they enjoy using.

In most cases, a news organization that wants to stay alive and serve the public interest has to look to the reader, for whom the thing was supposed to have been built in the first place. As the *Columbia Journalism Review*'s Ryan Chittum says: "If you want to have anything like the newsrooms we've been used to, online advertising is not going to support it. You've got to find other ways to bring in revenue. The two ways I know how to do that are from readers directly or from advertisers."

Thus, it appears to say make more sense to do business in order to practise journalism. Two emerging models of that approach are the *New York Times* and the *Guardian*. Both show promise for journalism; neither is necessarily applicable to a wide variety of circumstances; neither is compatible with slash-and-burn management.

The *New York Times* popularized the metered paywall and appears to be on the way to proving that a North American news organization can sustain itself mostly on audience support. It put itself in this position by settling for lower profit margins than most public news companies and by investing in journalism. In 2013, Chittum told me that the *Times*'s newsroom was roughly the same size it had been ten years earlier, but people were doing things they had never dreamed of a decade back. "The *Times* is a unique beast, but it has implications for other newspapers. I've estimated that it probably has $130 million in pure digital circulation revenue, and it's still growing …

I think it's reasonable to say that in five years they're going to have a million subscribers. If they continue to grow their digital revenue, they're going to make it pretty much as they've always done. They may be a little smaller, but they're not going to be an *L.A. Times* shell of themselves."

That is not to say the future is assured for the *Times*, or that the omens are all good. In October 2014, the organization announced it would eliminate one hundred jobs, owing to the disappointing performance of some of its digital products. "While there are promising signs in digital advertising and digital subscriptions," executive editor Dean Baquet wrote in a memo to staff, "the print business remains under pressure. And our new products are not achieving the business success we expected, even though they are journalistic sensations" (Mirkinson 2014). At around the same time, in its digital products, the *Times* was shrinking the type and modifying the language that identifies native advertising. The *Times* had been running sponsored content inside boxes surrounded by large blue borders, with advertiser logos displayed prominently, and the words, "Paid for and posted by ..." This was changed to a smaller and less obvious display, reduced prominence of company logos, and the label "Paid content." As *Advertising Age* noted, "A bit of reader confusion over what's an ad is inherent" (Sebastian 2014).

Operating under the stewardship of the Scott Trust, the *Guardian* maintains a newsroom of roughly 700 and has amassed an enormous international audience by giving its digital product away. (However, readers who wish to get their news free of "adverts" can pay a subscription price.) The organization can operate on sustainable losses, so long as the trust, aided by the newspaper's digital operations and advertising revenue, can raise enough to pay the bills. Another benefit of operating under the Scott Trust is that the *Guardian* is a rare media organization that can say in its charter that it is dedicated to freedom from corporate influence as well as government interference.

That last bit is key to the success of any news organization that chooses to trust its fate to audience support: it must serve the interests of the great community; it cannot cater to the rich and the powerful. It can transform itself into a marketing organization, or it can be put to work as a propaganda vehicle for special interests – but at risk of losing the confidence of its audience. That is one of the worries raised by the entry into the business of rich benefactors, such as the new owners of the *Washington Post, Boston Globe,* and *Orange County Register,* or the Koch brothers, who might be more than happy to put their mouths where their money is.

Ideally, news organizations must find ways to remain independent not only of government but of the corporate world as well. How to achieve that state is a problem that has eluded solution almost as long as we have had a free press, largely because of advertising, shareholders, and corporate ownership. When you practise journalism to do business, the product becomes a means to an end: advertising space to be sold, a property to be flipped, a source of wealth to be monetized. As observers from Walter Lippmann to Yochai Benkler have pointed out, the practice of journalism often poses a threat to these activities. In contrast, the more readers pay the freight, the more the newspaper is inclined to serve their needs.

Some operations, such as CBC, NPR, PBS, BBC, and various state news organizations, rely wholly or partly on funding from or through government, and that raises a whole new set of probems, as we have seen in the past two decades with the way sucessive Canadian federal governments have chipped away at the CBC. In June 2014, the broadcaster announced that it would cut as many as 1,500 jobs over five years, in addition to the 657 positions that were eliminated earlier in the year after the network lost the rights to telecast NHL games. Network president and CEO Hubert Lacroix unveiled a "digital first" plan to shift its focus from broadcast TV and radio to online and mobility, and announced that in-house production would be "significantly reduced" (Wong 2014). In March 2015, the reorganization began, as CBC management announced that it would eliminate 244 jobs in its local TV and radio operations across the country, and that it would add 80 positions in its digital operations (Houpt 2015). More than one commentator has pointed out how strange it seems that a public broadcaster is moving toward abandoning broadcasting.

As for the trust-fund model of finanacing the news, the closest thing to an organization like the *Guardian* on this side of the Atlantic is the *Tampa Bay Times*, owned by the Poynter Instutute. But Poynter has only $44 million in assets, compared to the estimated $1.5 billion the Scott Trust has at its disposal (Chittum 2014a). In Canada, we almost had a newspaper like the *Guardian*: the *Toronto Star*. When founding publisher Joseph Atkinson died in 1948, he willed his shares of the *Star* to the Atkinson Charitable foundation, so that the paper would "not fall into private hands" (Harkness 1963, 349). Within a year, however, following cries of outrage from the *Star*'s competitors – the *Telegram* and the *Globe and Mail* – Ontario's ruling Progressive Conservative government (long a favourite target of *Star* journalism) passed the Charitable Gifts Act, prohibiting charitable organizations from owning more than 10 per cent of a business (Hayes 1992, 60). Atkinson's biographer, Ross Harkness, wrote that this was "the final episode in the long dispute between Mr Atkinson, who believed that a little socialism now and again is a good thing, and those who presume private enterprise, spurred by the profit motive, will always run things better" (1963, 357).

That sentiment foreshadowed such late twentieth-century media critics as Ben Bagdikian, Noam Chomsky, Robert McChesney, John Miller, David Taras, Doug Underwood, and Robert Hackett and Yuezhi Zhao, among whom the general consensus appeared to be that the biggest threat to journalism was the profit motive of Big Media. At the time of writing, it has been a decade or more since that wave of criticism receded, and most of the large media companies have grown larger, for the most part to the detriment of journalists and their audiences, but to the great economic benefit of a few highly paid executives. The perpetuation of old-school ownership has meant bad habits and self-destructive ways are being imported to the Internet. As Dean Starkman wrote: "It has been unnerving to witness how the Internet's strengths – limitless space, a 24/7 publishing schedule, precise quantity and popularity metrics – have meshed with old-fashioned corporate imperatives of sped-up reporter productivity and indifferent journalism quality. High-flown rhetoric of futuristic digitism is deployed ... to justify reckless and unnecessary cost cuts to regional newsrooms and to marginalize reporting in the publc interest ... Unless rethought, it represents a darkening cloud over the future of news" (2014, 15).

It may be true, as Torstar's John Honderich says, that you can't cut your way to greatness, but more than a few newspaper owners are slicing their way to fat stacks of going-out-of-business bucks. What is sometimes forgotten in the process is that these companies are ruining properties that are also public services. As Ryerson University's John Miller says, there's a real danger that the news-lite products they put out will salt the earth – or choke the garden – so that nothing else can grow there. Time and again, we have seen big chains come to the brink – most dramatically the Tribune Co. and Canwest – only to see financial forces marshalled to keep them going as zombie corporations, struggling with debt loads that shackle otherwise profitable dailies to demoralizing rounds of staff cuts and subsequent reductions in community service. Or, in the case of companies like Gannett or Quebecor, they resort to systematic strip mining of assets deemed no longer worth sustaining.

In Canada, recent developments have pushed news-industry ownership back to the level of concentration we last saw in the 1990s. In October 2014, Postmedia Network Inc. and Quebecor Inc. announced a deal that would place the latter's 175 English-Canadian newspapers and its Web properties into the hands of the former. The transaction, which was approved by the Competition Bureau in March and finalized in April of 2015, puts Postmedia in control of every English mid-size to big-city print news product from Montreal to Vancouver, save the *Globe and Mail, Toronto Star, Hamilton Spectator, Waterloo Region Record, Winnipeg Free Press, Brandon Sun*, and *Lethbridge Herald*. In Vancouver, Calgary, Edmonton, and Ottawa, Postmedia owns both daily papers. It also owns two of the four dailies in Toronto, the only English-language newspaper in Montreal, and both of the big papers in Saskatchewan. With its own *Canada.com* and Quebecor's *Canoe*, it runs two of the half-dozen or so major English-language, national news websites.

One of the few hopes the recession had held out was that media organizations like Postmedia and the Sun chain would collapse and shatter into small, local publishing companies, and leave holes for new enterprises to fill. This almost happened with Canwest, but a complex financial arrangement involving US and Canadian hedge fund firms, led by New York's Golden Tree Asset Management, pulled Postmedia out of the rubble. Since Postmedia's creation in 2010, the investors "have pocketed an estimated $300-million … on Postmedia junk bonds that pay interest rates ranging between 8.25 per cent and 13.3 per cent" (McNish and Nelson 2014). Quebecor's Sun Media properties appeared to be on the way to extinction, until Postmedia stepped in and offered to pay $316 million for everything outside Quebec except the Sun News Network, which Quebecor abruptly shut down in February 2015 after failing to find a buyer for it.

Several Postmedia staff members have insisted to me that the financial favours bestowed by chains outweigh the burdens. The most commonly cited benefits are centralized advertising sales, the sharing of editorial content, and centralized production facilities. Yet, national advertising is declining almost as fast as classifieds did, and these same newspapers claim to be dedicating themselves to local news coverage – something that can hardly be strengthened by editing, graphic design, and content from hundreds or, in some cases, thousands of kilometres away.

Chains exist primarily to see to it that chains continue to exist, and there never seems to be an end to those who are willing to help finance the project.

Many news executives seem loath to accept the changes in the way the world works. For example, the *Globe and Mail* has announced that it is aimed at people who are making or have the potential to make more than $100,000 a year and is developing complicated ways of measuring what these people want to read (Basen 2013). This sounds like a throwback to newspapers' corporate strategies of the 1980s, when demographics and market research were hailed as the cures for declining circulation and an aging audience. It also appears to be designed to repel as many people as it attracts.

Many, if not most, news organizations are experimenting with sponsored content. For example, Postmedia aims to build online communities of foodies or entrepreneurs. It seems as if the roles of readers and advertisers consistently remain static; the product is intended as bait to draw the herd down the chute to advertisers. This is a strategy that flies in the face of the fact that readers and advertisers have many other options available to them. Also, in most cases, annual or even semi-annual layoffs have left these newspapers ghosts of what they were, yet the companies have begun asking readers to pay for an online product that is less than the one they had been used to getting for free. As the Montreal *Gazette*'s Raymond Brassard says, journalism is paying for three decades of bad management, and that is not just on the business side of the industry. The complaints and criticism of the news business have long centred on a journalism that has become increasingly timid, narrow, and elitist, and focused on the needs of the rich and powerful. *Globe and Mail* columnist Lawrence Martin has complained of a Canadian news industry that represents only the right wing, though polls have shown that Canadians lean mostly towards the progressive end of the political spectrum. Jay Rosen has argued that, in many cases, the majority of the audience lives in Daniel Hallin's sphere of deviance. As a result, journalism has tended to ignore or trivialize many of the things the audience holds dear or considers of pressing concern. Perhaps nowhere is this more obvious than in politics and business.

For example, the demoralizing lack of opportunity and crushing student debt afflicting much of our youth should be issues of abiding concern to a media supposedly preoccupied with finding ways to reach a younger audience. Instead, these issues are treated mostly as sideshows to a debate carried on by politicians and businessmen, who never present anything resembling solutions. Discussion focuses on ways to make tuition easier to finance or to extending repayment, ponders youth-training programs that never seem to get implemented, or examines new ways to finance student loans. Rarely discussed, at least beyond Quebec, is the possibility of public funding for post-secondary education, something common outside Canada, Britain, and the United States. What is consistently pushed into the sphere of deviance is the concept of investing in programs that pay back in social capital rather than dollars, and the topic of raising money for it through taxation – particularly corporate taxation – is almost taboo. The notion that everything should be run as a business and nothing should cost money has come to be taken for granted, an unassailable element of neo-liberal dogma.

Free-market ideology has come to dominate the public discourse, and the concerns of the so-called 99 per cent are being discussed everywhere but in our newspapers and on our newscasts. This goes a long way toward explaining the popularity among young people of *The Daily Show* and *Last Week Tonight*, where the main pastimes are exposing the hypocrisies and jeering at the stupidity of politics and the news media.

Similarly, the news industry has long paid lip service to the issue of diversity, while accomplishing little. As Carleton University's Catherine McKercher says, our newsrooms continue to be mostly the preserve of white, middle-class men:

We all know that journalism has traditionally been a man's business. If you go through current material on journalism and gender in every single area of journalism, men outnumber women. Still. And this is despite the fact that women have outnumbered men in journalism schools since at least the 1970s, and probably before that. We have more women graduating, but men outnumbering women. And it's past the point where there should be a generational shift. It's not quite as bad as it used to be, but it still is the case that men outnumber women [in the workplace], and the higher you go, the more likely you are to be a man than a woman. These old gender relations are still there. The one place in journalism where the women outnumber the men? Freelance writing. By two to one, women outnumber men. Which is the poorest-paid area of journalism? Freelance writing.

In the same way, the working class, Aboriginal people, and the poor are rarely if ever presented in the news as anything other than victims, social problems, or curiosities. Often, stories about people in these groups read like reports from anthropological expeditions to exotic lands. As well meaning as journalists may be – and, to be fair, the craft draws a lot of people who are open-minded and have a strong sense of social justice – it's just not possible for outsiders to adopt the point of view of insiders. "You seek out news from the kind of people you have always sought out for news," Ryerson University's John Miller says. "If you send a white reporter out on the street – I don't care how good they are – chances are, if they do a streeter, they're going to stop people who look like them. It's just an unconscious reaction, which is one reason some newspapers said, 'We're falling out of touch with who's who here, and the readers that we want and the advertisers we want, so we'd better make some changes.' Unfortunately, in this country, it never really took much hold."

Further serving to alienate journalists from their audience is the fact that almost all the blue- and pink-collar jobs that once existed in, or next to, newsrooms have been disappeared by technology. The secretaries, assistants, copy people, printers, engravers, proofreaders, and typesetters – the average readers who used to work alongside journalists – are mostly gone. Largely, what remain are privileged, university-educated, mainly white people who often live with and talk to other privileged, university-educated, mainly white people. Ethnic and gender diversity are rare; economic diversity may be rarer. And staff reductions have aggravated the news organizations' isolation from mainstream society. The single-minded pursuit of short-term gain has done enormous damage to their ability to evolve. When your main strategy is to cut staff, it becomes very difficult to pursue ethnic, racial, and gender diversity.

The situation is made worse by the fact that news organizations have been draining the pool from both ends. The people who tend to get cut or leave voluntarily are often the most valuable: the youngest and most enthusiastic, and the most experienced and knowledgeable. The people who can afford to take risks, to stand up to management or pursue unpopular story ideas – who don't have mortgages and growing families – are the young, and they are often the ones getting laid off or not hired. At the same time, early-retirement buyouts are depleting the news organizations' cultural memory and eliminating the people who could be training a new generation of journalists. "It's just shrinking and shrinking, and shrinking," *OpenFile*'s Wilf Dinnick says. "Look at the *Globe and Mail* and all the talent they lost. They had buyouts and all the most senior people go. And you create drainage. And it's very hard to attract young people. Do you want to work at a place where you're not going to learn a huge amount? … I know people who have worked at two of the big papers and they say about the people running their show, I wouldn't mind if they tried something and failed. I just don't like it chugging along the way it is."

The complaints about industrial journalism go back to the days of the Kent Commission. That nothing was done during the days of record profits is not surprising. That they persist in the face of an economic apocalypse is baffling and unsettling. With all the focus on the broken business model, the conversation about a broken journalism model seems to have been forgotten. As a consequence, many of the plans to revitalize journalism amount to little more than new ways of funding old ways, rather than reinventing the business by revitalizing the craft – or they involve transforming a public-service medium into a marketing one.

In 2014, when Margaret Sullivan, the public editor of the *New York Times*, looked for some of the "most interesting reading" on the subject of the newspaper crisis, she wrote that the oldest and most prescient item she could find was a blog post by Clay Shirky from 2009: "Newspapers and Thinking the Unthinkable." "When someone demands to know how we are going to replace newspapers," Shirky wrote, "they are really demanding to be told that we are not living through a revolution. They are demanding to be told that old systems won't break before new systems are put in place." However, in every revolution, he writes, the established order begins to crumble before something can be built to replace it. With newspapers, this is partly because the owners of the old stuff are clinging like misers to a niche in society that perhaps could be better filled by new stuff. Lest that be interpreted as a cold-hearted dismissal of the thousands of professional journalists thrown out of work, we should remember that what is bad for Big Media is not necessarily bad for journalism, and what is good for Big Media is not always good for journalism.

Many journalists who have lost their jobs are underemployed or struggling to earn a freelance living in a market where the value of their work is plummeting. Many are downgraded to reduced or part-time wages, or are out of the business altogether. However, there may be a bright side even to this. Non-profit organizations dedicated to investigative journalism are being formed and are looking for ways to fund journalism free of corporate and government interference, similar to the Scott Trust and Poynter arrangements. A few alternative news sites, like *The Tyee, iPolitics, allNovaScotia.com, Voice of San Diego*, and *Minnpost* are springing up. And some, like the underground papers of the 1960s and '70s, are doing more interesting and harder-hitting journalism than the dailies with which they are competing. Also, the concept of hyper-local journalism has created thousands of alternative opportunities for journalists who want to be their own bosses, expand the conversation, or give a voice to their communities; organizations such as Quebecor and Gannett have been working hard to create a need.

Despite its reputation for shortening attention spans, digital technology is proving useful to literary journalism, as we have seen with the many Web publications that have adapted it to serve long-form features. Thanks to e-readers and tablets, storytellers are able to market long investigative features directly to their audience. One example is Paula Todd's *Finding Karla*, a forty-six-page e-book the Toronto journalist wrote about tracking down convicted killer Karla Homolka and which she marketed in 2012 through the Internet. At the same time, organizations such as the *New York Times* and the *Guardian* are creating intricately designed, complex blends of traditional features, and graphic and multimedia storytelling.

On the negative side are the small dailies and community newspapers that have been hailed by some as a blueprint for survival. A closer look reveals a segment of the industry that is still largely flying fat, happy, and stupid. New technologies have made it possible for these organizations to serve their communities better than they ever have. Yet only a few have embraced digital technology and the new ways of telling stories. When your paper is 70 per cent filled with ads, as some are, there's little reason to look to a future in which the Internet will siphon off your revenue.

That leads us to what may be the most underappreciated effect of the disruption of the business of journalism: a convergence of technology and surplus talent that has the potential to create a wave of creativity that could swamp all the old boats. If anything could finish the job of breaking the old things and replacing them with the new, this is it. As the *Globe and Mail*'s Steve Ladurantaye says, once the mainstream alternatives to newsroom work begin to get scarcer, enterprising and talented journalists are going to begin eyeing markets that are ripe for takeover, and they have access to technology that allows them to be very competitive. The same goes for the waves of bright, dedicated, and talented journalism students who are graduating every year, some of whom would likely find it more interesting to contribute to the disruption than to support the status quo.

The process of things getting broken before new things get made creates a vacuum, and that invites intervention by special interests, hustlers, propagandists, and opportunists, many with stronger financial backing than any idealistic entrepreneur could hope for. In recent years, we have seen a new class of newspaper owner emerge, harking back to the era of the big-city news boss or, as Jack Shafer writes, to the days of wealthy patronage: the "new Medicis." Shafer coined that term in reaction to the news that investor Neil Barsky had hired former *New York Times* executive editor Bill Keller to head his new journalism organization, *The Marshall Project*. Barsky joins: Aaron Kushner of the *Orange County Register*; John Henry of the *Boston Globe*; Amazon's Jeff Bezos, who bought the *Washington Post*; Pierre

Omidyar, who invested $50 million in Glenn Greenwald's *Intercept*; Herbert Sandler and *ProPublica*; and even the latest generation of Thomson family owners at the *Globe and Mail*. What makes these people different from corporate owners, whose motive is profit, and journalists, whose motives are artistry, truth, and glory, Shafer writes, is that "the new Medicis want primarily to save the world."

"Pierre Omidyar ... has articulated his opposition to surveillance culture, the Kochs have their libertarian agenda, Neil Barsky is upfront about the *Marshall Project*'s goal being to 'help make criminal justice reform an important part of the national debate by the 2016 presidential campaign,' and Pete Peterson (*Fiscal Times*) has always hollered about the need for debt reduction" (Shafer 2014). That sounds very similar to a concept embraced by the new class of obscenely rich robber barons: voluntary taxation, the idea that the super-wealthy have earned the right to dictate where their tax dollars go. If society needs education, health services, public transit, and snow removal, and the rich want private schools, ballet-opera houses, executive air terminals, and heliports, guess what society gets? As Shafer points out, the problem with the very rich being in a position to dictate the issues upon which journalistic attention is focused is that, to us, "their investigations might constitute misinformation, subversion, agitprop or stupidity."

To be fair to the new Medicis, it's worth noting that owner meddling has not been unknown in the news business. Perhaps the most notorious case in Canadian media history is that of the Canwest newspapers of the early 2000s. Shortly after they took control of the Hollinger (formerly Southam) dailies from Conrad Black, the owners of Canwest issued an edict that the papers in their chain would run a quota of editorials from head office each week. As well, there were charges of corporate interference in the news pages. In a piece that was never permitted into print, *Halifax Daily News* columnist Stephen Kimber wrote: "CanWest's owners, Winnipeg's Asper family, which made its fortune in the television business, appear to consider their newspapers not only as profit centres and promotional vehicles for their television network but also as private, personal pulpits from which to express their views. The Aspers support the federal Liberal party. They're pro-Israel. They think rich people like themselves deserve tax breaks. They support privatizing health care delivery. And they believe their newspapers, from Victoria, BC, to St. John's, NF, should agree with them" (2001).

Though management there was never as heavy handed or as tone deaf to public opinion as the Aspers, when I worked at the *Toronto Star* we even had a code for "handle with care," High Corporate Interest. Just the initials, HCI, would abruptly end any debate over the merits of a story. The term said that powerful eyes were watching, and any editor or reporter who valued her or his paycheque would make sure those eyes liked what they read and where it appeared in the next day's paper. It could be an adjective or a verb: "This story is HCI." Or, "You had better HCI that story." To verify the accuracy of my memory, I emailed Kathy Muldoon, a former *Star* colleague and now director of the print journalism program at Oakville's Sheridan College, and asked if she recalled the term. "I just thought of that the other day, trying to tell my students that a story was a must-run even though we think it sucks," she wrote back. "We always said, 'HCI.' Yes, High Corporate Interest. Used in a sentence: '[A senior executive's] wife sits on the board of the diabetes society. How will you play that sugar-free cookie recipe?'"

As in other public-service endeavours, even the appearance of collusion with special interests can be damaging to a news organization's reputation. The 2014 Ontario provincial election offered two instances of apparent partisanship on the part of senior management of two of Canada's top newspaper companies.

Toward the end of the election, the *Globe and Mail* endorsed Conservative Tim Hudak, whom the national daily itself had characterized in a news story as an ultra-right-wing candidate who consulted "leading lights on the American right – from Tea Party-linked think tanks to anti-tax crusaders – in his effort to craft an unabashedly small-government platform" (Morrow 2014). After the election, Jesse Brown (2014) reported on his *Canadaland* blog that the *Globe*'s editorial board had planned to endorse a minority government for Liberal premier Kathleen Wynne but was overruled by management in favour of a Hudak endorsement.

On election night, one of the people interviewed by CBC at Hudak's headquarters was Postmedia chair Paul Godfrey, the top executive of the nation's most powerful print news organization. A viewer tuning in partway through the interview might have been forgiven for confusing Godfrey with a Progressive Conservative Party operative when he told CBC that Hudak had lost because he told people truths that they just didn't want to hear. Godfrey was proved right on that count: Hudak won just 25.2 per cent of the popular vote. A little less than a year later, Godfrey publicly endorsed Patrick Brown for leadership of the Ontario PCs. Asked whether this represented a conflict of interest, Godfrey told the *Globe and Mail*: "Conflict for who? This is a race between Tories. The media talks about transparency. I'm the most transparent guy of all because I say the things that I do" (Bradshaw 2015).

It is tempting to draw the conclusion that neo-conservative politics might be considered HCI at the *Globe* and Postmedia papers, regardless of appeal or lack of it among readers. This is not to say that the *Globe and Mail* or the vast Postmedia organization will suddenly begin behaving like the Fox News Network. However, it is likely that individual journalists, knowing the political bent of the top echelon of their news organization, might be reluctant to endorse or even discuss policy positions that lie in a perceived zone of deviance. This would imply not so much an attack on leftist or centre-left viewpoints as a void in the conversation where the left used to be.

Government and commerce have at times joined forces to discourage the dissemination of inconvenient information. Harvard's Yochai Benkler (2011) meticulously documented the concerted attacks by government agencies, online money-handlers, and various Internet service providers to disable WikiLeaks after the Bradley Manning revelations, and the *Guardian* has been threatened about its supposed lack of "social responsibility" by the Conservative-led government of David Cameron. Another example of government and commerce coming together to punish dissent is the way Beijing has moved to tame the once-unruly Hong Kong press. In early 2014, the tabloid AM730 announced that mainland Chinese firms had pulled all their advertising in response to the paper's criticism of Central Committee policies; this was expected to cost the paper $1 million per year (Chan 2014). Also, during the Occupy Central protests of October 2014, there were news reports of Beijing-sponsored gangs interfering with the distribution of *Apple Daily*, whose owner, Jimmy Lai, was a prominent supporter of the Hong Kong democracy movement.

It would be foolish to assume that East and West, and government and corporations, are not learning from one another when it comes to controlling information. As Evgeny Morozov (2011) points out, one of the tenets of cyber-utopianism has been that the forces of freedom are skilled at adapting new information technologies, while the forces of repression are too sluggish and dim to see their potential. Yet Morozov warns that "this belief in the democratizing power of the Web ruins the public's ability to assess future and existing policies, not least because it overstates the positive role that corporations play in democratizing the world without subjecting them to the scrutiny they so justly deserve" (40).

For better or worse, the players who have stepped up to plug holes in the line are bloggers, citizen journalists, activists, political parties, and NGOs. Often, they are as capable of reporting the news as any so-called reputable news organization. For anyone who simply wants game reports and statistics, cfl.ca or mlb.com will do the job better than any local newspaper. And, if you want the investigative reporting on funding college athletes, contract disputes, drugging, or head injuries, magazines like *Sports Illustrated*, *Hockey News*, or even *Atlantic Monthly* will deliver the goods. That leaves the local sports sections in limbo, especially the ones that don't consider recreation, amateur athletics, or the minor-leagues worth covering. Similarly, for someone looking for a response to official policy, there is a range of online alternative publications and think tanks ranging from the US Heritage Foundation to the Canadian Centre for Policy Alternatives. And unions, political parties, and activist groups of all stripes have strong presences online.

Anyone who can master WordPress, Blogger, or one of the other do-it-yourself Web design services can become a commentator or citizen journalist. The lowering of the entry fee for participation has made for a richer and more diverse public discourse, though it is a fragmented one. "It's just glorious," Jack Shafer says, "that for the price of cheap stereo back when we were kids, you can set up the equivalent of a full, high-powered printing press and keep a server up for a year. It's phenomenal that every citizen has the ability to be a pamphleteer and try to make their voice heard."

The operative word is "try." As Morozov, Robert McChesney, and David Taras have pointed out, the Internet is rapidly becoming a corporate, free-market institution dominated by a few gigantic players. Netflix, iTunes, Amazon, Google, Twitter, and Facebook are some of the large, noisy companies to which everyone pays attention. The rest, as Taras says, are the little guys who don't have much hope of reaching a wide audience. For the most part, Big Media is bringing old-media thinking to the Internet: establish a monopoly, nail it down, exploit it, dominate the market, cut expenses, increase profit, service debt, and make shareholders happy and executives rich. In Canada, mainstream companies such as Postmedia and BCE have designs on dominating the online world, and the unfolding narrative looks a lot like "meet the new boss, same as the old boss."

The handover of Sun Media properties to Postmedia aims not so much to create a massive chain of newspapers as a Canadian online megalith that can hold its own against the international brands. "We're not just buying a well known newspaper brand ...we're evolving into a news media company, with one print and three digital platforms – the Web, the smartphone and the tablet," Paul Godfrey said after the deal was announced. "Over time, it's our hope that *Canoe* and other related websites will become the jewel of the deal. Scale is important, particularly in the digital world" (Flavelle 2014). In Ontario, Torstar's Metroland chain of community papers is setting up a network of websites, such as *Inside Brockville*, *Inside Belleville*, and *Inside Ottawa Valley*, that aims to pre-empt attempts by independents to establish competitive sites. As slick-looking as they are, they contain a lot of non-local material and little that is innovative in the way of storytelling.

All the talk coming out of Postmedia after the Sun announcement was about strategy and tactics of market domination, and not about journalism. As the *Toronto Star*'s Rosie DiManno wrote: "*Synergies* mean layoffs. *Maximizing across multiple platforms* might mean collapsing and combining daily newspapers. *Re-imagined product strategy* could mean the unilateral pimping of a news chain's digital assets" (2014). The deal is the same old chain-ownership story of debt ($140 million of new debt for a total of close to $500 million) and shareholder equity ($186 million, purchased by Postmedia's backers), which is another form of financial obligation. As DiManno goes on to say, this is rarely good news for journalists or their audience.

Newspapers can provide several vital services in addition to the old-fashioned work of delivering objectively researched and intelligently interpreted accounts of current events, and keeping an eye on power: curating and filtering the white noise that makes the Internet such a tricky, devious source of information; funnelling and focusing the best new voices so that the real talents among the bloggers, citizen journalists, and online obsessives get noticed; exposing the special interests for what they are, and inhibiting their attempts to refeudalize the public sphere.

It's not so much that we are in danger of losing the information that we need to be democratic citizens. It's that we're losing the convenience and coherence of getting it in one or two places and delivered by organizations that at least operate under a doctrine of objectivity even if they occasionally stray from it. The argument that the diffuse and incoherent cacophony of the Internet constitutes a cognitive surplus or a democratic asset is cyber-utopian magical thinking. You can control information by limiting it, or by releasing it in such a flood that no one could hope to keep up with it. And it is extraordinarily naive to assume that, when people go looking for clarification, they will naturally gravitate to sane, objective sources of information.

Despite the persistence of the cyber-utopian mythology, people have less time to be informed or omnicompetent citizens, and we have more need than ever for watchdogs to keep an eye on wealth and power. The challenge lies in finding trustworthy sources of unbiased information that weigh the various points of view, and are open to new and alternative ideas. The news organizations that have preserved their brand and still inspire trust in their audience are most likely to survive. The material that simply blends in with the rest of the commercial messages and happy-talk infotainment is going to fade away or disappear into vanity projects of special interests. Those vanity projects may place the public sphere in more danger of becoming a marketing culture, and move us closer to the debased society and politics of selfishness that the Hutchins Commission, *Four Theories of the Press*, and the Kent Commission warned against.

Anyone who has paid attention to the newspaper crisis has noticed that it's the mid-market dailies that have suffered the worst. As we have seen, the mid-market papers also suffer from a host of pre-existing conditions that made them, at best, neutral parties in the conversation of the culture or, at worst, a menace to democracy.

When people say the news depresses them, it's likely they have more in mind than the ISIS horde, resurgent Russian empire, or an impending Ebola plague. In the United States, when a politician denounces global warming as bunk and invokes the "scientific proof" that, when an ice cube melts, the water level in a glass goes down, it is mostly left to Jon Stewart to point out that the politician's three main campaign funders are oil companies – and that it is the external meltwater running *into* the glass that should worry us. In Canada, the voices of dissent are so quiet that they are almost inaudible. Progressive media are few, ill-funded, and regionalized. *The Tyee* speaks to Vancouver, *Rabble* preaches to the converted, and, though "Metro Toronto" has become "The GTA," the *Toronto Star* still lives by its old slogan: "What does it mean to Metro?"

In Quebec, one company – Quebecor – controls the lion's share of newspapers, book publishing, magazines, print distribution, book stores, private TV, and Internet and cellphone service. The owner of that company leads the opposition Parti Québécois and has already openly lobbied the Quebec government on behalf of his properties, which are in a blind trust, though no one is under any illusions about who calls the shots. As columnist Lysiane Gagnon wrote in the *Globe and Mail* in 2014, "Quebec is a small society and Quebecor's weight in all the key areas of the province's cultural life, from book publishing to the film industry, is absolutely disproportional."

The CBC, which could be our last best hope, has been starved and threatened by successive Liberal and Conservative governments to the point that it has been turned into a dancing bear: mangy, emaciated, muzzled, fearful, and reflexive. Answering to a president and board with strong connections to the governing party and apparently living in mortal fear of offending those who feed and beat it, much of its output has become defensive, anodyne, and derivative. Witness the first few weeks of the Jian Ghomeshi scandal of fall 2014, which involved accusations that the high-profile CBC Radio One host had a history of assaulting women and abusing staff. On CBC TV, the main coverage consisted of playing catch-up to the *Globe and Mail* and *Toronto Star* on a story in which the network and one of its employees were the two main protagonists. CBC's first two "investigations" on the subject were a soft-news, millennial-bait feature about how the affair had tracked on Twitter, and a panel discussion about the use of anonymous sources in reporting. In the latter, Ghomeshi was mentioned once, in the form of an outburst by a panellist who seemed embarrassed by the proceedings. Finally, after several weeks, the network's current events series, *the fifth estate*, attempted to get to the bottom of the issue and was met by corporate sandbagging that played like a throwback to the Watergate era. Compare that to the extensive in-house investigations and coverage by the *New York Times* after Jayson Blair, one of its star reporters, was found to have been manufacturing news stories, and questions were raised about the impartiality of another, Judith Miller, in the march to war in Iraq.

As usual, the strongest stink comes from the head. Writing in the *Globe and Mail*, Patrick Lagacé, a columnist for *La Presse*, denounced CBC president Hubert Lacroix as "a political mouthpiece" who is acting as "little more than enabler for the steady, quiet dismantling" of CBC/Radio-Canada (2014).

None of this should be taken as a dismissal of the value of a free press in a democratic society. That many news organizations have failed to do their job very well, or have chosen to be irresponsible and sensationalistic, does not prove the job is not worth doing, or that journalists, given the opportunity, do not perform a vital public service.

"I wouldn't want to live in a community that doesn't have a daily newspaper," the *Globe and Mail*'s Steve Ladurantaye says. "Where else am I going to learn about why my taxes are going up and who's voting for it than my daily newspaper? Most people aren't going to go to a county website or a city council meeting. These are really basic things that people consume in their newspaper. Who's been arrested? What happened in court? These are vital, vital things for a community."

Unlike the emerging global news organizations, the mid- to large-market omnibus dailies have very limited appeal outside their market areas and face increased competition from blogs and news sites, city weeklies, tabloid give-aways, and myriad alternative options for advertisers and readers. They have also been hobbled by the demands of servicing their parent companies' debts and meeting shareholder expectations of high profit margins. This has led to severe cutbacks in staff that inevitably affect the quality of the product, and limit news organizations' ability to profit from the paywalls they have put in place. This explains the native-advertising fad. As *New York Times* reporter David Carr said, when you are drowning, everything looks like a life preserver.

Whether news executives have the resources, will, or imagination to recreate their products for various platforms is highly debatable. It often seems, especially in view of the Postmedia-Sun deal, that there is a relentless, grim continuity in the Canadian newspaper business, in which executives seek instant solutions in mechanics and ledgers, traditional business strategies, and audience-dazzling silver bullets. As in the 1980s, when much of the industry aped the USA Today formula of soft news, weather, and flashy graphics, and in the 1990s, when newspapers marched en masse into the dot-com bubble, news executives are embracing a strategy that mainly involves design and technological innovations, and does very little to address the issue of quality journalism.

Native advertising, algorithms that measure reader satisfaction, and mobile apps that play like video games are measures that sound complex and innovative, but are really very simple and predictable. Similarly, the obsession many news organizations have with social media is a promotional concern masquerading as an editorial one. Conversely, a much more simple-sounding plan – hire more journalists so you can produce better content, and give them the wherewithal to tell great stories – offers a very complex solution. Quality isn't easily measured or made; it's something that increases brand awareness in increments, story by story, photo by photo. As Stewart Brand said, bad content has the same value as good content – until good content proves itself consistent and worthwhile (quoted in Tofel 2012, 88).

The *New York Times* and the *Guardian* may not have mobile apps that are as pretty as the ones Postmedia is rolling out; in fact, the *Times* app looks a lot like a Web version of a traditional newspaper. However, neither company has reacted to economic pressures solely by attacking its workforce or focusing on marketing solutions disguised as journalism, and each is among the most successful news organizations on the Web. In Canada, with every news company, including the *Globe and Mail*, cutting back staff and farming out functions such as editing and design, there appear to be no contenders for the role of national news organization of record – at least not at the level of the *Times* or *Guardian*.

The country has devolved into a media oligarchy. Private TV is more or less completely owned by Bell, Shaw, Quebecor, and Rogers, which, along with Telus, dominate Internet delivery, telephone service, and online news. In print, most of Atlantic Canada is controlled by TC-Transcontinental; New Brunswick belongs to the Irving-owned Brunswick News Inc.; Quebecor dominates media in Quebec; Torstar rules the Kitchener-Oshawa corridor; Postmedia-Sun will have nearly everything else.

Even the community papers and small dailies are controlled by a handful of chains: TC-Transcontinental, Torstar's Metroland Group, Black Press, Glacier Newspaper Group, and Continental Newspapers Canada Ltd. With the takeover of Sun Media, Postmedia stands to pick up another 167 community papers, specialty publications, and small dailies across Canada including such important small operations as the *St Catharines Standard* and the *Kingston Whig-Standard*. If Postmedia decides to divest, these will almost certainly be gobbled up by the above-mentioned chains. At least that eventuality promises to create a few job opportunities, as the buyers will need to shore up local coverage to save many titles that might have remained viable had they not been bled dry by Quebecor over the past decade. Excluding the tiniest operations, that leaves seven organizations: the online and broadcasting services of the CBC; FP Publications' *Winnipeg Free Press* and *Brandon Sun*; the Thomson-owned *Globe and Mail*; Montreal's independent *Le Devoir*; Power Corp.-owned *La Presse* in Montreal; *Le Soleil* in Quebec City, acquired in 2015 by former federal Liberal cabinet minister Martin Cauchon; the independent *Halifax Chronicle-Herald*.

David Beers says he started Vancouver's *The Tyee* to broaden the discourse in a city dominated by one media company, but that was at a different time with a different Internet, one yet to be dominated by a few online entrepreneurs and media conglomerates. Now, it is highly debatable whether new voices will be able to enter the public discourse with any hope of being heard.

Conditions in the news business provide great potential for those in government and business to manipulate the public sphere. Overextended and often sympathetic news organizations are more willing to accept corporate and government handouts in the form of photographs, prepared news stories, or TV news video, as Canadian news agencies have with photo handouts from the PMO and US TV stations have with public service videos presented as news reports. Pseudo-news sites with agendas, or funders with deep pockets, can step in to provide "information" services. News agencies, such as the *Wall Street Journal*, Reuters, and Bloomberg, which serve special interests, become more powerful as public service news is impoverished. More and more journalists are relegated to the role of digital entrepreneur, enjoying the "freedom" to work unlimited hours for low pay, with no protection from litigation or harassment, should they choose to commit acts of accountability journalism. For the news consumer, it becomes easier to find out what is going on in London, Cairo, or Beijing, and more difficult to keep up with local politics and news.

The balance of power is tipping in favour of propaganda over information, further privatization of the public sphere, and more power for marketing over democratic discourse. "Historically, we have always had the elite communicating with each other, and that will go on no matter what," an anonymous reporter told me. "What I worry about is the cutting out of the middle class as partners in this public debate about the future of our democracies and economies, and the issues we should all care about. Perhaps what we're seeing is the final inning of the traditional newspaper industry being played out. Maybe it does need to die in its current form and be replaced by this digital platform that is really not so much about addressing the serious issues of the day ... Maybe, after some years of missing traditional journalism, there may come a demand for it. And there may then be a basis upon which to rebuild what we've lost."

Here, in Canada, the range of discourse has actually narrowed since David Taras wrote in 1999 that most of our news organizations were in the hands of right-wing ideologues. With the accelerating decay of the CBC, the creation of massive news monopolies, and the anti–free-speech attitude of the Harper government, the conversation is more focused than ever on the benefits of the few. A nation in which centrist news organizations such as CBC and the *Toronto Star* can be considered "far-left" (as so many of their critics persist in calling them) has a severely skewed political compass. Anything as mild as welfare capitalism or social democracy has been pushed into the sphere of deviance by a political discourse that ranges from a crazy crypto-fascist fringe to a great neo-liberal sphere of consensus. In this climate, John Diefenbaker could be branded a communist.

With apologies to Dorothy Parker, we are in danger of becoming mired in a public conversation that runs the ideological gamut from A to B.

In May 2014, at the *Toward 2020: New Directions in Journalism Education* conference at Ryerson University in Toronto, Robert Picard, director of research for Oxford University's Reuters Institute, laid an egg. At the same time, he unwittingly uncovered a couple of challenges to the future of journalism in Canada: how we train journalists and why we are allergic to criticism.

"Factory journalism" has seen its day, and good riddance, Picard said in his keynote speech to the event. Consequently, journalism schools must refocus, away from producing workers for the big media companies, and toward arming the most talented students with the tools they will need to act as free agents in a fluid economy. Then, he said two things that brought the house down – on his head: that roughly 10 per cent of students had the gifts to succeed at the upper levels of the craft, and that the surest way for a journalist to build a future is to develop a specialty. Both drew a scattered and hostile response from the audience. (At least the hostile ones were most vocal.) In response to Picard's comment about specialization, one man shouted from the back of the room, "That's the same as a beat."*

There are three interesting things about the audience reaction: the level, or at least the volume, of irritation and impatience with a journalism model that runs contrary to the status quo; the anger of the response to even mild criticism from an affable and highly qualified critic; that Picard's ideas were attacked but not questioned and debated.

Most people familiar with the thinness of skin among members of the Canadian media would not have been surprised by Picard's reception at Ryerson. In November 2014, following the Ghomeshi scandal, *Globe and Mail* TV critic John Doyle wrote a column in which he rolled his eyes at the Toronto media establishment. "We have a relatively small media in Canada," he wrote. "And most of it exists inside a bubble. To call it insular would be an understatement." Doyle went on to describe the media as a "gated community" and media criticism as non-existent. "Some journalism schools offer up their staff to do media analysis, but that usually amounts to interpreting 'spin' in a hot news story, which essentially means talking about PR, not journalism or media. Me, I have more or less stopped talking to the student-written *Ryerson Review of Journalism* because the writers seem to have conclusions wrapped up in advance and have no curiosity about

---

* For the record, the difference between a beat and a specialty is obvious: a beat is given to a reporter by an editor, and can be taken away by one; a speciality is constructed by the reporter, and cannot be taken away.

anything that challenges their existing views about television. Besides, most want into that gated community of Canadian media."

Very few Canadian journalists are cantankerous enough to take on the role of outsider when it comes to writing critically about the country's media establishment (as Doyle and the *Toronto Star*'s Rosie DiManno have). As for journalism schools, York University's Fred Fletcher once told me about asking the head of a prominent school why there is so little media criticism in the country. "We don't bite the hand that feeds us," was the reply.

The question of what can, will, or should be done to preserve journalism in Canada has not been addressed with anything resembling the vigour of the discussion that has taken place in the United States. And, to be fair, that question is something of an invitation to a mug's game. There are, however, a few things that cry out to be addressed, and one of the most obvious is the lack of an aggressive and popular media criticism. In the United States, the national conversation about the national conversation goes on at all levels of society, from *The Daily Show* and *Last Week Tonight* to the *Columbia Journalism Review*, to the annual *State of the News Media* reports from the Pew Research Centre's Project for Excellence in Journalism. In Canada, there is nothing resembling the PEJ. The only review of journalism is, as Doyle pointed out, written by students and aimed at reporting on the media rather than holding it to account. The website *J-Source* often looks critically at the news media, but it consists of journalists and academics talking to one another, and it lives inside the gated community. Finally, political satire in this country has been in a bad way since Rick Mercer took to sleeping over at 24 Sussex Drive and skinny-dipping with Bob Rae.

Next – and the unpopularity of this notion was highlighted in red during Picard's speech – journalism schools need to stop "preparing students to go to work for established news organizations." As Picard said, we do not train students in "entrepreneurship and independent journalism where employment opportunities are rising ... [or] how to establish themselves to work as individual journalists or in journalistic cooperatives" (2014). To that, I would add that we should be teaching our students a wide range of storytelling skills – and not simply how to be reporters. Those skills include: graphic design and digital storytelling for print and the Web; all types of editing (because they will need to exercise their own quality control, and be prepared to manage a news operation); basic photographic skills; data journalism; TV and radio production; business practices (if they're going to be "entrepreneurs," we need to teach them how to bill, get paid, keep books, and manage money). We also should insist that they have a grounding in English literature, political science, finance, and/or science.

There also needs to be a recognition that most of the opportunities and many of the best jobs in terms of professional satisfaction lie in small dailies and community newspapers, independent multimedia projects, free-agency, hyperlocal projects, and alternatives such as *The Tyee*. It won't do to simply add Twitter, Facebook, and various types of software coding to the old standard of training newsgatherers for the great newsrooms of the CBC, the *Globe and Mail*, and the *Toronto Star*. As Steve LaDurantaye said, we need to train journalists, not employees. We need to stop worrying about the dwindling job market in the factory newspapers, and start thinking about how widely useful journalism skills are – from law to the upper levels of business, to policy analysis, to fiction, showrunning, and screenwriting.

Next, we must save the CBC. There have been suggestions piled on suggestions, reports following reports, and unending attacks on the public broadcaster, much of it based on a myth: that the CBC is a waste of money and a service most Canadians could happily live without. In fact, a 2014 Nanos Research poll conducted for Postmedia showed that just 10 per cent of Canadians wanted to cut CBC funding. Forty-one per cent of respondents said the network's funding should be increased; 46 per cent wanted it kept at its present level. As for the notion that Conservatives are out to get the network: "Among federal Conservative supporters 51 per cent would like CBC funding to be maintained, 25 per cent would like to see CBC funding increased and 21 per cent would like to see funding decreased" (Csanady 2014). In other words, Conservative Party supporters don't dislike the CBC; they just like it at a slightly lower level than does the population at large.

Then, why has the network been subjected to more than twenty years of budget cuts? Because the past three federal leaders (two Liberal, one Conservative) *do* dislike the CBC, and they control the bank account. Thus, it seems clear that we need to remove the bottleneck in the flow of money from the public purse to the public broadcaster. That means stable, guaranteed funding pegged to inflation and controlled by some sort of non-government agency that lies beyond the reach of vindictive politicians. If support for the CBC is this high, why not let the service tax us directly, in the form of income tax vouchers or a broadcast-receiver licence, or, as the 1996 Juneau Report suggested, in the form of a small tax on cable and satellite bills?

Finally, it would be worthwhile to find ways to encourage the growth of alternative news media, made up of organizations like *The Tyee*, *iPolitics*, *OpenFile*, and *Canadaland*, that would be free of government or corporate interference. Perhaps something like Telefilm Canada could be established to help finance start-up news-media ventures, provided they agree to forgo native advertising and seek at least 50 per cent of their funding from their audience. Alternative-funding strategies have already begun to evolve, such as *The Tyee*'s blend of labour backing and reader support, and *Canadaland*'s pact with its podcast audience of 10,000: pay us a dollar each per month and we'll pour it into the show. A bit of public funding could jump-start a host of new projects that could go on to be self-sustaining and perhaps repay their financing, or be rejected by their audience and deserving of a quick death. At the same time, any laws or regulations that inhibit the ability of a news agency to operate as a trust or non-profit should be repealed, as Ontario's Charitable Gifts Act was in 2009. We badly need news organizations that are, as the *Guardian* is, beholden only to their audience.

Canada has a long history of indirectly subsidizing media companies (as does the United States), from preferred mail rates to the Income Tax Act, to Canadian content regulations, to the simulcasting rules that make it so profitable to be a private Canadian TV network. We must continue that tradition, but we need to stop subsidizing Big Media, which profits so well from its protected place in our system and contributes so little. Instead of continuing with this Bizarro World socialism, in which the fat and wealthy get the government aid, and the poor and struggling are left to die or be gobbled up, we need to start playing midwife to new ideas. In the past, we subsidized news businesses; now, we need to subsidize journalism.

To make public funding and audience support work, it takes a public and an audience that are aware of the value of a free press and the danger of one that does not serve the public good. We need media literacy in our elementary and secondary schools, and media criticism in our public conversation. To incubate new ideas, we need journalism education that is highly critical and independent of Big Media, and that trains its students to go out and build new structures to replace the crumbling old ones. We need to produce news-industry revolutionaries, not cannon fodder for establishment media.

To counteract the pervasive influence of corporate media, we need to level the playing field, so that new players don't get crushed by the old giants – and new ideas get a chance to grow into new projects. The Kent Commission showed the futility of trying to control Big Media. One thing we haven't tried is to help build competition for what is becoming a special-interest cartel controlling the conversation of our culture.

References

INTERVIEWS

Adam, G. Stuart, professor emeritus journalism, Carleton University, 12 August 2013.
Anonymous, a senior reporter who requested to have their name withheld, 29 July 2013.
Beers, David, founding editor, *The Tyee*, 31 July 2013.
Black, David, chairman, Black Press, 12 September 2013.
Blicq, Andrew, filmmaker, producer-director-writer, *Crackberry'd: The Truth about Information Overload. Doc Zone*, CBC, April 2011.
Boychuk, Rick, former editor-in-chief, *Canadian Geographic*, 24 July 2013.
Brassard, Raymond, former executive editor, *Montreal Gazette*, 22 August 2013. (Retired, September 2013.)
Chittum, Ryan, deputy editor, "The Audit," *Columbia Journalism Review*, 30 July 2013.
Chodan, Lucinda, regional vice-president editorial, Postmedia Network Inc.; editor-in-chief, *Montreal Gazette*, 25 July 2013.
Coombs, Stephanie, managing editor, *Edmonton Journal*, 13 September 2013.
Creighton, J. Douglas, founder, the *Sun* newspapers, 11 February 2002.
Dinnick, Wilf, founder, *OpenFile*, 12 August 2013.
Dorland, Michael, professor communication studies, Carleton University, 23 July 2013.
Dornan, Christopher, associate professor journalism, Carleton University, 28 August 2013.
Ferri, John, digital editor, *Toronto Star*, 23 July 2013. (As of 2014, vice-president current affairs and documentaries, TVOntario.)

Fletcher, Fred, professor emeritus communication and culture, York University, 31 July 2013.
Fulford, Robert, columnist, *National Post*, 1 August 2013.
Gibbons, Rick, radio host, former publisher the *Ottawa Sun*, 7 July 2013 (via email).
Gitlin, Todd, professor and chair PhD program, Columbia University Journalism School, 1 August 2013.
Godfrey, Paul, chief executive officer, Postmedia Network Inc., 13 August 2013.
Greenspon, Edward, vice-president strategic investments and new ventures, Star Media Group, 26 August 2013. (Since January 2014, editor-at-large, Bloomberg News Canada.)
Honderich, John, chairman, Torstar Corp., 23 July 2013.
Ladurantaye, Steve, media reporter, *Globe and Mail*, 29 July 2013. (Joined Twitter Canada, December 2013.)
Maffin, Todd, futurist, president of engageQ, for *Crackberry'd: The Truth about Information Overload*, *Doc Zone*, CBC, April 2011.
McKercher, Catherine, professor journalism, Carleton University, 24 July 2013. (Retired, June 2014.)
Miller, John, professor emeritus journalism, Ryerson University, 1 August 2013.
Muldoon, Kathy, director print journalism, Sheridan College, 14 March 2015 (via email).
Olive, David, business and current affairs columnist, *Toronto Star*, 25 July 2013.
Parrish, Wayne, chief operating officer, Postmedia Network Inc., 13 August 2013; 3 July 2003.
Pyette, Lester, former publisher and chief executive officer, *National Post*, 25 July 2013.
Raudsepp, Enn, distinguished professor emeritus journalism, Concordia University, 8 August 2013.
Rosen, Jay, professor of journalism, New York University (via SMS), 31 July 2014.
Salkeld, Stuart, editor, *St Albert Gazette*, 12 September 2013.
Shafer, Jack, media columnist, Reuters.com, 25 July 2013.
Stackhouse, John, editor-in-chief, *Globe and Mail*, 20 August 2013. (Left *Globe and Mail*, March 2014. Since January 2015, senior vice-president at the Royal Bank of Canada.)
Steward, Hartley, former publisher, *Toronto Sun*, 11 January 2002. (Died 5 June 2014.)

Taras, David, professor communication studies, Mount Royal University, 29 July 2013.
Unland, Karen, Capital Ideas, *Edmonton Journal*, 13 September 2013.
Waddell, Christopher, associate professor and director, School of Journalism and Communication, Carleton University, 29 July 2013. (Stepped down, July 2014. Now associate professor of journalism, Carleton University.)
Winseck, Dwayne, professor communication studies, 23 July 2013.

SECONDARY SOURCES

Adam, G. Stuart. 2006. "Notes towards a Definition of Journalism." In *Journalism: The Democratic Craft*, edited by G. Stuart Adam and Roy Peter Clark. New York and Oxford: Oxford University Press.
Adams, Larry L. 1977. *Walter Lippmann*. Boston: Twayne.
Advertising Age. 2011. "New York Times Introduces BETA620, a Public Site for Its Experimental Projects." 7 August.
Agence France-Presse. 2009. "Future of Newspapers Is Digital: Murdoch." 28 May.
– 2011. "Newspapers to Disappear by 2040: UN Agency Chief." 3 October.
Alterman, Eric. 1982. *Sound and Fury: The Washington Punditocracy and the Collapse of American Politics*. New York: HarperCollins.
– 2008a. "Out of Print: The Death and Life of the American Newspaper." *New Yorker*, 31 March.
– 2008b. "I Read the News Today ... Oh Boy." *Nation*, 4 August.
– 2009a. "Save the News, Not the Newspaper." *Nation*, 11 February.
– 2009b. "Lose the 'Business'; Save the 'News.'" *Nation*, 27 April.
Atrios. www.eschatonblog.com. Accessed 28 July 2012.
Auletta, Ken. 2012. "Citizens Jain: Why India's Newspaper Industry Is Thriving." *New Yorker*, 8 October.
Austen, Ian. 2010. "Globe and Mail Uses Old Weapons in Press War." *New York Times*, October 24.
Australian, The. 2010. "Newspapers Gone by 2022, Says Futurist," 24 August.
Bacon, Lise, et al. 2006. *Final Report on the Canadian News Media*, Standing Senate Committee on Transport and Communications. Parliament of Canada.
Bagdikian, Ben. 1990. *The Media Monopoly*. 4th ed. Boston: Beacon Press.
– 2004. *The New Media Monopoly*. Boston: Beacon Press.
Bailly, Nestor. 2009. "Dallas Morning News 'Draws a Line in the Sand' Regarding Cuts, Fights Back with Quality." World Editors Forum, 12 October. editorsweblog.org.

Ball, James. 2012. "Paul Dacre's Press Accreditation Plan Should Be Struck Off." *Guardian*, 8 February.
Baluja, Tamara. 2014a. "How Well Are Canadian Newspapers Doing with Paywalls, Tablets?" *J-Source.ca*, 24 January.
– 2014b. "Updated: Postmedia Eliminates Parliamentary Bureau." *J-Source.ca*, 4 February.
– 2014c. "Union: Globe Proposes Reporters Write Advertorial Copy." *J-Source.ca*, 8 May.
Banerjee, Sidhartha. 2010. "Journalists Decry Harper Gov't PR Control." Canadian Press, 10 June.
Barstow, David, and Robin Stein. 2005. "Under Bush, a New Era of Pre-packaged News." *New York Times*, 13 March.
Basen, Ira. 2013. "Opinion: Why the Globe Might Not Want to Target an Elite Audience." *J-source.ca*.
Bauder, David. 2012. "Tablets Drawing More People to News, but News Industry May Not Profit from It." *Toronto Star*, 19 March.
Beaujon, Andrew. 2013. "Nearly One-Third of U.S. Adults Have Abandoned a News Outlet Due to Dissatisfaction." Poynter.org, 18 March.
Beers, David. 2014. "Mr. Nuttall Goes to Ottawa (Thanks to You)." *The Tyee*, 18 August.
Beers, David, Geoff D'Auria, Julie Jenkins, and Phillip Smith. 2013. "Help The Tyee Go National." *The Tyee*, October 28.
Behling, Ellie. 2010. "How Publishers Are Making News More Personal." *eMedia Vitals*, 2 September.
Bell, Jocyln. 2000. "The British Are Coming, the British Are Coming: How Fleet Street Stormed Front Street and Colonized the Globe and Mail." *Ryerson Review of Journalism* (Summer).
Benkler, Yochai. 2006. *The Wealth of Networks; How Social Production Transforms Markets and Freedom*. New Haven and London: Yale University Press.
– 2011. "A Free Irresponsible Press: Wikileaks and the Battle over the Soul of the Networked Fourth Estate." *Harvard Civil Rights–Civil Liberties Law Review* 46: 311–97.
Bercovici, Jeff. 2010. "Times of London Paywall Paying Off Already." *Forbes*, 3 December.
BETA620.nytimes.com. Accessed 23 June 2014.
Bird, Roger. 1997. *The End of News*. Toronto: Irwin.
Bledstein, Burton J. 1976. *The Culture of Professionalism: The Middle Class and the Development of Higher Education in America*. New York: W.W. Norton.

Blethen, Ryan. 2009. "Recession Could Fuel New Era of Local Newspaper Ownership." *Seattle Times*, 12 June.
Boorstin, Daniel J. 1982. *The Image: A Guide to Pseudo-Events in America*. New York: Athenium.
Botelho, Stephanie. 2012. "The New York Times, The Daily and New Yorker Top Performing Titles on Apple's Newsstand." *Folio*, 13 January.
Bowden, Mark. 2009. "The Story behind the Story." *Atlantic Monthly*, October.
Bradshaw, James. 2014. "Ottawa Citizen's Redesign a Model for Postmedia." *Globe and Mail*, 20 May.
– 2015. "Postmedia CEO Wades into Ontario PC Leadership Race." *Globe and Mail*, 2 April.
Braganza, Chantal. 2015. "Winnipeg Free Press to Launch Micro-Payment Paywall." *J-Source.ca*, 31 March.
Briggs, Asa, and Peter Burke. 2005. *A Social History of the Media: From Gutenberg to the Internet*. 2nd ed. Cambridge: Polity.
Brown, Jesse. 2014. "Source: Globe Editorial Board Endorsed Wynne Liberals, Was Overruled." Canadalandshow.com, 11 June.
Brown, Tina. 2008. "Kill the Media Zombies." *Daily Beast*, 8 December.
– 2010. "Things to Stop Bitching About in 2010." *Daily Beast*, 3 January.
Bundy, Jeff, 2011. "Buffett on Newspapers: 'Enormously Useful Product.'" *Omaha World-Herald*, 4 December.
Bunz, Mercedes. 2010. "In the U.S., Algorithms Are Already Reporting the News." *Guardian*, 30 March.
Canadian Media Research Consortium (CMRC). 2004. *Report Card on Canadian News Media*. www.cmrcccrm.ca/english/index.html.
– 2008. The Credibility Gap: Canadians and Their News Media Five Years Later. cmrcccrm.ca/english/index.html.
– 2011a. "Canadian Consumers Unwilling to Pay for News Online." cmrcccrm.ca/english/index.html.
– 2011b. "Even in the Digital Era, Canadians Have Confidence in Mainstream Media." cmrcccrm.ca/en/projects/documents/CMRC_Trust_Report_11May.pdf.
Carey, James. 1997a. "Communications and Economics." In *James Carey, a Critical Reader*, edited by Eve Stryker Munson and Catherine A. Warren. Minneapolis: University of Minnesota Press.
– 1997b. "The Press, Public Opinion and Public Discourse." *James Carey, a Critical Reader*, edited by Eve Stryker Munson and Catherine A Warren. Minneapolis: University of Minnesota Press.

Carper, Alison, 1997. "Marketing News." In *Politics and the Press: The News Media and Their Influences*, edited by Pippa Norris. Boulder, CO, and London: Lynn Rienner.

Carr, David. 2009a. "Nonprofit Journalism: Not Necessarily on the Cheap." *New York Times*, 30 September.

– 2009b. "Newspapers Essential Strengths." *New York Times*, 4 May.

– 2009c. "After a Year of Ruin, Some Hope." *New York Times*, 21 December.

– 2010. "At Flagging Tribune, Tales of a Bankrupt Culture." *New York Times*, 5 October.

– 2011a. "At Media Companies, a Nation of Serfs." *New York Times*, 13 February.

– 2011b. "At Gannett, Furloughs but Nice Paydays for Brass." *New York Times*, 10 April.

– 2011c. "Why Not Occupy Newsrooms." *New York Times*, 23 October.

– 2011d. "When Truth Survives Free Speech." *New York Times*, 11 December.

Carr, Paul. 2010. "A Death of a Thousand Hacks: New Forbes Editorial Genius in Bold Plan to Kill Forbes." Techcrunch.com. 14 June.

Carroll Rory, 2013. "California Newspaper Defies Industry Wisdom to Stay Alive – and Prospers." *Guardian*, 23 July.

Carter, Bill, and Brian Stelter. 2010. "In 'Daily Show' Role on 9/11 Bill, Echoes of Murrow." *New York Times*, 26 December.

CBC.ca. 2013a. "Sun Media Announces 200 Layoffs." 4 December.

– 2014. "LaPresse to Cease Printing Newspapers – Eventually." 15 May.

Chambers, Sam. 2013. "Guardian Media Returns to Profit, Going against the Grain on Ads." Bloomberg.com. 16 July.

Chan, Wilfrid. 2014. "Hong Kong Journalists: Press Freedom Is at an All-Time Low." CNN, 24 February.

Chase, Stephen. 2009. "What's Wrong with These Pictures." *Globe and Mail*, 7 November.

Chittum, Ryan. 2009a. "Circulation Revenue Only Thing Growing at Newspapers. *Columbia Journalism Review*, 23 July.

– 2009b. "NYT Now Gets as Much Money from Circulation as from Ads." *Columbia Journalism Review*, 23 July.

– 2010a. "Parsing the Latest Online-Charging Poll." *Columbia Journalism Review*, 14 January.

– 2010b. "Newsday Paywall Is Barely Affecting Local Traffic." *Columbia Journalism Review*, 28 January.

- 2012a. "The New York Times Company in 2015." *Columbia Journalism Review*, 18 April.
- 2012b. "Paywalls: Maybe Not So Complicated after All." *Columbia Journalism Review*, 17 January.
- 2012c. "Newsweek and the (Relative) Health of Print Mags." *Columbia Journalism Review*, 24 October.
- 2014a. "The Trust-Fund Newspaper." *Columbia Journalism Review*, 30 January.
- 2014b. "The NYT on the Right Track." *Columbia Journalism Review*, 6 February.
- 2014c. "Gannett's Print-Focused Paywalls Flounder." *Columbia Journalism Review*, 6 February.
- 2014d. "NYT Hasn't Been Hit That Hard." *Columbia Journalism Review*, 7 February.

Chomsky, Noam. 1989. *Necessary Illusions: Thought Control in Democratic Societies*. Boston: South End Press.

Chyi, Hsiang Iris, Seth C. Lewis, and Nan Zheng. 2011. "A Matter of Life and Death?" *Journalism Studies* 13 (3): 306–24.

Clifford, Stephanie. 2009. "Online Rally May Sidestep Newspapers." *New York Times*, 26 October.

CNS News. 2013. "Newspaper Ad Revenue down 55% since Historic Peak in 2005." 5 August.

Cohen, Andrew. 2009. "Journalism's Amateur Hour." *National Post*, 3 December.

Cohen, Noam. 2010. "What Would Daniel Ellsberg Do with the Pentagon Papers Today?" *New York Times*, 18 April.

Cohen Noam, and Andrew Stelter. 2010. "Iraq Video Brings Notice to a Web Site." *New York Times*, 6 April.

Colbin, Kaila. 2011. "Shoptalk: The Value of User-Generated Content." *Editor and Publisher*, 31 May.

completure.com. Accessed 12 June 2014.

Cornies, Larry. 2009. "Why the Free Press Still Stands Tall." *J-Source.ca*, 11 April.

Coursey, David. 2012. "You Be the Judge: Are Bloggers Journalists?" *Forbes*, 2 January.

Coyle, Jake. 2012. "More than Just Cat Videos: Viewers Now Turning to YouTube for News." *Globe and Mail*, 16 July.

Coyne, Andrew. 2008. "How Journalists Got in the Way of the Election." *Maclean's*, 29 September.

Crawley, Phillip. 1998. "What It Takes to Survive: Ever-Tougher Competition Demands an Ever-Stronger Push for Quality Journalism." *Marketing*, 16 November.

Csanady, Ashley. 2014. "Majority of Conservative Voters Like the CBC: Poll." Canada.com, 5 September.

Curran, James, and Jean Seaton. 1997. *Power without Responsibility: The Press and Broadcasting in Britain*. 5th ed. London and New York: Routledge.

Dailing, Paul. 2009. "How to Become a 'Death of Newspapers' Blogger." *Huffington Post*, 25 March.

Darnton, Robert. 2009. *The Case for Books*. New York: Public Affairs.

Davey, Keith, et al. 1970. *The Uncertain Mirror: Report of the Special Committee on Mass Media*. Vol. 1. Ottawa: Information Canada.

Davies, David R. 2006. *The History of American Journalism: The Postwar Decline of American Newspapers, 1945–65*. Westport, CT, and London: Praeger.

Deans, Jason. 2014. Guardian Website Tops 100 Million Monthly Browsers for the First Time." theguardian.com, 17 April.

Deutsche Welle. 2014. "Citizen Journalism: Hyper-Local News App Apprazzi Lures Young Gossipers," 31 January.

Deuze, Mark. 1999. "Journalism and the Web: An Analysis of Skills and Standards in an Online Environment." *International Communication Gazette* 61 (5): 373–90.

– 2004. "What Is Multimedia Journalism?" *Journalism Studies* 5 (2): 139–52.

– 2007. *Media Work*. Cambridge: Polity.

Dewey, John. 1954. *The Public and Its Problems*. Athens: Swallow Press/ University of Ohio Press.

Diana, Alison. 2011. "Twitter Trends Driven by Mainstream Media." *InformationWeek*, 16 February.

Didion, Joan. 2006a. "Insider Baseball." *We Tell Ourselves Stories in Order to Live: Collected Nonfiction*. New York, London, and Toronto: Everyman's Library. Orig. 2001.

– 2006b. "The White Album." *We Tell Ourselves Stories in Order to Live: Collected Nonfiction*. New York, London, Toronto: Everyman's Library. Orig. 1979.

DiManno, Rosie. 2014. "Sun-Postmedia Merger Narrows Readers' Options, Fattens Paul Godfrey's Wallet." *Toronto Star*, 7 October.

Domingo, David. 2011. "Managing Audience Participation: Practices, Workflows and Strategies." *Participatory Journalism: Guarding Open Gates at Online Newspapers*. Malden, MA, and Oxford: Wiley-Blackwell.
Dornan, Christopher. 2012: "Newspapers and Magazines: Of Crows and Finches." In *Cultural Industries.ca: Making Sense of Canadian Media in the Digital Age*, edited by Ira Wagman and Peter Urquhart. Toronto: Lorimer.
Downie, Leonard Jr, and Michael Schudson. 2009. "The Reconstruction of American Journalism." *Columbia Journalism Review*, 20 October.
Doyle, John. 2014. "After the Ghomeshi Exposé, Where's the Media Analysis?" *Globe and Mail*, 5 November.
Drew, Jill. 2010. "The New Investigators." *Columbia Journalism Review*, May-June.
Dumenco, Simon. 2009. "Trashy Parasitism as a Get-Rich-Quick Scheme? Hi HuffPo." *Advertising Age*, 22 June.
Durrani, Arif. 2013. "Mail Online and Guardian Lead Record Highs for Newspaper Sites in January." *MediaWeek*, 22 February.
Economist, The. 2008. "Not All Bad News: Newspapers Are Thriving in Many Developing Countries." 24 July.
Edmonds, Rick. 2009. "Shrinking Newspapers Have Created $1.6 Billion News Deficit." Poynter Online, 10 October.
Edmonds, Rick, Emily Guskin, Amy Mitchell, and Mark Jurkowitz. 2013. "Newspapers: Stabilizing, but Still Threatened." *PEJ*, 18 July.
Eisenstein, Elizabeth. 1979. *The Printing Press as an Agent of Change*. Cambridge, New York, Melbourne: Cambridge University Press.
Engelhardt, Tom. 2012. "What Was the Most Underreported Story of 2012?" *Huffington Post*, 24 December.
Ernst and Young. 2013. *2012 Actual + 2013 Estimated Canadian Internet Advertising Revenue Survey: Detailed Report*. Sponsored by the Interactive Advertising Bureau of Canada, 18 September.
ethicsscoreboard.com/list/freeping.html. 2004. Accessed 23 June 2014.
Fetherling, Douglas. 1990. *The Rise of the Canadian Newspaper*. Toronto: Oxford University Press.
Financial Post. 2012. "Postmedia Network Announces Cost Transformation Plan." 11 July.
Fink, Conrad C. 1996. *Strategic Newspaper Management*. Boston: Allyn and Bacon.

Fitzgerald, Mark. 2010a. "Times-Picayune Super Bowl Victory Edition Sells 50,000-Plus Copies." *Editor and Publisher*, 8 February.
– 2010b: "Fireworks at Journal Register Co: 'Ben Franklin Project' Successful at All 18 Dailies." *Editor and Publisher*, 6 July.
Flavelle, Dana. 2014. "Postmedia Buys 175-paper Sun Media for $316 Million." *Toronto Star*, 6 October.
Flock, Elizabeth. 2012. "Are Syrian Citizen Journalists Embellishing the Truth?" *Washington Post.com*, 27 March.
Franklin, Bob. 2008. "The Future of Newspapers." *Journalism Studies* 9 (5): 630–41.
Free Press Newspapers. 2012. "FP Newspapers Inc. Reports Third Quarter 2012 Results and November 2012 Dividend." News release, 14 November.
Friend, David. 2009. "Star Announces Major Restructuring." *Toronto Star*, 3 November.
Fritz, Ben. 2010. "Most Original News Reporting Comes from Traditional Sources, Study Finds." *Los Angeles Times*, 11 January.
Gabler, Neal. 2013. "A Journalistic Revolution." Reuters, 31 October.
Gabriele, Sandra, and Paul S. Moore. 2009. "The Globe on Saturday, the World on Sunday: Toronto Weekend Editions and the Influence of the American Sunday Paper, 1886–1895." *Canadian Journal of Communication* 34 (3): 337–58.
Gagnon, Lysiane. 2014. "The Province of Quebecor?" *Globe and Mail*, 4 December.
Gatehouse, Jonathan. 2009. "The Short End of the Canwest Stick." *Maclean's*, 20 October.
Geary, James. 2006. "In Praise of the Tabs (Sort of)." *British Journalism Review* 17 (1): 196–208.
Geary, Joanna. 2012. "Paul Dacre's Old Media Thinking Threatens Citizen Journalism." *Guardian*, 8 February.
Gerard, Warren. 2005. "He Made His Mark on City and Nation." *Toronto Star*, 9 November.
Gillespie, Bruce. 2015. "Memo: Toronto Star to Hire 60 Staff for New Tablet Edition." *J-Source.ca*, 6 January.
Gitlin, Todd. 2009. "Journalism's Many Crises." www.opendemocracy.net, 25 May.
Globe and Mail. 2010. "Editorial Autonomy and Financial Acumen," 10 September.
Goodale, Gloria. 2010. "Colbert-Stewart Rally Raises Question: Where Is Journalism Headed?" *Christian Science Monitor*, 21 October.

Graham, Patricia. 2014. "Ombudsman: Should Brunswick News Have Taken Down Its Paywall Following the Moncton Shootings?" *J-Source.ca*, 12 June.

Gramsci, Antonio. 1971. *Selections from the Prison Notebooks*. New York: International Publishers.

Greisling, David. 2008. "Tribune Co.'s Crisis Has Been Years in Making." *Chicago Tribune*, 9 December.

Gross, Daniel. 2009. "Paper Hangers." *Slate*, 28 October.

groundreport.com. Accessed 10 March 2015.

Grueskin, Bill, Ava Seave, and Lucas Graves. 2011. *The Story So Far: What We Know about the Business of Digital Journalism*. New York: Columbia Journalism School Tow Center for Digital Journalism.

Guardian, The. 2011. "History of the Guardian: A Brief History of the Guardian Newspaper." www.guardian.co.uk, 28 October.

– 2014. "ABCs: National Daily Newspaper Circulation June 2014." www.theguardian.com, 11 July.

Guardian Media Group. 2014. "The Scott Trust." gmgplc.co.uk.

Gustin, Sam. 2011. "Murdoch's News Corp. Launches the Daily for Apple's iPad." *Wired*, 2 February.

Habermas, Jürgen. 1991. *The Structural Transformation of the Public Sphere: An Inquiry into a Category of Bourgeois Society*. Cambridge, MA: MIT Press. Orig. 1962.

Hackett, Robert A., and Yuezhi Zhao. 1998. *Sustaining Democracy: Journalism and the Politics of Objectivity*. Toronto: Garamond.

Hagey, Keach. 2013. "Tribune Co. Emerges from Bankruptcy," *MarketWatch*, 31 December.

Hallin, Daniel C. 1989. *The Uncensored War: The Media and Vietnam*. Berkeley and Los Angeles: University of California Press.

Hallman, Eugene, P.F. Oliphant, and R.C. White. 1981. *The Newspaper as a Business: Research Studies on the Newspaper Industry*. Royal Commission on Newspapers.

Halperin, Mark. 2010. "The Media Spiral: From O.J. to Sherrod." *Time*, 26 July.

Hambleton, Paul. 2009. "Dealing with User-Generated Content: Is It Worth It?" In *The Future of Journalism: Papers from a Conference Organised by the BBC College of Journalism*, edited by Charles Miller. London: CoJo.

Hansen, Susan. 2007. "Superiority Complex: Why the Brits Think They're Better." *Columbia Journalism Review*, 8 May.

Harkness, Ross. 1963. *J.E. Atkinson of the Star*. Toronto: University of Toronto Press.

Haughney, Christine. 2012. "Buffett Says He Remains Bullish on Newspapers, despite Closing One." *New York Times*, 27 November.

Hayes, David. 1992. *Power and Influence: The Globe and Mail and the News Revolution*. Toronto: Key Porter.

Herman, Edward S., and Noam Chomsky. 1988. *Manufacturing Consent*. New York: Pantheon.

Hernandez, Marco. A., District Judge. 2011. Opinion. *Obsidian Finance Group, LLC, and Kevin D. Padrick v. Crystal Cox*. United States District Court, District of Oregon, Portland Division. 30 November.

Hiar, Corbin. 2010. "Writers Explain What It's Like Toiling on the Content Farm." pbs.org, 21 July.

Hirschorn, Michael. 2009. "End Times." *Atlantic Monthly*, January-February

Hockenberry, John. 2005. "The Blogs of War." *Wired*, April.

Honderich, Beland. 1999. "How One Man's Crusade Changed Our Lives." *Toronto Star*, 13 December.

Hood, Duncan. 2008. "Could Canwest Go Bankrupt?" *Maclean's*, 22 December.

Houpt, Simon. 2012a. "A Seasoned David Gergen Decries Today's Pop-Up Pundits." *Globe and Mail*, 16 March.

– 2012b "Newspapers: A Good News Story Writ Small." *Globe and Mail*, 3 April.

– 2013. "Postmedia Drops Publishers." *Globe and Mail*, 30 April.

– 2015. "CBC Cuts 244 Jobs as Part of Its Plan to Eliminate 1,500 Positions." *Globe and Mail*, 26 March.

House of Lords Select Committee on Communications (Lords). 2008. *The Ownership of the News*. London: Authority of the House of Lords.

Hutchins, Robert M., et al. 1966. "A Free and Responsible Press: Report of the Commission on Freedom of the Press." In *The Responsibility of the Press*, edited by Gerald Gross. New York: Fleet. Orig. 1947.

Inpublishing. 2014. "The Guardian Reaches over 100 Million Monthly Unique Browsers." 22 April.

Isaacson, Walter. 2009. "A Bold Old Idea for Saving Journalism." *Huffington Post*, 8 March.

Jackson, Joseph. 1999. *Newspaper Ownership in Canada: An Overview of the Davey Committee and Kent Commission Studies*. Ottawa: Public Works and Government Services Canada, Political and Social Affairs Division.

Johnson, Gene. 2009. "Could Seattle Become a No-Newspaper Town?" Associated Press, 14 March.

Jones, Alex S. 2009. *Losing the News: The Future of the News that Feeds Democracy*. Oxford, New York: Oxford University Press.

Kamiya, Gary. 2009. "The Death of the News." *Salon.com*, 17 February.

Katz, Elihu, and David Foulkes. 1962. "On the Use of the Mass Media as 'Escape': Clarification of a Concept." *Public Opinion Quarterly* 26 (3): 377–88.

Kawamoto, Dawn. 2009. "Online Newspaper Readership Climbs 16 Percent." Cnet.com.

Kent, Tom. 1981. *Royal Commission on Newspapers*. Ottawa: Supply and Services Canada.

– 1996. "The Times and Significance of the Kent Commission." In *Seeing Ourselves: Media Power and Policy in Canada*, edited by Helen Holmes and David Taras. Toronto: Harcourt Brace Jovanovich.

Kesterton, W.H. 1984. *A History of Journalism in Canada*. Ottawa: Carleton University Press. Orig. 1967.

Kimber, Stephen. 2001. "Column by Stephen Kimber Spiked by Halifax Daily News." www.cwa-scacanada.ca/YourMedia/modules/canwest/chronicle/020104_kimber_column.html. Accessed. 19 May, 2015.

Kimmett, Colleen. 2013. "Target Globe Reader Has $120k Household Income, Editor Clarifies." *The Tyee*, 9 October.

Kinsman, Matt. 2010. "November Issue Is Biggest Revenue Generator in The Atlantic's 153-Year History." *Folio*, 12 October.

Kinstler, Linda. 2013. "The Times of London, Navigating Audience with a Strict Paywall, Retires Its Opinion Tumblr." Nieman Journalism Lab.

Kirby, Jason. 2010. "A Lord Resurrected: Legal Vindication, Yes, but More Surprising, Some of Conrad Black's Harshest Critics Admit They Were Too Quick to Judge." *Maclean's*, 13 December.

Kirchner, Laura. 2011. "John Paton's Big Bet." *Columbia Journalism Review*, July-August.

Kozlowski, Michael. 2013. "Publishers Begin to Abandon Apple Newsstand." *Good-E-Reader.com*, 5 October.

Krashinsky, Susan. 2010. "Why Carnage on the Newsstand Is Giving Way to Cautious Optimism." *Globe and Mail*, 15 May.

Kurtz, Howard. 2009. "As Mainstream Exits D.C., Niche Media Tide Rises." *Washington Post*, 11 February.

– 2010a. "In Journalism's Crossfire Culture, Everyone Gets Wounded." *Washington Post*, 2 August.

– 2010b. "Mindless March of the Media Herd." *Washington Post*, 23 August.

Kwong, Matt. 2015. "Facebook, New York Times Deal Could Change News Business." CBC.ca, March 27.

Ladurantaye, Steve. 2012a. "The Globe to Roll Out Metered Paywall as Industry Shifts to Digital Revenue." *Globe and Mail*, 15 October.
– 2012b. "Sun Media Dismisses Regional Publishers in Reorganization." *Globe and Mail*, 24 October.
– 2012c. "New York Times Advertising Pulls Back." *Globe and Mail*, 25 October.
– 2013a. "Canadian Newspapers Saw Revenue Fall 13% in Last Five Years." *Globe and Mail*, 5 December.
– 2013b. "Newspaper Revenue to Drop 20 Per Cent by 2017, Report Predicts." *Globe and Mail*, 5 December.
– 2013c. "Postmedia's Godfrey Saw Total Pay Rise 50 Per Cent Last Year." *Globe and Mail*, 28 November.
Lagacé, Patrick. 2014. "Enabler to a Media Hatchet Job." *Globe and Mail*, 6 November.
Lanham, Richard A. 2006. *The Economics of Attention: Style and Substance in the Age of Information*. Chicago: University of Chicago Press.
Layton, Charles. 1999. "Tea Leaves." *What Do Readers Want?* State of the American Newspaper. http://www.pewresearch.org. (No longer accessible; archives go back only to 2001.)
Lee, Edmund. 2013. "New York Times Tops USA Today to Become No. 2 U.S. Paper." *Bloomberg.com*, 30 April.
Levine, D.M. 2011. "Small Papers Lead the Way on Paywalls." *Adweek*, 3 June.
Levine, Josh. 2009. "Turning the Page: The News on Europe's Newspapers." *Time*, 19 February.
Lewis, Jemima. 2007. "There Is a Thin Line between Respectable and Supine, and U.S. Journalism Is on the Wrong Side." *Independent*, 30 June.
Lewis, Paul. 2011. "Crowdsourcing the News." Video. www.ted.com/talks/paul_lewis_crowdsourcing_the_news.html.
Liedtke, Michael. 2009b. "Small Is Becoming Beautiful for Many Newspapers in U.S." Associated Press, 15 August.
Linkins, Jason. 2009. "Online Poll: Jon Stewart Is America's Most Trusted Newsman." *Huffington Post*, 9 September.
– 2010. "Poverty Rate Report: The Day the Media Cared About the Poor." *Huffington Post*, 17 September.
Lippmann, Walter. 1963. "Why Should the Majority Rule?" *The Essential Lippmann: A Political Philosophy for a Liberal Democracy*. New York: Random House. Orig. 1926.
– 1978. *Drift and Mastery*. Westport, CT: Greenwood. Orig. 1914.

– 1993. *The Phantom Public*. New Brunswick, NJ: Transaction. Orig. 1925.
– 1997. *Public Opinion*. New York: Free Press Paperbacks. Orig. 1922.
– 2008. *Liberty and the News*. Princeton, NJ, and Oxford: Princeton University Press. Orig. 1920.
Lippmann, Walter, and Charles Merz. 2007. "A Test of the News." In *Killing the Messenger*, edited by Tom Goldstein. New York: Columbia University Press. Orig. 1920.
Lobdell, Scott, and Kenneth Rocafort. 2012. "They Will Join You in the Sun." *Superman* 13 (December).
Lodish, Emily. 2011: "Gaddafi's End: How Cell Phones Became Weapons of Choice." *Global Post*, 21 October.
Lotan, Gilad. 2012. "Bulgaria: Israeli Tour Bus Attacked." *groundreport.com*, 19 July.
Lynch, Lisa. 2010. "We're Going to Crack the World Open." *Journalism Practice* 4 (3): 309–18.
Lyons, Daniel. 2009. "Exterminate the Parasites: A Radical Plan to Save Old Media." *Newsweek*, 14 September.
MacAfee, Michelle. 2000. "Newspapers Not Keeping Up with Technology, Analyst Says." Canadian Press, 11 May.
MacPhail, Wayne. 2001. "Content? No Thanks!" *Rabble.ca*, 22 October.
Mak, Tim. 2011. "Pew: Opinion of Media Never Worse." *Politico*, 23 September.
Manjoo, Farhad. 2009. "The Newspaper Isn't Dead Yet." *Slate*, 18 June.
Martin, Lawrence. 2003. "It's Not Canadians Who've Gone to the Right, Just Their Media." *Globe and Mail*, 12 January.
– 2009. "To Save Journalism, Bring On That Jon Stewart Outrage." *Globe and Mail*, 19 March.
– 2011. "Has the Fourth Estate Lost Its Tenacity?" *Globe and Mail*, 24 May.
McArthur, Keith. 2000. "It's All in the Delivery," *Globe and Mail*, 29 April.
McCann, Nick. 2011. "Investigative Blogger Must Pay $2.5 Million." *Courthouse News Service*, 29 March.
McChesney, Robert. 1999. *Rich Media, Poor Democracy: Communication Politics in Dubious Times*. Chicago: University of Chicago Press.
– 2013. *Digital Disconnect: How Capitalism Is Turning the Internet against Democracy*. New York, London: New Press.
McChesney, Robert, and John Nichols. 2010. *The Death and Life of American Journalism: The Media Revolution that Will Begin the World Again*. Philadelphia: Nation Books.

McLaren, Leah. 2010. "A Globetrotting Canuck Journo Aims to Revolutionize Online News." *Globe and Mail*, 7 May.

McNair, Brian. 2000. *Journalism and Democracy: An Evaluation of the Political Public Sphere*. London, New York: Routledge.

McNish, Jacqui, and Jacqueline Nelson. 2014. "U.S. Junk Bond Specialists Behind Postmedia's Project Canada." *Globe and Mail*, 7 October.

McPherson, James Brian. 2006. *Journalism at the End of the American Century, 1965–Present*. Westport, CT, London: Praeger.

Meares, Joel. 2011. "Confidence in TV News and Newspapers (Slightly) Up. *Columbia Journalism Review*, 28 June.

Meek, James Gordon. 2010. "FBI: ACORN Gotcha Guy Busted for Bugging Landrieu." *Daily News*, 26 January.

Merced, Michael J. de la. 2008. "Tribune Files for Bankruptcy." *New York Times*, 8 December.

Merrill, John C., and John C. Nerone. 2002, January. "The Four Theories of the Press Four and a Half Decades Later: A Retrospective." *Journalism Studies* 3 (1): 133–4.

Miller, John. 1998. *Yesterday's News: Why Canada's Daily Newspapers Are Failing Us*. Halifax: Fernwood.

Mindworksglobal.com. "About Us." Accessed 20 February 2014.

Mirkinson, Jack. 2014. "New York Times Announces Deep New Round of Staff Cuts as Digital Initiatives Stall." *Huffington Post*, 1 October.

Mitchell, Amy. 2014. "State of the News Media 2014: Overview." *PEJ*, 26 March.

Moozakis, Chuck. 2009. "Papers Hope Web Holds Key to Future." *Newspapers and Technology*, April.

Morales, Lyman. 2010. "In U.S., Confidence in Newspapers, TV News Remains a Rarity." Gallup.com, 13 August.

– 2012. "U.S. Distrust in Media Hits New High." Gallup.com, 21 September.

Moroney, James W. III. 2010. "Newspaper Companies That Survive Will Not Consider Themselves Newspaper Companies." *Poynter Online*, October 1.

Morozov, Evgeny. 2011. *The Net Delusion: The Dark Side of Internet Freedom*. New York: Public Affairs.

Morrow, Adrian. 2014. "Hudak Revamped Policy after Visiting Stalwarts of U.S. Right." *Globe and Mail*, 1 June.

Morton, John. 2008. "It Could Be Worse." *American Journalism Review*. www.ajr.org.

– 2011. "Costly Mistakes." *American Journalism Review*. www.ajr.org.

Moses, Lucia. 2012. "Bloomberg and Reuters: The Future of News." *AdWeek*, 2 April.
Mutter, Alan D. 2009. "Mission Possible? Charging for Web Content." *Reflections of a Newsosaur*. newsosaur.blogspot.com. 8 February.
– 2011. "Newspaper Ad Sales Head to New Low: $24B." *Reflections of a Newsosaur*. newsosaur.blogspot.com, December 5.
– 2012. "Newsroom Staffing Hits 34-year Low." *Reflections of a Newsosaur*. newsosaur.blogspot.com, April 4.
Myers, Steve. 2010. "New York Times Embraces Collaborative Journalism with CUNY Hyperlocal Experiment." Poynter Online, 16 January.
Nader, Laura. 1997. "Controlling Processes: Tracing the Dynamic Components of Power." *Current Anthropology* 38 (5): 711–37.
Neil, Janice. 2011. "Quebec Journalists Approve Idea of 'Professional Journalist' Card." *The Tyee*, 13 April.
Nerone, John C., ed. 1995. *Last Rights: Revisiting Four Theories of the Press*. Urbana and Chicago: University of Illinois Press. Orig. 1956.
New Republic. 2009. "MSM RIP." 4 March.
Newspaper Guild. 2006. "Salary Info." http://www.newsguild.org/salary/2006reporterstart.php.
Newspapers Canada. 2012a. "2012 Daily Newspaper Circulation Report." http://www.newspaperscanada.ca/about-newspapers/circulation. Accessed 16 January 2014.
– 2012b. "2012 Net Advertising Volumes Canada Report." http://www.newspaperscanada.ca/sites/default/files/NAVCDA_Net_Advertising_Volume_Canada_2003-2012.pdf. Accessed 16 January 2014.
New York. 2010. "Tom Brokaw Agrees with Tina Brown: Young People Should Just Move to India." 10 October.
Nguyen, Linda. 2014. "Toronto Star Plans to Tear Down Paywall in 2015; Launch New Tablet Edition." Canadian Press, 5 November.
Nolen, Stephanie. 2011. "Black, White and Read All Over India." *Globe and Mail*, May 13.
Nordland, Rod. 2012. "Ghastly Images Flow from Shattered Syrian City." *New York Times*, 22 February.
Norris, Pippa. 1997. *Politics and the Press: The News Media and Their Influences*. Boulder, CO, London: Lynn Rienner.
– 2000. *A Virtuous Circle: Political Communications in Postindustrial Societies*. Cambridge: Cambridge University Press.
Norris, Pippa, et al. 1999. *On Message: Communicating the Campaign*. London, Thousand Oaks, CA: Sage.

Nussbaum, Emily. 2009. "The New Journalism: Goosing the Gray Lady." *New York*, 11 January.

nytimes.com. 2008. "Casualties of War." /ref/us/20061228_3000FACES_TAB2.html, 12 January.

– "The Lourdes of Twang." /packages/html/travel/20080222_MARTIN_FEATURE, 22 February.

– "The Collapse Sequence." interactive/2008/03/15/nyregion/20080315_CRANE_GRAPHIC.html, 15 March.

– 2011. "The Reckoning." /interactive/us/sept-11-reckoning/viewer.html. Undated.

O'Beirne, Ronan. 2014. "J-Source's Top 10 Journalism Stories of 2014." *J-Source.ca*, 19 December.

Olive, David. 2009. "My Stubborn Faith in Newspapers." *Toronto Star*, 19 October. thestar.blogs.com/davidolive.

Osborn, Andrew. 2013. "Britain's Cameron Says May Act against Newspapers over Spy Leak." Reuters.com, 28 October.

O'Shea, James. 2011. *The Deal from Hell: How Moguls and Wall Street Plundered Great American Newspapers*. New York: Public Affairs.

Ovide, Shira, and Russell Adams. 2009. "As Decline Grips Big U.S. Dailies, Investors Rush to the Small Towns." *Globe and Mail*, 28 April.

Paper Cuts. 2012. "Layoffs and Buyouts at U.S. Newspapers." newspaperlayoffs.com/maps/2007-layoffs.

Paton, John. 2012. "Another Tough Step." jxpaton.wordpress.com, 5 September.

Patterson, 2009. "Buffett Sees Unending Losses for Many Newspapers." *Wall Street Journal*, 2 May.

Paulussen, Steve. 2011. "Inside the Newsroom: Journalists' Motivations and Organizational Structures." *Participatory Journalism: Guarding Open Gates at Online Newspapers*. Malden, MA, and Oxford: Wiley-Blackwell.

Pérez-Peña, Richard. 2008. "Newspapers: A Hot Commodity after Obama's Win." *New York Times*, 6 November.

– 2009. "Seattle Paper Is Resurgent as a Solo Act." *New York Times*, 10 August.

Peters, Jeremy W. 2010. "Not on His Watch: USA Today Founder Says." *New York Times*, 30 August.

– 2011. "Carlos Slim Adds Stake in Times Company." *New York Times*, 23 August.

Peters, John Durham. 2003. "Retroactive Enrichment: Raymond Williams's *Culture and Society*." In *Canonic Texts in Media Research: Are There*

Any? Should There Be Some? How about These? edited by Elihu Katz et al. Cambridge, UK: Polity.
Peterson, Andrea. 2013. "Here's What You Miss by Only Talking to White Men about the Digital Revolution and Journalism." *Washington Post*, 10 September.
Pew Research Center. 2008. "Internet Overtakes Newspapers as News Source." pewresearch.org/pubs.
– 2009. "Stop the Presses? Many Americans Wouldn't Care a Lot if Local Papers Folded." pewresearch.org/pubs/1147/newspapers-struggle-public-not-concerned.
– 2010. "Facebook Is Becoming Increasingly Important." 9 May. journalism.org/analysis_report/facebook_becoming_increasingly_important.
Pfanner, Edward. 2009. "European Newspapers Find Creative Ways to Thrive in the Internet Age." *New York Times*, 30 March.
– 2010. "In Britain, a Laboratory for Newsprint's Future." *New York Times*, 4 April.
Pfeifer, Stuart, and Andrew Khouri. 2014. "Long Beach Register Stops Publishing." *Los Angeles Times*, 28 December.
Picard, Robert G. 2008. "Shifts In Newspaper Advertising Expenditures and Their Implications for the Future of Newspapers." *Journalism Studies* 9 (5): 704–16.
– 2010. "A Business Perspective on Challenges Facing Journalism." In *The Changing Business of Journalism and Its Implications for Democracy*, edited by David A.L. Levy and Rasmus Kleis Nielsen. Oxford: Reuters Institute for the Study of Journalism.
– 2014. "Deficient Tutelage: Challenges of Contemporary Journalism Education." Keynote Speech to the *Toward 2020: New Directions in Journalism Education* conference, 31 May 2014 at Ryerson University in Toronto. http://www.robertpicard.net/files/Picard_deficient_tutelage.pdf.
Pincus, Walter. 2009. "Newspaper Narcissism." *Columbia Journalism Review*, May-June.
Pompeo, Joe. 2010. "The Daily Is Murdoch's 'No. 1 Most Exciting Project.'" *Yahoo! News*, 17 November.
Poniewozik, James. 2009. "Doing Less with Less: What Are You Willing to Give Up from Journalism?" *Time*, 16 December.
Ponsford, Dominic. 2014. "Guardian's £600m Trader Media Group Windfall Puts It in Sight of £1bn Trust Fund to Protect Its Journalism Forever." *Press Gazette*, 22 January.

Postmedia Networks Inc. 2014. "Postmedia Network Reports First-Quarter Results." Company news release, 9 January. http://www.postmedia.com/wp-content/uploads/2014/01/Postmedia-Network-Reports-First-Quarter-F14-News-Release-FINAL.pdf.

Preston, Peter. 2011. "Will the iPad Tablet Really Be the Cure for Newspapers' Ills?" *Guardian*, 5 June.

Project for Excellence in Journalism (PEJ). 2007a. *The State of the News Media*. stateofthemedia.org/2007.

– 2007b. *Anna Nicole Smith: Anatomy of a Feeding Frenzy*. Pew Research Centre, 4 April. http://www.journalism.org/2007/04/04/anna-nicole-smith-anatomy-of-a-feeding-frenzy/.

– 2009. *The State of the News Media*. stateofthemedia.org/2009.

– 2012a. *The State of the News Media*. stateofthemedia.org/2012.

– 2012b. "YouTube and News: News Videos Compared with the Top Videos," 16 July.

Pulitzer.org. 2013. "Nomination for the 2013 Pulitzer Prize. Category: Feature Writing." Date unknown. www.pulitzer.org/files/2013/feature-writing/branchentryletter.pdf.

Quateman, Lily. 2009. "Wiki Journalism." *New York Review of Ideas*, June.

Rachman, Gideon. 2008. "American Journalism Still a Model." *Financial Times*, 14 July.

Rainey, James. 2010. "Freelance Writing's Unfortunate New Model." *Los Angeles Times*, 6 January.

Rainey, James, and Michael A. Hiltzik. 2008. "Tribune Co. Files for Chapter 11 Bankruptcy Protection." *Los Angeles Times*, 9 December.

Rainie, Lee, Paul Hitlin, Mark Jurkowitz, Michael Dimock, and Shawn Neidorf. 2012. "The Viral Kony 2012 Video." Pew Internet and American Life Project, 15 March.

Reader's Digest. 2010. "Top Jobs: The Professions We Trust Most." 11 April. www.readersdigest.ca.

Reich, Zvi. 2011. "User Comments: The Transformation of Participatory Space." *Participatory Journalism: Guarding Open Gates at Online Newspapers*. West Malden, MA, and Oxford: Wiley-Blackwell.

Renzetti, Elizabeth. 2013. "You Won't Believe What the Press Just Did: Their Jobs on the Public's Behalf." *Globe and Mail*, 18 October.

Rich, Frank. 2006. *The Greatest Story Ever Sold: The Decline of the Truth from 9/11 to Katrina*. New York: Penguin.

Riggio, Ronald E. 2009. "Why Jon Stewart Is the Most Trusted Man in America." *Psychology Today*, 24 July.

"RMP." 2010. "Bigger Is Better" comment. Torontosunfamily.blogspot.com, 10 September.

Roberts, Jeff. 2010. "Canwest Shows No Appetite for Piecemeal Bids." *Globe and Mail*, 19 January.

– 2012. "Why Warren Buffett Is Buying Newspapers." *Time*, 21 May.

Robillard, Alexandre. 2013. "Pierre Karl Péladeau Invited to Key Cabinet Meetings." *Globe and Mail*, 9 October.

Robinson, James. 2010. "Huffington Post Is among 'News Parasites,' Says Washington Post Man." *Guardian*, 23 September.

Roosevelt, Theodore. 1906. "The Man with the Muck Rake" speech, 15 April. www.infoplease.com/ipa/A0900141.html.

Rosen, Jay. 1999. *What Are Journalists For?* Hartford, CT: Yale University Press.

– 2006. "The People Formerly Known as the Audience." PRESS*think*, 27 June. journalism.nyu.edu.

– 2009. "Audience Atomization Overcome: Why the Internet Weakens the Authority of the Press." PRESS*think*. journalism.nyu.edu, 12 January.

Rubenstein, Will, Liv Combe, Alegra Kirkland, and Samantha Link. 2012. "Editorial: Fearless? Not Re: the Internet." *Oberlin Review*, 27 July.

Rusbridger, Alan. 2009. "First Read: The Mutualized Future Is Bright." *Columbia Journalism Review*, 19 October. www.cjr.org.

– 2010. "The Hugh Cudlipp Lecture: Does Journalism Exist?" 25 January. guardian.co.uk.

Sanchez, Raf. 2013. "Boston Marathon Bombings: How Social Media Identified Wrong Suspects." *Telegraph*, 19 April.

Schaffer, January 2009. "First Read: Follow the Breadcrumbs." *Columbia Journalism Review*, 19 October.

Schudson, Michael. 1978. *Discovering the News: A Social History of American Newspapers*. New York: Basic Books.

– 1995. *The Power of News*. Cambridge, MA: Harvard University Press.

– 2003. *The Sociology of News*. New York: Norton.

– 2008. "The Lippmann-Dewey Debate and the Invention of Walter Lippmann as an Anti-Democrat 1986–1996." *International Journal of Communication* 2: 1031–42.

Seattlepi.com. 2014. Accessed 25 January 2014.

Seattletimes.com. 2014. Accessed 25 January 2014.

Sebastian, Michael. 2014. "New York Times Tones Down Labeling on Its Sponsored Posts." *Advertising Age*, 5 August.

Sebelius, Steve. 2013. "Trust the Media? Most Don't, but We're Beating Politicians." *Las Vegas Review*, 18 December.

Segar, Mike. 2012. "Buffett Snaps Up 63 Newspapers for $142 million." *Reuters*, 17 May.
Seitz, Matt Zoller. 2010. "Why I Like Vicious Anonymous Online Comments." *Slate*, 3 August.
Selley, Chris. 2009. "Who Died and Made Andrew Cohen the Journalism Gatekeeper?" *National Post*, 4 December.
Shafer, Jack. 2006. "The Tipster in Wolfe's Clothing." *Columbia Journalism Review*, March-April.
– 2009a. "Not All Information Wants to Be Free." *Slate*, 18 February.
– 2009b. "Democracy's Cheat Sheet: It's Time to Kill the Idea that Newspapers Are Essential for Democracy." *Slate*, 27 March.
– 2009c. "Bring Back Yellow Journalism." *Slate*, 30 March.
– 2009d. "Hello Steve Brill, Get Me Rewrite." *Slate*, 17 April.
– 2012a. "So Warren Buffett Likes Newspapers Again?" *Reuters*, 18 May.
– 2012b. "How the Byline Beast Was Born." *Reuters*, 6 July.
– 2012c. "The Daily Didn't Fail – Rupert Gave up." *Reuters*, 3 December.
– 2014. "Who'll Fund Journalism? Meet the New Medicis." *Reuters*, 26 February.
Shahid, Sharon. 2011. "2011 First Amendment Survey: Public Supports Watchdog Free Press." Newseum.org, 12 July.
Shapiro, Ian. 2009. "The Death of Newspapers (Gawker Edition)." *Washington Post*, 2 August.
Shapiro, Michael. 2012. "Six Degrees of Aggregation: How the Huffington Post Ate the Internet." *Columbia Journalism Review*, June.
Shearer, Harry. 2012. "The Sometimes Picayune: Want to Damage New Orleans (Again)? Decimate Its Newspaper." *Columbia Journalism Review*, 6 June.
Shirky, Clay. 2008. *Here Comes Everybody*. London: Penguin.
– 2009 "Newspapers and Thinking the Unthinkable." www.shirky.com, March.
Siebert, Fred S., Theodore Peterson, and Wilbur Schramm. 1963. *Four Theories of the Press*. Urbana and Chicago: University of Illinois Press. Orig. 1956.
Silverman, Craig. 2015. *Lies, Damn Lies, and Viral Content: How News Websites Spread (and Debunk) Online Rumors, Unverified Claims, and Misinformation*. A Tow/Knight Report. Columbia University Journalism School (Tow Center for Digital Journalism).
Singer, Jane. 2011. "Taking Responsibility: Legal and Ethical Issues in Participatory Journalism." *Participatory Journalism: Guarding Open Gates at Online Newspapers*. Malden, MA, and Oxford: Wiley-Blackwell.

Smillie, Dirk. 2009. "Journalism's Hottest Job." *Forbes*, 9 December.
Smith, Charlie. 2009. "Vancouver-Based Glacier Media Posts $28.3 Million Profit." Straight.com, 23 March.
Solomon, William S. 1995. "The Site of Newsroom Labor: The Division of Editorial Practices." In *Newsworkers: Toward a History of the Rank and File*, edited by Hanno Hardt and Bonnie Brennen. Minneapolis: University of Minnesota Press.
Sotiron, Minko. 1997. *From Politics to Profit: The Commercialization of Canadian Daily Newspapers 1890–1920*. Montreal and Kingston: McGill-Queen's University Press.
Spears, Borden. 1984. *Borden Spears: Reporter, Editor, Critic*. Edited by Dick MacDonald. Markham, ON: Fitzhenry and Whiteside.
Spears, Tom. 2010. "Quake Couldn't Shake Loose Government Red Tape." *Ottawa Citizen*, 28 December.
Starkman, Dean. 2012. "On Blaming The Daily's Demise on Purely Technical Causes: Was It Any Good? Who Knows?" *Columbia Journalism Review*, 5 December.
– 2013. "No Paywalls, Please: We're the Guardian." *Columbia Journalism Review*, 10 October.
– 2014. *The Watchdog that Didn't Bark: The Financial Crisis and the Disappearance of Investigative Journalism*. New York: Columbia University Press.
Starr, Paul. 2004. *The Creation of the Media: Political Origins of Modern Communications*. New York: Basic Books.
– 2009. "Goodbye to the Age of Newspapers (Hello to a New Era of Corruption)." *New Republic*, 4 March.
– 2010. "Governing in the Age of Fox News." *Atlantic Monthly*, January-February.
Steel, Ronald. 1980. *Walter Lippmann and the American Century*. Boston: Little, Brown.
Stelter, Brian. 2011. "Protest Puts Coverage in Spotlight." *New York Times*, 20 November.
Stephens, Mitchell. 2007. "Beyond the News." *Columbia Journalism Review*, January-February
Stepp, Carl Sessions. 1999. "Paradise Lost." The Project for Excellence in Journalism (PEJ). http.//ajr.newslink.org/special. (No longer available.)
Stoeffel, Kat. 2012. "RIP Newscore: News Corp.'s Weird News Wire Goes Dark, Sheds Staff." *New York Observer*, 11 July.
Strupp, Joe. 2009. "New York Times R&D Team Seeks Next Big Things." *Editor and Publisher*, 8 October.

Sturgeon, James. 2012. "CRTC Blocks BCE Bid for Astral." *National Post*, 18 October.
Sullivan, John. 2011. "True Enough: The Second Age of PR." *Columbia Journalism Review*, May-June.
Sullivan, Margaret. 2014. "'Journalism Oracle'? What Was I Thinking?" *New York Times*, 26 February.
Surowiecki, James. 2008. "News You Can Lose." *New Yorker*, 22 December.
Taras, David. 1999. *Power and Betrayal in the Canadian Media*. Peterborough, ON: Broadview Press.
Taylor, Adam. 2011. "Paywall Fail: Times of London Circulation Collapses as Company's Online Strategy Falters." *Business Insider*, 10 June.
Teel, Leonard Ray. 2006. *The History of American Journalism: The Public Press, 1900–1945*. Westport, CT, London: Praeger.
Thornton, Emily, and Ronald Grover. 2008. "Sam Zell's Deal from Hell." *Businessweek*, 30 July.
Timmons, Heather. 2008. "Newspapers on Upswing in Developing Markets." *New York Times*, 20 May.
Tobaccowala, Rishad. 2010. "Papers Aren't Going Anywhere." *Adweek*, 1 September.
Tofel, Richard, J. 2012. *Why American Newspapers Gave Away the Future*. Now & Then iBook.
torontosunfamily.blogspot.ca. Accessed weekly, 2007–15.
Turner, Dan. 2005. "Canadian Journalism: Pretty Good. Not Really. Ughhh. Better and Worse than What the Yanks and Brits Get. It Sure Could Use a Lot More of This. Much Less of That. Can It Be Saved? Hell, No. Then Again ... Maybe." Ottawa: Public Policy Forum.
Underwood, Doug. 1995. *When MBAs Rule the Newsroom*. New York: Columbia University Press.
US Census Bureau. 1999. "20th Century Statistics." *Statistical Abstract of the United States*. www.census.gov/prod/99pubs/99statab/sec31.pdf.
Vanderklippe, Nathan. 2015. "China Seeks to Export Its Vision of the Internet." *Globe and Mail*, 1 January.
Van Praet, Nicolas. 2012. "Huffington Post Debuts in Quebec under a Cloud." *National Post*, 8 February.
Warnica, Richard. 2013. "Behind the Paywall: The Truth on the Move to Paywalls." *Canadian Business*, 26 February.
Watson, Thomas. 2010. "Media War 2.0." *Canadian Business*, 13 September.
Watt, Nicholas. 2013. "David Cameron Makes Veiled Threat to Media over NSA and GCHQ Leaks." *Guardian*, 28 October.

Webbyawards.com. Accessed 22 June 2014.

Weingarten, Marc. 2005. *The Gang that Wouldn't Write Straight*. New York: Three Rivers Press.

Wemple, Erik. 2012. "Warren Buffett Buys Newspapers. Is He Nuts?" *Washington Post*, 17 May.

Whittaker, Zack. 2011. "UC Davis: Official Spin Crumbles in the Face of 'Too Many Videos.'" *ZDNet*, 20 November.

Williams, Raymond. 1978. "The Press We Deserve." In *The British Press: A Manifesto*, edited by James Curran. London and Basingstoke: Acton Society Press Group.

– 1983. *Culture and Society, 1780–1950*. New York: Columbia University Press. Orig. 1958.

Wilson, Jeff. 2010. "Analyst's View: Flipboard for iPad Is Rupert Murdoch's Nightmare." *PC*, 11 August.

Wilson-Smith, Anthony. 1998. "A New Embrace: Quebecor Proposes a Friendly Takeover of Sun Media and Pushes Torstar to the Sidelines." *Maclean's*, 21 December.

Wingrove, Josh. 2013. "Fifteen Tory Motions to Know About from the Convention." *Globe and Mail*, 13 November.

Wolfe, Tom. 1973. *The New Journalism*. Edited by Tom Wolfe and E.W. Johnson. New York, San Francisco, London: Harper and Row.

Wolff, Michael. 2009. "Rupert to Internet: It's War." *Vanity Fair*, November.

Wong, Jan. 2013. "Canadian Media Guild Data Show 10,000 Job Losses in Past Five Years." *J-Source.ca*, 19 November.

Wong, Tony. 2014. "CBC to Lose up to 1,500 More Jobs." *Toronto Star*, 26 June.

Wyatt, Nelson. 2002. "Canadian Media Biased – Poll." Canadian Press, 5 May.

Yarow, Jay, and Kamelia Angelova. 2011. "Chart of the Day: How Much Is Apple Making on the App Store?" *Business Insider*, 11 July.

Yarrow, Charlene, 1993. "Hail and Farewell to the Whig." *Ryerson Review of Journalism*, Summer.

YouTube. 2010. "Newsday Commercial: iPad Is Not a Paper." www.youtube.com/watch?v=Rtdq87nX6EA&feature=related. Posted 29 November. Accessed 25 January 2014.

Yu, Roger. 2014. "OC Register, Press-Enterprise Cut about 70 Jobs." *USA Today*, 17 January.

Index

accountability reporting. *See* investigative reporting
accreditation and definition of journalists, 224–8
Adam, G. Stuart, 6, 54
advertising: "advertising rags," 137; classified, 89, 101, 109–11, 112; and competition bureau, 69; digital, 3, 17, 96, 100–8, 115, 123–4, 140–1, 182, 236, 122–3; diminishing role in newspaper finances, 11, 114–15; display, 47, 57, 112, 115; global spending on, 133; pulling out of newspapers, 237, 251; retail, 113–14, 235–6; revenue from, 101, 108–9, 114, 119, 140, 235; small papers, 130; traditional role of, 23–5, 28, 40–1, 76–7. *See also* native content
Advertising Age, 239
aggregation: and newspapers, 104–5, 134, 137–8, 183–4; and online news consumption, 4; structure of, 70, 90, 100; tablets, 187. *See also* blogging
Alliance Atlantis Communications, 119, 121

Alterman, Eric, 10, 11, 16, 50–3, 146–7
alternative weeklies, 56–7; online alternative publications, 159, 212; underground press, 55–6, 213–14
American Society of News(paper) Editors (ASNE), 64
anonymous senior reporter, 15, 88, 147, 197, 259
Apple, 122, 142, 152, 186, 190
Aristotle, 7, 11–12
Armadale. *See* Saskatchewan newspapers
Assange, Julian, 175–6. *See also* Benkler, Yochai; Manning, Chelsea (Bradley); WikiLeaks
Astral Media, 124–5
Atkinson, Joseph, 31–3, 52, 66, 219, 241
Atkinson Charitable Foundation, 241
Atlantic Monthly, 21, 57, 128, 154
Atrios, 219
Auletta, Ken, 133

Bagdikian, Ben, 40, 42, 70, 72, 80
balance and objectivity: byproduct of art, 57–8, 223; core belief of

journalism and rise of the pundits, 48, 50–3; definition of and confusion with balance, 8–10, 77, 216–17
Baltimore Sun, 28
bankruptcy: and Chapter 11, 16, 118–19, 121, 157, 200; and Companies' Creditor Arrangement Act, 120–1
Baumgartner, Travis, hearings, 166, 172–3
BBC, 150, 156–7, 223, 240
BCE Inc. (Bell Media): Astral Media Inc. takeover, 124–5; and consolidation of ownership, 253, 257; corporate strategy, 90; TV holdings, 46; and *Globe and Mail*, 70
Beers, David, 170–1, 212–13, 258
Ben Franklin Project, 157
Benkler, Yochai: attacks on WikiLeaks, 8, 63, 176, 251; press monopolies, 82, 209. *See also* Assange, Julian; Manning, Chelsea (Bradley); WikiLeaks
BETA620, 158
Bezos, Jeff, 145, 152, 233, 248
Big Media: attempts to regulate, 67; encouraging competition 263–4; market complacency, 4–5; online 151, 253; as threat to journalism, 98, 241
Bird, Roger, 83
Black, Conrad: as media personality, 75; and *National Post*, 194–5; opinion of news media, 198–9; press acquisitions, 45, 70; as right-wing ideologue, 73, 86. *See also* Hollinger Inc.
Black, David, 83, 131
Black Press, 83, 131, 258
Blethen family, 129

Blicq, Andrew, 149
blogging/bloggers: and definition of "journalist," 224–8; ethics, 32; free news content, 104–5, 137; in the military, 174; and public trust, 204; resemblance to early newspapers, 22; as unpaid freelancers, 184. *See also* aggregators
Bloomberg Business, 100, 258
Bogart, Leo, 81
Boston Globe: and John Henry, 233, 240, 248; paywall, 141; sale of, 108, 145
Boston Marathon bombings, 178
Bourque, Justin, shooting rampage, 142
Brand, Stewart, 99–100, 257
Brassard, Raymond, 108, 189, 243
Breitbart, Andrew, 183, 215, 218, 233
Briggs, Asa, and Peter Burke, 34
Broadcasting Act of 1932, 38
broken business model: and advertising model, 113; definition of, 1; focus of crisis coverage, 97, 138, 193, 199; and technology, 151
Brown, Jesse. *See Canadaland*
Brown, Tina: on British journalism, 223; India, 133; news management, 9, 146, 151, 193–4
Brunswick News, 142, 257
Buffett, Warren, 126–7

Calamai, Peter, 86
Calgary Herald, 112, 121, 190, 221
Calgary Sun, 43
Cameron, David, 8, 63, 223, 251
Canadaland, 250, 263
Canadian Media Research Consortium, 203–4

Canadian Radio-television and Telecommunications Commission (CRTC), 125
Canon of Journalism. See American Society of News Editors
Canwest: bankruptcy, 119–21, 124, 200, 242; BC coastal monopoly, 213; Hollinger takeover, 16; and ideology, 75, 249
Carey, James, 11, 60, 84. *See also* Dewey, John; Lippmann, Walter; *The Phantom Public*; *The Public and Its Problems*; *Public Opinion*; Schudson, Michael; Williams, Raymond
Carr, David: and definition of journalist 225–6; and management excesses 199–200, 256; and online strategy, 154, 185
CBC: and Bangladesh factory tragedy, 22; competition for newspapers, 39, 150, 157; funding, 143, 255; importance of, 262–3; Jian Ghomeshi scandal, 255–6; 2015 staff cuts, 240
CBC *News Sunday*, 99
centralized production, 70, 115–16, 129, 201, 243. *See also* Mind Works Global Media; outsourcing
Charitable Gifts Act, 241, 263
Chicago Sun-Times, 45, 47, 121
Chittum, Ryan: charging for content, 10, 104, 114, 139, 193, 238; media companies' business strategies, 98, 119; non-profit news organizations, 234; *Orange County Register*, 144–5; outlook for *Guardian*, *New York Times*, Gannett, 135–6; outlook for magazines, 128; tablets, 189

Chodan, Lucinda, 86, 113
Chomsky, Noam, 8, 72, 76, 241; and Edward S. Herman, 71–2
circulation of Canadian dailies, 112–13
citizen journalism: and accreditation 227; bearing witness, 173–80; collaboration with professionals, 169–70, 252; organizations, 162–3; and public journalism, 60; public perception of, 204; replacing professional journalism, 3–4, 9, 98; and technology, 150, 153. *See also* collaborative journalism; crowd-sourcing; participatory journalism; user comments; user-generated content
civic journalism. *See* public journalism
Clark, Ruth, 80–1
Cohen, Andrew, 224
Colbert, Stephen, 183, 214
collaborative journalism, 166, 150–1, 168–9, 180, 198. *See also* citizen journalism; crowd-sourcing; participatory journalism; user comments; user-generated content
Columbia Journalism Review, 261
community newspapers: impact of recession, 6, 17, 130–2; and Postmedia, 74; and Quebecor, 115; strengths of, 83; and Warren Buffett, 127. *See also* small dailies
concentration of ownership, attempts to limit, 67–70; collapse of Canwest, 120–1; conditions leading to, 40–2; and Hollinger, 86; on the Internet, 152; and Postmedia-Quebecor

takeover, 241–2; in Quebec, 19–20
Consumer Reports, 100, 238
content farms, 134, 230
convergence, 46, 248
Coombs, Stephanie, 106, 166, 172
Cox, Crystal, 225–6
Coyne, Andrew, 75, 207
CPM, 103, 105–6, 114
Cramer, Jim, 215
Crawley, Phillip, 48, 87, 194
credibility of news media, 93–4, 203–6
Creighton, J. Douglas, 45
crowd-sourcing, 150, 155, 157, 161, 171. *See also* Lewis, Paul
CTV, 46, 70, 124–5
Curran, James, and Jean Seaton, 66
cutbacks, 107–8, 195–6, 198, 201, 256. *See also* layoffs; *Paper Cuts*
cyber-utopianism, 4–9, 13, 197, 251, 254

Dacre, Paul, 224–7
Dailing, Paul, 99
Daily, the, 186–8
Daily Mail, the, 135, 140, 198
Daily News, the, 44, 104, 127, 143
Daily Show, The, 214, 224, 244, 261. *See also* Stewart, Jon
Darnton, Robert, 150, 191
data journalism, 149, 155, 171, 262
Davey Committee, 68
death of newspapers, 14, 95–6, 99
debt: and acquisition strategy, 15, 79; Canwest, 119–21, 124, 242; and economic crisis, 10; Postmedia and Sun takeover, 253; and quality, 91, 101–2, 107–9; Sam Zell and the Tribune Co., 47, 118–19

democracy: Aristotle, 12; and learned societies, 49; newspapers and preservation of, 200–8, 209, 216, 229; in online society, 13, 151; and penny press, 28; the press and political communication, 3–8, 59–61; and reliability of the news, 71, 85; and sensationalism 65–7
demographics, 27, 44, 85–6, 236, 243
Deuze, Mark, 172, 197
Dewey, John: involved public, 6, 94, 151; on journalism, 53, 60; and Walter Lippmann, 11–13, 50–1. *See also* Carey, James; Lippmann, Walter; *The Phantom Public*; *The Public and Its Problems*; *Public Opinion*; Schudson, Michael; Williams, Raymond
Didion, Joan, 53, 92, 207
digital audience, 17, 104–5, 123, 135
Digital First Media, 157–8. *See also* Ben Franklin Project; Paton, John
digital journalism: and the CBC, 240; community papers, 198, 248; employment, 6, 188; long-form journalism, 21, 155, 247; mobile apps, 17; multimedia, 150–5; vs print, 11–12, 97; viral content, 179
digital revenue: "digital first" 120, 124, 128, 168, 240; effect on revenue model, 105–7; *Guardian*, 135–6, 239; *New York Times*, 238–9; pay plans, 123
DiManno, Rosie, 253
Dinnick, Wilf, 161–2, 170, 246
disruption, 6, 37, 43, 113–14, 248
diversity, 18–19, 65, 244–6

Doctor, Ken, 127, 200
Dornan, Christopher, 13–14, 82
dot-com bubble, 3, 108, 257
Doyle, John, 260–1

Editor and Publisher, 79
Edmonton Journal: "Capital Ideas," 86, 170; Michener Award, 221; online, 172; and Postmedia, 121; women executives, 19
Eisenstein, Elizabeth, 24
Ellsberg, Daniel, 180
end of news, 83, 99, 102
Engelhardt, Tom, 208
evening newspapers, 43, 128, 189
executive compensation, 146, 197, 199–200

Facebook: and audience for news, 166–7, 177; newsgathering, 179; as promotional tool, 182–3. *See also* social media; Twitter
Fédération professionnelle des journalistes, 224
Felker, Clay, 55
Ferri, John, 162
Final Report on the Canadian News Media, 68
Fireside Chats, 38, 150
Fletcher, Fred, 69, 210, 261
foreign newspapers, 17, 132–5
four-platform strategy, 189, 253, 256. *See also* Postmedia
Four Theories of the Press, 7, 61–4
Fox News Network, 51, 73, 75, 216, 221
FP Publications (defunct chain), 41–3
FP Publications (*Winnipeg Free Press, Brandon Sun*), 129, 142, 258
Franklin, Bob, 10–11, 132–3

Free and Responsible Press, A, 64–6, 254. *See also* Hutchins, Robert M.
Freedom Communications, 144. *See also* Kushner, Aaron; *Orange County Register*
freelancing: and aggregators, 184; definition of journalist, 225–6; in new economy, 197, 230–2, 258; and New Journalism, 56; women, 245. *See also* content farms
freeping, 167
Frontline, 229
Fulford, Robert, 96, 157

Gabler, Neal, 49, 58, 218
Gagnon, Lysiane, 255
Gannett Company: executive compensation, 199; harvesting, 146; paywall, 141; profit margins, 46, 98, 136. *See also* USA *Today*
Gazette, the, 43–4, 113, 121, 190
Gergen, David, 219
Ghomeshi, Jian. *See* CBC
Gibbons, Rick, 122, 201
Gitlin, Todd: alternative media, 213–14; chain ownership, 145–6; five wolves at the door, 193; on the *New York Times*, 220; rebirth of journalism, 217; universities as publishers, 234
Globe and Mail: and BCE, 46; competition from *National Post*, 194–5; demographic marketing, 210, 243; growth of mobile app, 168, 188; layoffs, 117, 246; national edition, 40, 43, 44–5; and native content, 236; online classifieds, 110; paywall, 141; purchase of presses, 127; target audience, 87; 2014 Ontario

election, 250; and Woodbridge, 124–5
Godfrey, Paul: on classified advertising, 110; compensation, 200; digital strategy, 74, 120, 253; on journalism, 75; and the Ontario Progressive Conservatives, 250–1; on paywalls, 137. *See also* Postmedia Network Inc.; Sun Media
Golden Tree Asset Management, 242
government support for media, 24–5, 38, 41, 240, 263. *See also* Broadcasting Act of 1932; Income Tax Act
Gramsci, Antonio, 64, 70
great society and great community, 6, 34, 152
Greeley, Horace, 29, 50
Greenspon, Edward, 180
Greenwald, Glenn, 198, 223, 249
groundreport.com, 162–3
Groupe Vidéotron, 46
Guardian: classified ads, 111; free content 14, 132; freedom from influence, 135–6; interactive, 170–1; as international news organization, 6; and Manning leaks, 175; online audience, 17, 238–9; online innovation, 155–6; and Snowden leaks, 8, 251. *See also* Lewis, Paul; Rusbridger, Alan

Habermas, Jürgen, 35. *See also* public sphere
Hackett, Robert A., and Yuezhi Zhao, 241
Halifax Chronicle-Herald, 141, 258
Halifax Daily News, 249
Halifax Gazette, 25

Hallin, Daniel C., 71–2, 160, 219, 244
Hambleton, Paul, 187
Harkness, Ross, 241
Harper, Stephen, 231–2
Harper government, 207, 211, 259
Harper's Weekly, 164
harvesting, 146, 201–2
Hayes, David, 43–4
Hearst Newspapers, 66, 110, 121, 158, 233
Hedges, Chris, 161
Hollinger Inc., 45–6, 73, 86, 249
Homolka, Karla. *See* Todd, Paula
Honderich, Beland, 33, 52–3
Honderich, John, 102–3, 117, 136, 180, 241
Hong Kong, 251
House of Lords Select Committee on Communications, 104, 111
Houston Post, 52
Huffington Post, 183–4, 187, 188, 230
human flesh search engine. *See* Boston Marathon bombing
Hutchins, Robert M., 64. See also *A Free and Responsible Press*
hyper-local news, 153, 177, 198, 201, 247

Income Tax Act, 41, 45
India, 17, 133–4, 183
insider baseball, 92, 207
interviews, 29
inverted pyramid, 29, 83, 172, 187–8
investigative reporting: difficulties of, 91, 226; high-tech, 175, 229; in the 1970s, 56; non-profits, 247; and the penny press, 23, 30. *See also* Assange, Julian; muckrakers; WikiLeaks

iPad, 122, 185–7
Iraq War, 8, 94, 174, 211, 203
ISIS, 176

Jefferson, Thomas, 22
Jones, Alex S., 201–2
Journal de Montréal, 44, 45, 83, 116
Journal de Québec, 45, 116
Journal Register Co., 167. *See also* Ben Franklin Project; Paton, John

Katz, Elihu, and David Foulkes, 54
Kent, Clark, 196
Kent, Tom, 69
Kent Commission. *See* Royal Commission on Newspapers
Kent State University, 173
Kesterton, W.H., 25
Kimber, Stephen, 249
King, Rodney, 173
Kingston Whig-Standard, 46, 237, 258
Koch brothers, Charles and David, 145, 234, 240, 249
Kony 2012, 178–9
Kushner, Aaron, 144–5, 233, 248. *See also* Freedom Communications

labour reporting, 220
Lacroix, Hubert, 240, 256
Ladurantaye, Steve: on bad newspapers, 5, 82, 201; interactivity, 168; journalism training, 262; paywalls, 104, 122; Quebecor, 196; rethinking the daily, 128; Twitter, 181; value of newspapers, 256
Lagacé, Patrick, 256
Langewiesche, William, 57–8

Lanham, Richard A., 106–7
La Presse, 31, 44, 141, 158, 188, 258
Last Week Tonight, 214, 244, 261. *See also* Oliver, John
layoffs, 115–17, 129, 243, 253. *See also* cutbacks; *Paper Cuts*
Layton, Charles, 78
Le Devoir, 44, 258
Le Jour, 44
Le Soleil, 45, 258
leveraged acquisition: and Canwest, 119–20; consolidation of ownership, 124; effect on news content, 15; independent ownership, 129; process, 107–8; Tribune Co., 118
Lewis, Paul, 180–1
Linkins, Jason, 220
Lippmann, Walter: as anti-democrat, 13; and Dewey "debate," 6, 11–12, 50, 152; framing the news, 8, 20, 60–1, 76; and Charles Merz, 70–1; as model modern pundit, 51–3; at the *New York World*, 33; and the phantom public, 6, 165, 186; political philosophy, 64. *See also* Carey, James; Dewey, John; *The Phantom Public*; *The Public and Its Problems*; *Public Opinion*; Schudson, Michael; Williams, Raymond
literacy, 23–7, 31, 34
literary journalism, 52, 54–7, 77, 194, 247–8
Los Angeles Times, 118–19, 138, 145, 159, 239

Macdonald, Neil, 210
MacPhail, Wayne, 90
Maffin, Todd, 190

magazines: continental medium, 38; economic recovery, 21, 109, 114; and freelancers, 230; and muckraking, 30; and New Journalism, 55–7; popular apps, 188
MailOnline. See *Daily Mail*
mainstream media: advertising, 103; audience confidence, 204; bloggers and aggregators, 137; criticism of, 3, 9, 211; depleted resources, 208; digital developments, 162; influenced by new media, 213–6; and New Journalism and underground press, 55–6
management by objective, 77–8
Manning, Chelsea (Bradley), 63, 175–6, 251. See also Assange, Julian; Benkler, Yochai; WikiLeaks
Martin, Lawrence, 74–5, 207–8, 244
McCain, John, 153
McChesney, Robert, 85, 89, 151, 252; and John Nichols, 5, 9, 143, 210
McKercher, Catherine, 37, 202, 230, 244–5
Megarry, A. Roy, 76
Mencken, H.L., 64, 145
Mercer, Rick, 261
Merrill, John C., 7, 62. See also *Four Theories of the Press*; Nerone, John C.
Metroland Newspapers, 102, 131, 201, 253, 258
metropolitan omnibus daily, 28, 131, 197, 228, 256
Michaels, Randy, 199–200
Miller, John: on conventions of news coverage, 84, 208; cutbacks, 202; diversity, 18, 245; news management, 15–16, 195

Mind Works Global Media, 134, 144. See also centralized production; outsourcing
MinnPost, 112, 144
Montréal Matin, 44
Montreal Star, 31, 40, 43
Moroney, James W., III, 95–6
Morozov, Evgeny, 152, 251–2
Morton, John, 101, 108
muckrakers, 30, 51, 52, 218, 223. See also investigative reporting
Muldoon, Kathy, 250
multimedia, 12, 119, 169
Munsey, Frank, 41
Murdoch, Rupert, 47, 183, 185–7, 222–3
Mutter, Allan D., 101, 231

Nation, 29, 41
National Post: Canwest collapse, 121; elimination of Monday editions, 128; founding, 45, 194–5; Gastropost, 86, 170
National Public Radio (NPR), 114, 150, 156–7, 221, 240
native content, 17, 86, 236–7, 239
neo-conservatism, 73, 214–15, 251
neo-liberalism, 62, 244, 259
Nerone, John C., 7, 61–5. See also *Four Theories of the Press*; Miller, John C.
network society, 11
Neuharth, Allen, 203
new journalism. See literary journalism
new media, 5, 8–9, 30, 215–17, 229
new Medicis, 248–9
New Republic, 51, 70, 204, 206
New York Herald-Tribune, 55, 53
New York magazine, 55, 153–4
New York Post, 44, 47
New York Sun, 27–8

New York Times: Boston Globe ownership, 108, 145; circulation, 104, 136–41; commitment to journalism, 220, 238–9; coverage of Bolsheviks, 70–1; coverage of newspaper crisis, 95; culture of self-criticism, 256; digital experimentation, 153–6, 159, 169–70; loan from Carlos Slim Helú, 128; mission statement at launch, 50; mobile app, 188, 257; paywall, 138–41; revenue, 11, 111, 211
News Corp., 222–3
News of the World, 47, 222–5
news you can use, 80, 90, 158
Newsday, 118, 140, 185
newspaper chains: aversion to risk, 75, 82, 209; in Britain, 66–73; business strategies, 14, 91, 98, 145–6, 253; and community papers, 258; criticism of management, 146–7, 214; vs family ownership, 79–80; rise of, 8, 37, 41–6; survival, 242–3
Newspaper Guild, 117
Nieman Foundation for Journalism / Journalism Lab, 18, 64, 189
Norris, Pippa, 59, 92

Obama, Barack, 72, 131, 205, 233
objectivity. *See* balance and objectivity
Occupy Central. *See* Hong Kong
Occupy Wall Street, 72, 160, 221
Ochs, Adolph, 31
O'Keefe, James, 178, 216, 233
old media: adaptability, 12, 20, 100; and information gathering, 137; online alternatives, 213, 216, 229, 253
Olive, David, 94, 158

Oliver, John, 214. *See also Last Week Tonight*
Omidyar, Pierre, 198, 233, 249
online readership. *See* digital audience
OpenFile, 161–2, 170, 212, 263. *See also* Dinnick, Wilf; Ferri, John
Orange County Register, 134, 144–5
Original Sin, 101, 104, 136
O'Shea, James, 199. *See also* Tribune Co.; Zell, Sam
Ottawa Citizen, 13, 116, 121, 189, 195
Ottawa Journal, 40, 43, 69. *See also* Southam Newspapers; Thomson Newspapers; *Winnipeg Tribune*
Ottawa War Memorial shooting, 174
outsourcing, 116–17, 120. *See also* centralized production; Mind Works Global Media

Pacific Press, 43, 121
page views, 87, 105–6, 114, 140
Paper Cuts, 117. *See also* cutbacks; layoffs
Parrish, Wayne: on audience engagement, 106; "base unit of content," 187–8; classifieds, 111; newspaper competition, 195; paywall, 137, 146
participatory journalism, 9, 150, 153, 160, 168–9. *See also* citizen journalism; collaborative journalism; crowd-sourcing; user comments; user-generated content
Paton, John, 157–8. *See also* Ben Franklin Project; Digital First

paywall: argument against, 132; and audience engagement, 114; growth of, 14, 104–5, 140–4; hard paywall, 105; origins, 137–8; and revenue, 91, 111, 122–3, 211; value of content, 10, 193
PBS, 229, 240
Péladeau, Pierre, 41, 45
Péladeau, Pierre Karl, 41, 73–4
penny papers, 27–34, 48, 218, 223
Pentagon Papers, 56, 180
Peters, John Durham, 12
Pew Research Center: confidence in newspapers, 204–5; industry profitability, 123; mobile apps, 188; old media, 137; social media, 182; YouTube, 178–9. See also Project for Excellence in Journalism
Phantom Public, 51, 61, 165, 186. See also Carey, James; Dewey, John; Lippmann, Walter; *The Public and Its Problems*; *Public Opinion*; Schudson, Michael; Williams, Raymond
Picard, Robert G., 108, 133, 259–61
Plato, 7, 11, 62
Politico, 229
politics, coverage of: effect of ideology on, 244, 250–1; insider baseball, 206–7; newspaper influence, 70, 84–5; in partisan press, 32; punditry, 92–3. See also Coyne, Andrew; Didion, Joan; insider baseball; Martin, Lawrence
postal systems, 24–5, 150
Postmedia Network Inc.: creation of, 120; cutbacks, 143; debt, 15; digital strategy, 86, 188–90; executive compensation, 200; paywall, 141–2; revenue, 101, 104; Sun Media takeover, 73, 74–5, 116, 146, 200–1, 242–3, 258
Poynter Institute, 112, 178, 240
Press Gazette, 135
profit margin: current, 101–2; and debt, 126; harvesting, 202–3; long-term repercussions, 98; shareholder pressures, 46, 80–2; Tribune Co., 118
progressive movement, 30, 40Project for Excellence in Journalism, 83–4, 93–4. See also Pew Research Center
ProPublica, 97, 144, 220, 229
Province (Vancouver), 43, 44
Public and Its Problems, The, 61. See also Carey, James; Dewey, John; Lippmann, Walter; *The Phantom Public*; *Public Opinion*; Schudson, Michael; Williams, Raymond
public journalism: criticism of traditional journalism, 84; and *New York Herald*, 50; online, 11, 172–3, 217; persuasion, 60–1; social responsibility, 63
public opinion, 28, 35, 203–4, 232, 237
Public Opinion (book), 51, 60, 61, 76. See also Carey, James; Dewey, John; Lippmann, Walter; *The Phantom Public*; *The Public and Its Problems*; Schudson, Michael; Williams, Raymond
public relations, 35, 228
public sphere, 35–6, 92, 254, 258–9. See also Habermas, Jürgen
Pulitzer, Joseph, 30, 33, 34, 49, 219
Pulitzer newspapers, 30, 33
Pulitzer Prize, 155, 156, 159, 229
Pyette, Les, 97

Quebec Gazette, 25
Quebecor: dominance in Quebec, 19–20, 255; ideology, 73; labour disputes and cutbacks, 115–16, 196, 198, 200–2; purchase of Sun Media, 45; sale of Sun Media, 120, 242–3; Vidéotron takeover, 46, 146

Radler, David, 73
Raudsepp, Enn, 207
Reader's Digest, 204
recession: coverage of 2007–8, 5, 93, 94; of 1990 and newspaper profits; 46–8; of 2008 and media revenues, 108–9; and newspaper crisis, 14, 17, 101–2, 111, 129–30
Reflections of a Newsosaur. See Mutter, Alan D.
reform and anti-reform newspapers, 26, 31
Renzetti, Elizabeth, 232
Reuters, 100, 175, 233
RMP, 15–16
Rocky Mountain News, 121, 158
Rogers Communications, 46, 124, 257
Roosevelt, Franklin D., 38. See also Fireside Chats
Roosevelt, Theodore, 30, 51. See also muckrakers
Rosen, Jay, 84–5, 172, 219, 244
Rusbridger, Alan, 132, 156–7, 217. See also *Guardian*; Lewis, Paul

St Catharines Standard, 46, 258
Salon.com, 21, 57, 138, 155
Saskatchewan Newspapers, 45, 74, 242
Schudson, Michael: and Leonard Downie, 110, 130, 143; "field with a mission," 7; Lippmann-Dewey "debate," 13, 165; literacy, 34; New Journalism, 54–5; partisan press, 22; professionalism, 48; public sphere, 35; sphere of deviance, 72. See also Carey, James; Dewey, John; Lippmann, Walter; *The Phantom Public*; *The Public and Its Problems*; *Public Opinion*; Schudson, Michael; Williams, Raymond
Scott Trust. See *Guardian*
Scripps, Edward Willis, 41
Seattle Post-Intelligencer, and seattlepi.com, 121, 129, 158–9
Seattle Times, 105, 129, 159
Shafer, Jack: on accrediting journalists, 226–8; Warren Buffett, 127; citizen journalism, 252; New Journalism, 57–8; new Medicis, 248–9; newspaper collapse, 101–2; paid Internet, 100, 238; yellow journalism, 30, 218, 222; threat to democracy, 200, 229
shareholders, 46, 80, 91, 98, 101–2
Shaw Media, 121, 124, 125, 257
Shearer, Harry, 121–2
Shirky, Clay, 150–1, 169, 226, 227–8, 247
Silver, Nate, 149
Silverman, Craig, 179
Slate, 21
small dailies, 17, 126–7, 130–1, 248, 258. See also community papers
Smith, Anna Nicole, 94
Snowden, Edward, 8, 63, 156
social media: advertising, 100–2, 114; human flesh search engine, 178; and news, 166, 171, 179, 180–3, 188, 257; and politics, 232

social responsibility, 8, 63, 66, 235, 251. *See also* Facebook; Twitter
Social Responsibility Theory of the press, 7, 62–4, 65
Southam Newspapers, 41–3, 45, 69–70, 237. See also *Ottawa Journal*; Thomson Newspapers; *Winnipeg Tribune*
Spears, Borden, 68
Spears, Tom, 231
Stackhouse, John, 87, 142, 183
staff reduction. *See* cutbacks; lay-offs; *Paper Cuts*
Starkman, Dean, 186, 211, 241
Starr, Paul, 25, 215–16, 228–9
State of the News Media reports. *See* Project for Excellence in Journalism
steam press, 23–4, 28, 150
Steel, Ronald, 13
Stepp, Carl Sessions, 48, 83–4
Sterne, Rachel. *See groundreport.com*
Steward, Hartley, 109
Stewart, Jon, 214, 255. See also *The Daily Show*
sub-prime mortgage crisis, 211, 214
Sullivan, Margaret, 246
Sun (UK), 47, 223
Sunday newspapers, 24, 31, 116, 126
Sun Media: cutbacks, 115–16, 201; paywalls, 141; Postmedia takeover, 73–4, 242–3, 253, 258; Quebecor takeover, 45, 109. *See also* Creighton, J. Douglas; Postmedia; Quebecor; Steward, Hartley
Sun News Network, 73, 75, 116, 215, 243
Super Bowl, 131
Superman. *See* Kent, Clark

Tampa Bay Times, 127, 240
Taras, David, 19–20, 73–4, 252–3, 259
telephone hacking scandal. See *News of the World*
Thompson, Hunter S., 57–8
Thompson, Robert, 214
Thomson, Roy, 128
Thomson family, 124–5, 249, 258
Thomson Newspapers, 41, 43, 45–6, 69–70. See also *Ottawa Journal*; Southam Newspapers; *Winnipeg Tribune*
Thomson-Reuters, 100, 233
Times (London), 105, 111, 137–8, 140, 223
Times of India, 133, 148
Times Mirror Co., 118
Times-Picayune, 121–2, 131, 229
Todd, Paula, 271
Tofel, Richard, 202–3
Torontoist, 212,
Toronto Star: digital, 142; and Charitable Gifts Act, 240–1; cutbacks, 116–17; high corporate interest, 250; and ideology, 259; parochialism, 255; transition from yellow journalism, 52
Toronto Sun, 83, 194
Toronto Sun Family, 15–16, 201
Torstar, 14, 45, 102, 124, 257
Tribune Co., 46–7, 118–19, 145, 146, 199–200. *See also* O'Shea, James; Zell, Sam
Trilling, Lionel, 54–5
trolling, 65, 170. *See also* freeping
Truthdig, 72, 76, 160–1, 212. *See also* Hedges, Chris
truthiness, 181, 216
Twitter, 171–3, 179–80, 181–2, 252. *See also* Coombs, Stephanie; crowd-sourcing; Facebook; Lewis, Paul; social media

Tyee, The, 143, 170–1, 212–13, 255, 258. *See also* Beers, David

underground papers. *See* alternative weeklies
Underwood, Doug, 77–8
Unland, Karen, 115, 131, 170, 172, 182–3
Urban, Christine, 89
USA Today: coverage of newspaper crisis, 95; creation of, 41; front-page ad, 203; paywall, 141; style of journalism, 80–1; success story, 83; trendsetter, 257. *See also* Gannett Company; Nueharth, Allen
user comments, 150, 159, 161, 164, 165–9
user engagement, 106, 161, 172, 179, 210
user-generated content, 160, 177, 180. *See also* citizen journalism; collaborative journalism; crowd-sourcing

Vancouver Sun, 43, 121, 212–13
Victoria Times Colonist, 43, 131, 213
viral content, 107, 114, 179
Voice of San Diego, 144

Waddell, Christopher, 229
Wall Street Journal, 41, 60, 95, 100, 258
Warhol, Andy, 107
Washington Post, 56, 126, 131, 145, 233
Watergate, 56, 165
Webby Awards, 156–7

WikiLeaks, 8, 63, 175–6, 192, 251. *See also* Assange, Julian; Benkler, Yochai; Manning, Chelsea (Bradley)
Williams, Raymond, 12, 14, 49, 67, 217. *See also* Carey, James; Dewey, John; Lippmann, Walter; *The Phantom Public*; *The Public and Its Problems*; *Public Opinion*; Schudson, Michael
Winnipeg Tribune, 40, 43, 69. See also *Ottawa Journal*; Southam Newspapers; Thomson Newspapers
Winseck, Dwayne, 125, 152
Wolfe, Tom, 53, 56–8
Woodbridge. *See* Thomson family
world newspapers, 6, 12, 256
World Trade Center attacks, 93, 108, 140, 155

yellow journalism. *See* penny press
Young, Brigham. *See* Greeley, Horace
YouTube, 160, 169, 174–6, 178–9

Zapruder, Abraham, 173
Zell, Sam, 118–19, 146, 199. *See also* O'Shea, James; Tribune Co.
Zuckerberg, Mark, 152
Zuckerman, Mort, 104, 127, 143